RULING PASSIONS

Ruling Passions

A Theory of Practical Reasoning

SIMON BLACKBURN

Humean scepticism about reason.
+
Expressivism about morality.

CLARENDON PRESS · OXFORD
1998

Oxford University Press, Great Clarendon Street, Oxford OX2 6DP
Oxford New York
Athens Auckland Bangkok Bogota Bombay Buenos Aires
Calcutta Cape Town Dar es Salaam Delhi Florence Hong Kong Istanbul
Karachi Kuala Lumpur Madras Madrid Melbourne Mexico City
Nairobi Paris Singapore Taipei Tokyo Toronto Warsaw
and associated companies in
Berlin Ibadan

Oxford is a trade mark of Oxford University Press

Published in the United States
by Oxford University Press Inc., New York

British Library Cataloguing in Publication Data
Data available

Library of Congress Cataloging in Publication Data
Blackburn, Simon
Ruling passions : a theory of practical reasoning / Simon Blackburn.
Includes bibliographical references.
1. Ethics, Evolutionary.   I. Title.
BJ1311.B53   1998   171´.2—dc21   98–3781
ISBN 0–19–824785–0

1 3 5 7 9 10 8 6 4 2

Typeset by Invisible Ink
Printed in Great Britain
on acid-free paper by
Biddles Ltd, Guildford and King's Lynn

PREFACE

This book defends a particular view of practical reasoning. Since practical reasoning is characteristic of us as living human beings acting in the world, it defends a particular view of human beings. The British moral philosopher Elizabeth Anscombe once said, rightly, that there could be no philosophy of ethics that was not founded on a proper philosophy of mind. I do not say that this book provides the foundations she was looking for, but it is an attempt to clear some of the ground involved in doing this. It is only when we have human nature under some control that human ethical nature comes under control.

The outline of the investigation is as follows. In the first chapter I set the scene, describing some of the emotional and practical features of ethical thought, and assessing from this standpoint the position of critics of ethics. Chapter 2 describes some of the ways in which we moralize: the features of situations that set us off, and the priorities philosophers have attempted to give them. The third chapter presents my expressivist or projectivist way of understanding moral thought. Here as well we explore a naturalistic account of what it is to value something, and thence what we are expressing when we voice our values. The fourth chapter turns to other theories of the moral proposition: the focus of our thoughts as we wonder what to do, or what it is right to do or best to do. I take issue with various attempts to understand this proposition.

Chapters 5 and 6 pursue the theory of motivation, first via an extended treatment of the idea that we either are, or ought to be, 'self-interested', and second via an investigation of rational agency as it is construed in decision theory and game theory. I argue against the supposed 'rational' or normative implications of these theories, seeing them instead in terms of an interpretative grid from which we read back the subject's real concerns or preferences. The following two chapters contrast broadly 'sentimentalist' with broadly 'Kantian' models of decision-making, arguing the superiority of the tradition derived from David Hume and Adam Smith. In the final chapter I turn to some of the staple problems of the theory of ethics: the bogeys of subjectivism and relativism, and the way to counter them in the light of what has gone before. This chapter completes the examination of strategies for 'placing' ethics in the natural world, and for demystifying the very concept of ethical truth and knowledge. It may be surprising to find these topics coming so late, but I consider that they need the setting to be appreciated properly.

The book defends a certain kind of theory of ethics in a tradition that includes Aristotle, Hume, and Adam Smith. I spend some time denying that certain alternative traditions, whose heroes might be Kant or Ross, or even Plato or Leibniz or Descartes, deliver the benefits they promise. This is unfashionable, even in some eyes almost indecent. In my years of teaching and discussing these issues I find that the position I am supposed to represent is thought of as sceptical, or relativistic, or somehow slightly less than fully respectful of the awful majesty of ethical thought. Many people think in their hearts that the 'quasi-realism' I defend smells of sulphur. This book is my answer to that doubt. I do not expect it to succeed in laying to rest the doubt in every reader. The contemporary academy is in the grip of several contrary currents. People think that only Kant (or Plato) keep their dignity as rational agents intact. They think that any attempt to understand ethics as a natural human phenomenon somehow taints it, and that any such explanation rubs the bloom off the flower. I do not think these fears can be automatically dispelled by argument, even when I think that they ought to be. In fact, I suspect that people get the theory of ethics that is true of them, and if they cannot respect human sentiments, including such sentiments as benevolence, or respect for conventions and contracts, then they cannot be brought to accept a theory that puts them at the foundations of ethics. If they are disgusted at human nature, they will want to keep the good and the right free of it. If they feel in themselves that people would be apt to behave badly if it were not for the dictates of God, or Reason, or some other independent authority, then they will not believe that ethics can be given secure foundations without such bricks. This is no more surprising than a politician whose funding comes from tobacco companies being impervious to argument that nicotine is harmful. It is just an example, although an interesting one, of an emotional state swaying what ought to be an intellectual matter. I hope that here there are some considerations that sway some people the other way, and for good reason.

The book was a long time in the making, and has benefited from innumerable discussions. I began the project as a Fellow of the Institute for the Arts and Humanities at the University of North Carolina in 1994. I wrote the first draft and talked about it at length while enjoying the hospitality of the Research School of Social Sciences at the Australian National University in 1995. I am grateful to Geoffrey

Brennan for my Adjunct Professorship at that idyllic institution, and to the University of North Carolina for the Kenan Fellowship that enabled me to spend the time there. I owe thanks to Frank Jackson, Philip Gerrans, David Braddon-Mitchell, Richard Holton, Rae Langton, Philip Pettit, and Huw Price for conversations on these themes. At that time too I profited from an invitation to take part in a centenary conference in Glasgow, in honour of Lewis Carroll's paper 'What the Tortoise Said to Achilles'. I owe thanks to Nick Zangwill and Pat Shaw for that opportunity. Since then I have exposed the material to seminars in Chapel Hill and benefited from the detailed attention of colleagues and students. Jay Rosenberg and Tom Hill tried to ensure that Kant was given due respect; Geoff Sayre-McCord, Dorit Bar-On, Keith Simmons, and many students also helped enormously. Margaret Walker has been a sensitive and sympathetic commentator on several chapters. Michael Smith has been a particularly close collaborator and critic of this work, both in Australia and America, and I fear that the sections in which I dissent from his approach do scant justice to this. In the summer of 1997 I gave a National Endowment for the Humanities Summer Seminar for college teachers, and enjoyed yet another audience of outstanding merit. I probably learned more from Eric Cave, Maudemarie Clark, Eva Dadlez, Steven Daniel, Justin D'Arms, Richard Galvin, Jeanine Grenberg, Bennett Helm, Amy Ihlan, Daniel Jacobson, Mark Lovas, Andrew Valls, Kit Wellman, Chris Williams, and Patrick Wilson, than they did from me. I owe thanks too to Christine Korsgaard and Alasdair Macintyre for being willing to visit this seminar and brave my Humean scepticism about their own approaches to these matters. It will be obvious to anybody reading this book how much it shares with the work of Allan Gibbard. From the time we first discovered the parallels between our work, and the seminars we gave together in Oxford in the late 1980s, it has been a constant pleasure to me to compare my work with his, and I have profited greatly by doing so. Among my own students, I would particularly like to thank Sean McKeever and Valerie Tiberius, both for research assistance and for considerable philosophical help and challenge.

CONTENTS

Organizing Practice:
The Elements of Ethics

We, the public, are easily, lethally offended. We have come to think of taking offence as a fundamental right. We value very little more highly than our rage, which gives us, in our opinion, the moral high ground. From this high ground we can shoot down at our enemies and inflict heavy fatalities. We take pride in our short fuses. Our anger elevates, transcends.

Salman Rushdie, 'At the Auction of the Ruby Slippers', *East, West*

1. A PRACTICAL SUBJECT

Ethics is about how we live in the world. It separates the things we will do gladly from those we will not do, or not do without discomfort. It classifies the situations we aim for, and those we seek to avoid. It is displayed in our attitudes to ourselves, such as pride, or self-satisfaction, or guilt, or shame. It is also displayed in our attitudes to others: whether they behaved well, or went the extra mile, or did their bit, carried their burdens, lived or died in ways we admire. Our ethics is shown in the things we forbid, or tolerate, or require. It is shown in the reactions we have as we think of the characters of people, or the events they cause, or the nature of the societies they form. To develop an ethical personality is to become sensitive to different aspects of things, and to be disposed to use them to influence or determine attitudes, emotions, and choices. Ethics is a practical subject, manifested in our reactions to things and the motivations we feel. Ethics puts pressure on our choices, and we use ethical considerations to guide the choices of others. The practical role of ethics is what defines it. This is what ethics is *for*. If there is such a thing as ethical knowledge, it is a matter of knowing how to act, when to withdraw, whom to admire, more than knowing *that* anything is the case. A conversation drawn by Jane Austen or George Eliot can reveal volumes about the characters' ethics, although no overtly moral language is used and no moral opinions are delivered.

This means that our ethics is manifested in our practical reaction to things. It is not simply a matter of the situations we find ourselves in, but of how we respond to them. We are born into a social world of values and duties, that is, a world of human norms and pressures and ways to behave which we learn, very quickly, to absorb. We take them in with our mother tongue. Perhaps it is in principle open to us not to be interested in what we are taught. At the limit, such a distance might become inhuman: a child might observe the entire world of values, emotions, norms, in a totally alienated spirit. Autistic children are often described as being like that. But normally values are contagious. We grow up absorbing them. Some people later rebel in some ways. But even thoroughgoing rebels need some way of voicing what they *are* concerned about and what they find important and demand from themselves and others. Then these other concerns show what their ethics really is. Our ethics is shown by the things that matter to us, and the things that do not. It is shown, too, by the way things matter and the practical stances we take up. In this sense, *there is no getting behind ethics*. It comes unbidden. It comes with living.

Still, ethical commitments have their specific nature. They feel different from 'mere' desires or preferences. To some they have a peculiar majesty, a sovereignty over our other desires. But as the quotation at the head of this chapter suggests, to others they present a darker appearance. Ethics has its detractors. Moral certainties, and the causes and crusades mounted in their name, are dangerous things. The history of human moralizing is as grey and dismal, patchy and stained as any other part of human history. Perhaps it is even more so, for the moral cloak conceals our crimes even from ourselves. People find it easy to man the Gulag or the guillotine while intoning about justice, equality, and liberty, and they seldom treat each other as badly as they do when they feel they have a right or preferably a duty to behave as they do.[1]

We are also right to mistrust being told what to do. People who moralize too readily arouse our suspicions. To be able to give somebody a bad conscience is to have a hold over them, and people like this power. They may claim quite spurious authority, from sacred traditions, or convenient pieces of text, in holy books or holy constitutions,

---

[1] The connection is horrifically described by Elaine Scarry, *The Body in Pain* (New York: Oxford University Press, 1985), ch. 1.

or from inner voices. They may be hypocrites, or they may be just stupid, blind to the real complexities of situations people find themselves in, and perhaps they are glib with justifications for their own doings. And in response other people often claim that they have enough to do, wrapped up in pursuing their own personal concerns, without worrying about telling others what to do, or becoming obsessed with 'impractical' issues of conscience. People individually, and perhaps more especially companies and nations, dislike occasions when ethics intrudes upon their decision-making, and there is a strong temptation to reject its voice as cant: insubstantial or irrelevant, fit only for dreamers.

Moral judgement is indeed used to coerce, and cajole, and to judge: when it is internalized, its victims may walk around under a burden of guilt and anguish. People who talk much of obligation approach practical life with a certain kind of armoury, and one that may make them insensitive, cruel, inhospitable to understanding and excuses. We might hear them say, for example, that people who live in the inner cities are under an obligation to respect the principles of property and the laws against drugs or vagrancy. And we know what this means. We are entitled, if we agree, to coerce, to use force, to turn our backs on do-gooders, on social workers, on liberals, or on attempts to understand or improve the environment, and so on. Instead, peoples' failure to live up to their obligations licenses our anger, resentment, punishments, and violence. History shows plenty of examples where moralizing brings nothing but disaster. The Christian Church's history of seeing mental illness in terms of witchcraft and devil's work is not unusual in this respect. During the Cold War, regarding communism as 'evil' was both a handy substitute for any thought about the intolerable social structures that led to good men seeing it as their only hope. It discouraged any such thoughts as akin to treachery, just as on the other side, seeing capitalism as evil often prevented any attempt to understand the liberal optimism that leads reasonable people to suppose that markets work. A contemporary example would be the hysterical certainty that heroin (or even marijuana) is evil that leads governments and doctors to deny them to terminally ill patients in terrible pain. At the time of writing, moral attitudes in Islamic countries, China, and much of central Europe have prevented governments from making half-way adequate provision for education in ways to avoid AIDS. Moral crusades strangle thought, and the attitudes of those who promote them are frequently repulsive.

Hence we find the insecurity about the authority of ethical thought that infuses the Western tradition. Thrasymachus in the *Republic* splendidly maintains that ethics is merely a device of the powerful for furthering their own interest.[2] Plato's spokesman for relativism, Protagoras, seems to think ethics is simply a matter of conformity to local custom.[3] Callicles, by contrast, in the *Gorgias*, is supremely contemptuous of the whole subject.[4] It is these attitudes that Plato or Socrates sets out to oppose, but they live on at least as vigorously as the arguments mustered against them. The theme of ethics as the fig-leaf for power recurs in the writings of Marx and Engels.[5] Nietzsche is the philosopher who most famously takes on the task of outright opposition to morality, although the picture here is blurred at best, since Nietzsche is at least as often railing against what he regarded as the soggy, self-abasing side of Christian morality, in favour of a proper aristocratic pride, rather than railing against ethics itself. Wanting to substitute something more pagan for an entrenched Christianity is not rebelling against ethics, but making a move within it.

To balance the picture a little, one thing we might remark at the outset is that it is not obviously the defender of ethics who is impractical and unworldly. To imagine a human world without ethics, but in which life goes well, it is necessary to suppose a golden age: a world without competition, or causes of strife, or clashing desires, or envy or malice. Certainly, we would not need to campaign for humane prisons if nobody committed crimes and got into prison in the first place. We would not need conventions on the treatment of prisoners of war if there were no wars. But given the tendencies of human beings, as we know them, we do need these things. So it is not the proponent of ethics, but the detractor, who seems to be the more out of touch with what is needed to sustain human society. It is no accident that the critics of morality already mentioned—Marx, Engels, Nietzsche—go on fairly unashamedly to moralize themselves. They have their views about what makes life admirable or tolerable.

2. INPUTS AND OUTPUTS

How is ethics to be thought about? Our attitudes and practices arise in response to features of the world around us. We represent the world around us in one way or another, and because of that we end up

---

[2] Plato, *Republic*, Bk. I, 338c.   [3] Plato, *Theaetetus*, 172a–c.
[4] Plato, *Gorgias*, 484c–486c.
[5] Karl Marx and Friedrich Engels, *The German Ideology*, in *The Marx–Engels Reader*, ed. Robert C. Tucker, 2nd edn. (New York: Norton, 1978), 154–5, 172–4.

behaving one way or another. So we can usefully compare the ethical agent to a device whose function is to take certain inputs and deliver certain outputs. The *input* to the system is a representation, for instance of an action, or a situation, or a character, as being of a certain type, as having certain properties. The *output*, we are saying, is a certain attitude, or a pressure on attitudes, or a favouring of policies, choices and actions. Such a device is a function from input to output: an ethical sensibility.

Analogously, a skilled sportsman, for example, is sensitive to features of the delivery and flight of a ball, and for each way the ball is delivered, makes the appropriate response. A less good player either notices the wrong features, or fails to notice the right ones, or, even if he does so, makes a less effective response. The player needed training to learn to separate the important features from the 'noise' or useless information that meets the eye. Similarly the good person has learned to select some features of situations as demanding some responses, and to ignore others as unimportant. The question is how to analyse this organization of input and output.

Speaking in terms of input and output will prove useful, but it is right to register two warnings. First, it does not prejudge the question of how much thought or how much rationality may be involved in the transition. It is not intended to imply a simple chute or conveyor belt whereby we mechanically or automatically find some things generating some responses. The response can indeed be automatic, as when 'without thinking' we find some behaviour repellent, or the reverse. But there may be nothing mechanical or automatic about it. On the contrary, it may take the most delicate exercise of observation and imagination to represent a situation to ourselves in ways that even suggest a particular reaction or verdict, and even then, we may draw back from giving it, demanding further knowledge, or further thought. Sometimes we may scarcely know what to look for, or what to find relevant. Selecting certain features of a situation as the ethically salient ones is a process that we practice, and that will change with education and experience. It may surprise us that some things matter in the way they do to other people, and we may learn to emulate them or to oppose them. It is a process that we discuss, and sometimes criticize. All that the input/output terminology insists upon is that we recognize the distinctness of the starting-point in the features of a situation that we believe to be present, and the upshot of taking them as salient, which is the output of practical policy, attitude, or emotion.

The second warning is that talk of an input/output function may imply too much of a one-way street, whereas the truth is more complex. Attitudes and emotions determine the features of things and people that we notice. They organize our experience, determining how we construe situations. Loving or hating someone we highlight, perhaps unconsciously, features that make them lovable or hateful, sometimes even inventing ones for the purpose and suppressing what does not fit. In the light of emotion things which we would otherwise see become invisible, while others thrust themselves onto our attention. Just after Anna Karenina has met and fallen in love with Vronsky, she meets her husband:

> As soon as the train stopped at Petersburg and she got out, the first person to attract her attention was her husband. 'Goodness, why are his ears like that?' she thought, looking at his cold, distinguished figure and especially at the cartilages of his ears, pressing up against the rim of his round hat.[6]

Some philosophers suggest that we should not even separate input from output. Their idea is that all we should find is the one unified mental act: judging a situation in moral terms, or seeing the situation as demanding in some specific ways. Such philosophers like to think in terms of a unitary, 'thick' rule or concept, a single principle of organization that in one movement determines both how we see the situation and, seamlessly included in that, determines our reaction to it. They then refuse to distinguish fact (input) from value (output). They think this distinction is due to a simplistic idea of there being a 'fact–value' gap. The issue here is delicate, and I shall have much more to say about specific proposals of this type throughout the book. But a preliminary remark is in order. Someone may clearly just 'see' a situation in value-laden terms. From the inside, as it were, there is just that one movement of the mind and a judgement comes out in value-laden terms: the action was heroic, the boy is a nerd, the man is a cad, the snake is slithery. In George Eliot's words that I quote later, a feeling can become 'an idea wrought back to the directness of sense, like the solidity of objects'. In other words, for the agent, there is just the one movement of the mind, a 'felt thought', as literary critics like to put it. It seems just obvious that the boy is a nerd, or the snake slithery—as obvious as the fact that the table is solid or the sunset crimson.

But this does not destroy a more reflective view, which sees very well that in deploying these terms the subject is exercising an input/output function. She is in fact taking some features of a situation, usually identifiable in a more neutral way, and in their light

---

[6] Leo Tolstoy, *Anna Karenina*, trans. David Magarshack (New American Library, 1961), Pt. I, ch. 30.

entering into a practical state: admiration for the bravery of whatever deed was done, contempt for the person who enjoys mathematics and computers, condemnation of the man whose actions were not those of a gentleman, or disgust and fear at the mode of motion of the snake.

It is only by thus 'splitting' the input and the output that the reaction can be seen sufficiently clearly for what it is. And this is important because only then can the reaction itself be intelligently discussed, and perhaps, as in at least two of these cases, seen as highly questionable. The splitting may take some analysis and critical thought, because the moral and emotional lens is not readily visible to the person who sees situations through it.

Consider how in just the same way the sportsman's only thought might be that the coming ball needs such-and-such a treatment. Yet, if his response is inappropriate, we need to factor out what it was about the delivery that made him think that, and then perhaps get him to practice a different reaction to balls of that kind. The subject may even fail to see that in calling a boy a nerd he is reacting unfavourably to an interest in mathematics and science (and that this in turn is a function of disturbing social arrangements, themselves cemented in place and expressed partly by the very existence of the term with its current flavour). But this is what he is doing, and if on reflection he can be brought to see that this is so, then perhaps improvement is possible. Refusing to 'split' begins to sound like a refusal to think, perhaps symptomatic of a complacent belief that the emotional and moral lenses through which we see deserve no critical attention themselves.

Because ethics is essentially practical, there arises a query about the extent to which we might be in the domain of reason, knowledge, or cognition, and truth or falsehood. For most philosophers one leg, certainly, is in this domain: the part in which we represent the world to ourselves in some way, believing some features to characterize the situation to which we are reacting. But since the other leg stands in the domain of practice there seems always to be a part of the function which is not so clearly under the control of reason and cognition. This is the active or dynamic part that translates what is cognized or apprehended as true into a motivation or real pressure on action.

This seems true even if we have a very generous conception of what is truly apprehended. For example, in the philosophy of Kant people are supposed to be able to apprehend when something is contrary to a moral law whose credentials are those of reason itself. But even with such a highly charged input, unless we *respect* the law, this apprehension could remain inert, no more a part of our practical lives than the parking regulations are part of the practical lives of those who more or less successfully take no notice of them. Respect is here the dynamic element that translates knowledge into practice.[7]

Many philosophers, perhaps professionally wedded to the sovereignty of reason, have tried to bring the whole process under the control of rationality. They do not want to acknowledge any element of contingency or happenstance, or of cultural or imaginative or emotional factors, in the step that has to be made from the representative to the practical. This book is intended to make that acknowledgement comfortable without denying that it needs to be made.

3. EMOTIONAL ASCENT

Ethics does not concern the whole of human choice and action, although it structures a surprisingly large amount of it. We react badly to the taste of something and throw it away, or react well to the price of some commodity and buy it instead of a competing brand, but in these cases at first blush ethics is not involved. We act from desire, and certainly without even thinking of the rights or wrongs of what we are doing. Perhaps we are just disgusted, or attracted. But, of course, it may be that ethics lurks in the background: the food may taste disgusting because of a culturally embedded association of foods of that kind with prohibitions (does snot or earwax actually *taste* disgusting?—but what could be more loathsome than tasting it?), or the commodity appeals to us in the first place because of its association with status and an implicit demand on the admiration of others. What, then, distinguishes the obvious territory of ethics?

We could approach this question by discussing the kinds of thing that set us off delivering judgements of value, or that prompt us to invoke obligations, duties, and the rest. But I am going to postpone discussion of that for the following chapter, in favour of thinking first about the output side.

It is hard to imagine a human life going on at all without an implicit awareness of some values of some kinds. If we are not allowed to compare whether under one regime life goes better than under another, then how is choice and action possible at all? The Shakespearean characters Hamlet, and Jacques in *As You Like It*, are each examples of

---

[7] Kant thought that this respect is, however, 'necessary'. It is not a function of culture or temperament, but characterizes rational agency as such. See, for instance, *Critique of Practical Reason*, trans. Lewis White Beck (New York: Macmillan, 1959), 73–7. I discuss this further in Chapter 8.

people who have lost their values. The world for them is just 'weary, stale, flat and unprofitable'. As a result there is nothing left for them but melancholy, listlessness, and incapacity for action. Conversely, if we are condemned to act in the human world, then by the same token we are compelled to rank situations and actions as better or worse. At the very least, we must prefer some things to others. In Chapter 3 I shall locate our values in effect as our stable concerns, and living requires that we have stable concerns.

But there is more to the output side. What kind of thought or feeling is involved when we have a moral reaction to some conduct or some situation? Centrally, a moral transgression is something that is other peoples' business, something that is against the mores or norms. It is some kind of trespass. As such it is of legitimate concern to others. This is not a strict definition, since itself it involves ethical terms (we are talking of when it is proper or allowable for others to be concerned, and this is to make an ethical judgement). But it points to the right area.

We should think in terms of a staircase of practical and emotional ascent. At the bottom are simple preferences, likes, and dislikes. More insistent is a basic hostility to some kind of action or character or situation: a primitive aversion to it, or a disposition to be disgusted by it, or to hold it in contempt, or to be angered by it, or to avoid it. We can then ascend to reactions to such reactions. Suppose you become angry at someone's behaviour. I may become angry at you for being angry, and I may express this by saying it is none of your business. Perhaps it was a private matter. At any rate, it is not a moral issue. Suppose, on the other hand, I share your anger or feel 'at one' with you for so reacting. It may stop there, but I may also feel strongly disposed to encourage others to share the same anger. By then I am clearly treating the matter as one of public concern, something like a moral issue. I have come to regard the sentiment as legitimate. Going up another step, the sentiment may even become *compulsory* in my eyes, meaning that I become prepared to express hostility to those who do not themselves share it. Going up another level, I may also think that this hostility is compulsory, and be prepared to come into conflict with those who, while themselves concerned at what was done, tolerate those who do not care about it. I shall be regarding dissent as beyond the pale, unthinkable. This should all be seen as an ascending staircase, a spiral of emotional identifications and demands.

The staircase gives us a scale between pure preference, on the one hand, and attitudes with all the flavour of ethical commitment, on the other. The scale is not *only* emotional, in the sense that it is measured by strength of feeling, although we might notice that this is a natural enough phrase to use. But in this sense strength of feeling is also a matter of the degree to which things capture our attention, our degree of engagement, and our readiness to deploy pressures on other people to conform or to change.

At the bottom end we located genuine idiosyncratic likes and dislikes, such, perhaps, as the brute, given, facts about our natures that lead us to prefer some tastes or smells or colours to others. If someone has slightly different preferences, or if I find my own preferences changing over time, then that is just how it is. There is not an issue to be fought over here. We need have no engagement with such preferences. *De gustibus non disputandum*: tastes are not to be disputed. But there are actually surprisingly few cases of pure preference that invite no judgement. Even simple pleasures of the palate can give rise to moral and social judgement. It is not only that societies are quite strict about which foods are permissible, as well as which ones would honour or dishonour a guest, for example. It is also that if someone deliberately chooses what is disgusting then they become the target of moral reactions. In his recent book William Ian Miller described the revolting case of St Catherine of Siena who mortified her flesh to the extent of drinking the suppurations of one of her patients.[8] Not surprisingly, this disconcerted everyone, including the patient, who 'came to believe that whenever the holy maid was out of her sight . . . that she was about some foul act of fleshly pleasure'. We can understand the patient believing that if you will do *that* you will do anything, and also recognizing that she herself, the patient, has been relegated to being a mere occasion for St Catherine's own performance, a 'prop in her play', as Miller describes it.

St Catherine was not indulging a taste, one hopes. Perhaps in our culture we cannot moralize so tellingly about a real taste: a preference for sweet crude wine over more finely balanced wine for instance. But it does not escape dimensions of criticism altogether. One would not expect too much, in some directions, of someone with the first taste. One would wonder what caused them never to *learn*. Laziness? Puritanism? Pride in vulgarity? Some might think of such a taste as slovenly, akin to slovenliness in dress or cleanliness. Those are certainly qualities that invite moral reactions, although how far up the staircase of emotional ascent we then climb is also subject to dispute.

---

[8] William Ian Miller, *The Anatomy of Disgust* (Cambridge, Mass.: Harvard University Press, 1997).

The pure gourmet or aesthete who climbs too quickly is himself the object of certain kinds of scorn, including amusement.

However, it is with the palate, only a little beyond lies aesthetic taste. But here disputation is more evidently in order. We enter the domain of judgement, and have a clearer conception of a *fault:* a sensibility that prefers what is worse to what is better. A person who is blind to the beauty of a poem or the harmony of some music is missing something. If they prefer the cheap, or glib, or sentimental, then this in turn is akin to a moral fault. It is something we could want to engage. Or, if for instance they are resolutely blind to the interest of art from other cultures, we might suspect that this illustrates a blinkered vision, parochialism, or even an incipient racism. We might want to educate them out of it. If their aesthetic taste goes on to include such things as a relish for violence, or depictions of groups in humiliating or other lights, then our engagement becomes overtly moral: we want to change them, and we may deploy various sanctions to do so, mobilizing social pressures, and eventually even soliciting for legal powers in order to express disapproval or bring about reform.

As an aside, we may notice that the interplay between aesthetics and more overtly ethical issues is complex and interesting. It was a topic of major concern in the eighteenth and nineteenth centuries. It is not a topic of significant concern in contemporary philosophy, and this reflects our late-twentieth-century Western inability to articulate aesthetic ideals as genuinely binding and obligatory, not to mention our artistic inability to give expression to human or moral themes. This is one of those peculiarities of our situation that seems so natural that it is invisible, but that nevertheless plays a part in defining the distinct ethical texture of our time. In general there is often a perfectly proper question whether some lapse of taste is itself to be thought of as an appropriate target for moral or ethical valuation, or whether it should simply be left alone, passed by with a smile rather than a frown. Thus, we may laugh at Ruskin's view that only moral goodness makes a person beautiful. But there are certainly cases where aesthetic and moral values interpenetrate. It may be hard to say, for instance, whether an affection for some way of life, such as that of the village, or monastery, or army, is more aesthetic or moral.

Consider as well such problems as expressing genuine respect for the wildernesses of the world, or for the diversity of living species, except in unconvincing terms about how useful they are, for example as sources of medicine. Here we need to find a moral force behind respect for the independence, or grandeur, or sublime nature of the wilderness, although we find it difficult to do so without sounding sentimental or romantic. But take the actual case in which an advertising concern hatched the plan of putting a disk into space, about the apparent size of the moon, on which advertising slogans and images would be generated, thereby becoming compulsory and permanent sights in the night sky. It is hard in conventional terms to show that anyone is 'harmed' by such a project—for why should it be more harmful to look at the Coca-Cola logo than to look at the moon?— indeed, if the product advertised is beneficial, perhaps some 'good' would be done. And doubtless some people would *like* it. Yet it is not over-delicate to see the proposal as disgusting, a violation, a symptom of a break in the tie between humanity and the cosmos, an outrage against the dignity of the natural order of things. Indeed (climbing the staircase) I would say that it is barbaric to see it otherwise. One would feel contaminated, polluted, by belonging to a culture in which such a thing could be thought of. Aesthetic revulsion here blends seamlessly into moral revulsion.

It is naturally the actions of other people that concern us the most. But ethics does not only concern actions: we may think that in some circumstances people ought to *feel* various ways. We go some way up the staircase when we moralize about moods, for instance resenting someone who fails to feel meditative gazing at the night sky, or uplifted by a mountain landscape, or tranquil by the lake. Again, there are levels of ascent here: as with the aesthete, a significant moral question is how far up the staircase, how quickly, it is appropriate to go. People who climb too quickly give us our bigots and fascists, and are as much of a nuisance as the lukewarm, who scarcely ever get off the ground.

At the top end of the emotional scale are cases of harm and evil where dissent is not tolerated. I think it is wrong to hurt children for fun, and here there is nothing left of *de gustibus non disputandum*. If you do not think this, then I am against you too, and my opposition may show itself in any number of ways, from avoiding your company, to advising others to do so, to seeking to change you, to constraining you as I can, or deploying social and legal pressures of all kinds against you.

The reactions we have identified may seem surprising foundations for the high and pure subject of ethics. When some people think of ethics they highlight the lofty conscience, the sense of righteousness and duty that animates good people and is capable of motivating acts of nobility and heroism. I have started with feelings of disgust, contempt, anger, or feelings of shame and guilt, together with a staircase of attitudes such as disgust at those who are not disgusted, or anger at those who remain calm. At present I shall just remark that these are quite sufficient to give us the heartland of everyday ethics. Consider how the God of the Old Testament defines his morality mainly by a series of commands, coupled with a ready disposition to unleash his anger on anyone disobeying them. That is what his morality consists in. A moralistic society is one in which a large variety of things arouse the anger and censure of others; a tolerant or tranquil society is one in which only certain behaviour does so. We best observe the morality of a society by noticing such patterns, and observing when hostility gets public acceptance and expression (that is, when such anger is not itself the subject of a hostile reaction on the part of significant numbers). To moralize, we might say, is to insist on emotional responses. But in saying this we must not forget that as well as emotions such as anger there are the reverse. Encouragement and admiration are also important. When people go beyond what can be required of them—that is, they go the extra mile, well beyond any baseline below which anger would have been appropriate—they deserve and sometimes receive our admiration. And this carrot is frequently more effective than any stick.

While I think there is no doubt about the central ethical role of disgust, anger, and contempt, it is easy to oversimplify the reactions involved. Ethics is not always emotional: a prohibition or permission can be issued in a perfectly clinical frame of mind. It is clearly not simply a matter of likes or dislikes or preferences, as those are usually understood, for ethics often opposes our likes and our preferences in the name of principle (although the issue here is delicate, and returns in Chapter 4). Rather, ethics involves the *full* dynamic range of our practical natures. An ethic may be shown in perfect calm. I may not be angry at someone who steals my goods, nor even hold him in contempt, but nevertheless think he ought not to do it, and here the output is expressed in terms of my preparedness to encourage restraints and boundaries within which people should be forced to act. As Gilbert Ryle put it, ethics involves the 'tempers, habits, dispositions, moods, inclinations, impulses, sentiments, feelings, affections, thoughts, reflections, opinions, principles, prejudices, imaginations and fancies'.[9] A picture that leaves out any of these is to that extent impoverished.

Analytical philosophers demand definitions, but I do not think it is

no def of
moral

---

[9] Gilbert Ryle, 'Jane Austen and the Moralists', *The Oxford Review* (1966), repr. in S. P. Rosenbaum, ed., *English Literature and British Philosophy* (Chicago, Ill.: University of Chicago Press, 1971), 182.

profitable to seek a strict definition of 'the' moral attitude here. Practical life comes in many flavours, and there is no one place on the staircase that identifies a precise point, before which we are not in the sphere of the ethical, and after which we are. We find things important in different ways, and different reactions, emotionally and practically, may equally qualify as expressions of our ethics. An ethic may characteristically express itself in disdain of those who do not measure up, rather than anger at them, or in colourless administrative controls on conduct, rather than emotional public demonstrations. But this difficulty of definition arises not because the subject is mysterious, or especially 'sui generis', or resistant to understanding in any terms that enable us to understand the rest of our emotional and motivational natures. It arises because of the polymorphous nature of our emotional and motivational natures themselves.

4. GUILT, SHAME, AND THE REJECTION OF ETHICS

Critics of ethics sometimes express themselves by saying that it is 'all a matter of words', or 'depends on what you mean by' various ethical terms. We can now see that this cannot be right. Ethical disagreement is essentially practical. It concerns who gets approval, and who gets the reverse, and the words with which it is conducted are not simple counters that we can use as we like without dispute. This simple point can be buttressed by a number of arguments, of which the most famous is the 'open question' argument propounded by G. E. Moore.[10] Thus, it might naively be thought that ethical terms are given their meaning entirely by those features that we select as good or bad. These features determine the application of ethical verdicts to things. So, for instance, I may care about whether something creates happiness, in order to decide whether it is good. You, on the other hand, might care more about whether it shows respect for nature. Does this mean that we just talk past each other if, for instance, I describe contraception as good, and you deny it? Is our disagreement 'merely one about words'? Not at all. This is not a standard case of one person using a word to mean one thing, and someone else using it to mean another. Our dispute cannot be settled by the method appropriate to verbal disagreement, namely head-counting or other purely linguistic investigation into usage. Even if it turned out clearly that most people

---

[10] G. E. Moore, *Principia Ethica* (Cambridge: Cambridge University Press, 1903), 10–20.

used the word as you do, it remains open to me simply to say that you are all wrong. You have inappropriate standards, according to me. Applying the term to the wrong things, you approve of the wrong actions and forbid the wrong actions. You no doubt will retort the same to me. Our dispute is one over the kind of feature that *ought* to determine our verdicts, and this is not a purely verbal dispute. It is a dispute about how to react to different features of things, and how to act and choose. In effect, Moore pointed out that it is always an open question, something that can be discussed and denied, whether some given feature of things is the thing that determines whether they are good.

If it is hard to see a disagreement over which standards to use as more than verbal, this is because the boot is often on the other foot: many disputes that may seem to be purely verbal are at bottom ethical. Words are contested because they illustrate attitudes, and have other consequences, and these can rightly cause concern. Many terms in a language combine a descriptive and evaluative element, and their application is contested as a matter of ethics. The most familiar are racist and sexist epithets, but, as anybody who has tried to find 'neutral' terminology to describe any social or political matter knows, ethical shades and colours cling to nearly all the words describing social life, and the choice of one description or another will be in part an ethical choice. Words typically nudge people, with more or less subtlety, towards attitudes to the things they pick out, and rejecting or accepting these attitudes then pitches us into an ethical, not a verbal, issue. This is so even at the most sensory end of things, where philosophers might have expected a purely descriptive, empirical vocabulary. But, for instance, there is probably no neutral way to describe the textures of things that are disgusting to the touch. Slimy, viscous, greasy . . . are all heavily loaded words. [*is how split?*]

We can now return to the suspicion of ethics voiced in the first section. We can interpret the critic as suggesting that it would be better if we lost these tendencies to such things as socially coordinated anger. The tendency to such reactions is part of a defective way of life. The idea is that the ethical vocabulary is typically used to cement and enforce unfortunate psychological attitudes, disguising power, discouraging thought, and perhaps acting as a fig-leaf for what may at bottom be an exploitative social order.

Morality, as we have identified it, encourages coercion and rejection, and as such needs careful employment. The question will be whether the attitudes with which it can be associated, and upon which the critic seizes, count as an *abuse* of the notion, or an integral part of any use of it. If the latter, then we may hear ourselves saying, for example, that there are no obligations, thereby wishing to cleanse our practical lives of the attitudes that go along with anger, resentment, exclusion, punishment, and to foster instead sympathy, acceptance, inclusion, and perhaps a relatively fatalistic acquiescence in human nature in all its manifestations.

To see how it might go, we can reflect for a moment on a concept that has lost a great deal of its popularity, that of sin. Sin deploys the emotion of disgust in the service of a particular kind of ethics. The sinner is foul or vile, and his or her sins raise a stench. They are loathsome: they fill God with pain. If it were just a question of the sinner being contemptible, God could look the other way, but one is *afflicted* with disgust, whereas one is not afflicted with contempt. Sinning is supposed to bring with it the particular pain of self-disgust: the sinner is not only bad, but unclean. The sinner ought not just to feel guilty, but ought to loathe himself, ought to hide himself from the sight of others and the sight of God.

Now it is not very difficult to think that these emotions can be overdone, and were undoubtedly typically overdone in the Christian centuries. Let us do away with them. But if we learn to soft-pedal sin, what next? Guilt is the most obvious next candidate for criticism. Guilt is the badge of a moral style that puts the anger of others where sin puts their disgust. We feel guilty when we know that the anger of others would be justified. That feeling has an imperial manner: thinking in terms of it may make me into a 'servant of the world', unable to live my own life or pursue the partial, limited, even selfish projects that alone would allow me integrity and dignity, if I could only let them do so.[11] Guilt is quickly inclined to go bad, becoming obsessive and neurotic.

Once more, there is also a great deal of force in this critique. As already conceded, it would often be a good thing if moralizing occurred less and were less unpleasant when it did occur. Many people want to demonize and criminalize lives that they don't like and don't understand. Parents meet the emotions of their growing children with moralistic antagonism, and families and people are destroyed by the habit. People are destroyed by neurotic and obsessive misplaced guilt as well, and the feeling of having let themselves or others down, when no such feelings are appropriate.

So is guilt wholly bad? If others moralize against us, there are three

---

[11] This is a paraphrase of (part of) the Bernard Williams's critique of the 'morality system'. See especially *Ethics and the Limits of Philosophy* (London: Fontana, 1985).

broad possibilities. We may resent their criticism, thinking it was none of their business, or that the standards they are applying are inappropriate, and we will either return their hostility, or at best shrug it off as the reaction of people who are best ignored. Or, we may engage with them, and seek to justify our action. Finally, we may recognize that they are right: that is, we see our own behaviour as they do, and ourselves feel guilty.

Guilt is the emotion that arises when we feel we could not defend ourselves against the anger of others. We have 'internalized' the voices of others, and recognize that we have no defence against their reaction (it is the very reaction we would have to them, had they done what we did). Guilt co-ordinates the hostility of others with preparedness to undergo it on the part of the subject.[12] Perhaps it would be better to downplay it, like sin. If we get rid of sin and guilt, however, we are still left with a third moral style. Shame is similar to guilt but usually described as differing by internalizing the contempt or disdain rather than the anger of others.[13] When we are ashamed we think that we are in a position where others who witness us would or could despise us. Fear of shame, or shame itself, motivates us to hide ourselves from the gaze of others. We feel ashamed in situations in which we are not up to scratch, even when no question of guilt arises.

There are three main differences that have been suggested between guilt and shame. The first, and most important, is that guilt is associated with our own agency: we are typically guilty through having done or failed to do something. By contrast, shame may attach to features where there is no question of one's own agency. I may be ashamed of my unmusical voice, but I cannot feel guilty about it, because I do not believe it was any doing of mine that created it, nor that any effort of mine would have significantly improved it. I may be ashamed of my bodily figure, but I can only feel guilty about it if I think that I brought it about by, for instance, failing to exercise or by over-eating. To feel guilty, it seems, I must feel responsible for whatever needs putting right.

Arising from this is the second difference. Shame typically motivates us to *concealment*. We try to hide the failure or the flaw from others. Guilt, on the other hand, typically motivates us to *reparation*, which can include 'setting things right', apologizing, confessing, expiating, and getting back onto all fours with the others. Guilt can

[12] Allan Gibbard, *Wise Choices, Apt Feelings: A Theory of Normative Judgment* (Cambridge, Mass.: Harvard University Press, 1990), 67–8.

[13] For a recent treatment, see Bernard Williams, *Shame and Necessity* (Berkeley, Calif.: University of California Press, 1993), 219–20.

motivate us to expose ourselves. Guilt is especially supposed to work even although others do not know what we have done. It is enough that we have internalized their voices, and this means that our discomfort is not dependent upon the actual accusation of others. We can imagine what they would say about us, and find it uncomfortable, even if in fact nobody was there to point the finger of anger. Shame is not quite so indifferent to the absence of others. It connects with concealment differently in different cases. There are things that we are not ashamed of doing, but where we would be ashamed to be observed, such as exercising natural bodily functions. Here, shame only arises from the actual gaze of others. In the other kind of case shame is more like guilt. We may be ashamed although there were no actual witnesses. I may be ashamed of my poor piano-playing, although I take care to practise in private, or ashamed on re-reading a clumsy paragraph I have just written but that nobody else has read. Because these performances are deficient, I am glad they are hidden from others.

3.   The third and related mark of difference we have already mentioned. This is that guilt is typically associated with the potential anger or hostility of others, whereas shame anticipates their disdain or contempt. If I am ashamed of my lame performance at the piano, I anticipate that anyone hearing it would find it regrettable or miserable, but not that they might be angry at me for it (if they might be, it would be because my agency is involved—I failed to practise as I should have, or as I promised to, for instance).

It is sometimes thought that guilt is irrational if it is engendered via elements of a situation that were bad luck or beyond our control. I engage more with this range of thoughts later. But I can remark here that this is not how we actually think about it. Suppose I sometimes drive paying a little too much attention to my mobile phone, and too little to the road. I do not feel guilty. But if by bad luck a child runs out and I kill it, then I do, even if that extra aspect of the situation was quite beyond my control. And I am supposed to feel guilty: if I do not feel guilt, having run over the child because I was paying attention to my mobile phone, I am likely to be regarded as some kind of monster. In our actual moral world, in such a case contrition and some instinct to reparation are compulsory. In fact, the link with responsibility should not be thought of as fixed and a priori. It may permit of cultural variation, so that it is just a fact about the West that we typically restrict guilt to occasions for which we feel responsibility.[14] And even

---

[14] This theme is emphasized in Rom Harré, *The Social Construction of the Emotions* (Oxford: Oxford University Press, 1986).

in the West, we can understand the guilt of someone who feels that they have been or are part of some infamous collective process, regardless of their responsibility for it. We feel guilty about just being complicit. People can feel guilty about their parents' doings, and we can feel guilty about our generation's destruction of the environment, although here the thought 'I should do or should have done something about it' may not be far away.

Finally, it is worth remarking that the three features we have noticed that distinguish guilt from shame—the involvement of agency, the disposition towards reparation and contrition, the internalized anger rather than disdain of others—are typically intermingled, so that it is seldom clear-cut which it is that we feel. Feeling ashamed of something is often not readily distinguished from feeling guilty about it. It would be a fine call, for instance, to say whether typical anorexics or bulimics feel guilty about eating or ashamed of eating. Often this is because we can become obsessed by the false idea that a deficiency must have been due to our own agency. In low-church cultures, for example, illness or handicap can be moralized into something about which to feel guilty: a punishment for some imagined transgression. Furthermore, guilt and shame almost inevitably go together for another reason, which is that when we feel guilty it is typically because we have behaved as we did because of emotions or desires or motivations of which we are ashamed. Here the impulse to confess clashes with the impulse to conceal, and the resulting conflict makes our state multiply unpleasant.

With this much understanding of these emotions, then if we also *better off without the emotions?* concede that societies can be too moralistic, too quick to react to too many kinds of behaviour with anger and guilt, or contempt and shame, is it coherent to suggest that we would get by better without any such emotions at all? The idea might be that we could still rank some situations as better than others, and try to bring them about, and we could still admire some human characteristics more than others, and try to encourage them and imitate them. It is just that we would not feel angry or ashamed or guilty at the failures of others and ourselves. We would accept more, and judge less. This might seem to be pure gain, for anger and shame and guilt are unpleasant emotions.

There is a way of thinking, more common in popular psychology texts than in philosophy or literature, that invites us to think of guilt and shame as bad feelings, like nausea, that we ought just to wish away. They are there to be cured. But that is too simple. Guilt, for instance, typically involves the wish to have done otherwise, and if I really wish to have done otherwise, I won't find that wish just a brute uncomfortable fact about my own consciousness, one that I might in turn wish away. I don't just wish myself to be free of that wish. My last word is not 'this is a nasty state to be in, so I wish I could get rid of it'. My last word is 'I wish I had done otherwise'. This is the intentionality or directedness of emotional states, including desire, and will be a major element in understanding desire. I return to it in later chapters. Misunderstanding it prompts entire philosophies to mistake the nature of deliberation.

The cost, obviously, of getting rid of guilt or shame will be one of *motivation*. Without these emotions, the motivation to act well is diminished. If there is no fear of the anger of others, or no internalization of their potential rejection, then a central buttress of good behaviour has been lost. If there is no inclination to make reparation, or to undergo the hostility of others, then our responses are unco-ordinated and social dissolution becomes more likely. For how do the happy people who are innocent of guilt or shame comport themselves? It would be left to other motivational states to keep them behaving well. But it is not at all clear what these would look like, for too many of the normal boundaries on action are dependent upon entrenched emotions. Fear of discovery, for example, presupposes that discovery will be a bad thing, yet if it never arouses the anger of others, it will not be a bad thing. Desire for the admiration of others may not be so urgent if the admiration goes without some kind of ranking, whereby actions that are not admired eventually provoke at least some kind of disdain. Unless I am sometimes ashamed of my piano playing, and sometimes even guilty about failing to practise, I am not likely to improve very fast. Pride is a pleasant state, and the prospect of a proper pride is a great motivator, but it only exists at its best when the situation was one in which a shameful outcome was possible, but avoided.

Some philosophers, notably Bernard Williams, have portrayed guilt as part of a culturally specific 'morality system' which we would be better off without. But I doubt if this is right. Of course, both guilt and shame can both become obsessive and neurotic. But the co-ordinating function and the motivating function of these emotions are enough to give them a place in the well-tempered psychology. (Other aspects of Williams's critique, including the idea that guilt trades on an unrealistic fantasy of pure freedom, occupy Chapter 8.)

In the Oresteian trilogy of Aeschylus, Orestes, having killed his mother, who had herself killed his father, is pursued by the 'Eumenides', initially the Furies, whose hate and fury signify the sense of guilt and shame that corrode Orestes. But when the situation is finally resolved by the goddess Athene, the Eumenides are not banished. They are not regarded as formless diseases. Their role has been perfectly honourable, and they are given a place at the foundation of Athens, that is, at the foundations of civic life. 'For what man who fears nothing at all is ever righteous?' The Eumenides then, as it were, grow into deserving their name (the 'well-wishers'), because their presence under the civic order is its necessary guarantee against anarchy and wrongdoing.

We can certainly campaign for a society to becomes less moralistic and more forgiving. We can campaign for it to pay more attention to the social conditions that lead people to behave badly and less to the individual who is a victim of those conditions. And we can certainly attempt, as Nietzsche does, to revalue our values: in other words, to rethink whether some conventionally accepted goods or virtues really are so. But none of this amounts to a wholesale rejection of ethics. It is still making moves *within* ethics: changing the key, not refusing to play the tune. And in fact our reflections suggest that the rejection of ethics is not really an option. As we already saw, there is no getting behind ethics, because the decision to live a tolerant 'non-judgemental' life is itself an ethical decision, and not obviously one that can be sustained for very long, or defended for very long as likely to lead to wholly good consequences. Certainly people may moralize too much and too quickly and about the wrong things. But people may also be too slow to praise good behaviour, or to feel anger at behaviour that deserves it: cruelty, ingratitude, injustice of all kinds.

5. PRIVACY AND PRINCIPLE

Is there any other way of criticizing ethics as such, as opposed to crit-icizing the particular attitudes held by some people at some times? We have already come across the idea that we often do not want ethics to intrude into practical living, not because we feel guilty about what we are doing, but because it introduces 'one thought too many'. In a personal relationship, for example with one's partner or children, the last thing one wants is that people are acting with an eye to behaving well, or out of a sense of duty. Parents are to cherish children out of spontaneous love of them, not because they feel they ought to do so, or that it is what the world expects, or that somewhere in the future some good might come of it. A partner who realizes that the other is meeting them not because they want to, but out of a sense of duty, thereby recognizes that the relationship is lost. We do not want anything specifically ethical to intrude: a lover or parent who acts out of love, but at the same time is always checking what ethics requires of them or is mainly pleased that he or she is acting dutifully, is inadequate. The delicate adjustment of one to another that communication needs is incompatible with one party having half a mind on duty or consequences, just as rapt engagement with a play is incompatible with having half a mind on the cost of the ticket. There are places, it seems, where only spontaneous emotion will do, and where ethical thinking should not intrude. If we think all practical living is like that, then ethical thought is left with no respectable place in our lives.

It is only a highly imperialistic conception of ethics that is under attack here: a conception according to which ethics is to intrude into everything. This just means that an ethic which recommends that we feel no attitudes and emotions without ethical thought is unfit for human beings, and on that account alone ought to be rejected. We need and cherish spheres within which we are completely absorbed by private concern and emotion, just as we need spheres of private property. But it is a fantasy to suppose that all areas of practical life might be like that. We have to think in terms of obligations and duties sometimes, and when we do they are important (although not, perhaps, important enough to trump everything. Rebellion has its own allure, and virtuous people may sometimes kick over the traces. I talk more of admirable naughtiness in Chapter 3).

We might have as a kind of Utopian ideal a world in which, without social penalties or rewards, people spontaneously act out of love, trust, benevolence, and care; where they do not have to think what they are doing, or pay attention to the consequences, or worry about the resources they are demanding from others, or about the amount they are contributing to the common good. This is the simple 'peasant goodness' recommended, for example, by Tolstoy, and by Christianity in its aspect of opposition to the rigid law-governed social world of Judaism. In the real world, however, utterly simple, innocent, inarticulate goodness is a rare bird (the idea that it belongs naturally to children, and equally to peasants, is of course sentimental rubbish). And it is hard to imagine it existing at all without education via mechanisms of admiration or disdain, reward and even punishment, or the setting of boundaries that are articulated in a common ethic. We may indeed hope that when an ethic is firmly in place, people spontaneously find themselves wanting to do only what it is right for them to do. But even if such a Utopian moment came about, there will be the constant need to pass on the success to new generations, and that means communicating and co-ordinating our attitudes in public discussion. In other words, simple, inarticulate, good conduct may be admirable, but it no more supplants the need for articulate ethics than simple, inarticulate, consummate musicianship supplants the need for musical education.

There is another aspect of this that I am not here engaging: the wisdom of conducting political affairs on the presumption that ethics is more steam than substance: the duty of the lawgiver to presume that all men are wicked. The whole theory of constitutional design, from Machiavelli, through Hobbes, to the American revolution, is (rightly) based on this maxim. But that is not because the maxim is necessarily true, but because it is true often enough for a state to need the checks and balances to prevent one group from predating upon the others.[15]

The plot of the rest of the book is as follows. In the next chapter I look at the restless relationship between deontological, consequentialist, and virtue ethics. I then turn to the moral proposition and I introduce and defend a particular view of this, and compare it with other attempts to understand it. I then discuss the nature of human motivation, and in particular the question of our egoism or selfishness. Are people incurably selfish? Are they driven by selfish genes, and what implications does this have for their behaviour? Does it show us what rationality demands in various kinds of decision-making problem? I then turn to the problems of freedom and rationality as they work themselves out in two great rival traditions: the naturalistic tradition of Hume, and the rationalistic tradition of Kant. I turn to confront the problem of authority, and the nagging doubts of scepticism and relativism. Learning how to confront those, we emerge into relative daylight, able finally to give a satisfactory account of moral thought, its credentials, its scope, and its limits.

---

[15] Paul Rahe, 'Antiquity Surpassed: The Repudiation of Classical Republicanism', in David Wooton, ed., *Republicanism, Liberty, and Commercial Society, 1649–1776* (Stanford, Calif.: Stanford University Press, 1994).

2

Things that Concern Us

'But I plainly see that everything is going to sixes and sevens and all order will soon be at an end throughout the Kingdom.'

'Not however, Ma'am, the sooner, I hope, from any conduct of mine,' said Catharine in a tone of great humility, 'for upon my honour I have done nothing this evening that can contribute to overthrow the establishment of the Kingdom.'

'You are Mistaken, Child,' replied she; 'the welfare of every Nation depends upon the virtue of its individuals, and any one who offends in so gross a manner against decorum and propriety is certainly hastening its ruin . . .'

Jane Austen, *Catharine*

1. VIRTUES, ENDS, DUTIES

Our aim is to understand our capacities for ethics, and more widely, for practical reasoning in general. To do this we must give an adequate conception of the deliberating agent and of the moral commitments she forms. It is not my intention to defend one ethic or one specific style of ethics above others. So in this chapter I only sketch enough of the philosophy of the input side to enable us to proceed to the rest of the theory.

We classify actions as cases of telling what is not true, or promise-breaking, or killing, or theft, or alternatively as examples of loyalty, integrity, or principle. When such characterizations of action give us our input, the ethics that emerges will be one of right and wrong, obligations and duties, prohibitions and permissions. This gives us a duty-governed or *deontological* system. The Ten Commandments and other lists of religious ordinances telling us what we may or may not do are the best-known examples of ethics of this type. The moral philosophy of Immanuel Kant is their best-known philosophical expression. Kant's concern was to give a systematic description of the real obligations and duties under which we lie, and to show that they all derive from a fundamental principle, binding upon all rational agents. This, the 'categorical imperative', occupies us in due course. It gets different formulations, each of which is recognizable as a version of the demand that to act well you have to act in ways in which you would wish everyone to act.

We think deontologically when we think that there are some things that we 'simply must' do, or others that we 'simply will not' do. And such thoughts might strike us as the prime data of ethics. On such an account, each of us, as a deliberating agent, asks what we must or must not do here and now. Our ethics lies in the boundaries to action that present themselves to us from within this deliberative perspective. We may feel that our way of being in the world would be destroyed by cheating or killing or whatever. Our identity would be violated: we would fall apart if we acted in such a way. Such boundaries, according to the deontologist, are the fundamental facts about a well-shaped ethic; they are the place where ethics touches the ground. Often the boundaries present themselves as principles that are simply beyond debate. If people want to argue about them, the deontologist may just turn away in disgust: such people show corrupt minds; they are not worth taking seriously. Correlated with what we must do, of course, will be a lively sense of what other people must do as well. When *their* duty is to treat *me* in some specific way, then I have a right against them. It is more agreeable to most people to think in terms of rights than duties, but they are essentially two sides of the same coin.

The obvious reaction to this is that it might be all right if everyone shared the same boundaries. But in human life as we have it, things are not like that: some people simply will not do things that others think they ought to do, such as eat meat, or join the army, or help pregnant girls not to become mothers. One person's principle is another person's fetish. Furthermore, the boundaries themselves require definition, and the definitions introduce choices about which people differ. We may all feel revulsion against telling a lie, but what about telling a white lie, or telling a lie to someone who has no right to the truth, or in order to deceive the enemy, or to protect a friend? What of concealments that are not lies, but mislead, and the stratagems we use for throwing people off the scent when it comes to our private opinions and emotions? Such questions are certainly not solved by a natural light of conscience, for people find it easy to differ over them. A deontological theory, then, will typically try to do something to systematize the apparent grab-bag of principles and boundaries that determine practical life.

In order to do this, we may ask whether things go well or badly when various principles guide peoples' choices. This introduces a different kind of subject: the relative values of states of affairs. Actions produce consequences, and some are better than others. A world in which people are fearful and ill and starving is worse than one in which they are secure and healthy and fed. We aim for better situations, and try to improve worse ones. An ethics in which this kind of subject fills the foreground is _consequentialist_, supposing that things are to be evaluated by estimating the likely good of the consequences resulting from them. The best-known example of an ethics of this type is utilitarianism, in which the fundamental subject-matter is the value of different possible outcomes of action, measured by considering the sum total of 'utility', usually thought of in terms of human happiness or misery, in each of them. The aim of action in general is to maximize this utility, just as the aim of economic action is to maximize profit.

Utilitarianism, as it came to prominence as the social and political philosophy of the early nineteenth century, was first and foremost a public moral philosophy, trying to express the principles that ought to drive fair public administration, including virtues such as the impartial treatment of all persons as equals.[1] In the hands of reformers like Jeremy Bentham, utilitarianism proposed a measure for weighing social institutions, and in particular the law. Laws would be justified in so far as they contributed to the public good, just as traffic rules are justified in so far as they contribute to road safety. Similarly, utilitarianism also proposes a method for drawing the boundaries that impress the deontologist. We ought to promote rules whose observance maximizes the general good; rules which do not fulfil this function, however firmly they may be embedded in peoples' consciences, are impostors and should be scrapped.

The exact nature of the impartial public good that utilitarianism puts at the centre of things is problematic. Thinking only in terms of happiness is apt to promote indeterminate debates in which we consider different conceptions of what is finally worth aiming for: for instance, whether more happiness is produced by less security but more wealth, or vice versa. One tradition hopes to inject something objective, or even quantifiable, by considering only individual desires, and measuring the good by the number of these that are satisfied. Society is decomposed into an aggregation of individuals, and an individual considered purely as the locus of a succession of desires. But quite apart from the first step, which occupies us later, the second step of taking desires as simply _given_ is quite inadequate. A moment's

---

[1] An aspect well brought out in Robert E. Goodin, _Utilitarianism as a Public Philosophy_ (Cambridge: Cambridge University Press, 1995).

thought reveals that desires are themselves largely downwind of ethics, formed in the light of socially conditioned forms of esteem, serving the end of attracting the honour and admiration of those around us, which they will only do against a background of a socially active conception of what counts as success.[2]

Even a public ethic may consider situations using other measures than pure utilitarian ones. That is, an ethic may be teleological or consequentialist, but be constructed in terms of promoting values other than human happiness. One might look at some social arrangement not only in terms of happiness but also in terms of security, or health, or the capacities people exercise, or their opportunities for self-development. The elusive goal of a 'high quality of life' is not only measured in terms of the equally elusive notion of happiness, but also in other currencies: opportunities, health, freedom from ignorance, a sense of dignity and social solidarity. Allied to this, the source and nature of the happiness matters. Suppose people are only content because they are under an illusion about themselves. Perhaps they acquiesce in myths determining their own subservience, as feminists claim is often the case with women. In that case, we need to criticize the state of affairs not on grounds of happiness, for the women in question may be happy enough, but on grounds of justice or truth.

Perhaps it is also better to think in terms of public bads from which we need protection, rather than public goods at which to aim. If happiness is elusive, misery at least is not. It is easy to get agreement on the ills from which a public polity may try to preserve us, for it is easier to know when life is going badly than when it is going ideally, just as hell is easier to describe than heaven. Public polity must at least aim at freeing us from universal obstacles to happiness: want, ignorance, pain, disease, fear, subjection to the arbitrary power of others. We can recognize the value of such freedoms without thinking of them as automatic means to that nebulous thing, happiness.

Whatever currency we use to measure it, some situations are worse than others, and the ethic of any society is in part an articulation of which such situations are to be avoided and which others are to be promoted.

A third kind of subject-matter is the *character* of agents: a large part of ethics is concerned with delineating human character, and describing the positive traits or virtues, and negative traits or vices, that they illustrate. An ethic that finds this kind of judgement fundamental is a

---

[2] The classic assault on utilitarianism from this standpoint is F. H. Bradley, *Ethical Studies* (Oxford: Oxford University Press, 2nd edn., 1927).

virtue ethics. Its topics are such approved traits as courage, sympathy, industry, generosity, and self-control, or, on the negative side, features of which we disapprove, such as cowardice, indifference, laziness, avarice, envy, and other vices and weaknesses (for just as consequentialism can concentrate upon bad consequences to be avoided, so virtue ethics can concentrate on vice). This is the part of ethics that concerns educators, trying to turn out people of the right sort. A great deal of popular moralizing consists in rumination on the advantages of virtue and the disadvantages of vice: the one-and-a-half million purchasers of William Bennett's collection, *The Book of Virtues*, are simply following a tradition which is equally visible in medieval wall-paintings, illuminating the contrast between the paths of virtue and those of sin, and in innumerable sermons, fables, and novels before, in between, and after. Hume describes this species of 'easy and obvious' philosophers as follows:

As virtue, of all objects, is allowed to be the most valuable, this species of philosophers paint her in the most amiable colours; borrowing all helps from poetry and eloquence, and treating their subject in an easy and obvious manner, and such as is best fitted to please the imagination, and engage the affections. They select the most striking observations and instances from common life; place opposite characters in a proper contrast; and alluring us into the paths of virtue by the views of glory and happiness, direct our steps in these paths by the soundest precepts and most illustrious examples. They make us feel the difference between vice and virtue; they excite and regulate our sentiments; and so they can but bend our hearts to the love of probity and true honour, they think, that they have fully attained the end of all their labours.[3]

The task for the less easy and obvious philosopher is to inject some order into the apparent jumble of features that strike us as virtues or vices, and to articulate some account of how traits get onto the list. Much writing in this tradition takes the moral philosophy of Aristotle as its inspiration. Its reflections are in effect those of the novelist whose delineation of the fine gradations of character expresses and perhaps imparts a fine nose for the dimensions of merit and fault, their interrelations and the kinds of life that embody them. The connoisseur of character knows just where proper pride turns into vanity, where courage turns into bravado, where sustaining kindness becomes suffocation, and so on. This is called experience. There is considerable resistance, in the philosophical expressions of this tradition, to sup-

---

[3] David Hume, *Enquiries concerning Human Understanding and concerning the Principles of Morals*, ed. L. A. Selby-Bigge, 3rd edn. revised by P. H. Nidditch (Oxford: Oxford University Press, 1975), sect. 1, pp. 5–6.

posing that it can be reduced to rule, or even taught effectively. Aristotle himself thought that people should not begin to study ethics until they were over 30. Knowing about these things takes maturity, wisdom, judgement. It also tends to defences of the Socratic ideal of the unity of the virtues, resolutely refusing to separate what is necessary, for instance, for true justice, from true benevolence, or true mercy or courage.

The virtue tradition prides itself on its ruminations on life and the way to live it, hoping to identify the virtues necessary to flourishing. It inspires as well its fair share of scepticism. Locke puts it in his cautious and sober way:

The mind has a different relish, as well as the palate; and you will as fruitlessly endeavour to delight all men with riches or glory (which yet some men place their happiness in) as you would to satisfy all men's hunger with cheese or lobsters; which, though very agreeable and delicious fare to some, are to others extremely nauseous and offensive: And many people would with reason prefer the griping of an hungry belly, to those dishes which are a feast to others. Hence it was, I think, that the philosophers of old did in vain enquire, whether summum bonum consisted in riches or bodily delights, or virtue, or contemplation. And they might have as reasonably disputed, whether the best relish were to be found in apples, plums, or nuts; and have divided themselves into sects upon it.[4]

More spirited reactions come in literature from Fielding's *Shamela* to Jane Austen's *Catharine*, to Hilaire Belloc's *Cautionary Verses*. And there is something slightly ridiculous about some of the tradition's more flowery constructions. In the gigantic woodcut 'The Large Triumphal Chariot of Maximilian I', Dürer shows the emperor on a chariot driven by Ratio or Reason (who has what appears to be an ominously empty bubble coming out of her head), on wheels called Dignity, Magnificence, Honour, and Glory, while Justice, Fortitude, Prudence, and Temperance accompany the emperor on pedestals. As Willibald Pirckheimer, who designed the symbolism, wrote of these virtues:

These four virtues are interrelated and cannot be separated. If one virtue is lacking, the others are imperfect. Likewise the ancillary virtues which spring from these four are interrelated and fused one to the other. Because Justice requires truth, she holds the wreath of truth in her left hand. It is touched by her right hand signifying temperance. Where there is no truth there cannot be justice. Also temperance divorced from truth cannot be termed temperance. The right hand of Justice touches the wreath of clemency. This is to show that

---

[4] John Locke, *Essay Concerning Human Understanding*, ed. P. H. Nidditch (Oxford: Oxford University Press, 1975), II. xxi. 5.

justice must not be too severe but should be tempered with clemency. The wreath of equitability is linked to the former, for justice should be neither too mild nor too severe, but equal and constant. Without such Justice of equality it cannot be sustained.[5]

And so on and so on. Constancy, Bounty, and Security are also on board, together with Clemency, Truth, and Equitability. For good measure the reins that Ratio holds are inscribed with Nobility and Power, while the twelve cart-horses drawing the chariot are accompanied by excited ladies representing Moderation, Providence, Alacrity, Opportunity, Velocity, Firmness, Acrimony (?), Virility, Daring, Magnanimity, Experience, and Perseverance. No wonder Victory crowns the whole show, and it is a pity that the emperor died before the work was published.

Returning to earth we could say that these focuses of attention— duty, situations, and virtue—correspond, respectively, to the ethics of police and lawcourts, the ethics of planning and managing, and the ethics of educators and schoolteachers.

But we also want to be alert to distinctively ethical judgements that do not centre upon any of these things. There are characteristic ethical textures to periods of history, or cultures, or to forms of art, literature, or religion, and these can matter as much or more than the doings of individuals. Such features of our own culture are also less visible, hidden within what 'goes without saying', or, sometimes, hidden in what goes with saying—that is, what is already presupposed by the language we use. There is a position in social psychology called 'methodological individualism', which would try to reduce social facts, including here social ethical facts, to facts about individuals: to whether they did their duties, or to the consequences of their acts, or to the virtues and vices they possessed. But methodological individualism is forcefully countered by noticing that some facts about individuals, notably the ways they think, are themselves only identifiable in terms that presuppose the social. So, for instance, the fact that an individual is motivated to avoid some action because it is dishonourable would only be possible because of a specific conception of what counts as honour in her culture. And in turn, the salient question becomes not so much whether to admire or condemn the individual, but what to think about a social system in which this conception of honour is embedded. Amongst its many other infirmities, most analytical moral philosophy proceeds without ever clearly focusing on the

---

[5] I owe the quotation to Walter L. Strauss, ed., *Albrecht Dürer: The Woodcuts and Woodblocks* (New York: Aberis, 1980), 537.

social as a determining feature of individual action and motivation. One of the advantages, I shall urge, of talking of moral attitudes and stances, in place of simple moral beliefs, is that it forces us to confront the variety of ethical styles available, including the important one that is all too often invisible, namely our own.

Returning to duties, consequences, and virtues, we might remark that in practice we tend to find ourselves noticing all these features of things, and we are not very inclined to separate them. Considering a particular action we may say that it was wrong (deontological: trespassing against a duty), or that the upshot was distress and unhappiness, or disappointment, or hurt and the violation of their security (teleological: bad consequences), or that the agent was being insensitive or ungrateful (based on a negative assessment of virtue: vices are exhibited). It is no accident that we expect all three to pull together, for we surely tailor our view of what counts as duty, as better or worse states of affairs, and as good character precisely so that this is so. Perhaps Willibald Pirckheimer was wiser in throwing good things from all three areas in together than contemporary philosophical tradition is in trying to separate them.

It would certainly be impractical to suggest that we care only about one aspect of these things—only about duty, or only about situations, or only about virtues. We may, for instance, often concentrate upon virtues and vices, but an ethic will also have to concern itself to some extent with permissible and forbidden actions. A functioning society may have to compel people to do what they would naturally do if they were virtuous, but fail to do as things are. The fundamental fact about a good soldier or a good bank-clerk is that he does what his duty requires of him; the question of whether some virtuous impulse, or mere fear of detection, prompted him is secondary, and often irrelevant.

Also, consequences matter. Often, indeed, describing the virtue of a person is simply a way of describing which consequences of actions matter to them. Admiring someone as environment-friendly is admiring them because they take impact on the environment as an important consequence of actions, for good or ill. If someone is kind, this means that the consequences of their actions for the welfare of those around them is important to them. And although we might applaud the virtuous impulse of someone, the question of whether a virtue actually does any good is never out of place. Kindness is a virtue, but kindness has associations with contempt, and we know of the person whose kindness swamps others, or whose concern is fundamentally patronizing, or masks an exploitative relationship, or simply leads to resentment, and although things are sometimes meant kindly, they do damage none the less. The novelist who has us discriminate more finely within general categories typically does so by showing the good effects of one variety of trait compared with the bad effects of the neighbouring varieties. Life and art reveal cases when virtue does harm and its absence does better, or where the performance of an obligation will have worse consequences than its neglect.

2. VIRTUE FIRST?

Suppose we start by asking if considerations of virtue may be the fundamental basis of ethics. As already remarked, different conceptions of virtue exist. One conception is that virtue is simply rectitude or righteousness. It is the principle of action that keeps us in the path of duty. In the deontologist Kant, for example virtue is 'fortitudo moralis' (moral strength): 'Virtue is, therefore, the moral strength of a *human being's* will in fulfilling his *duty,* a moral *constraint* through his own lawgiving reason, insofar as this constitutes itself an authority *executing* the law.'[6] Virtue is the strength we muster against the 'brood of dispositions opposing the law'. It is 'the strength of man's maxims in fulfilling his duty'. Virtue in Kant is only visible in the conformity of the will to the commands of duty ('the will's firm resolution to conform with every duty'). This stony emphasis on rectitude paints one picture of virtue. If we adopt it, then clearly duty is the fundamental concept in ethics. Virtue is simply the handmaiden of duty.

On the other hand a more amiable, less duty-ridden conception of virtue is also possible. We expect that the exercise of virtue promotes human happiness. So Hume, for example, thought that the virtues are simply traits that give us pleasure to contemplate, because they are 'useful or agreeable to ourselves or others'.[7] The Humean virtues are sunny members of our brood of dispositions, such as good cheer or perseverance or benevolence, or civility and courtesy. For Hume, a cheerful nature is as much or more of a virtue as a gloomy devotion to duty. The blockhead who forces his stupidity upon us is as bad, in

---

[6] Immanuel Kant, *The Metaphysics of Morals*, trans. Mary Gregor (Cambridge: Cambridge University Press, 1996), 164. The following quotation is from the same paragraph.

[7] David Hume, *Enquiry Concerning the Principles of Morals*, IX. 1, p. 268.

Hume's book, as the knave who sets about cheating us.[8] In fact rectitude has only a back-seat position. It only comes in as a kind of reinforcement for other motivations, rather as the traffic police and the fear
they inspire may come in to reinforce a natural desire to drive safely.
Putting a sense of duty at the foundation of ethics, for Hume, would
be absurd because an action only gets classed as a duty in virtue of first
having some characteristic about which we care. So caring about doing
one's duty has to be secondary, a reinforcement or back-up for whatever makes us care about actions in the first place. So if there is a distinct notion of righteousness, or 'fortitudo moralis', it is only a
secondary virtue. By analogy, a miser may care above all else about
money. But that concern cannot be the fundamental economic motive,
for if money did not independently have an economic function, there
would be no point in caring about it, and indeed, since it would not
exist, no possibility of doing so. So it is that function which needs treatment in fundamental economic theory, not the motivations that then
parasitically cling to it.

We return later to the contrast between Kant and Hume on this point
and on the nature of practical deliberation. But it is clear that just as for
Kant virtue is subordinate to duty, so on the Humean picture it looks
as though virtue has a less fundamental status than sources of happiness or pleasure, which the virtues exist to cultivate. The picture here
is a little more complicated, however, by a thought present in Hume
and prominent in Aristotle, that happy living involves action, and may
be inseparable from acting well. A comparison is the way that the
pleasure of playing golf is inseparable from in fact playing golf. It is
incoherent to imagine getting just that pleasure any other way. In
Aristotle virtue and personal happiness or well-being ('eudaimonia')
pull together in this way. Eudaimonia consists in living virtuously. It is
not simply that virtue is a way to buy happiness, thought of as an inde- ✓
pendent state that might, in principle, be secured by other means.
Rather, true well-being involves the exercise of virtue, in the way that
true health, one might say, involves physical exercise. If you are truly
healthy you *want* and enjoy physical activity. In fact, in Hume's view
a major part of happiness lies in the consciousness of merit and of
behaving well, and to be conscious of that means in fact behaving
well.[9]

---

[8] David Hume, *Treatise of Human Nature*, ed. L. A. Selby-Bigge, 1st edn. (Oxford:
Oxford University Press, 1888), III. iii. 4, p. 607. See also *Enquiry Concerning the Principles
of Morals*, Appendix iv.
[9] *Treatise*, III. iii. 6, pp. 618–21.

Naturally, different cultures emphasize different components of virtue: Christian virtue is not the same as pagan virtue. Military and aristocratic castes go in for the heroic virtues of *superbia*: pride and courage, a short fuse, an exaggerated sense of punctilio and honour. By contrast prudence, decorum, and self-control characterize the gentry and the bourgeoisie. Humility and self-abasement mark the Christian, in theory at any rate. Once brought up in a certain culture the properly educated person will find a good deal of what counts as virtue in that culture automatic. Someone's modesty or politeness or good humour can be quite unselfconscious. It takes no thought to exercise it, any more than it takes thought for the trained batsman to execute the flawless stroke. But just as the input/output function that produces ethical motivations is not necessarily mechanical or automatic, virtue need not be mere disposition to behaviour, unthinking and, after appropriate training, automatic. It can also consist in knowingly acting for a reason, or in having a disposition to act controlled by the right kind of reflection on the situation.

In the virtue tradition, there is no embargo against thinking to some extent in terms of the consequences of action. Such thought is sometimes regarded as equivalent to asking what *benevolence* requires in a situation. But benevolence is not the only virtue involved when we pay attention to which situations are better or worse than others. We may value the wilderness, or the diversity of species, or the cleanliness of the oceans or atmosphere as ends in themselves, as things that it would be bad for us to destroy. Here our values are consequentialist, for they concern the ranking of states of affairs or outcomes of actions. But the currency is not 'human happiness', but the survival of things we value for their own sake.

Virtue requires thinking of consequences. The environment-friendly person thinks of impact on the environment, the kind person thinks of the good of others, the courageous person stands fast in the face of risk, that is, in the face of possible or probable consequences that he regards as undesirable. This suggests that judgements of virtue cannot have a fundamental status apart from other thoughts about what has value.

Virtue is also not alone the fundamental concept in ethics, because we can always ask how something gets on the list of virtues. What if you think chastity is a virtue, and I do not? Surely we have little alternative but to argue about the place chastity holds in human life. This may partly consist in an attempt to place it amongst other virtues—modesty, fidelity, filial piety—but any such reflection seems only to postpone the looming question of whether it 'does any good', that is, benefits its possessors or those around them, or in some other way promotes ends that we admire. But we are then involved in a consequentialist argument.

An argument about whether chastity 'does any good' is going to invoke consequences, but that is not to say that it presents us with a simple sum: find the amount of happiness or utility in a society that honours chastity, then find the amount lost or added by deleting that feature. The suggested change in social texture changes everything: people would start living quite different forms of life as a result. It is most unlikely that there could be any intelligent assessment of such a change along one linear dimension: more happiness or less? Rather, a comparison would have to be given in terms of other activities and social relations. The gains or losses would themselves be described in terms of virtues: whether people are any longer loyal or reliable, or whether they make good parents or dull company. Obviously, a medley of considerations clamour for attention, and equally obviously no one dimension of measurement seems to emerge. If a society which honours chastity turns into one that does not, as when the circle of Cromwell was succeeded by the court of Charles II, things become different, and any attempt to say that they have become better or worse looks hopelessly simplistic. The attempt to calculate all losses and gains in a single currency, that of utility, occupies us further in Chapters 5 and 6.

Some theories are called 'virtue ethics' because they concentrate upon the virtues required of the good judge of values. But that is a little careless. If the ideal judge is to look, for instance, solely at consequences, as in some versions of 'ideal observer' theories, then the theory is more properly called consequentialism. If the ideal judge focuses exclusively on duty and lapses from it, the theory is deontological. Such a theory is only properly a virtue theory if the ideal judge concentrates upon the virtues and vices displayed on occasions of action. But this exclusive attention is, as I have argued, unwarranted.

The reason that recognition of traits of character as virtues cannot by itself provide a basis for our moral thought is that we must recognize the value of situations we promote or avoid. Like Catharine in the epigraph to this chapter, we have to worry whether our traits of character are such as to hasten to ruin the welfare of the nation. But we can acknowledge this even while remembering the converse Aristotelian thought that virtue should not be regarded simply as a means to some quite separate end, human happiness, for example. We can acknowledge that we have no handle on what it is to live happily that does not invoke some conception of living virtuously: in harmony with others,

with self-control, with temperance, courage, and foresight. We simply
need to accept that conceptions of virtue and of other values are
inevitably intertwined.

There is an important caveat to be entered about virtue ethics. There
is significant empirical work in social studies that suggests that we are
not nearly so well-described in terms of virtues and vices as people
think.[10] That is, while we characterize ourselves and others as courageous, modest, prudent, sympathetic, and so on, it turns out that we
are much more fragmented and contextually variable than these terms
suggest. Much work in social psychology suggests that people act
more from moods and forces that are themselves set by situations,
rather than from settled dispositions such as prudence, kindness, and
the rest. In other words, while we attribute behaviour to standing dispositions of character, in ourselves and others, we are often wrong to
do so. This being so, the virtue tradition at least needs complicating. It
might retreat to talking of higher order dispositions, such as the disposition to let a context or a mood affect one in one way or another.
And it then turns out that people do not differ very markedly in these
dispositions and our common belief that they do is simply an illusion.
We might worry that in its recent concentration on virtues, at the
expense of consequentialism, analytic moral philosophy is in effect
turning its back on social and political situations and needs (not that it
was ever brilliant at looking them in the face), preferring instead lux-
urious and wholly unrealistic fantasies about what is possible for
human beings.

We do not like being told that we are typically under illusions about
the characters we attribute to ourselves and to each other. It is hard for
us to accept that our 'common-sense' approach to personality is typically far from the truth. And for the virtue tradition, the result may not
be quite as catastrophic as it seems. If we were forced to give up the lay
characterizations of persons in terms of virtues and vices, we could no
longer talk of someone being, for instance, courageous *tout court*. But
we can still share the educator's ambition to bring up people to behave
courageously in some circumstances, and hopefully more often than
they would have managed without the education. And that may be
enough to justify at least some claims of the virtue tradition. Even if
our characters are not as durable and steadfast as we like to think, still,
they can surely be better or worse. Adjectives like 'industrious' or

---

[10] The evidence from social psychology is collected and assessed in Lee Ross and
Richard Nesbitt, *The Person and the Situation* (Philadelphia, Pa.: Temple University
Press, 1991).

'mean-spirited' have some application, after all, even if there are situations in which the otherwise industrious person becomes lazy, or the mean-spirited person becomes generous. The elements of the virtue tradition that will be jettisoned are those that rhapsodize over the special nature supposedly belonging to virtuous persons, such as their special immunity to temptation, or the way in which their virtue 'silences' all their other dispositions.[11] For it seems to turn out that this god-like nature belongs to nobody, and represents an ideal to which nobody can approximate.

3. DUTY FIRST?

Consider next the relation between consequences and duties. Suppose we think of the consequences of actions in terms of better or worse states of affairs, and suppose we put on one side the problem of measurement. If we put a conception of better or worse states of affairs at the foundation, we would first claim that the boundaries we feel as we deliberate cannot be accepted just as data. They are where they are because they have a function: the boundaries to our actions are justified because they enable us to get along, or avoid conflict, or in other words promote the social good or help avoid social distress. Similarly, the rules of a game are where they are in order for the game to be a good one: it offers a fair opportunity to each player, exercises abilities, and causes pleasure. The deliberating player just obeys the rule; facts about why the rules are as they are do not concern him. Nevertheless, there are such facts, and to understand the place of games in human life we would need to know them.

But as we have seen, according to the deontologist, ethics touches ground in what I as an agent will do and will not do, here and now. It does not touch ground in the benefits or disasters it brings to people. According to the more rigorous versions of this approach, consequences and context have nothing or next to nothing to do with it. A stock example would be of a person who is in a position in which, if he kills one innocent person, he averts the deaths of many others, or in which if he tells one lie, many more truths will end up being believed. What is important to the deontologist's favourite kind of agent is that

[11] John McDowell, 'Are Moral Requirements Hypothetical Imperatives?' (*Proceedings of the Aristotelian Society*, supp. vol. 52 (1978), 13–29. The problem for the virtue tradition is explored in John Doris, *People Like Us: Personality and Moral Behavior* (Cambridge: Cambridge University Press, 1998).

he or she does not kill or lie, even in these diabolical situations. He or she is concerned to respect the value or the duty in his or her own behaviour, regardless of whether any good, even that good which the value or duty specifically concerns, is thereby brought about. You don't lie even if, foreseeably, because of your lie the audience will come to believe the truth. You don't kill, even to save life.

This way of thinking is intrinsically concerned with one's own agency: the descriptions one could give of one's own actions. It is as if our overwhelming concern is with the history of our own doings, told in a few rather simple terms. This may seem strange, but the way of thought is not unfamiliar, and nor is it especially confined to ethical contexts. Our own agency matters. Consider, for instance, someone bent on revenge. It may matter to him that *he* destroys his enemy; it would not be the same, it would not do, if someone else got in first. He does not just want the outcome that his enemy be destroyed. What matters is that he does it himself. Similarly, if I promise to tell someone the good or bad news, it may matter to me that I do the telling (this is what I promised); if the upshot, that the person gets the news, occurs some other way, I may feel disappointed or guilty. The deontologist is concerned with what he or she does, rather than with upshots or outcomes or consequences. The deontological cast of mind can thus lead to such a person simply refusing to do what would nevertheless be for the greater good, and seeing the refusal as a matter of principle: a principle that governs their actions, regardless of the rest of the world.

To the consequentialist all this is absurd. While it is good that people should feel strong inhibitions against various kinds of action, the *authority* of these inhibitions actually lies in the good they do, or the evils they avert. Giving the principles a life of their own, even when no good or much harm comes from doing so, may be understandable, but according the consequentialist, it is all the same indefensible. For the deontologist gives her private 'no-go areas' a dignity and authority that are actually borrowed from the public function of ethics. Ethics has its importance because of its place in co-ordinating our social lives. It makes things go better. Taking a 'matter of principle' as authoritative when it fails to play any such role is quixotic. It is elevating the ornament above the building. However firmly an English gentleman has internalized the duty of never eating dinner without wearing a dinner jacket, he ought to be aware at some level that it would be extremely stupid to starve to death for lack of one.

The issue between deontologists and consequentialists here is venerable. The reason is that each side has its strong card. The consequentialist's strength lies in understanding the social function of ethics. To have evolved at all, moral attitudes must have some kind of function, and then the only function worth citing seems to be their value in co-ordinating human actions, avoiding conflict, generating conventions, promoting the possibility of flourishing existence. But, says the consequentialist, once we understand what ethics is for, this understanding also dictates the shape our first-order ethics ought to take. It ought to be such as to promote our goals, and that means that promotion of the goals should be an aim or ideal. We should act so that the good for which ethics exists is maximized.

From this perspective the deontologist, it seems, has nothing very impressive to offer. He seems to present us only with the picture of the slave of duties and boundaries, solipsistically protecting his or her own conscience for no other apparent reason than that this is how he or she feels they must behave, or, in the more elevated language of Kant and Rousseau, because they have 'legislated' these duties for themselves, like fetishes or rituals. But the deontologist has a reply. The strength of the position is that it seems to fit better with the standpoint of the deliberating agent: the participant in practical reasoning who will indeed feel that he or she simply must do this or cannot do that. Not only will people feel this, but it seems that we must allow them to feel this, or encourage them to feel it. For a radical consequentialism that seeks to overthrow normal deliberation in favour of a model in which everyone, all the time, thinks in terms only of consequences and outcomes is hardly likely to improve human life and action. Just as we have to approve of unselfconscious, uncalculating involvement with others, so, according to the deontologist, we have to approve of unself-conscious, uncalculating dispositions to stay within the well-defined boundaries of duties and obligations.

If each side has its strength, then either can gain an advantage by explaining and perhaps justifying in its own terms the thoughts that lead to the other. Thus, just as a virtue theorist can notice benevolence, so a deontologist might acknowledge a duty of paying attention to the general good (even if only the good of a tribe or limited group of insiders) as one amongst other boundaries on conduct. But it has to be said that it is not obvious how that would sit comfortably with other prohibitions and duties: what importance it would deserve, or how it should be ranked among other objects of concern. If the agent is now enjoined, for instance, not only to concern himself that he tell the truth, but also to concern himself with the general good, he can hardly avoid internal conflict in the difficult cases where he can only further the general good by telling a lie. The problem here is quite general: a reflective deontology needs not only its list of boundaries, but some kind of story about how anything gets on the list, and some kind of advice on how to rank the different prima facie obligations when they clash. To do this it is necessary to defend some conception of the rules involved as neither purely self-justifying, nor as mere means to an independent end, and this is not easy to do. We return to far the most impressive attempt on the problem, the philosophy of Kant, in Chapters 7 and 8.

4. EXPLANATION AND JUSTIFICATION

It certainly appears easier for the consequentialist to *explain* the ways of thinking that impress the deontologist. The place to start is with the institutional roles which we frequently occupy. Consider the example of a referee in a game. His role demands that he administer the rules fairly, punishing infringements and leaving play that accords with the rules alone. This is his *participant's* perspective, and it gives his deliberations a deontological cast. The only thing he must bear in mind is how the rule applies to the situation in front of him. But now suppose he *reflects* on the point and purpose of game-playing: the exercise it gives the players, or the pleasure of the participants or spectators, or the reinforcement of ancient tradition, or the ritual defusing of tension between neighbouring communities, or whatever else occurs to him. The point of game-playing is here like the social good, or the overall point of the institution. There is nothing to prevent the referee taking up a reflective stance whereby these things become of interest to him.

Now suppose that on an occasion it may be apparent that the point is better served by bending a rule. Perhaps a false line-call will prolong the intensely pleasurable competition, or falsely giving the batsman as out will prevent the match becoming lopsided and uninteresting. A referee may find himself tempted to give the false call. But he should not, and if he does not he can reflect with satisfaction on his dispositions. Because the nature of the game and the role of referees within it demands that no such temptation be admissible. If people knew in advance that this sort of consideration would be in the referee's mind and able to sway his decisions, then the whole nature of the game would change. Indeed, it might well collapse, because the whole point of a properly conducted game is that the participants understand themselves to be bound by the rules, and understand that everyone else understands that too. If it is known in advance that this is not so, the game does not get played, and we lose whatever benefits that game-playing brings. So the referee could not himself admire a fellow referee who took the law into his own hands, and would not expect the admiration of others in turn.

Here the consequentialist stresses the overall benefit of the deontological cast of mind. We have a 'two-level' structure in which one kind of thinking is validated by a very different kind of justification.[12] We have a consequentialist argument for non-consequentialist ways of thought. This can seem paradoxical, but it is not so really. The same structure is found in many human affairs. The lawyer is to administer the rules of justice, or the soldier obey the command of superior officers, without exercising their own judgement about whether the rules or commands further one end or another. But the rules or commands are there for serving ends. Legal and military institutions do not exist as of right: they have a social function, and are doing well only when they fulfil it. But to fulfil it they may require the unreflective, rule-governed, participation of members of the institution. And as we have already seen, a person's role as a spouse or lover requires spontaneous, unreflective involvement in the life of the partner. It requires thinking, sometimes, that one simply must do something because the other wants it, or needs it. Nothing could be more insulting than a spouse or lover who only behaves by conscientiously computing what the role requires. One wants absorption within the role, not a sideways consultation of what it requires, and still less of whether another role might meet its purposes better.

We saw that, for the consequentialist, ethics touches ground in the promotion of various values and ends without which human life goes badly, and with which it goes well. We now see that while it touches ground here, it does not follow that it recommends that on each occasion each participant in any human affairs bears the consequences in mind. Indeed, as in the case of the referee or the lover, it might positively require that they do not. What we get, as we have seen is a distinction between the *participant's* stance and the *reflective* stance. But there is no fracture, no lack of harmony, in a life in which we occupy each stance successively. We act, perhaps impeccably, as referees or lawyers or lovers even while we are capable of understanding that our roles are only possible, and certainly only admirable, because of their place in the ongoing attempts of human beings to promote the good and ward off the bad.

There is a mistaken thought that sometimes surfaces here, and has

---

[12] R. M. Hare, *Moral Thinking: Its Levels, Method, and Point* (Oxford: Oxford University Press, 1981), is the central recent exposition of this kind of structure.

occasioned much discussion in the literature. According to the position here located, consequentialism applies to thinking about the good of institutions (such as traffic rules, legal systems, or games) but it is not to determine the thoughts of participants in those institutions. The objection is that this combination is somehow unstable. For what is to stop the participant from being alert to situations in which the general good is indeed furthered by his breaking a rule? Surely the very story we tell about the good generated by the institution must allow that there should be such cases, and that the participant would do better to exploit them. For, *ex hypothesi*, they are cases in which the good is furthered by the infringement. So we can have the general good plus the surplus good created by occasions of departure from the rules. And in that case surely any consequentialist ought to hold this is what we should aim to produce. So, it appears, a truly alert referee should have one eye cocked on the possibility of beneficial bending of the rules, or, if he does not, he should feel somehow ashamed of his unthinking 'rule worship'.

The mistake in this tempting line of argument is in supposing that we *can* have the general good plus the surplus. The incoherence of this as a general recommendation is already apparent. For if it were generally known (for example) that referees were disposed to give false decisions when they judged that in that way the interests of spectators and players would be better served, then, as we have seen, the entire structure collapses. The knowledge common to players, spectators, and referee that they are playing according to such-and-such rules is destroyed, and with it the whole point of the activity. You do not get the sum of two utilities (that of the game, plus that of the infringements), but instead end up with neither. On the other hand, if the suggestion is that secretly each referee should harbour thoughts of useful false decisions, then again nothing but disaster is predictable. A referee, however alive to the general purposes served by a game, can scarcely expect to sustain a career of deception: his 'one thought too many' would become apparent as inevitably as the conduct of the participant in a conversation who only listens out of a sense of duty, or the lover who has one eye on future financial advantage. It is hard enough concentrating on the play, without thinking of other things as well. So there is no consequentialist reason to encourage consequentialist thoughts from the participants.

What is here stressed is the consequential value of institutions, in which people play definite roles that demand of them more or less mechanical adherence to certain rules. The curiosity is that to take on such a role is to forswear consequentialist thinking: the consequentialism is 'self-effacing' or, as I once saw it put in a marvellous misprint, 'self-defecating'. For if *all* of the best kind of life we can envisage were occupied by such roles, then we get an ethic of 'my station and its duties'. We would be endorsing a way of life in which people occupy themselves solely with what their role demands, seeing themselves as simply a part of a wider social organism.[13] There is a certain kind of tranquillity in such a life. If I am a foot-soldier in the army, I do not have to think about what to do. Uncertainty and dilemmas melt away if the manual prescribes for every situation.

So now we can see how a deontologist might reply. True, he should say, we can have the consequentialist *explanation* of the ways of thought. But we should not confuse explanation and *justification*, and deontology is a thesis about justification. In other words it concerns the right structure of reasons as they present themselves in peoples' deliberations. In the referee case, the consequentialist may explain the existence of the game in terms of the benefits it brings about to players and spectators. But the justification of the referee's way of thinking (that is, the rule-governed, or deontological way) is simply given by his role *within* the game. His thinking has to be like that for him to play that role. Similarly, the justification of any piece of ethical reasoning, for instance the prohibition against lying or killing or fraud or injustice, is given *within* the structure of rights and duties which themselves shape the form of our lives. Our thinking has to be like that for us to live those lives as we do. The consequences of a form of life may indeed explain its successful emergence, just as the social and psychological functions of a game may explain its emergence. But those consequences do not play any justificatory role.

Perhaps then the right thing to say is that ethical reasoning should be deontological all the way down. If practical reasoning were encoded in a manual, it would be a manual like that determining how to play chess or bridge. There is no reason to include any chapter on why chess or bridge is worth playing. That is a different enterprise altogether.

5. CONSEQUENTIALISM FIRST: ONE THOUGHT TOO FEW?

Although this counterattack may sound persuasive, it does so mainly because it imagines that there is indeed a manual for each occasion. It

---

[13] See Bradley, 'My Station and Its Duties', in *Ethical Studies*, ch. V, pp. 160–213.

invites us to see life in terms of the permanent assumption of a role: each of us is a foot-soldier in some army of the righteous or good, and none of us will face problems whose solution is not antecedently prescribed. The trouble is that there is no such manual. Or rather, there are different ways of reading such tatters and shreds of manuals as we have. The truth is that just as it is wrong to think that consequentialist thoughts should *always* come back, thereby wrecking the role of the parent or lover or referee, so it is wrong to think that they should *never* come back, prescribing changes in the rules, or the neglect of some roles in favour of others. Here the example of self-contained rule-governed activities, such as games, may be misleading. The pleasures of bridge are indeed irrelevant to the manual on how to play it. But promoting good and avoiding bad consequences each have a justificatory as well as an explanatory role in the story of life. Understanding that there is a point to the rules must coexist with proper devotion to them. We see this well enough when emergencies force revaluations, like the starving Englishman forced to wonder whether he can eat without his dinner jacket.

Let us consider in closer detail the intelligent participant. On the one hand, as participant, he is to concentrate only on what is required by the rules. On the other hand, as reflective thinker, he knows that the rules are there only for a purpose, and that this purpose may be better served by occasional infraction. How is he to know, we might ask, when to occupy the unthinking internal role, and when to adopt the more thoughtful, external perspective? When is he to let consequential considerations invade his role, and when is he to shut them out? The deceptively simple but untenable answer to this is: let them in when good is gained by doing so. But this will act as a blanket permission to behave as the bad referee or soldier, forever prepared to betray his role. So it cannot be so simple.

The boring but true answer is that it will require judgement and training to know when a situation is a real emergency, one where for the sake of avoiding harm or doing good one should grasp the nettle and bend or abandon a prescribed role. This does not sound like much of a guide for the perplexed. But is perplexity at this point a real burden? Difficulties only become apparent either in an emergency in which our role is rightly suspended, or alternatively when the purposes of the institution no longer commend themselves to us. For the first kind of case, imagine a referee able to give a false call that terminates the otherwise endless game of bowls that is preventing Sir Francis Drake from going off to engage the Armada. Surely it is just obvious that this is what to do: Drake's dedication to the game is preventing (suppose) the saving of the nation; so it is right to bring the game to an end by any possible means.

For the second kind of case, imagine a person whose whole self is bound up with his role as a soldier and who becomes gradually aware that the main function of the rules and rituals he unquestioningly implements is to promote a habit of mindless obedience, and in turn that the main function of this is to enable the army to kill people the better. And suppose he becomes disenchanted with the role of expert killer. Then, naturally enough, his dedication to unquestioning obedience, and to the rules and rituals that nourish it, will likely diminish. In like manner a lawyer who becomes convinced that his branch of law exists in order to protect extant distributions of property, and who begins to think that those distributions are themselves disastrous, may reasonably lose his enthusiasm for the rules of law that he has been trained to enforce. But, far from being an objection to the intrusion of consequentialism, such examples show its merits: it is natural and good that disenchantment with the consequences should feed back into disenchantment with the institutions and the rules that exist to promote them. A deontologist who is insulated from this feedback is, like the man who starves for want of a dinner jacket, a lunatic rather than a saint. He has the converse vice of the man who has 'one thought too many', namely, that of having one thought too few.

But this, in turn, is not to suggest that it is always easy to decide that one is facing an emergency, or that disenchantment with the perceived consequences of an institution is justified.

It seems, then, that a suitably guarded consequentialism can do much to justify, and explain, the concentration on particular duties and particular roles stressed by the deontologist. Since consequentialism has in addition a natural, functional story about the nature of ethics, it seems that it maintains the advantage.

To a deontologist, naturalistic stories about why we feel the pressures we do can feel threatening. It is as if the awful seriousness of duty were being compromised. A deontologist may feel that something is lost if we allow the explanation, as if just by touching the flower we rubbed off some of its bloom. Consider, for instance, some serious rule, such as the prohibition on incest. Suppose we come to believe that the function of this rule is something in which we have some interest, but not an overriding interest: for example, preserving the availability of children to cement interfamily alliances, or maintaining the diversity of the gene pool. Then the explanation may be felt to soften or even undermine the prohibition: if *that* is all it is about, someone might feel, then it is not such a bad thing to break the rule now and then. After all, it is not compulsory to care about interfamily alliances, nor about the diversity of the gene pool. People in religious traditions often find the natural explanations of dietary prohibitions unsettling. If it is the distressing tendency of meat and shellfish to go rotten in the heat that explains why there is a rule forbidding their consumption, then why doesn't the arrival of refrigerators undermine the rule? And then participants may feel as if something sacred has been profaned.

If they do so, then obviously the right thing to think is that the rule must for them, now, be fulfilling some other function than that which explains its origin. By now, it may be defining a form of life, or be a symbol of their identity. Breaking the rule might be like burning the flag: not a particularly villainous action in itself, in that flags are cheap and replaceable, but highly significant and emotionally charged as a rejection of a policy or a culture or a country.

If we want to say that the fundamental place that ethics touches the ground is in what I do here and now, we would need to say that the authority of rules and prohibitions does not derive from naturalistic stories about their function. But while this is an understandable emotional need, it is hard to regard it as intellectually respectable. For, first, naturalistic, historical, and evolutionary stories about the emergence of rules and prohibitions might be true, regardless of whether we like them. And, secondly, if they are true, they may reveal a deliberative boundary as highly dysfunctional, or as only functional if taken up to a point and no further. And it is surely impossible to believe that the authority of the rule somehow sits above such considerations, unless we subscribe to some mythical origin for it: the voice of reason, or the voice of God. It is therefore no accident that the great naturalists, theorists who have sought to understand ethical thought as part of the natural world—notably Hobbes and Hume—are also inclined towards ethical rules whose authority eventually derives from promoting the common good, or, perhaps, avoiding the common bad.

I have not, in this chapter, said much about consequentialism in itself. This is because to do so requires a much more subtle investigation of the concerns that actually motivate us in our lives. The only general thing to be said at this point about consequentialist reasoning is that it is essentially forward-looking. It looks to what action will bring about. Once that is done different features of the consequences may matter. But in later chapters we shall have cause to reject purely consequentialist deliberations. We shall find that the past and present matter as well, and independently of their role as a signpost to the future.

We now turn to present a positive theory of the focus of ethical thought. This focus is any proposition couched in ethical terms: a proposition claiming that something is good, or admirable, a duty or a right, or a virtue or a vice. In the next chapter I give my positive theory of such thoughts. I explain their function as the locus of practical reasoning. In the following, optional, chapter, I suggest why this approach escapes the problems lying in front of other contemporary approaches. This is before turning to the further investigation of the actual shape of our practical reasonings, in the second half of the book.

3

Naturalizing Norms

We are all of us born in moral stupidity, taking the world as an udder to feed our supreme selves: Dorothea had early begun to emerge from that stupidity, but yet it had been easier to her to imagine how she would devote herself to Mr Casaubon, and become wise and strong in his strength and wisdom, than to conceive with that distinctness which is no longer reflection but feeling—an idea wrought back to the directness of sense, like the solidity of objects—that he had an equivalent centre of self, whence the lights and shadows must always fall with a certain difference.

George Eliot, *Middlemarch*, ch. XXI

1. IN THE BEGINNING WAS THE DEED

The natural world is the world revealed by the senses, and described by the natural sciences: physics, chemistry, and notably biology, including evolutionary theory. However we think of it, ethics seems to fit badly into that world. Neither the senses nor the sciences seem to be good detectors of obligations, duties, or the order of value of things. As everyone knows, nature is heartless; the universe runs as much in accordance with its own laws when it brings suffering and ruin, as on the occasions when it brings peace and prosperity. Human beings too run as much in accordance with their own mixed and fallen natures when they do each. Iago is just as natural as Mother Theresa, and on a head-count perhaps more so. It may once have been a consolation, but it is so no longer, to think that the order of the universe is an ethical order. It is not, and even if it were, we would have no access to what the order is.

To be a naturalist is to see human beings as frail complexes of perishable tissue, and so part of the natural order. It is thus to refuse unexplained appeals to mind or spirit, and unexplained appeals to knowledge of a Platonic order of Forms or Norms; it is above all to refuse any appeal to a supernatural order. After that, the degrees of austerity that naturalism imposes can be variously interpreted: some philosophers are more relaxed than others about reconciling the world as we know it, 'the manifest image', with the world as science tells us it is, 'the scientific image'. But we nearly all want to be naturalists and we all want a theory of ethics. So the problem is one of finding room for ethics, or of placing ethics within the disenchanted, non-ethical order which we inhabit, and of which we are a part.

'Finding room' means understanding how we think ethically, and why it offends against nothing in the rest of our world-view for us to do so. It does not necessarily mean 'reducing' ethics to something else. Reductionism here, as elsewhere in philosophy, implies seeing one thing as if it were another. Fastidious philosophers are rightly suspicious of it: as Moore famously said, quoting Butler, 'everything is what it is and not another thing'.[1] Nevertheless, the reconciliation of the normative and the natural must be carried out somehow, so if we are not reductionists we must find some other strategy.

I said in the first chapter that ethics was more a matter of knowing how (to behave), or knowing whom (to defer to, or punish, or admire), or knowing when (to act, or withdraw), than a matter of knowing *that* something is the case. Ethical knowledge, unlike knowledge of physics or history, can be quite inarticulate, and a novelist can paint a subject's ethics without ever showing them saying anything ethical. Whereas you could not paint a subject's knowledge of physics or history without showing them saying things belonging to those disciplines. If ethics is not in fact inarticulate, this is because we need to discuss how to behave and whom to admire, and to pass on the solutions to such problems that we find. Ethical sentences are the focus of these transactions.

The theory I want to defend is one that gives a story about the way in which ethical thought functions. Valuing something, it says, is not to be understood as *describing* it in certain terms, any more than hoping for or desiring something are describing it in particular terms. Rather, the state of mind of one who values something is distinctive, but nevertheless it is itself a natural, and naturally describable, state. Once we find ethics here, we understand the essential phenomenon, which is that of people valuing things. When they value things, they express themselves in terms of what is good, bad, obligatory, right, justifiable, and so on. When they wonder what to value, they express

[1] G. E. Moore, *Principia Ethica*, epigraph.

themselves as not being sure what is good or justifiable; when they achieve a certain kind of confidence, they say they know what to value, or what is valuable. The ethical proposition gets its identity as a focus for practical thought, as people communicate their certainties, insistences, and doubts about what to value.

This strategy—that of expressivism—leaves ethical properties and propositions alone with their own specific identities. They are the counters in our transactions with our values, just as a piece of money is a counter in financial transactions. To understand the value of a piece of money it is no good staring at it. It is necessary to understand the processes of human economic behaviour. You need to approach the token not with a microscope and a scalpel, but with an eye for large patterns of human interactions. Similarly, to understand the ethical proposition, it is no good looking for a 'concept' or 'truth condition'. We need the same eye for whole processes of human action and interaction. We need synthesis, not analysis.

So the expressivist thinks we can say interestingly what is involved for a subject *S* to think that *X* is good. It is for *S* to value it, and this can be explained in natural terms. Nature itself may be heartless and free of desires, but amongst the creatures it has thrown up are some which are not heartless, and not free of desires. We understand our values by understanding ourselves as valuing, and this we can do. If you go on to ask this strategist what it is for something to *be* good, the response is that this is not the subject of this theoretical concern—that is, not the subject of concern for those of us who, while naturalists, want a theory of ethics. Either the question illegitimately insists that trying to analyse the ethical proposition is the only possible strategy, which is not true. Or it must be heard in an ethical tone of voice. To answer it then would be to go inside the domain of ethics, and start expressing our standards. In this sense we may discuss whether promoting human flourishing, or manifesting respect for nature, or for liberty and equality, are good. But this kind of discussion is not furthering the project of explaining ethics in natural terms. It is taking ethical thought for granted, and trying to express and systematize our actual values.

Expressivism denies that when we assert values, we talk about our own states of mind, in actual or potential circumstances. It says that we *voice* our states of mind, but denies that we thereby describe them.[2] Similarly, if we are sincere when we say that 'the time is midnight' we voice our belief, but we do not describe ourselves as having a belief.

---

[2] Huw Price, 'Truth and the Nature of Assertion', *Mind*, 96 (1987), 202–20.

Our having the belief is not what makes it true that the time is midnight. It is only what makes us sincere when we say it.

Wittgenstein said, after Goethe, that in the beginning was the deed: *im Anfang war die Tat*. Words are themselves deeds ('words can be hard to say').[3] That is, it is only through understanding the *activities* associated with particular linguistic transactions that we understand the words used in conducting them. Amongst the activities involved in ethics are these: valuing, grading, forbidding, permitting, forming resolves, backing off, communicating emotion such as anger or resentment, embarrassment or shame, voicing attitudes such as admiration, or disdain or contempt, or even disgust, querying conduct, pressing attack, warding it off. When I say that these are involved in ethics, I mean what I have already adverted to, that by describing the contours of a character in terms of doings like these, a narrator can tell us all that is important about the character's ethics, regardless of the words said.

Should all these activities be herded together as 'expressing ethical beliefs'? It is hard to see how that could be useful to do so. It would be labelling at a level of abstraction that makes the interesting detail invisible. A philosopher might carelessly regard this as harmless: perhaps he sees it as simply revealing the 'depth grammar' or 'logical form' behind the rather ragged surface of linguistic behaviour. But it is not harmless. When we voice our ethics we have a distinct conversational dynamics. People are badgered. Reproaches are made and rejected. Prescriptions are issued and enforced. Resentments arise and are soothed. Emotions are tugged. The smooth clothing of statements proposed as true or denied as false disguises the living body beneath. The expressivist task is to reveal that clothing for what it is—but that is not to say that we should always try to do without it.

2. PRELUDE: NORMS AND FUNCTIONS

The evaluative proposition is the focus for practical discussion: what to do, what to admire, whom to badger, when to repent, and so on. But although Wittgenstein may have been right that in the beginning was the deed, it is still true that deeds need interpretation. We do not know what someone is doing until we can see their mere movements as expressions of purpose and intention, conducted in the light of beliefs about their situation, desires, and emotions. So before tackling

---

[3] Ludwig Wittgenstein, *Philosophical Investigations*, trans. G. E. M. Anscombe (Oxford: Blackwell, 1953), § 546.

the evaluative proposition head-on, I wish to consider for a while the theory of interpretation in general. What are states of mind?

States of mind are natural states. They are extremely hard to define. There is one well-known reason for this: the famous 'holism of the mental'. This view can best be understood by contrast with the view that it superseded, which was the view often called logical behaviourism, particularly associated with Gilbert Ryle.[4] Logical behaviourism proposed that each state of mind of an individual, such as their desiring this or believing that, could be defined in terms of the characteristic behaviour that would be expressive of that state of mind. The objection on the grounds of holism is that there simply never exists a characteristic piece of behaviour of the kind required. How people behave in the light of their beliefs depends upon what they desire. But how they behave in the light of their desires depends upon what they believe. If I believe that it is a fine day, this may prompt me to go for a walk, but only if I like that kind of exercise, and if nothing else interferes. If I fear ultra-violet light, it might make me stay indoors. It might make me say 'It is a fine day', but only if I want to tell the truth; others might be prompted to deny that it is a fine day, depending on what stratagems they have in hand. And so on. On this view a person's entire mentality forms a kind of web or field or force in which no single element has its own self-standing connection with action. Different beliefs and desires (and perhaps other states, such as emotions, attitudes, wishes, fantasies, fears, and of course values) come together to issue in action. But the contribution of any one of them will vary according to what else is in the mix, and therefore resists definition in terms of behaviour.

Holism means that we must beware of over-simple connections between values and action. But, in spite of holism, values, along with every other mental state, are eventually read back *en bloc* from peoples' doings. Values, like desires, are manifested in behaviour, even if they are only manifested as part of a crowd of other mental states, some of which, sometimes, do a good job of obscuring them.

Philosophers of mind have learned to live with the holism of the mental. Few deny the phenomenon, but few think of it as posing an

---

[4] The association with Ryle is loose. Ryle himself was at best a half-hearted reductionist in the philosophy of mind. First, his conception of a 'multi-track' disposition shows a realistic appreciation of the holism of the mental, and the diversity of ways in which a mental state may issue in actual behaviour, depending upon what other things the subject believes or desires. Secondly, Ryle is quite happy to use mental vocabulary on the right-hand side of his equations. There is no implication of reduction to behaviour as it is witnessed by the camera or Martian.

insuperable threat to any kind of naturalism. It shows that it was wrong to go for a simple item-by-item analysis of mental states in terms of overt behaviour. But it does not show that it is impossible to isolate the function of a particular belief or desire in the rest of a cognitive economy. And it emphatically does not show that the whole system is somehow unnatural, or magical, or resistant to natural identification.

But there is another aspect, which we can call the pervasiveness of normativity. The idea is this. Holism does not seriously threaten our naturalistic hopes in the philosophy of mind. It only suggests that the mind is like a complicated causal field in which many factors combine to influence any outcome. A belief or desire can be defined by its effect over all such fields: what it would do if found in combination with one or the other mix of other beliefs and desires. The pervasiveness of normativity denies that it is just like that. What it suggests instead is that when we are in the domain of the mental we are in an order of *rationality* rather than an order of *causality*. In Sellars's famous phrase, we are in the 'logical space of reasons'.[5] In other words, we can say what a person *ought* to do or what it *makes sense* for them to do if they have ought/will such-and-such a belief, coupled with such-and-such other beliefs and desires. But we cannot directly, on this account, say what they *will* do. Mental states are located not by their place in a causal structure, but by their place in a rational structure. And 'rational' here means normative: it tells us how it would make sense for a person to factor a belief or desire into a pre-existent matrix of mental states. A desire for an apple is something that makes sense of an agent's action of picking up the apple, given of course a normal human background of other beliefs and desires. But it equally makes sense of an agent's avoiding the apple, given that he has an overwhelming religious desire to mortify the flesh.

This way of looking at it is encouraged by much writing about the situation of the 'radical interpreter'. This is someone thought of as facing the problem of identifying a subject's beliefs, desires, and other mental states on the basis of their linguistic and other behaviour, but without prior acquaintance with the language they speak. It is supposed that investigating the *epistemology* of this enterprise is the best way of understanding the *ontology* or nature of mental states in general (this is the doctrine called interpretationism in the philosophy of

---

[5] W. F. Sellars, 'Empiricism and the Philosophy of Mind', reprinted in *Science, Perception and Reality* (London: Routledge & Kegan Paul, 1963), 169. Sellars actually only makes the claim about imputations of knowledge, but it is natural to generalize it.

mind, most notably associated with Donald Davidson and Daniel Dennett).[6] It is then added that the epistemology is best seen as normative in its essence. It is a matter of 'rationalizing' the subjects, hypothesizing that they believe what they ought to believe, and desire what they ought to desire, or at least what it makes sense for them to desire. Such a principle is known in various forms as a principle of charity or principle of humanity. Given this, mental states turn out to get their identity from a network of normative considerations.

There are two more buttresses to this view that I shall mention. One is that any exercise of judgement requires a subject who is not only disposed to apply or withhold terms, but who regards it as *correct* to apply or withhold terms. Speaking meaningfully is more than regularly producing noise. What animates words or gives them their life is the way in which their application is correct or incorrect, and this means that they are subject to evaluation. Obviously in human life this evaluation is a public matter and involves a community of speakers, although it is controversial whether this is necessarily so. But even if one lonely speaker, a congenital Robinson Crusoe, is a possibility, if he or she uses words then he or she must have established norms for their correct application. A second buttress to the view is the plausibility of a theory of interpretation also allied to that of Dennett and Davidson. On Collingwood's account, to understand your doings and sayings I must see them as the things *to have* done and said in the light of your grasp of the situation.[7] And that means making your words and sayings my own, in the sense of thinking the situation through 'in your shoes' or from your point of view, and then realizing that you did what was to be done, or that you said what was to be said. That process of rationalization also requires evaluation, in this case my own evaluation of sensible actions and the appropriate applicability of terms in your situation. It does not prevent me from discounting for things, say, that I know and you do not. But it does require me taking my own thinking and reasoning skills into your situation. In so far as I cannot see myself saying or doing what you did on any account of the matter, I do not understand you.

It is essential to realize that, in the view of writers in this tradition, the principle of charity is not here an optimistic and optional assump-

---

[6] For Davidson, see the essays collected in *Essays on Actions and Events* (Oxford: Oxford University Press, 1980). For Dennett, see *The Intentional Stance* (Cambridge, Mass.: MIT Press, 1987).

[7] R. G. Collingwood, *The Idea of History* (Oxford: Oxford University Press, 1946).

tion about how well we are doing. It is a 'constitutive' rule, or a principle that governs the very essence of mental states. It is not open to empirical rebuttal: it is a tautology, or principle that defines its subject-matter. Writing it in a form on which we can focus, we have an a priori principle of interpretation (API):

> (API) It is <u>analy</u>tic that creatures with beliefs, desires, and other states of mind, behave in ways that (best) make sense (and not in ways that make no sense), given those states of mind.

The idea behind calling this a <u>constitutive rule</u> is that it tells us *what it is* to have beliefs and other states of mind. According to API, then, it is analytic that creatures *conform* to the normative or rational order. A creature which appears not to do so is either a creature that we have misinterpreted, or a creature that has no mental states, but merely exhibits movements.

With API in place, it turns out not to be a simple empirical matter to describe a creature as believing this and desiring that. It turns out that issues of attitude are involved. To interpret someone as believing that the glass contains benzene and to loathe the idea of drinking benzene is partly to be poised to inveigh against them if they drink what is in the glass. But this is just what is involved in locating mental states in a normative space, rather than in purely causal terms.

The normative dimension to interpretation might seem to be consistent with a view of the normative which is non-naturalistic. That is, the existence of 'oughts' of rationality could be a real, Platonic mystery, for all this approach tells us. They could obtain in virtue of highly mysterious, *sui generis* facts about the rational order: facts which bear only a strange relationship to the natural order, and whose own credentials and authority remain shrouded in obscurity. If we think of it like this, then the expressivist strategy for naturalizing values runs into trouble. For it pins its faith on the possibility of a natural account of the state of valuing something. If no such account is forthcoming, because valuing, like other mental states, is identifiable only through the existence of a network of norms whose own nature is entirely mysterious, then the promise collapses.

But this is over-pessimistic. Suppose a principle or 'platitude' governing how to attribute a mental state such as fear of dogs to someone contains clauses such as this:

> <u>X fears dogs</u> ≡ X is in a state which, in conjunction with the belief that a dog is about, means that (other things being equal) it makes sense for X to flee; in conjunction with the belief that the

dog's owner is present, means that it makes sense for X to ask him to hold the dog, etc.

non-norm 'ought' of expectation

Then the question is how to take the references to 'making sense' in these clauses. They seem to be statements about what you would expect from an agent. It would surprise you, and lead you to scramble for another interpretation of X, if X does not behave in ways that make sense. Similarly we might say that the circuit is wired up if it is in a state such that, when the key is turned, there ought to be a spark. But the 'ought' here speaks not of duties and values, but just about what you would expect. If there is no spark, then something has gone wrong, but this too means simply loss of expected or intended function. The ignition creates the current; that is what it is for. The fear prompts the flight; that is what it is for.

To focus our thoughts, let us return to the apparent rival to the normative way of thinking about the mental. The functionalist rival at first either rejects the pervasiveness of normativity, or defuses it in the way suggested by the example of the circuit. It simply cites what we think mental states *do*, not what we think they ought to do. According to functionalism, any state of mind is located in essence by a trio of causal relations the state may have. It is caused by some things; it causes other mental states; and in conjunction with other beliefs, desires, and values it has various effects on action. The state is located by its typical causes, its mental relations, and behavioural effects. Saying that if you fear dogs, then when you come upon one you ought to flee, is just saying that this is the kind of behaviour you would expect of people who fear dogs. There is no implication that if you do not flee, you are somehow irrational. You are only to some extent doing something unexpected, to be explained with further investigation, and even indicative that your fear of dogs is not all that real.

Functionalism identifies mental states by their place in causal networks, not by their place in systems whose principles of construction are normative. We can 'solve for' fear of dogs at the same time as we solve for other elements of such a network. But in all of this there is nothing specifically normative involved. There are just dispositions to actions, and solutions for the elements in the causal field that give rise to action. States of mind are just there, identifiable in the psychologies that make people act as they do. Of course, the functionalist can add to the story some of the ingredients that impress those who put normativity in a central place. We represent the world to ourselves. If we represent it wrongly, plans and projects based on the misrepresentation are apt to fail. If too many fail, evolution sweeps us away. If our desires do not bear some relationship to our needs, the same happens. We ourselves deploy norms in these areas: we decry badly formed belief as misrepresentation of the world; we decry non-adaptive desires as disagreeable or useless to those who have them and those around them. There is nothing unnatural in our valuing accurate belief and healthy desire, once valuing is itself registered as one natural state among others.

Is there any opposition between the first, norm-centred approach to rationality, and the second, cause-centred approach? The first is, apparently, evaluative where the second is, apparently, empirical or causal. But this opposition seems to be markedly softened when we take into account API, the 'constitutive' role of the principles of rationality. For API means—this is something of a mouthful—that it is analytic that (typically) creatures exhibit a causal structure that is *isomorphic* with the rational structure that the normative approach prizes. For example, suppose it makes sense for Fred to drink a glass of benzene because Fred wants to drink a glass of gin, and has been plausibly but misleadingly told that the glass is full of gin. And suppose it would make no sense at all for Fred to drink what is in the glass if the deception is revealed. Given API, Fred's desire for gin will cause him to drink the liquid in the first scenario, but will not cause him to drink it once the deception is revealed. If Fred did drink the liquid after the deception comes to light, we have to search again for interfering factors: perhaps this makes sense because Fred wants to see what happens, or wants to exhibit a reckless machismo. Given such wants, it makes sense for Fred to drink the benzene, and if Fred does so it will be one of these wants that explains why he does so. In such a way, it is not only true, but a matter of definition or analytic, that Fred's desires and beliefs form a causal structure that mirrors the structures of what it makes sense for him to do. If they don't, then we have to reinterpret him.

How can API be true? How can it be a matter of trivial, analytic or definitional truth that people conform to a certain normative order? It would seem to be contingent, and even on the face of it optimistic, to suppose that by and large they do what they ought to do, in the domain of rationality just as much as in that of morality. But we can answer the question like this. Consider the example of game-playing. Here, too, there is a definitive normative order: a game is defined by its rules. There is a limit to the extent to which people can fail to conform to the rules. A rule may be broken now and again, but systematic and acknowledged breaking of the rules becomes not that, but a change of the game. Yet it is largely an empirical matter which game people are playing. Their behaviour tells us which patterns they *do* conform to and that in turn tells us which game they are playing: that is, which are the rules to which they *ought* to conform. Roughly: to play football is to behave in any of the large variety of ways that are licensed by the rules of football. It includes avoiding those actions that are prohibited by the same rules. It is also, in self-conscious beings, to have behaviour guided by explicit or implicit knowledge of what the rules are. There cannot be a total mismatch between what people in fact do on the playing field and what they ought to do. Similarly, to have the desire for *F* is to be disposed to behave in any of the variety of ways that are made sense of by having the desire for *F*. To have the value *V* is to be disposed to behave in those ways that are made sense of by having that value. There is, in other words, an assimilation of the normative and the causal order. We know what a desire is by knowing what it would make sense to do in the light of having the desire; but then we know whether someone has the desire by seeing if this light is one that makes good sense of what they do. API can be true because desires and beliefs are defined by what it is that they make sense of. But they are attributed by what they make people do, under the rubric that people do what makes sense to them. If we try to suggest cases where creatures (systematically) do what makes no sense to them, we end up denying the application of beliefs and desires at all. We are left only with behaviour, bodily movements that are not actions. This being so, the 'rational order' talked of in the theory of interpretation cannot be any very mysterious order of normative structures. For, if it were, it would inevitably be contingent whether people manage on the whole to conform to it—and that conflicts with API.

The theory of mind that is suggested by these considerations is twofold. On the one hand, the concept of a belief or desire, or any other state of mind, is identified using normative terms. These are defined in terms of what it makes sense to do in the light of them, given other states similarly defined. On the other hand, their presence in any subject is identified empirically, in terms of the causal structures visible in the actions the subject performs, and those she would perform in other circumstances. Any apparent mismatch is averted via the analytical principle API.

Where computation fails in the rational order, rules for prediction fail in the natural order. Computation fails because we may not be sure in advance how new cases may strike us, or strike others. This means that we recognize the *permeable* nature of the mind: new things catch our attention. New experiences, new angles of vision, new comparisons, new wishes, fantasies, memories, moods, emotions occur, and each of these can influence what it seems to us to make best sense to do. Revisiting the factors in a deliberation is like revisiting old friends. Much of what happens is predictable, but surprises and reval-uations do occur, and are always possible. But the causal order shows exactly the same permeability, for exactly the same reason. When new things catch our attention, or we become subject to new moods or memories, they influence what we think it makes sense for us to do, but, equally, they influence what we do in fact do. They act as new causal factors. So uncodifiability in the rational domain is matched by causal complexity in the natural domain, and indeed, given API, this has to be so.

We draw some morals from the theory of interpretation when we look at preferences, utilities, and choices in Chapters 5 and 6. We shall find that the theory of expected utility conforms to this model, impos-ing a parallel logical or normative structure on agents whose behavi-our makes them eligible for interpretation as agents in the first place.

3. STATES OF MIND: SATAN AND OTHELLO

Let us now concentrate on what we regard as a person's values. Expressivism requires a naturalistic story of the state of mind of valu-ing something. We then go on from that to give an account of the pro-cedures of valuation that we adopt; the modes of expression that are appropriate; and finally the logic and theory of meaning of our typi-cal expression of values. We have already seen that we locate a per-son's values in the light of a number of manifestations: what they say, what they do, what they regret in themselves, what they encourage in others, what they forbid or what they insist upon. Sometimes these elements pull together, and we have no doubt what someone values. Sometimes they do not harmonize all that well, and suggest various interpretations. Someone may sincerely believe that something is best, but not do it. There may be states of loathing of ethics, or of desire to be bad, or of maliciousness or waywardness, as well as despair or lethargy (what Aquinas called *accidie*), all of which can interfere with a simple attempt to read anyone's values straight back from their choices. Nobody lives up to their better selves all the time; some people only do it very little of the time.

There are interestingly different, although related, ways of inter-preting a lot of such cases. If a person fails to live up to their professed values enough of the time, we start to doubt whether the professions

are sincere, or, if they are at least sincere, we may wonder about self-
deception. One class of cases is the simple 'inverted commas' type of
case, where an agent pays lip-service to a value that they do not really
hold, either through hypocrisy or self-deception. This is no problem:
a person says that an action other than the one he intends is the 'good'
action, and means only that it is what the others call 'good' (there is a
specific sneering intonation that is typically used when we so speak).
Another very different class of case is where something is given an
evaluative label through *inertia*, even after the usual connection
between valuation and motivation has been severed. For example, we
deem a wine good in light of the pleasure we take in tasting it. This is
the typical or basic case. But if, for some reason, we have lost our taste
for wine and take no pleasure in tasting any, we could still call some
wine good if we know that it once merited the label. This has an obvious point: it serves the public function of grading the wine, or encouraging others to try for the pleasure. A third class of case I would like
to distinguish is different, although related. Here evaluative words
have also 'gone dead' and retain a use only to specify the class of
things meeting the standards that apply. Consider this conversation
from Jane Austen's *Emma*:

> 'Mr. Dixon, you say, is not, strictly speaking, handsome.'
> 'Handsome! Oh! no—far from it—certainly plain. I told you he was plain.'
> 'My Dear, you said that Miss Campbell would not allow him to be plain,
> and that you yourself—'
> 'Oh! as for me, my judgment is worth nothing. Where I have a regard, I
> always think a person well-looking. But I have what I believed the general
> opinion, when I called him plain.'

Here Jane Fairfax, the second speaker, does not put inverted commas
around 'the general opinion', yet the word 'plain' is applied in accordance with it, rather than as an expression of her own judgement. The
use is in a certain sense deferential to normal opinion. But, of course,
the valuation still lies in the background. It provides the reason why
Mr Dixon is called plain even if, in the mouth of Jane Fairfax, it
expresses no aesthetic attitude of her own. Jane is part of the social
practice of rating people on their looks. If she is spectacularly out of
line with the others, she will be criticized by them for misleading
them, and this is what she seeks to avoid in the conversation.

Other cases are more interesting, because a person's own values are
involved, yet there is only a shaky or perverted connection with
motivation. On occasion, clearly, a person can act, knowingly and
intentionally, against her values: she may have desires that overcome

her scruples, or just knowingly succumb to temptation. Doing wrong even has its own allure. But if the values are really there, we will expect them to manifest themselves somewhere else: in regret or remorse, or in guilt or shame. Yet even that may be too simple, and some philosophers ('externalists') have suggested that there can be agents in whom a pure cognizance of ethics has no practical effect: they know what is good to do, and simply do not care. Perhaps it is only good people who care to do what they know to be good. Perhaps there are bad people who know what it is good to do and then deliberately direct their wills the other way. Thus in Book IV of *Paradise Lost* Satan describes his motivation for bringing about the Fall with the chilling resolution 'Evil be thou my Good' (l. 110). For Satan, the ↳ judgement that something is evil acts as an attraction. And the fact that this possibility makes sense casts some doubt on the very close identification I have been urging between ethics and practical, motivating states of mind. If externalists are right, perhaps we have to see ethics more in terms of awareness of fact, with it then being up to us whether we care about the perceived fact one way or another. Philosophers resisting this ('internalists') have to say how they interpret the persistent, careless person who sees what is good, and doesn't care, or who, like Satan, sees what is good, but goes the other way.

My own judgement on this debate is that externalists can win individual battles. They can certainly point to possible psychologies about which the right thing to say is that the agent knows what it is good or right to do, and then deliberately and knowingly does something else. And they can point to psychologies like that of Satan, in which it can become a reason for doing something precisely that it is known to be evil. But internalists win the war for all that, in the sense that these cases are necessarily parasitic, and what they are parasitic upon is a background connection between ethics and motivation. They are cases in which things are out of joint, but the fact of a joint being out presupposes a normal or typical state in which it is not out.

To understand this, it is useful to think of another analogy. Consider the complex of dispositions involved in being in love with cf love someone. This typically includes taking pleasure in their company, wanting above all to be with them, wanting to give them pleasure and take pleasure from them, and so on. Nevertheless there are cases in which one person is in love with another, but wants not to see them (it would be too painful), or even wants to hurt them (jealous revenge). These cases are necessarily parasitic upon the normal in the sense that they require a background of the normal dispositions, which have then been wrenched out of order, giving rise to jealousy or the desire for revenge: love coexisting with hatred. But it would be absurd to conclude that being in love with someone is therefore a purely cognitive state, having no necessary connection with emotion or attitude.

We can approach the issue by another ethical illustration, here a public act rather than a private attitude. What is it to forbid something? To issue an injunction against it—but what is that? We might talk of communicating an intention to invoke sanctions or to become in one way or another set against anyone who disobeys the injunction. Surely 'forbidding' inhabits that neighbourhood. But can't you forbid someone from doing something, while all the time intending to forgive them if they do it? The case skates perilously close to pretence, or play-acting. But we might allow it: parents, for example, seem to tell their children what not to do, but without any apparent intention of doing much about it when they are disobeyed. If we allow it, we should say that the case exists, but is parasitic on a more robust social connection between forbidding and the disposition to sanction. The link is put out of joint by half-hearted parents, but it exists as the background to their activities, and is necessary to make those activities possible. Once more, it would be wrong to conclude that there is no necessary connection between an act of forbidding and an intention to invoke a sanction. That has to be the typical case that any others exploit.

Coming back to the individual psychology, Milton's Satan marvelously illustrates the point. Before saying 'Evil be thou my Good' he makes the terrible renouncement:

> So farewell Hope, and with Hope, farewell Fear
> Farewell Remorse: all Good to me is lost . . .
>
> (*Paradise Lost* IV. 108–9)

and Milton tells us:

> Thus while he spake, each passion dimmed his face
> Thrice chang'd with pale, ire, envie and despair,
> Which marred his borrowed visage, and betrayed
> Him counterfeit, if any eye beheld;
> For heav'nly minds from such distempers foul
> Are ever clear . . .
>
> (IV. 114–19)

Satan is racked with all the 'foul distempers' going. His position is exactly analogous to that of the jealous or despairing lover who wants to harm the beloved. It is his perpetual curse that he remembers how things could have been otherwise (he and God, representing the Good, could still have been together, as they once were); Milton's whole poem describes how his resolution to do evil is a response to this nightmarish predicament. It is a reaction against an acknowledged, internalized, active set of concerns, which align with those of the good. This is why his predicament is one of rebellion not only against the good, but against part of himself. In other words, this is not a psychology in which 'knowledge of what is good' is emotionally or practically inert. It is a psychology driven by reaction *against* the emotional and practical force that knowledge exerts. Such a psychology represents an ultimate conflict within the agent, and perhaps is as likely to issue in suicide as murder. The point is made in the myth: Satan's knowledge of what is good is established by his being a *fallen* angel, in whom the appropriate attitudes and emotions were once in place.[8] Similarly, in order to be jealously murderous, a lover must once have loved in more normal ways, and been dislocated from them.

Is it a conceptual truth, or a truth of empirical psychology, that the subject must originally be one way, and only later get out of joint, for these interpretations to earn their keep?[9] If the latter, we might talk of 'projection' or 'dislocation' simply as psychological mechanisms, useful for explaining how a good person becomes attracted to the bad or how a lover becomes murderous. If the former, we would deny that there are even possible cases in which the love of the bad comes about except through a previous love of the good going out of joint. My own opinion inclines to this, although it is not essential to the main message of expressivism. The main message can allow that in principle an individual may love the bad without ever having loved the good, provided enough social context, in which motivations are aligned with the good, is provided.

In Shakespeare's play, Othello still loves Desdemona as he smothers her. One might prefer to say that his love has turned to hate. But I think this would be simplistic, or even just unkind (for these verdicts will carry moral implications).

During the crisis, Othello is never simply somebody who hates Desdemona, and to say that would not explain the eventual size of his remorse when he knows what he has done. His love is far from

---

[8] The phenomenon is superbly treated in Salman Rushdie's *The Satanic Verses*, 424–7.

[9] I am grateful to Margaret Walker for forcing me to confront this question.

extinguished, but only temporarily overcome. Even when he is accusing her, Desdemona is

> There where I have garnered up my heart,
> Where either I must live or bear no life,
> The fountain from which my current runs
> Or else dries up—

IV. 1. 59–62

And after the murder:

> Had she been true,
> If heaven would make me such another world
> Of one entire and perfect chrysolite
> I'd not have sold her for it.

V. 2. 150–3

The problems with Othello are his fears and his conception of honour, not his attachment to Desdemona. But we look further in Chapter 5 at the sinister way in which egoistic motives might underlie even the most fervent and sincere attachments.

In any fully realized case of love behaving as hatred does, or of evil being someone's good, we can provide more or less plausible empirical speculations about how the joint gets to be out. It is here that we talk of displacement and egoism and pride and immaturity, or whatever strikes us as the best history of the conflicts within the breast.

Of course, there are many less extreme examples of dislocation between ethics and action. I might recognize that it is my duty to do something, and resent that fact because I resent having been put in that position. I still have to be the victim of a foul distemper for this to happen.[10] But I might just feel like being mischievous, or even malicious for once (this can be *delicious*). If I am very dutiful normally, but the others are having more fun, I might want to join them. But, again, these cases only exist against either a *psychological* background of motivation by what is perceived as duty, or a *social* background of insistence upon duty as a practical constraint. That is, even if we try to stretch the case away from the Satan/Othello model by sketching an agent who has absolutely no conflict, but views duties with the utmost unconcern, we will find that he exists only against a backdrop in which talk of duty does express concern.

If there is nothing but settled, cold unconcern from an agent for

---

[10] Hume describes the nice case of an historical situation in which because of too much prating about ethics, a 'peevish delicacy' led people to belittle its claims: *Enquiry Concerning the Principles of Morals*, VI. 1, p. 242.

what he verbally acknowledges as his duty, then of course we do begin to talk of mere lip-service. The agent is using evaluative vocabulary in a parasitic way, as mere labelling for what other people regard as good. He may be like Jane Fairfax, or the wine-taster who has lost pleasure in wine, using the word as a label for the kind of wine in which he would expect others to take pleasure. But we are, rightly, not quick to reach for these interpretations in ethics. Partly this is because, if the agent has a normal history, we would expect internalized values still to operate at some level. There will be incipient conflict. Partly it is an exercise of a general interpretive strategy, which is to hold people to the literal meanings of their words. Unless agents deliberately indicate the inverted commas we take them literally, as indeed Jane Fairfax was taken in the conversation quoted above.

Doing what you know to be bad is bad. We might describe it as irrational, and since Plato many philosophers have done so. But that is not, as it stands, a very interesting thing to say, for it is not at all obvious what further or different specific kind of charge it makes. Satan's pride got him where he is, but his pride is not inexplicable or unintelligible. It is not as if he insists that $7 + 5 = 13$, or that he is a teapot. In fact, Milton's poem is so great because Satan is not only intelligible, but not wholly unadmirable. His reaction to God's suffocating superiority makes sense. If a loving but strict parent lays down all kinds of constraints on a child's conduct, we understand the child being naughty and we might admire her for it, even if, as she is being naughty, she is in conflict with herself and as a result unhappy. In fact, parents are often more or less quietly proud of naughtiness in their children. Rebelliousness takes courage. Similarly, jealousy may be a very bad emotion to feel, but it is not clear what is meant by saying that it is irrational to feel it. It makes sense, in human terms, as a response to fear of loss or betrayal, even if heavenly minds are clear of it. Satan is not irrational, but bad. And if that is true of Satan, it is still more so of the more mundane cases of human weakness: we are depressed, we let ourselves be led, we succumb to temptation, we even make little attempts to break the moral mould. We are not irrational, but weak. Or, if 'rational' implies boundless strength of mind in pursuit of the good, say that we are irrational. But we are perfectly intelligible, and may deserve sympathy, and if our characters require improvement, it is not usually in the direction of better calculation or logic.

So externalists can have individual cases, but internalism wins the war. Ethics remains essentially practical, a matter of attitude, disposition, and emotion. When a psychology contains other elements, the

way these issue in action becomes surprising, or even in a way contradictory, in the way that Othello's final expression of his love of
Desdemona contradicts that emotion. And that is just the way it is
with the relationship between attitude and action, in beings as complex as we are.

How, then, do values relate to other practical states, and notably to
desires? Do they constitute a special *sui generis* motivational state, one
of 'normative governance' rather than normal desire? Gibbard talks
of a state 'identified by its place in a syndrome of tendencies towards
action and avowal—a syndrome produced by the language-infused
system of coordination peculiar to human beings'.[11] I think this is
right, although I shall later caution against supposing that the motivational system in question is special or extraordinary. And I shall
return to some of the detail of coordination later. But I doubt if anything more direct would be right. Philosophers have often suggested
equating an agent's values not simply with what she desires, but with
what she desires to desire, or with her highest-order desire, thought
of as the desires she 'identifies with', or has no tendency to wish
away.[12] This, too, is surely along the right track, although it does not
work well with Satan. Satan does not at any level desire to desire as
the good angels do, happy indulging in monotonous worship, even
although he knows that in rebelling against that status he rebelled
against being good. He feels the most intense pressure towards repen-
tance, yet he does not desire to repent, and neither does he desire to
desire it. This is partly because he is well aware that if he were to
repent and become good again, the whole process would start all over
again (IV. 93–100). So Satan's genuine present sense of evil and of the
good he has lost does not coincide with present *desires* at any level,
although it may align with regret and wishes that things might have
been otherwise.

Our values also do not seem quite the same as our highest-order
desires for another reason. It seems natural to interpret some agents
as regretting having the values they do: a person of unswerving
integrity, for instance, might at some level wish that he was a little
more relaxed, if those who cut corners or bend the rules just a little
seem to be having more fun or getting on better in the world.

---

[11] Allan Gibbard, *Wise Choices, Apt Feelings*, 75.

[12] The classic papers by Harry Frankfurt, particularly 'Identification and Whole-
heartedness', are collected in his *The Importance of What we Care About* (Cambridge:
Cambridge University Press, 1988). See also Gerald Gaus, *Value and Justification*
(Cambridge: Cambridge University Press, 1990).

Obviously, however, if this wish starts to dominate his practical life, then his integrity has been compromised, and we might prefer to say that his values have changed, at least temporarily.

I may desire to eat ice cream, but be quite calm contemplating a future state in which I would not desire it. I need not resist processes that change my desires. In fact, I might welcome them. Whereas, when values are involved, we typically resist anything likely to destabilize them. Such processes would be regarded as undermining and threatening. So, if we imagine the general field of an agent's concerns, his or her values might be regarded as those concerns that he is also concerned to preserve: the ones by which he stands. He would contemplate losing them only with dismay. It is because a child or an animal has no such protective concerns that they are thought of as 'wanton'.[13]

To hold a value, then, is typically to have a relatively stable disposition to conduct practical life and practical discussion in a particular way: it is to be disposed or *set* in that way, and notably to be set against change in this respect. This way of being set is such as to align values and motivations. And, characteristically in philosophical psychology, although this may be the paradigm, typical case, there are also others. We are often not aware of what we value, or how much we value it. We may not be all that disposed to protect and cherish a concern, but, when things go wrong, realize how much it mattered. It may only be retrospectively that we discover that we have valued something. Here the disposition is not one of being set to foster a concern, but being set to feel pain when it is threatened or vanishes.

Because we are talking about the way an agent is set, there is a speed limit on change of values. Someone who one day professes one set of concerns and priorities, but another day a quite different set, is not someone who has many values, albeit for a short time each, but someone who has no real values at all. Over sufficient time, of course, a person's concerns and interests and priorities can change, although it is also worth noticing that values one thinks one has suppressed can be surprisingly resilient: habits of valuing, like habits of deference or old superstitions, tend to come back to haunt us. It is difficult to shake off their grip, and there is often something off-colour about the professions of a convert, just as there is about professions to be cured of different emotions.

What has been said here concentrating upon the notion of a value, which might typically get expression by saying that something is

---

[13] I am indebted to Valerie Tiberius for emphasizing this.

good, or that some character trait is a virtue, can be adapted quite easily to the vocabulary of right and duty, rights and obligations. Here we find states of mind further up the staircase of emotional ascent: ones that prime us to insistences and to hostility to others. But the connection with action is obvious in typical cases, and subject to the same kinds of interpretative subtleties when normal links are broken.

seen

   To sum up, then: to hold a value is to have a relatively fixed attitude to some aspect of things, an attitude with which one identifies in the sense of being set to resist change, or set to feel pain when concerns are not met. That fixed attitude typically issues in many dispositions, at various places on the staircase of emotional ascent I described in the first chapter. When things are not out of joint, values align with motivations. But we understand quite profound misalignments in terms of intelligible internal conflict. If the conflict is sufficient, we will not know what to say, just as we do not know when to say that love coincides with hate, or when it has been replaced by it. When things get out of joint the normal or typical expression of the attitude can be perverted; reactions set in, and under sufficient stress we have the person of weak will, who knowingly succumbs to temptation, or more interestingly the Satanic figure who is knowingly attracted to evil. To merit such an interpretation, however, and not to be put down merely as a hypocrite who pays lip-service to values he does not really hold, an agent must show a dynamic pattern of change and stress. There has to be a history, and an internal conflict. Not everyone who murders someone is murdering someone he loves, but occasionally some do, and sometimes we understand why.

4. THE ETHICAL PROPOSITION AND FREGE'S ABYSS

So what at last is said when we say that something is good or right? Following Moore, we do not expect to identify the content in other terms. We can now say, however, what is done when we say such things. We avow a practical state. 'Avowal' here means that we express this state, make it public, or communicate it.[14] We intend coor-

---

[14] We are not prepared to avow all the norms that influence us. Gibbard makes the useful distinction here between accepting a norm, which includes preparedness to avow it, versus being in the grip of a norm, which means being subject to its sway, perhaps unwillingly or guiltily, as in the case of a not-quite-liberated racist or sexist, who knows how he ought to be, but does not quite measure up in his snap emotional reactions (*Wise Choices, Apt Feelings,* 58–61).

dination with similar avowals or potential avowals from others, and this is the point of the communication. When this coordination is achieved, an intended direction is given to our joint practical lives and choices. Saying that something is good when we do not really value it is either deceiving others about our state, or is the result of self-deception. But because we have to accommodate the flexible, many-layered nature of our minds, we may sincerely say that something is good when we are not, unhappily, motivated to pursue it, provided one of the diagnoses sketched in the previous section applies.

If I permit smoking in my house, but you forbid it in yours, we do not necessarily disagree about anything. Similarly, some evaluations are happily relativized: the weather is good from the farmer's point of view, but bad from the tourist's point of view, or good in so far as it helps the crops, bad in so far as it spoils the holiday. But with much ethics there is no scope for this coexistence. If I am minded to permit smoking in our house, and my wife is minded to forbid it, we do disagree. Only one of these practical attitudes can be implemented, and I am for one, and she is for the other. When we discuss ethics with each other, we are typically talking about 'our' house, or in other words practical issues on which we want to coordinate, or have to coordinate. In that case difference of attitude means disagreement, just as surely as difference of belief does. If the case is like that of separate houses we can sometimes 'agree to differ', and drop the conversation. But sometimes, even if we do not have to coordinate our actions, we cannot agree to differ, for serious enough differences cannot be tolerated. I return to this when we discuss relativism, but meanwhile the point remains that the typical, default, position is that difference in attitude is treated as disagreement.

Ethical avowals, like decisions and verdicts, require grounds. If I grade one paper higher than another, I must be prepared to indicate some relevant difference between them. We acknowledge the need to point to something that grounds our judgement, in virtue of which one is better than the other. But, as we shall see in the next chapter, discussing Cornell realism, no complete theory of ethics can simply point to the grounding properties, and suppose that evaluations are given their meaning by their relationship to them. We need first to understand the evaluative stance.

Expressivism claims that the ethical proposition is something that we synthesize for a purpose. Its role is to act as a focus for practical thought. So what is it to believe that something is good, wonder whether it is good, to deny that it is good, to be undecided, or to know that it is good? In basic or typical cases:

believing that *X* is good or right is roughly having an appropriately favourable valuation of *X*;

wondering whether *X* is good or right is wondering what to
do/what to admire or value;

denying that *X* is good or right is rejecting a favourable attitude
to *X*;

being undecided is not knowing what to do/what to admire,
etc.;

being certain that *X* is good or right is having a settled atti-
tude/rejecting the possibility that improvement could result in
change;

knowing that *X* is good is knowing to choose *X*/admire *X*, etc.

Here the practical states on the right-hand side are voiced and discussed in terms of attitudes to the saying or thought on the left. This
is what I mean by saying that the moral proposition is designed or
invented or emerges naturally as the focus for our practical transactions. And in the previous section we established the natural credentials of the states on the right and their intricate connections with
other attitudes and emotions.

The reason expressivism in ethics has to be correct is that if we supposed that belief, denial, and so on were simply discussions of a way
the world is, we would still face the open question. Even if that belief
were settled, there would still be issues of what importance to give it,
what to do, and all the rest. For we have no conception of a 'truth condition' or fact of which mere apprehension by itself determines practical issues. For any fact, there is a question of what to do about it. But
evaluative discussion just is discussion of what to do about things.

However, many writers have insisted on a 'Fregean abyss' separating expressions of attitude from expressions of belief. They point out
that evaluative commitments are expressed in ordinary indicatives,
and that this enables them to occur in indefinitely many 'indirect' contexts. We not only say that *X* is good, but that either *X* is good or *Y* is,
or that if *X* is good such-and-such. Some think that this puts a weighty,
or even insupportable, burden on expressivism. For all the expressivist has given us is an account of what is done when a moral sentence is put forward in an assertoric context: an attitude is voiced.
What then happens when it is put forward in an indirect context, such
as 'if *X* is good, then *Y* is good too' and no attitude to *X* or *Y* is voiced?

It is worth asking how other parts of language answer this problem. Suppose I say that the sentence 'Bears hibernate' expresses a belief. Well, it only does so when the sentence is put forward in an assertoric context. So what happens when it is put forward in an indirect context, such as 'If bears hibernate, they wake up hungry'? For here no belief in bears hibernating is expressed. The standard answer is to introduce a proposition or thought, regarded as a constant factor in both the assertoric and the indirect context. When we say bears hibernate, we express or assert the proposition, and represent ourselves as believing it; when we say 'If bears hibernate . . .' we introduce the proposition in a different way, conditionally, or as a supposition. Frege thought that in this second kind of context we refer to the thought that we assert in the assertoric context.

If this is allowed to solve the problem for ordinary beliefs, it might simply be taken over by the expressivist. In the Fregean story a 'proposition' or 'thought' is simply introduced as the common element between contexts: something capable of being believed but equally capable of being merely supposed or entertained. So why not say the same about an 'attitude'? It can be avowed, or it can be put forward without avowal, as a *topic* for discussion, or as an alternative. Just as we want to know the implications of a proposition or a thought, so we want to know the implications of attitude. What implies it, what is it right to hold if it is to be adopted?

If we want to know in other terms what is going on when we so put forward an attitude, we must look to the function of the indirect contexts in question. The key idea here is one of a functional structure of commitments that is isomorphic with or mirrored by the propositional structure that we use to express them. Thus someone may be what I called 'tied to a tree': in a state in which he or she can only endorse some combination of attitude and belief. Suppose I hold that either John is to blame, or he didn't do the deed. Then I am in a state in which *if* one side is closed off to me, I am to switch to the other—or withdraw the commitment. And this is what I express by saying 'Either John is to blame, or he didn't do the deed', or equally, 'If John did the deed, he is to blame'. By advancing disjunctions and conditionals we avow these more complex dispositional states. Taking advantage of the theory of interpretation sketched above, we can regard the state in question not just in functional terms, but also in normative terms. By using the disjunction I am presenting myself in a way that will deserve reproach and bewilderment if, without explanation, I go on to suppose both that John did the deed and is blameless. This makes no sense, unless I have changed my mind about something.

There has been some scepticism about whether this approach can deliver the mighty 'musts' of logic.[15] But we now see that it can do so perfectly well. Consider the example made famous by Geach, of inference according to the pattern of modus ponens. Someone saying each of 'p' and 'If p then q' has the premises of a modus ponens whose conclusion is q. He is logically committed to q, if he is committed to the premises. To put it another way, if anyone represented themselves as holding the combination of 'p' and 'If p then q' and 'not-q' we would not know what to make of them. Logical breakdown means failure of understanding. Is this result secured, on my approach, for an evaluative antecedent, p? Yes, because the person represents themselves as tied to a tree of possible combinations of belief and attitude, but at the same time represents themselves as holding a combination that the tree excludes. So what is given at one moment is taken away at the next, and we can make no intelligible interpretation of them.

We can put the point another way. A mental state, I have said, is identified by what it 'makes sense' to hold in combination with it. To avow a mental state is therefore partly to express acceptance of certain norms. To avow anything of the form 'If p then q' is to commit oneself to the combination 'Either not-p, or q' and to be tied to that combination is to disavow the combination of p with not-q. Holding both together is therefore unintelligible. Logic is our way of codifying and keeping track of intelligible combinations of commitment.

We might usefully compare the situation to that in the theory of probability. The basic psychological reality as we contemplate the chances, for instance in a horse race, may be one of vague differences of confidence, reflected as dispositions to bet (under idealized circumstances) at various prices, or within various ranges of prices. If we choose to voice these confidences, for instance by saying that Eclipse has no better than an evens chance, or that 100 to 12 sounds a fair price on Sunrise, then we enter a more structured normative space. We only make sense if the chances we assign to the different horses in the field obey well-known classical rules of probability, and those rules dictate inferences. For instance, in a two-horse race, if we think one horse has a better than evens chance, then we must infer that the other has not.

[15] Bob Hale, 'The Compleat Projectivist', *Philosophical Quarterly*, 36 (1986), 65–84. Related work includes G. F. Schueler, 'Modus Ponens and Moral Realism', *Ethics*, 98 (1988), 492–500; M. H. Brighouse, 'Blackburn's Projectivism—An Objection', *Philosophical Studies*, 59 (1990), 225; Nick Zangwill, 'Moral Modus Ponens', *Ratio*, 5 (1992), 177–93; Mark van Roojen, 'Expressivism and Irrationality', *Philosophical Review*, 105 (1996), 311–35.

Our dispositions to bet at different prices only make sense if they can be represented as beliefs in probabilities, satisfying those laws. Working in terms of 'belief in classical probabilities' does not, then, necessarily reflect a prior commitment to the metaphysical hypothesis that there are such things, as it were hovering above and around horse races. More economically, it simply shows us working through the implications of various dispositions to accept and reject betting prices. The 'probability proposition' is a focus for our thoughts about where to put our money. And expressing ourselves in terms of probabilities imposes a necessary logic.[16]

Similarly, if we start with a set of beliefs and attitudes, we can put them into a structured normative space by representing them as beliefs in the ethical proposition. Accepting conditionals and disjunctions shows us working out the implications of various combinations of attitude, or combinations of attitude and belief. We crossed Frege's abyss by creating the ethical proposition, and it is there in order to generate public discourse about which actions to insist upon or forbid, and which attitudes to hold or reject.

A development of this approach has been elegantly presented by Gibbard.[17] Gibbard talks in similar terms of the disjunction: 'Either packing is now the thing to do, or by now it's too late to catch the train anyway', where 'packing is now the thing to do' are words simply expressing the decision to pack. Because decisions can be contested, discussed, disagreed with, we have the indicative form, and we have the devices of propositional logic to keep track of reasoning about decisions. Gibbard develops his own semantics in terms of the notion of a 'hyperdecided state': one in which 'I have a complete view, correct or incorrect, about everything that might be the case in the world, and I would have a universal plan for life, a plan that covers, in detail, every possible situation one could be in that calls for decision'. One can then specify the content of a complex statement involving components expressing decisions by seeing in which hyperdecided states one would not have changed one's mind about them. Logic follows from the conception of consistency: a state of mind is inconsistent if

---

[16] Why necessary? Because flouting the classical laws corresponds to a disposition to combinations of bets that would lead us to lose whatever happens. This is the 'Dutch book' theorem.

[17] Allan Gibbard, 'A Natural Property Humanly Signified', forthcoming. This presentation is, I think, more perspicuous than that in *Wise Choices, Apt Feelings* because the notion of a completed state is easier to grasp than that of a 'factual-normative' world, which is part of the earlier exposition. But the approach remains essentially the same.

there is no hyperdecided state I could reach from it without changing my mind about something.[18]

Among the most important indirect contexts are those conditionals that express our standards. 'If a person told a lie, then she did something wrong.' Dissent would be dissent from the standard, refusal to be tied to that tree, and we make this refusal if we want to accommodate blameless lying. Among suspect conditionals would be ones expressing what we might think of as a bourgeois morality, which finds rightness or wrongness purely in our gaze: 'If we/enough of us/ . . . think something is wrong, then it is wrong.' This is a tree we would well want to be free from, for we recognize the possibility of correctly dissenting from the herd. Similarly, 'If we had not disapproved of it, it would not have been wrong' only expresses the bourgeois view that our disapprovals actually create the wrongness. Sometimes, this is so. The variable obligations of etiquette, for example, enjoy this status. But usually it is not. Cruelty is not wrong because we disapprove of it, but because it causes pain and anguish.

It is sometimes incorrectly suggested that a 'Humean' must avoid conditionals with factual antecedents and evaluative consequents, because of his embargo on deriving an ought from an is. But this is simply a mistake. Hume can and does vigorously assert the conditionals that express standards. All he denies is that they are truths of reason, having an a priori or analytic status, or one guaranteed by logic alone.

There are other indirect contexts that can appear puzzling. Imagine the case in which you come to me and tell me something using an evaluative term. If you say, for instance, 'If an act creates happiness then it is good,' I will understand you well enough: this is voicing a certain standard, and acknowledging that standard means being disposed to value things on the basis that they create happiness. And values we already have under control. But suppose you are rather more enigmatic, and deploy your values only indirectly. Suppose you say: 'Johnny will do three good deeds by lunch time,' but I don't know what in your estimate counts as a good deed. Can I understand you, when you do not directly express an attitude of evaluation to anything? Since deeds are good in virtue of satisfying standards, and I presume you to understand as much, then I know in principle what will count for you as a vindication of what you say. Johnny will three times perform deeds with a quality X that *you* regard as sufficient to

---

[18] I would only add here that this requires some preceding notion of consistency in a plan, which would be identified with there existing a possibility of it being realized.

justify an attitude of admiration. I also know what will have to be true for *me* to agree with you. Johnny must perform three deeds with a quality Y that *I* regard as sufficient to justify that attitude. X may or may not be identical with Y. In the upshot, Johnny might perform to your satisfaction but not to mine or vice versa. If the issue is important enough, we are then in disagreement over the standards, and this we express in the propositional way: you think that X makes deeds good, and I think Y does, and you think Johnny did his three good deeds, while I do not.

For experts in the philosophy of language, it is pleasant to notice that construing such indirect contexts is directly parallel to the construction of indirect contexts in minimalist or 'deflationist' theories of truth.[19] Since these occupy us again in Chapter 9, it is appropriate to introduce them now. According to deflationism, 'is true' is basically a device of disquotation, whose meaning is given by instances of the famous schema:

$$\text{(T)} \quad \text{`}p\text{'} \text{ is true if and only if } p,$$

where the inverted commas imply mention of a sentence, or in some versions a proposition, or in others an understood-utterance, on the left-hand side, with the same utterance used to talk about whatever it does on the right-hand side. The detailed differences between interpretations of the truth-schema are not important here. But, according to deflationists, (T) encapsulates all we need to know about truth. This is variously expressed by saying either that 'is true' is not a property of utterances, or that it is not a robust or substantive property. It is not one that invites difficult philosophical questions. The idea, in its original formulation by Tarski, is that if we had a sentence of this form for every sentence of a language, and if on the right-hand side we never made use of semantic vocabulary ('is true' or 'refers') then we could, as it were, nevertheless equip a mind that is blind to semantics with enough to give a truth value to every sentence. And this would show that there is no need for such a mind to judge in terms of truth or reference itself in order to be in full cognitive command of the language.[20]

Whether it does show this is controversial. In any event, everyone agrees that something must be added to the schema to enable us to

---

[19] For an introduction, see my *Spreading the Word* (Oxford: Oxford University Press, 1984), chs. 7 and 8, or Paul Horwich, *Truth* (Oxford: Blackwell, 1990).

[20] Alfred Tarski, 'The Concept of Truth in a Formalized Language', in *Logic, Semantics, Metamathematics* (Oxford: Oxford University Press, 1956).

understand indirect mention, in which the actual proposition asserted remains hidden: 'What Johnny said this morning was true,' for example. We might try a direct quantification: there is a p such that Johnny said 'p', and p.[21] But many philosophers are uncomfortable with this, for it looks as though 'p' is treated as a variable ranging over propositions at one point, and as an assertion at another. If we avoid this quantification, the neatest way to solve the problem is in terms of an indefinitely large disjunction of conjuncts:

Either Johnny said 'p_1' and p_1, or Johnny said 'p_2' and p_2, or . . .

where $p_1, p_2, \ldots$ represent the possible things Johnny might have said. It is easy to verify that Johnny will have said something true if, but only if, at least one of these alternatives obtains. So similarly in the present case, when you tell me Johnny will do something good, I can reoresent the content of your saying in terms of a disjunction of conjuncts:

Either Johnny will do a deed X_1 and X_1 deeds are good, or Johnny will do a deed X_2 and X_2 deeds are good, . . .

Interestingly, just as disquotationalists in the theory of truth have some trouble with constructing their list, especially when we turn to consider utterances in a foreign language, we might have some trouble constructing a plausible list of possible standards, especially when we are confronted with the possibility of thoroughly alien standards. So there is an element of idealization involved in supposing that there is some definite list of utterances exhausting the things the reporter might have said, or the list of standards he might have had in mind. But we can well live with that. In each case we would know what is meant by adding 'and so on'. The disjunction sums up that we know what is going on. When someone reports that Johnny did something good, there is some property of deeds that the informant admires, and she believes Johnny did a deed with that property. Notice, however, that the truth of her remark is not simply guaranteed by Johnny doing such a deed: this is the issue of whether $X = Y$ again. I myself expect to be able to voice one of the disjuncts, thereby deploying my standards, in order to regard the remark as true.

With indirect contexts under control, we have now provided all the essential ingredients for a natural account of moral thought. We understand sufficiently what it is to hold something as a value, and to

---

[21] For experts: this would properly use a substitutional quantifier. The difference does not affect any of the points in the text.

express it using the locutions of belief in a proposition. We understand the ethical proposition as a focus for practical thought.[22]

What should a theory of this kind be called? I have called it 'projectivism', but that can sound misleading. It can make it sound as if projecting attitudes involves some kind of mistake, like projecting our emotions onto the weather, or projecting our wishes onto the world by believing things we want to believe. This is emphatically not what is intended. Gibbard calls the view 'expressivism', and I now think that is better. A full-dress title might be 'non-descriptive functionalism', or 'practical functionalism'. In any event, a term I used in my first paper on the subject remains appropriate.[23] There I said that the moral proposition was a 'propositional reflection' of states that are first understood in other terms than that they represent anything, and that remains the core claim. It is the isomorphism between propositional structures and necessary practical states that is the heart of things.

It remains to expand the account, by addressing worries about authority, scepticism, and relativism, and the possibility of moral knowledge, but the core ingredients are now in place.

5. REPRESENTATION AND MINIMALISM

There is a sophisticated position in the philosophy of mind and language which would not query the story so far. But it would query whether it makes the ethical proposition anything very special: anything deserving, for instance, special treatment, as the expressivist or projectivist seems to think. The position I have in mind pushes minimalism or deflationism through one more turn. It can usefully be introduced by looking again at the later philosophy of Wittgenstein.

Nobody can deny that Wittgenstein tried to understand many areas of discourse in terms other than those of 'representing the facts'. According to Wittgenstein, whole areas of language that look as if they are dedicated to describing how things are must be understood in other terms. If we think of the areas treated in his later philosophy—the nature of philosophy itself, the nature of self-knowledge, of necessity, of mathematics, of certainty, of religious belief and of ethics—we find that in every case Wittgenstein's approach is to suggest a different

---

[22] This construction of the ethical proposition is the exercise that I have christened 'quasi-realism'.

[23] 'Moral Realism', reprinted in *Essays in Quasi-Realism* (New York: Oxford University Press, 1994), 111–29.

function for thought in the area. We are doing such things as: laying down rules of grammar, making avowals, making frameworks of description, giving voice to metaphors or the way in which we are seized by a picture, or expressing attitudes. At various times a timid representationalist puts his head over the parapet, and Wittgenstein always dismisses him with a curt reminder of minimalism or deflationism in the theory of truth:

Someone may say, 'There is still the difference between truth and falsity. Any ethical judgment in whatever system may be true or false.' Remember that '*p* is true' means simply '*p*'. If I say 'Although I believe that so and so is good, I may be wrong': this means no more than that what I assert may be denied.

Or suppose someone says, 'One of the ethical systems must be the right one—or nearer the right one.' Well, suppose I say Christian ethics is the right one. Then I am making a judgment of value. It amounts to adopting Christian ethics. It is not like saying that one of these physical theories must be the right one. The way in which some reality corresponds—or conflicts—with a physical theory has no counterpart here.[24]

The implication is that we can talk of metaphysical, mathematical, modal truth because that is just to repeat our commitments in these areas. But what is going on when we have such a commitment is to be understood in other terms. Wittgenstein often associates this with a verificationist point: we only understand what is meant by making an assertion, or equally by calling it true, in so far as we have a grasp of the procedures that justify or verify the assertion.

Wittgenstein's thought here is the same as that of F. P. Ramsey, whose famous paper 'Facts and Propositions' argues that it is not by staring at the word 'true' that progress is made, but by understanding the function of various kinds of judgement in behavioural terms.[25] Because of the minimalism we can have for free what look like a ladder of philosophical ascent: '*p*', 'it is true that *p*', 'it is really and truly a fact that *p*' . . ., for none of these terms, in Ramsey's view, marks an addition to the original judgement. You can as easily make the last judgement as the first—Ramsey's ladder is lying on the ground, horizontal.[26]

Wittgenstein seemed to think that representation was one thing, but

[24] Rush Rhees, 'Some Developments in Wittgenstein's View of Ethics', *Philosophical Review*, 74 (1965), 23.

[25] F. P. Ramsey, 'Facts and Propositions', *Foundations: Essays in Philosophy, Logic, Mathematics and Economics*, ed. D. H. Mellor (London: Routledge, 1978), 40–57.

[26] See also Chapter 9, where I discuss philosophies that take advantage of the horizontal nature of Ramsey's ladder to climb it, and then announce a better view from the top.

all these different 'language games' did different things. But did he? After all, the minimalism about truth allows us to end up saying 'It is true that kindness is good'. For this means no more than that kindness is good, an attitude we may properly want to express. We can say that the proposition represents the fact that kindness is good. The ethical proposition can be put in the T-schema:

$$\text{'}X \text{ is good' is true} \equiv X \text{ is good}$$

Anyone understanding the sentence will be prepared to assert the right-hand side if and only if they are prepared to assert the left, in each case voicing the attitude of approval to X.

Minimalism seems to let us end up saying, for instance, that 'kindness is good' represents the facts. For 'represents the facts' means no more than: 'is true'. It might seem, then, that our investigations have ended up with a position remarkably like that of Moore. The ethical proposition is what it is and not another thing; its truth means that it represents the ethical facts or the ethical properties of things. We can throw in mention of reality: ethical propositions are really true. Since we already have a sketch of a minimalist theory of ethical cognition, saying that we talk of knowledge that p when we are convinced that no improvement has a chance of reversing our commitment to p, we might even find ourselves saying that we know moral propositions to be true. Or, really true, or really factually true, or really in accord with the eternal harmonies and verities that govern the universe, if we like that kind of talk. We can add flowers without end: 'it is good to be kind to children' conforms to the eternal normative structure of the world. For this means no more than that it is good to be kind to children.[27] And rather than saying that we hold that it is good to be kind to children, we can if we like say that as we hold that it is good to be kind to children our minds are in harmony with the eternal normative order of things. For this just means the same. I return to this surprising way of looking at things in Chapter 9.

Superficially this might seem like an objection to the investigation, as if the 'quasi-realist' construction has bitten its own tail. It starts from a contrast between expressing belief and expressing an attitude, which it then undermines, by showing how the expression of attitude takes on all the trappings of belief. Since we can handle the ethical proposition exactly like any other, it is not mistaken to say that we voice belief in it, when we do.

---

[27] 'Eternal' gets in because, I should judge, nothing is going to change to make it other than good to be kind to children.

R

But in fact this is no objection, and there is no tail-biting. We must remember Wittgenstein's dismissive attitude to invocations of truth and representation when he is dealing with the kinds of commitment that interested him. Just *because* of minimalism about truth and representation, there is no objection to tossing them in for free, at the end. But the commitments must first be understood in other terms. Once more, 'we remain unconscious of the prodigious diversity of all the everyday language games because the clothing of our language makes everything alike'.[28] Our understanding of the kinds of activity involved in specific, ethical, states of mind remain in place, driving the construction of the moral proposition. If we started and finished with a special, *sui generis* representation of moral aspects of the world, we would be drawing a blank. But by starting elsewhere, we can see what is right and justified about finishing saying some of the things Moore did when he spoke in these terms. By getting there this way, however, we have a complete answer to difficulties that destabilize Moore's own package, notably the questions of epistemology, and of why we should be concerned about the ethical properties of things. For we have the answer: what we describe as the ethical properties of things are constructed precisely in order to reflect our concerns.

[more explan
pours]

If we were discontented with minimalism about representation and truth, we might wonder how the story would go with a thick theory of representation to hand. Would that deliver a contrast between 'representing the ethical facts' and 'representing natural facts'? It is hard to say. Obviously there will be some differences between 'ethical facts' and the others. The fact that there is a cannonball on the cushion explains why it is sagging in the middle. The fact that kindness is good explains no such kind of thing. We do not expect laws of ethics to play a role in treatises of physics. Probably the most promising way of finding contrasts would be to think more about the adaptive mechanism that make us sensitive to physical fact, in contrast with the adaptive mechanism that give us an ethical motivational system. The adaptive stories will surely be sufficiently different to give vastly different accounts of 'representation'.

Wittgenstein himself, in the passage quoted above, suggests that with physics 'correspondence' has a different application. But he does not tell us why he thinks this.

We have, however, already met a cluster of considerations that might be drawn from Wittgenstein's later work and that also confuse the picture. We can list:

[28] Wittgenstein, *Philosophical Investigations*, II. xi, p. 224.

.

(1) The pervasive presence of normativity in any exercise of thought.

(2) The contingent exercise of sensibility involved in apprehending a principle of classification; *hence* perhaps the general impropriety of drawing a fact–value distinction

(3) The *practices* involved in any use of concepts. There are implications for mental action just as much as visible action in the application of any predicate—*hence* the idea that evaluations have a different 'direction of fit' from other representations is blunted.

The drift is that since all exercises of thought, all representation of things as being one way or another, involve evaluation and practice, evaluation should not be thought of as distinct from representation.

But even if this were right, it would not follow that there is anything misdirected about the approach we have adopted. For theorizing about evaluation and values as we have done is quite consistent with supposing that the dispositions of the mind that they consist in are as pervasive as these ideas suggest.

Let us consider an example of the presence of normativity in, say, a simple classification: 'X is a cat.' Suppose we concede that norms govern the activity of making the judgement. That is, if something is a cat then it is wrong to think of it as any number of things—canine, or insensible, or made of silicon. And it is right to think of it as born of a cat, possessing retractable claws, and so on. To judge that X is a cat (sincerely, in full understanding) entails being disposed not to judge that it is a dog, and being disposed to hold that it was born of a cat. Anyone failing to make these moves is apt to forfeit the interpretation. Any judgement has its a priori implications and exclusions. This fact must be couched in normative terms, in terms, that is, of what it is right to conclude, or right to exclude, in light of the proposition.

So now we are back with the idea that in the domain of psychology the normative is everywhere. Psychological states, as explained in the second section of this chapter, relate not by what they typically cause, but what 'makes sense' as an expression of one, or what counts an implication of one, or a reason for one. How exactly does this amount to a strike on behalf of some other theory, and against quasi-realism? Suppose the other theory dislikes e.g. talk of 'attitudes' and likes talk of 'normative beliefs'. Then the two offerings might be:

> (Realism) To believe there is a cat on the mat is to be in a normative space, which is in turn to believe that one ought to . . ., or to be subject to other people believing that one ought to . . ., or to be

disposed in conjunction with other things to believe that one ought to . . .

(Quasi-Realism) To believe there is a cat on the mat is to be in a normative space, which is in turn to have the attitude that one ought to . . ., or to be subject to other people having the attitude that one ought to . . ., or to be disposed in conjunction with other things to have the attitude that one ought to . . .

There is no reason to suppose that the first offering is *ex officio* the default, preferred account. In fact, if anything it looks subject to worrying regresses and circularity (beliefs requiring other beliefs of at least equal and apparently greater complexity). Escape into a different notion, such as sets of norms being embedded in communities and/or psychologies in various ways, alleviates this. Via such a notion we can understand what this normativity amounts to. Without it normativity remains an unmoved mover.

We have to avoid a regress, whereby every belief requires a further background belief about what ought to be held given the first belief. The mistake would be akin to holding that behind every interpretation stands another, rightly opposed by Wittgenstein. To understand the predicate is to *internalize* this system of norms governing its application. It implies a skill, something that can be done better or worse, accurately or ineptly. But it does not imply capacity to articulate a normative structure, capacity to articulate the norms involved in something being a normative structure, and so on.

These reflections show that how we understand the world in one set of terms, or how we understand one part of the world, has normative implications for how it is right to represent it in other terms, or how it is right to understand other parts of it. This is one of the morals of 'holism', although it depends on only a very dilute and uncontroversial version of the doctrine. But it does not break down the distinction between how we understand the world and what we are motivated to do about it. The understanding is practical within the sphere of understanding; our evaluative and ethical life is practical *tout court*.

The upshot is straightforward. In all spheres of thought we make judgements, and judging is subject to standards of correctness. To represent the world as one way or another is to stand ready to be corrected. But in so far as this breaks down a distinction between representation and evaluation, it does so on behalf of evaluation. It is the Apollonian side of the mind, representation and truth, that cannot do without its Dionysian cousin. This only adds importance to the specific investigation of the attitudes, and the other mental dispositions involved in practical reasoning.

It would be possible now to go straight on to explore the structures of motivation and deliberation that we need to understand. Readers impatient to do this should skip the next chapter, which is simply a comparison of the theory I have just presented with other contemporary approaches. This comparison and the criticism of other theories are not essential to understanding the theme of this book. But it may help to locate the exact nature of the view, by better distinguishing it from others with which it could be confused. And it should help to appreciate its strengths if we can maintain a firm grasp of the difficulties in front of alternatives.

4

The Ethical Proposition:
What it is Not

You see these compartments are the haunts of the Aristockracy said the
earl and they are kept going by peaple who got something funny in their
family and who want to be less mere if you can comprehend
    Indeed I can said Mr Salteena
    Personally I am a bit parshial to mere people said his Lordship but
the point is that we charge a goodly sum for our training here . . .

Daisy Ashford, The Young Visiters

1. DIONYSUS AND APOLLO

Moral philosophers like to concentrate on an object of thought, something that we can ponder and know to be true: the moral proposition.[1]
For people who want to think of themselves as objectivists, absolutists,
and realists, the moral proposition is a genuine aristocrat, something
sublime, authoritative, an independent object of attention. For them, it
is vitally important to recognize these propositions as true when they
are. They have their own truth-conditions, and magnetize our wills.
Kant wrote that two things command our respect and wonder the
more we think of them: the starry heavens above and the moral law
within. Moral truths make up the law. Only it is not a human law, or
even a divine law, but sits in judgement on all manufactured laws,
human or divine. For we can always ask of those whether they measure up, whether they are as they ought to be. When we focus on the
moral proposition, we focus on a true sovereign. It has absolute
authority, and measures other authorities. When we ask if something
is justifiable, we may have in mind only whether we can justify it to

---

[1] To avoid misunderstanding: I talk of 'the moral proposition' in the spirit in which
Kant talked of 'the judgement of taste': the label covers any of the things we assert when
we are presenting ethical and moral opinion. Differences and nuances within the family are not being ignored. They are mentioned when they crop up as important.

some human audience, such as our partner or our boss. But we can also have something else in mind, something less fallible and partial. We wonder whether our actions are *really* justifiable, as it were in the eyes of God.

For this reason most analytic philosophers agree all too literally with the fourth Gospel, that in the beginning was the word. They think that their starting-point should be the content of our ethical sayings: the propositions or sentences that we might use when we do get round to voicing our ethical points of view. Their enterprise is to understand such propositions, to 'give an account' of their 'content' or their 'truth conditions'. The question is what we are thinking when we think that such-and-such an action is obligatory, or that one state of affairs is preferable to another, or that chastity is a virtue, or the fact that the piano is on your foot provides a reason for moving it. Following entrenched, although unfortunate, philosophical usage in this chapter I shall call this approach 'cognitivism'. The usage is unfortunate, because there is nothing to stop us from talking of ethical knowledge in the light of the construction of the last chapter. I return to this in Chapter 9.

The default cognitivist position this century was set by G. E. Moore, in *Principia Ethica*. Moore approached the question of getting absolutely clear what was meant by ethical and moral propositions, and met a blank wall. So he concluded that there is no way of saying what they mean except in more or less identical terms. This means that we can sometimes give paraphrases, but these will not help us to understand what we want to understand: they will not give us a useful theory of knowledge for ethics, or way of understanding what we are doing when we talk about values or duties. We can paraphrase, for example, 'Love is good' in ways like 'An ideal adviser would advise you to love' or 'Love is fit to be chosen' or 'Love is desirable', but these paraphrases simply keep us *within* the sphere of the ethical; they do not tell us anything interesting *about* the ethical. Moore's procedure for securing this result is the 'open question argument' we met briefly in Chapter 1. For any proposed reduction of the ethical proposition, Moore points out contexts which show us treating the ethical proposition differently. It occupies a different niche in our thoughts. Thus, if someone proposes that the proposition 'X is good' just means the same as 'X creates happiness', Moore counters that we know perfectly well what it is to doubt whether all and only things that create happiness are good. This is a question we can ponder, even when we know perfectly well what each element means. It is an open question. We can augment his point by adding that we understand perfectly well what people are doing who deny that all and only things that create happiness are good, and who show in their practical lives that they accept no such inference.

Moore's argument has been controverted in detail, but it clearly contains an important insight. We might see it as hinging on the fact that valuing and other ethical activities are *different* from describing and explaining, or from purely scientific representations. Something special, and further, is involved in seeing anything that creates happiness *under the heading* of good, beyond just describing it as creating happiness. This further special thing characterizes those who use the property as a standard or ground for their valuations. Some people do, but others don't, and neither side can convince the other by pointing purely to meaning or semantics. Moore himself did not, however, conclude that valuing is different from describing. He concluded that ethical propositions were *sui generis*: they presented a special 'non-natural' area of facts distinct from facts of psychology or natural history or science. We know things about this area, fortunately, by means of a faculty called 'intuition'.

Moore's negative argument against identifying moral propositions in different terms remains convincing.[2] I believe he was absolutely correct about the content of the moral proposition. It is what it is, and not another thing. But this is not to succumb to intuitionism. It shows that we must approach the content of that proposition another way. We must synthesize it, rather than discover it by analysis. In other words, it is not Moore's arguments about ethics that were wrong. It was his conception of the possibilities open to philosophical method. Certainly the intuitionism with which he ends up is a blank wall. This is because it goes with no epistemology (no way of distinguishing better or worse intuitions) and especially because it goes with no account of why we should be remotely interested in what we are intuiting. Thus in Moore's picture an underlying fact, such as that an act is of a kind that promotes happiness, may 'give rise to' its being a good act. Some persons may be motivated to do this act (or to approve of it or encourage it) because it is an act that promotes happiness. But then there are other

---

[2] The only respectable way of controverting it is to urge the possibility of hidden analytic structure, whereby people in fact mean some complex by a term, even although they are not aware of this. The fact that they mean it is shown by their 'implicit' inferential dispositions. But Moore can and should reply that there are no implicit inferential dispositions at work to show that to think in terms of values is just to think in terms of natural descriptions, rather than to take up a stance or attitude to those descriptions. On the contrary, our implicit dispositions, such as who to regard as a partner in an ethical conversation, reveal nothing but the loosest relations to such descriptions.

persons who first apprehend that it is good, and are then motivated to do it, or to have the other attitudes, just because of its *goodness*. These people end up in the same place as the others, but they have had to go through *two* extra stages to get there: first apprehend the added value, the goodness; then be drawn to the action just because of that. There is extra apprehension and extra motivation. But why believe in these extra layers? Why not instead see there just being people who are motivated to care about the promotion of happiness, and who as a result are motivated towards the act, and, equivalently, are inclined to see it as good?

If Moore successfully attacks reductive theories, and this kind of argument successfully attacks Moore, as I believe it does, then we might conclude: so much the worse for the cognitivist approach by way of meaning, or content, or truth conditions. For it should have been obvious from the beginning that since moralizing and valuing are distinctive activities, the words we use to communicate our morals and our values will have their distinctive meanings. Why try to square the circle by going bull-headed for an illuminating 'account' of their 'truth conditions'?

Philosophers are not so easily put off. In the following sections of this chapter I am going to compare three attempts to drill holes in Moore's blank wall. The first approach takes as its inspiration Wittgenstein's rule-following considerations. It interprets these as showing that there is no sharp or interesting distinction between facts and values, so that there is no need to find anything special about the moral proposition. It suggests that the idea that there is something special is the residue of an 'eighteenth-century psychology', a faculty psychology that sharply distinguishes representing the world from responding to it, or Reason from Passion. The most influential contemporary exponent of this view is John McDowell. The second approach tries for an analysis of what is thought: a way of revealing what the words involved 'really' mean. This is a close descendant of classical philosophical analysis, aiming to reveal the real structure of our thought by expressing it more perspicuously, laying bare its real meaning. I shall discuss here a cluster of positions, more or less approximated by Michael Smith, Frank Jackson, Mark Johnston, and Philip Pettit. A different approach is centred on the idea that we don't have to say what moral terms mean to give a satisfying picture of ethics. If we can find the properties they refer to, that is enough. The position here is associated with David Brink, Richard Boyd, Nick Sturgeon, and Richard Miller. It is sometimes known as Cornell realism. Cornell realism thinks we can identify the 'truth-makers' for our ethical thoughts, identifying what properties of things make them true, rather as the scientist identifies the property of stuff that identifies water or gold. Success in this enterprise would be to show that when we think in ethical terms we are referring to this or that property of things, identified in other terms.

So in this chapter I discuss what I regard as the three most prominent contemporary approaches to giving an account of the moral proposition. I shall argue that they are each inferior to the expressivist or projectivist option that I introduced in the last chapter.

But first, why should we start with 'beliefs' and propositions rather than with other states of mind? There is, in the philosophical culture as much as in the everyday culture, an enormous pressure to do so. The pressure comes from the following picture:

Dionysus			Apollo
Emotions	*Desires*	*Attitudes*	*Cognition*
Upsets	Impulses	Stances	Representations
Passions	Whims	Dispositions	Knowledge
Arousals	Lusts	Sentiments	Truth
Excitement	Urges	Postures	Reasons

When people think of ethics, the elements in the three left-hand columns seem uninviting allies. They are an unruly crew, and generate a distinct set of associations in peoples' minds. They are subjective, whereas those on the right are objective. They are contingent, or variable, those on the right are timeless, or abiding. Things on the left are relative, those on the right are absolute. They answer to rhetoric; the others answer to thought. Things on the left buffet, prick, prod, spur, and goad us. Sometimes they overwhelm us; they make us lose our heads. But on the right we guide and pilot ourselves. Things on the left come in gusts and assail us; on the right we control them and fortify ourselves against them. We might fear that we are passive before the things on the left, when on the right we are active (in Kantian terms, when the left moves us we are 'heteronomous', moved from without, and when the right does we are 'autonomous', or self-controlled). Perhaps things on the left are passions, meaning that we are passive before them.[3]

In a word, things on the left belong to the dark, and those on the

---

[3] In the sense of Locke, for example: 'For when the ball obeys the motion of a billiard stick, it is not any action of the ball, but bare passion', *Essay*, II. xxi. 4.

right to the light. They are lower; those on the right are higher. In the bad old days, they were feminine, whereas the exercise of reason was masculine. Or, if we are biologically inclined, we might find ourselves associating those on the left with primitive sub-cortical structures; those on the right belong to the cortex. On the left we have flesh and the id, on the right, intellect and the superego.

Unlike Daisy Ashford's earl (in the epigraph to this chapter) philosophers are not traditionally partial to the lower orders. They talk disparagingly of mere emotions, mere desires, mere attitudes.[4] Nobody talks of mere knowledge, or mere truth. Nobody says that a reaction is merely reasonable, or that an opinion is just reason talking. And since philosophers want their ethics not to be 'merely' this or that—for what is less mere, more sublime, more aristocratic, more worthy to control us than respect for the right and the good?—ethics is to be placed firmly on the side of Apollo. Only on the right do we find truth. And we want our ethics to be true. Ethics belongs to the government, and not to the rather mere things that need governing.

Some philosophers are a little more partial to creatures of the left, because they conceive of them as getting virtue from the right. That is, they think of emotions as themselves cognitive in nature. If anger, for instance, can be classified as essentially a perception or cognition, such as a representation of oneself as having received some kind of threat or insult, then it possesses the virtue of the cognitive relation of perception. On such an account the authority of the right can seep through to the left. But this is, of course, an entirely Apollonian picture of the emotions. Although I shall not say much about it directly, I should say, first, that it is not in itself all that plausible as it stands, for one can think of oneself as having been threatened or insulted without being angry about it. One might even be amused by it. Secondly, it is not all that clear that thinking in terms of threat and insult is purely representational. Each term itself suggests attitudes and stances. Thirdly, as we have seen, ethics is not just about emotions, but also about other practical stances, and the prospect for finding them all 'cognitive' or purely representational is extremely dim.

Moore was really following the Platonic tradition. There is a very special property, the Good or the Form of the Good, that can be dis-

[4] See for instance, Judith Jarvis Thomson, in her contribution to G. Harman and J. J. Thomson, *Moral Relativism and Moral Objectivity* (Oxford: Blackwell, 1996): attitudes, displays of attitude, even a sea of attitudes, are 'mere' on almost every occurrence, e.g. pp. 97, 99, 102, 200, 201, 202, 206. This sniffiness goes back to Kant, of course, where 'the constraining power of the moral law' fights to get the better of 'merely sensible incitements'. I talk further of Kantian objections to mere emotions in Chapter 7.

cerned by the elite. It is intensely magnetic: once discerned it draws those who have known it irresistibly. It bends their wills, driving out the shades of Dionysus. And we can see why this picture will appeal to those who claim authority: why it informs the rhetoric of the mandarin classes. If you stalk Washington or Paris or London, framing policy and advising governments, the last thing you want to admit is that all you have in your pocket is a tissue of attitudes, or desires, or emotions. In a recent article, Ronald Dworkin magisterially denounces those who think that ethics might be a creation of imagination and culture, presumably because these things affect only the left, and have nothing to do with the pure cognitions on the right. Otherwise it is hard to see why we should applaud unimaginative and uncultured ethics.[5]

'But we use our values to criticize even our own desires and attitudes, and even those of our culture.' Indeed we do—but that, I argued in the last chapter, is because we call 'values' just those desires and attitudes that stand fast when we contemplate others and try to alter them. Even self-criticism has to stand somewhere, and what it stands upon most firmly we call our fundamental concerns, or in other words our values. What we have is not Apollonian bedrock, but relatively stable and abiding members of the Dionysian circle.

There is an insuperable obstacle to keeping ethics under the rule of Apollo. Suppose we think our ethics is entirely exhausted by our beliefs. What then? Even the most magnetic star does not attract everyone. Beliefs do not normally explain actions: it takes in addition a desire or concern, a caring for whatever the belief describes. The information that in my absence my partner has painted the bedroom yellow matters to me only in so far as it interacts with other concerns: hatred of yellow, or worry because it is Fred who is known to prefer yellow, not me. The belief that the piano is on your foot matters to me, and makes me act to remove it, because I believe it is causing you pain, and I am concerned at that. Suppose the philosopher valiantly identifies the moral belief and insists on its status as belief, and nothing else. Then—dreadful thought—what if someone doesn't care about the truth the belief represents (an upshot that would seem all too probable on the Moorean picture, of course)? This would be very regrettable no doubt, but would it be more regrettable than not caring about the pain in your foot? And if the latter concern is a brute emissary from the realm of Dionysus, what is to prevent caring for the truth of the moral

---

[5] Ronald Dworkin, 'Objectivity and Truth: You'd Better Believe It', *Philosophy and Public Affairs*, 25 (1996), 87–139.

belief from being just the same thing? In other words, we seem to be faced with the following zig-zag structure. We start with something bad such as the piano being on your foot. An agent is concerned about that. A novelist might leave it there: we have a piece of sympathy and right attitude, a modest indication of the agent's ethics. But the philosopher worries that this is very *mere* attitude or emotion on the part of the agent. So she substitutes, as the focal point of ethics, that the agent believes that she ought to help—a belief that is true, and carries the authority of truth. So if an agent fails to believe that she ought to help, it would be an Apollonian defect, not merely one of Dionysus. But then, alas, there are immoral and amoral agents, who know this truth and do not care about it. Are they 'merely' wrong on the Dionysian side? Perhaps we had better find a property of the moral belief that should sway them; for instance, that it is reasonable to be swayed by it and only it. Then the amoralist or immoralist fails to believe something that they should (we represent their defect as Apollonian, again): they do not realize (intuit) that failing to be concerned by moral beliefs is unreasonable. But suppose they do know that it is unreasonable, but just don't care about that? Then we drag the defect back to the right by finding another term: 'irrational' or 'normative' or whatever. But suppose they don't care about rationality or normativity . . .? Eventually, we will be bound to finish by appealing to Dionysus for help: 'But *don't* you care about things going well, or flourishing or social coordination, or peace, or contracts?' Fortunately, most agents do care, but then after all we started with someone who cared to get the piano off the foot, and in a well-functioning society, most agents care to do that. All the zig-zags have given us is a delaying tactic, for, as Hume saw, somewhere there will always have to be a practical, dynamic state: a concern or stance or attitude involved in translating belief into action.

This is so even if we go as Apollonian as we can. Suppose we find with the Kantian that moral duties, for example, are necessarily to be legislated by all rational agents as maxims governing their conduct (on which more later). We still face the fact that we have to motivate people to bother about that. We have to get them to love the law, or at least to respect it, and this is another piece of brute care and concern. But how sorry to labour to place ethics entirely in the light, only to find this creature of the night, this dark, contingent frog, this visceral, fleshy daughter of Dionysus, at the bottom of the Apollonian well![6]

---

[6] This paragraph incorporates material rather differently laid out in my 'Practical Tortoise Raising', *Mind*, 104 (1995), 695–711, and in my review of G. Harman and J. J. Thomson, *Moral Relativism and Moral Objectivity*, in *Philosophy and Phenomenological Research*, 58 (1998), 195–8.

McDowell

2. CONCEPTS, RULES, AND FORMS OF LIFE

A very sophisticated and influential attempt to get beyond Moore's blank wall is presented by John McDowell's writings on ethics. These come out firmly in favour of a position he calls cognitivism. But his cognitivism is not Platonic or Moorean. It is presented as fully informed by an understanding of the integral place that sentiment and attitude play in ethics. McDowell understands the danger of the kind of approach that leads to Moore's blank, or equally to the zig-zag structures of the last section. He damns such approaches as involved in a mythical 'Platonism'. He thinks that, in recoil from this hyper-objective Platonism, many people topple into an unhappy subjectivism, and ethics becomes merely a kind of 'sounding off' (this is how he thinks of expressivism, but the charge is unfounded). Happily, however, there is a 'fully satisfying intermediate position' deriving from the work of Wittgenstein, which shows how to understand these and other matters, providing we learn to avoid a certain kind of mistake.[7] The mistake is one about the perspective from which moral (and, for instance, logical or mathematical) demands are perceptible. They are perceptible, McDowell argues, from within the practices, or forms of life, or 'whirls of organism' that constitute moral, logical, or mathematical practice. They are not perceptible—but this should not worry us—from outside those forms of life, from the standpoint of the alien, or the cosmic outsider. In an analogous manner, the colours of things are not perceptible from outside the standpoint of those with colour vision, but this tautology should not lead us to doubt that colours are 'really' there, or to doubt whether we communicate truths and facts when we retail the colour of things to each other. Nor should we doubt that seeing things as coloured is genuine *receptivity*, or a response to what is 'there, anyway'. So realism (cognitivism) and truth attach to ethics, just as much as they do to colour judgements.

The appeal to Wittgenstein picks up the 'rule-following considerations' that dominate much of the first part of the *Philosophical Investigations*. To introduce these we can set the scene like this. The goal is to understand the ethical proposition, and to understand it as a real proposition, putting forward a truth or a falsehood as the case may be. Let us take the simplest case, of application of an evaluative term to a subject, and for example let us also take a case in which a fairly specific virtue is in question, such as '*X* behaved kindly'. Suppose this involves

---

[7] 'Non-Cognitivism and Rule-Following', in S. Holtzman and C. Leich, eds., *Wittgenstein: To Follow a Rule* (London: Routledge, 1981).

a favourable evaluation of what X did, which is why we are in the domain of ethics. Let us say we will understand the proposition if we understand who is referred to, and understand the *concept* of 'behaved kindly'. So what is it to understand a concept? It is to master a rule of application, a rule determining to which things it is correct to apply it, and to which things it is incorrect (and to which things it is indeterminate, if there exist such cases). Wittgenstein, now, is taken to teach us that mastery of such a rule is in effect identical with involvement in a form of life. McDowell quotes with approval a passage from Stanley Cavell: ·

We learn and teach words in certain contexts, and then we are expected, and expect others, to be able to project them into further context. Nothing insures that this projection will take place (in particular, not the grasping of universals, nor the grasping of books of rules), just as nothing insures that we will make, and understand, the same projections. That on the whole we do so is a matter of our sharing routes of interest and feeling, senses of humour and of significance and of fulfillment, of what is outrageous, of what is similar to what else, what a rebuke, what forgiveness, of when an utterance is an assertion, when an appeal, when an explanation—all the whirl of organism Wittgenstein calls 'forms of life'. Human speech and activity, sanity and community, rest upon nothing more, but nothing less, than this. It is a vision as simple as it is difficult, and as difficult as it is (and because it is) terrifying.[8]

The immediate application is that we see how 'behaved kindly' can be subject to a rule. The rule will only be applicable by those sharing 'routes of interest and feeling'. But that is true of *all* rules. So it marks nothing peculiar (nothing particularly soft or subjective) about 'behaved kindly' that it does so, in spite of it implying an evaluation. In this way the rule-following considerations can be taken to assimilate ethical judgements to every other judgement. We can no longer regard them as special just because they are shared only by those who share routes of interest and feeling.

So far I would claim that there is much to admire. The ingredients with which McDowell is working are the right ones: human sentiments and routes of interest and feeling, rebukes, appeals, senses of fulfilment or outrage, imagination and culture. We might agree that it is only people who share such things who can be said properly to share an ethic, and their ethic will be voiced when they say things like 'X behaved kindly'. What then happens when disputes break out? All we can do, it seems, is appeal to a 'hoped-for community of human

---

[8] Stanley Cavell, *Must we Mean what We Say?* (New York, Scribner's, 1969), 52; quoted in John McDowell, 'Non-Cognitivism and Rule-Following', 149.

response'.[9] We deploy whatever methods we can to try to get the other side to see it like we do. But this is not *less* than we need, because we never get *more* than this in any area, even in areas where we are inclined to talk about proof, for example.

Actually, this is contestable. Wittgenstein implicitly contrasts ethics and other subjects at *Investigations* § 240: 'Disputes do not break out (among mathematicians, say) over the question whether a rule has been obeyed or not. People don't come to blows over it, for example.' Here the organisms all whirl the same way, and indeed perhaps they have to do so to succeed in engaging in mathematics at all. It may be that Wittgenstein thinks that this is *sufficient* to ground a practice of talking about objectivity and proof. What is more disturbing is that consensus may also seem *necessary*, for otherwise we simply seem to have organisms that react one way, and ones that react another. One side, for instance, finds it natural and inevitable to classify a very young foetus as a baby, and the other side finds it grotesque, and classifies it as a complex of cells. And since we have abandoned any Platonic, external standpoint from which one can be seen to be doing the right thing and the other the wrong thing, any claim on behalf of one side to receptivity, cognition, truth, objectivity will at this point ring hollow (they may *make* claims in these words, but that will just be another part of the way they happen to whirl). In other words, if the hoped-for community of response is clearly not forthcoming, the status of the dispute, in Wittgensteinian terms, is at best unclear. This is more dramatically so when we think, as we might, that the majority of organisms are whirling the wrong way on such an issue. It is not a philosophical truth that the majority determine what is right.

This point, although significant, does not get to the heart of the matter. Self-criticism must be possible, and it would be an immediate crippling objection if the Wittgensteinian approach failed to make room for it. But perhaps the Wittgensteinian position can be defended by the reflection that part of our whirl of organism is to reflect upon and worry about and sometimes try to dislodge some of the very classifications suggested by our whirl of organism.

A more secure objection at this point arises if we ask whether the considerations so far have actually identified the ethical proposition as a genuine object of thought, or identified ethical concepts as genuine concepts, or justified thinking of us as genuinely *receptive* to anything. To show why this remains open, I shall take a simple case. Consider a culture in which excess body fat is regarded as perfectly all right, or

---

[9] McDowell, 'Non-Cognitivism and Rule-Following', 153.

even desirable. Now suppose that fashions change and there are ~~fat~~ ↓
people (slim, active, lithe teenagers, perhaps) who begin to find fat
people disgusting. Suppose they register this by a characteristic sneering tone of voice: 'What is your brother like?', 'Oh, he is *fat*'—which I
shall write as 'he is fat↓'. Only people who share the disgust will ever
be heard using the term with that tone. Others will not typically register dissent by saying 'No, he is not really fat↓', repeating the tone, for
that is what to say when you share disgust at fat, but deny that X is so.
People who want to reject the sensibility will say things like 'Don't say
that!'

Now, 'fat↓' is a term that can be used, and people who share the disgust will use it similarly. It is associated with a rule, in the
Wittgensteinian sense, and will be applied and withheld by people in
rough agreement (Wittgenstein himself said 'You might say that certain words are only pegs to hang intonations on').[10] We can read down
Cavell's list, and see how the shared use of the term depends upon features shared by the users: here their capacity to detect fat, and their disgust. But do we have a distinctive concept here, and a distinctive
proposition, capable of truth and falsity? Are those who use the term
'receptive' to a property that is there independently? On the face of it,
nothing of this sort is true. We would not credit the teenagers with a
conceptual advance when they come to share this disgust. We certainly
would not be likely to say, for example, that there is a distinctive property of fat↓ness, and that the teenagers' shared reactions now enable
them to detect it, discovering a new kind of truth. On the face of it,
there are just fat people, and the teenagers' expression of their disgust ✓
at them.

McDowell might even agree about this, for he specifically exempts
'disgust' from what he wants to say about 'the field of ethics'.[11] The difference is that 'disgust and nausea' are 'self-contained psychological
items, conceptualizable without any need to appeal to any projected
properties of disgustingness or nauseatingness'. I should say at once
that this is a strange concession, for as I described in Chapter 1, disgust
is an emotion capable of structuring a great deal of ethics (and politics),
and is recruited to do so by notions like sin and defilement. In cultures
with caste systems, disgust is a prime arbiter of moral status. The
moral worlds of *Hamlet* and *King Lear* (and even of *Oedipus Rex*) are
defined and sustained by disgust. So if, as McDowell wants, a moral

[10] Wittgenstein, *Philosophical Grammar* (Berkeley, Calif.: University of California
Press, 1974), 66.
[11] See 'Projection and Truth in Ethics', in S. Darwall, A. Gibbard, and P. Railton, eds.,
Moral Discourse and Practice (New York: Oxford University Press, 1997), 215, 218.

sentiment like contempt is to be thought of when things go right as a perception, an awareness, or cognition of the genuinely contemptible, it will be hard to see why justified disgust does not show a similar perception, awareness, or cognition of the genuinely disgusting (and it should be noticed that disgust is quite unlike nausea, in being not a generalized feeling of malaise, but an emotion with an object: we are typically disgusted at something or at the very thought of it).

In any event, whatever the place of disgust, McDowell wants to develop the rule-following considerations in other cases to enable us to say that there are moral concepts, and moral properties discerned by those who use them. We are to be given something more aristocratic than associations of description with (mere) attitude. How does this further move go?

It is not entirely easy to be sure, but one key idea is that in serious ethical cases there is no 'disentangling' of the factual from the evaluative. In the case of 'fat↓', and similarly, surely, in the case of pejorative racial slurs, we know what the response is, and what are the features that prompt it. But McDowell think that there are cases in which it is not like that:

McD

> Now it seems reasonable to be sceptical . . . about whether, corresponding to any value concept, one can always isolate a genuine feature of the world—by the appropriate standard of genuineness: that is, a feature that is there anyway, independently of anyone's value experience being as it is—to be that to which competent users of the concept are to be regarded as responding when they use it; that which is left in the world when one peels off the reflection of the appropriate attitude.[12]

The argument for this, in turn, is that when we consider a specific conception of some virtue in a moral community, it might be impossible to teach an outsider the *extension* of the term. In order correctly to predict future applications, the outsider must at least 'embark on an attempt to make sense of their admiration'. McDowell is specific that in order to learn to anticipate the way insiders will apply the term, the outsider need not share the community's admiration ('there need be no difficulty about that'). But the outsider does need to understand their special perspective, and to that extent enter into a community with them.

We can see the plausibility of this thought if we consider some evaluative practice to which we ourselves are outsiders. Suppose I am enticed to a high fashion show. A lot of clothes are exhibited, which all

---

[12] 'Non-Cognitivism and Rule-Following', 144.

look much the same to me. But the rest of the audience reacts differently. For them, and we can suppose unhesitatingly, some clothes are
divine and elicit ecstasy, and others are 'gross' and elicit derision.
There may be total consensus amongst the insiders in these reactions.
But I simply do not get it. It would need an induction course, an acculturation, for me to approximate to their reactions.

McDowell is perfectly right to notice the phenomenon. What is
much harder to follow is why it supports any genuine 'perception' or
sensitivity to a property which has a cognitive status: a property to
which the elite are genuinely responsive. It is really rather odd to think
that because of the situation just described, the fashion elite can *perceive* something I cannot: divinity or grossness, properties that are just
there, anyway.[13]

3. EIGHTEENTH-CENTURY PHILOSOPHY OF MIND?

But here there are slightly different points to be made. For McDowell[18]
also associates the impossibility of disentangling with an attack on the
'eighteenth-century philosophy of mind' that makes a separation
between genuine cognition, on the one hand, and passions and sentiments on the other (between the creatures of Apollo, and those of
Dionysus). It is this philosophy of mind that stops us from thinking as
he recommends, that is, thinking of 'exercises of our affective or conative natures either as themselves in some way percipient, or at least as
expanding our sensitivity to how things are'.[14] So where we thought
we had the affective on one side and the cognitive on the other, we now
have only unified, single-rule guided, cognitive/affective states:
'besires', as these have been christened.[15]

To assess this we should ask three things: what is difficult about disentangling, whether it indeed undermines the eighteenth-century
philosophy of mind, and whether in the light of that we can usefully
see exercises of our conative natures as percipient, or expanding our
sensitivity to how things are. The implications are by no means trans-
parent.

---

[13] Simon Blackburn, 'Reply: Rule-Following and Moral Realism', in Holtzman and
Leich, *Wittgenstein: To Follow a Rule*.

[14] 'Non-Cognitivism and Rule-Following', 143.

[15] J. E. J. Altham, 'The Legacy of Emotivism', in Graham McDonald and Crispin
Wright, eds., *Fact, Science and Morality: Essays on A. J. Ayer's* Language, Truth and Logic
(Oxford: Blackwell, 1986).

For here is one clear way in which disentangling might be difficult, by the standard on offer, namely that someone who has no appreciation of the evaluative point of a term cannot predict its extension. Just suppose that the reaction, perhaps interacting with other aspects of a person's 'whirl of organism' plays a major role in determining the extension. This is how it is with us and what we find amusing. Someone with no sense of humour will not succeed in predicting what we will find amusing. Or, imagine our teenagers becoming slightly more discriminating. Their disgust is not now uniform across fat people. They only call some of them fat↓—those they are disgusted by. Quite fine differences elicit different verdicts. Indeed their own attempts to state criteria tend to founder. Again, this is how it is with us with 'funny', where we only partially understand the bases of our own reactions of amusement. Here the attitudes or emotions drive the extension, so the outsider who cannot share or understand the emotions is at a loss. But should this by itself undermine the eighteenth-century distinction, suggesting that these attitudes or emotions are themselves some kind of cognition? It is hard to see how it works. To return to the fashion example, it seems obvious that the ecstasies and derisions, themselves caused by various features (originality, cost, surprise factor, impracticality), drive the application of 'gross' or 'divine', but not at all obvious that the situation is usefully thought about in terms of perception of grossness or divinity.

When these situations arise, the class of things eliciting the reaction seems what I christened 'shapeless', except in the fact that they do elicit the reaction. Shapelessness in this sense is supposed to be compatible with the supervenience of the moral, or the funny, or the divine on underlying features. McDowell acknowledges the plausibility of a supervenience requirement in ethics, and distinguishes it from the requirement that the things judged the same at the supervening level should form a 'kind recognizable as such' at the subjacent or underlying level.[16] So the salient question is why, when a reaction is elicited by members of an otherwise shapeless class, it should be deemed a cognition, a recognition that 'the members of some specific set of values are genuine features of the world', rather than, say, an attitude or emotion, or eighteenth-century passion or sentiment.

I see no answer to this question. The rival views line up like this:

Cognitivism: Shapeless underlying class → shapely property M → perception of it by those with proper affective dispositions ≡ perception of a reason for action → action

[16] 'Non-Cognitivism and Rule-Following', 145.

Margin notes: connoisseurship of fat! · FUNNY [all need say!] · shapeless ↦ 7BDM

Non-cognitivism: Shapeless underlying class → attitudes in those
with specific affective dispositions → action

where the arrows indicate some explanatory story. But if that is the
line-up then we would have to ask what extra explanatory weight is
added by the mention of the shapely property at the moral level, and
by the talk of perception, and there is no evident answer. Grossness
and divinity are playing no explanatory role in the phenomena of fashion. (To be fair, again, McDowell might choose to align these with the
excluded emotion of disgust, but again the question will be whether
there is any principle enabling him to do so.)

A very similar theory is advanced by David Wiggins, with the
exception that Wiggins is, plausibly, not concerned to classify the result
as a kind of 'realism' about ethics, but is concessive to the idea that it
represents a sophisticated subjectivism.[17] Talking about the thick ethical concept of cruelty, Wiggins too gives us a story in which we classify actions as cruel because they affect us in some specific way. They
do this in virtue of the 'marks' of cruelty that they possess, 'what cruelty consists in on the level of motivation, intention and outcome'.[18] So
far we have familiar ingredients on the input side. But he too wants the
'property' (although he says he would have preferred to work in terms
of 'concept') of cruelty to play a critical role in the story; a role showing that it is a 'sibling' of the ouput, rather than in any sense its creation.

I suspect the best way to read what is good in this story is as a nota-
tional variant of the theory I have presented. If it implies more, then I
think we should see it as deconstructing itself in the telling. For
although early in his paper Wiggins, like McDowell, makes much of
the mysterious *sui generis* response of those who sensitively use the
term ('there will often be no saying exactly what reaction a thing with
the associated property will provoke, without direct or indirect allu-
sion to the property itself'),[19] he then goes on quite cheerfully to
describe just what the right responses to cruelty are: Russell, he says,
should remind himself as thoroughly and vividly as he can of just what
it is that he 'dislikes, abhors, detests' about it.[20] There is no hint of a
special reaction, finding something cruellish, perhaps, on the lines of
finding it amusing, or seeing something as yellow. And this, of course,
is only common sense, for there is no special reaction, distinct from

---

[17] David Wiggins, 'Towards a Sensible Subjectivism', in Darwall, Gibbard and
Railton, *Moral Discourse and Practice*.   [18] Ibid. 240.
[19] Ibid. 232.   [20] Ibid. 240.

horror, detestation, and abhorrence. This strongly suggests not the existence of a special property or even concept in any interesting sense, but the existence of a term standing as the focus for discussion of which attitudes to have to particular actions and their amalgams of motive, intention, and upshot.

But perhaps McDowell and Wiggins do not intend an explanatory story. Perhaps the mention of perception is in a sense incidental to the main point, which is the fusion of conation and cognition. To go further, then, it is worth insisting how very strange a claim the denial of the eighteenth-century distinction is. In another influential paper McDowell talks of a non-virtuous person 'not knowing what it means to be shy and sensitive' if they do not react to a shy and sensitive person's needs in the right way. But he acknowledges that this kind of 'not knowing what it means' is highly loaded, since it is ('of course') compatible with 'competence by all ordinary tests, with the language used to describe the circumstances'.[21]

What this comes to, then, is that boys at a boarding school may know by all the ordinary tests that a newcomer is shy and sensitive: they can sort out the shy and sensitive as well as anyone. But if they go on to tease him just because of that, this shows that in some special strong sense they do not know what it means: they lack the full amalgam which makes up the unitary psychological state that is only improperly split into perception and attitude.

Why should we believe in this special strong sense or this special amalgamated state? A natural way of saying it is that the boys see what the newcomer is like, and that is why they enjoy teasing him. This is what their cruelty consists in. They do not react to what they know as virtuous people should. But for McDowell they simply lack a unitary state that the virtuous person has.

Now it may sound as though anything sayable in the one idiom is translatable without gain or loss into the other. So we might not be very enthusiastic for a debate over whether to classify some disposition or pattern of action either as the result of a single special-perception-had-only-through-affective-state, a 'besire', or as the result of two vectors: beliefs about what the situation is like, and motivations to do one thing or another about it. It might sound like arguing whether 'north-east' is one direction ('in its own right' we might say), or the vector resulting from two directions, North and East. But in fact, I believe the eighteenth century got it right, and the proposed substitute is inferior.

---

[21] McDowell, 'Are Moral Requirements Hypothetical Imperatives?', 22.

4. THE CUTE AND THE LEWD

This can be seen if we consider the example of 'thick' terms like 'cute' or 'lewd'. Take cuteness first. Here we imagine a man happily deploying this term, and happily possessed of a perceptual/affective amalgam corresponding to it. He and his cohort see women as cute. They have no trouble teaching the term, and agreeing about new cases. They have read McDowell, and take themselves to have a new, genuinely cognitive, sensitivity to the cuteness of some women. If other people, and especially women friends, do not see the world that way, then they can urge them along, try to get them to whirl the same way. Sometimes they succeed, and sometimes they do not. Often they succeed with women, who strive hard to appear cute, and blame themselves and feel ashamed if they are not.

Cuteness, our man says, elicits and justifies various affective reactions. It is hard to specify them except as perceptions of cuteness, but perceiving cuteness in women, when all goes right elicits and justifies reactions along the lines of admiration and arousal in men, or envy or admiration, from women. Indeed, there is a thick evaluative practice, together with procedures for regulating dissent, involved. Those who talk of cuteness are all 'regular' (virtuous) guys, but there is to-and-fro over whether some features are incompatible with cuteness, such as intelligence, age, or big feet. But that is how it is in ethics. And, he may add, if it comes to votes, maybe a majority of people see it like him and his friends. For most men do, and many women too: just look at role models in popular magazines.

Now it is *morally* vital that we proceed by splitting the input from the output in such a case. By refusing to split we fail to open an essential specifically *normative* dimension of criticism. If the last word is that these people perceive cuteness and react to it with the appropriate cuteness reaction, whereas other people do not, we have lost the analytic tools with which to recognize what is wrong with them. What is wrong with them is along these lines: they react to an infantile, unthreatening appearance or self-presentation in women, or overt indications of willingness to be subservient to men, with admiration or desire (the men) or envy and emulation (the women). Cute things are those to which we can show affection without threat, or patronizingly, or even with contempt. Children and pets are quintessentially cute. Applied to women, this, I say, is a bad thing. Once we can separate input from output enough to see that this is what is going on, the talk of whirls of organism, or single 'thick' rules, or a special perception available only to those who have been acculturated, simply sounds hollow: disguises for a conservative and ultimately self-serving complacency.

We need to say what is good about the virtuous and bad about the vicious. If our last word were to be that the virtuous see things one way, and the vicious another, we lose the normative space that opens up when we say that the virtuous react to things in the right way, whereas the vicious do not. The boys at the school were not locked into some barely interpretable amalgam of 'besire'. They saw that someone was shy and sensitive, and were moved to humiliate him. That is what is wrong with them.

Perhaps McDowell can admit that, as a bare fact, when we declaim against the lover of the cute as suggested, this may influence him for the better. It is an obvious fact that it can. But from the 'besire' standpoint, it must do so by misdescribing him. It describes him by decomposing his mental states, but these are states that, *ex hypothesi*, resist decomposition. So in principle, whether or not he is in fact embarrassed by the critique, he has a perfect defence against it. The critique starts from a misdescription, and why should we listen to critiques that start that way? My position, by contrast, is that the critique starts not from a misdescription, but from an essential insight.[22]

To return to the navigational analogy, it could indeed be important to see north-east as a vector. Suppose (as is actually the case) that it is one thing to determine latitude, and another to determine longitude, and hence one thing to lay down a rate of travel northward, and another to lay down a rate of travel eastward. Then there are two distinct and independent ways in which a navigator can go wrong in determining from the chart if he is travelling north-east. If he is not directed as he should be, we have to ask which one is at fault. This is how it is with the boys at school, or the man and his reaction to women.

And, in fact, we are entirely at home with the eighteenth-century distinction. Whenever there is a 'thick' term it is *easy* to see both its general descriptive orientation, and its general practical or attitude-giving one. This is what Wiggins had to admit about cruelty, in the course of officially denying it. We know that someone described as courageous is usually approved of for overcoming difficulties and dangers that would daunt others, that someone described as niggardly is attracting obloquy for being too careful with his money, and so on. There is a circumscribed range of inputs and outputs. And this is how it has to be, for we have to know the kind of thing, at the 'subjacent' level, to retail in order to engage someone's will when we are prescribing courses of

---

[22] I am grateful here to remarks by Sean McKeever.

[Handwritten margin notes: lose power for criticism if reject go for perception model. [no- cohon sum () however - not really hung]]

action. We have to know why to educate our child to be courageous, say, and this involves turning over the features involved, and, in the light of other attitudes of course, buttressing or undermining our commitment to it as a value.

But this is not to say that either input or output is fixed by any kind of definition or purely linguistic convention. They are malleable, and change with the importance we attach to things and to our reactions to things. To take another example used in this context by Allan Gibbard, we recognize that people will tend to call something 'lewd' if it involves some kind of transgressing of normal boundaries on accepted sexual display or reference, and if as a result they find it shocking or disapprove of it. But each element can be moulded in different ways. I may not find Titian's juxtaposition of fur and skin, or contemporary teenage dress, lewd, and I might disapprove of you who do. Or, I may find them lewd—recognize some deliberate testing of the boundaries—and rejoice in them on just that account. Censoriousness may be the last thing on my mind. Sexuality and its mockery are too important to call forth just one attitude.[23]

This connects with another strand in McDowell's thinking. He suggests that if we go in for the eighteenth-century split we are forgetting that there may be no way of specifying the objects of a person's desires or other attitudes, except from within a shared evaluative framework, or at least from a position that involves what he earlier described as 'an attempt to make sense of' their framework. This was the reason why 'disgust' was exempted from his lexicon of the genuinely ethical, because it was (wrongly, as I argued) regarded as a non-intentional self-standing sensation, like nausea. But the example of lewdness shows the mistake that is involved here. It is tempting to say that the attitude associated with lewdness resists identification in other terms, and hence can only be understood from within some shared community of response: a community with those who find themselves naturally thinking 'How lewd!' This in turn may tempt us to say that there is a specially elusive 'thick' state here, whose components cannot be factored out. But this would be a mistake. The reason that it is hard to identify such a thing as *the* attitude associated with regarding something as lewd is that there is no such thing as *the* attitude. The verdict can interact with intention and desire and action in a whole variety of ways, different in different people and on different occasions. 'It'

---

[23] See the pair of papers by Allan Gibbard and Simon Blackburn, 'Morality and Thick Concepts', *Proceedings of the Aristotelian Society*, supp. vol. 66 (1992), 267–83 and 285–99.

resists identification because there is no 'it' to identify on each occasion of use. Sometimes there is censoriousness, sometimes amusement, sometimes horror, sometimes we are minded to give a bit of lewdness a bold blessing, thanking goodness that we can laugh at ourselves; sometimes we are disposed to give it a rather more furtive blessing in the privacy of our closets. And these reactions can pass over our countenances in quick succession.

In this section I have applauded some things McDowell emphasizes, and resisted others. The good things—the emphasis on affective dispositions, and the way in which our moral voices are essentially voices from within shared practices—are better seen as an end-point of the different expressivist journey, variations on a position that captures with more certainty and less mystery the way the task of understanding the moral proposition must be conducted. The bad things include the unearned emphasis on 'receptivity' or the belief that some kind of cognitivism has been established, and the unfortunate hostility to the essential business of factoring out the inputs and the outputs of our evaluative practices. Meanwhile, there are other approaches to consider.

5. RESPONSE-DEPENDENT ACCOUNTS[24]

There is a different way of cooking with some of the ingredients we have been talking about. If our problem is finding an ethical proposition, capable of truth or falsity, when sentiment and attitude is so much to the forefront, we can at least reflect that some things elicit our attitudes, and other things do not. That much, at least, sounds like a natural truth. So why not locate the truths of ethics just there, in the fact that some things affect us, or some of us, in some ways? The moral proposition becomes a proposition about our own motivational responses or attitudes to the world. As such it can be a belief, because there are true and false things to be believed about our own responses and attitudes. I might believe that most people dislike ice cream, when in fact they love it, or that I am not motivated by ambition, when in fact I am, and so on.

The central idea is to apply a form of analysis to concepts that seem somehow anthropocentric, used and understood only because we have particular sensory or affective systems. The standard examples

[24] This section and the next draw on material from my paper 'Circles, Finks, Smells, and Biconditionals', *Philosophical Perspectives*, 7 (1993): *Language and Logic*, 259–79.

include concepts of colour and other secondary qualities, concepts like being fashionable or chic that centrally reflect the tastes of some identifiable group, or those like being boring or comical, where the application clearly depends somehow on the reactions of people (or some particular people). The idea rapidly generalizes to values themselves.

The starting-point for this approach is that we analyse ethical concepts in 'response dependent' terms, that is in terms of actual human responses: attitudes and desires, for example. The proposal develops by considering familiar kinds of equivalences or 'biconditionals':

X is good/right/justifiable ≡ [persons] are disposed to [reaction] under [circumstances]

A variation on this equation would be:

X is good/right/justifiable ≡ X tends to elicit [reaction R] from [persons P] under [circumstances C]

The brackets indicate choice points. What kinds of choice? Amongst the possibilities we have:

[persons]: myself, all of us, those who are normal, the experts, us as we actually are, us as we would be in some given circumstance, or after some specified empirical process. Or: us as we would be if we were improved in some way: rational, or ideal, for example.

[reaction]: a non-cognitive reaction, a cognitive reaction, a judgement that something is good/right/justifiable, a judgement couched in other terms, an attitude or emotion or posture of the mind, an experience, a piece of behaviour.

[circumstances]: common conditions of acquaintance, standard conditions, conditions appropriate especially to X, conditions of paying some specified kind of appropriate attention to X or having X as an 'intentional' object or object of thought, ideal conditions, whatever-conditions-it-takes.

Response-dependent accounts have recently become one of the most popular games in town, and the reasons for this are not hard to seek. First, they bid fair to do justice to the non-cognitivist's concerns: they give some prominence to the 'responses', which may be other than propositional attitudes but include desires or other stances, or even emotions. Second, however, in so far as they see us as *describing* ourselves, they remain thoroughly cognitivist, and in principle able to draw up a truth-condition for evaluative remarks. Third, they have obvious flexibility. Not only are there the bracketed choices, but there is also room for manœuvre about the status of the biconditionals involved: whether they are analytic, or a priori, or reductionist in intent, or none of these. Fourth, they seem plausible in many areas: there must be something right about thinking that the boring things are those that bore us, or the funny things those that amuse us, just as the red things are those that we perceive as red, at least under good conditions. And finally, we can point to everyday language as well. In the classroom, for example, there is not much difference between the teacher instructing 'Evaluate this poem' or instructing 'Describe your responses to this poem'.

In spite of all this, I shall argue that there is something badly amiss about all such accounts. I shall summarize my objection in advance: *either* they give us no real theory of the ethical proposition, but simply substitute one way of putting it for another. *Or* they confuse speaking from within a moral perspective with *describing* those who speak from within it. I shall eventually argue that there is something seriously wrong about seeing ethics as, at bottom, self-description. But I shall start by introducing a problem that has to be avoided. Consider, for instance:

> (I) *X* is good ≡ *X* is such as to elicit approval from good people under the ideal circumstances (that is, whatever circumstances it takes for people to approve of good things).

It is not that this is objectionable in itself. In fact, it is true. It is trivially true that good things are such as to elicit approval from good people in ideal circumstances (especially where these are whatever circumstances it takes for good people to value good things). But the trouble is exactly that it is trivial. By substituting it we advance the naturalistic project no further. We only have an equation *within* the domain of the ethical. We do not have a way of tethering the ethical to the natural earth. As far as that project goes, we are simply running on the spot. We have passed no starting-line, let alone any finishing-line.

For the moment I shall let (I) stand as an awful warning, rather than explore with more precision the shape of the boundary it marks. That is, it may be quite delicate to know how near we can approach (I) without betraying the naturalistic project. Clearly, however, the obvious diagnosis is that triviality arises because of the overt reintroduction of evaluative vocabulary on the right-hand side: to know which people are good, or which circumstances are ideal, we ourselves have to deploy values. In other words, we have to make the very kind of judgement that is targeted on the left-hand side. We cannot therefore be said to have related the ethical to any other kind of judgement.

There are many ways in which evaluations can creep into the right hand side of these equations:

(M) X is good/right/justifiable $\equiv$ X merits/deserves/ought to elicit a positive valuation from [P] in [C].

Again, no doubt this is true for a wide variety of [P] and [C]. Saying that something is good or right or justifiable is certainly equivalent to saying that it deserves a positive evaluation—even, perhaps, a positive evaluation from *anyone* in *any* circumstances. But again, the problem is that this only takes us to the starting-line. The one evaluation is merely being presented in other, slightly different terms. If we are trying to understand ethics, such an equivalence is useless. It takes us nowhere outside the ethical circle. It only gives us different ways of saying the same thing. In particular, a non-cognitivist, denying that the way to understand the left-hand side is in terms of belief in a particular proposition, will simply say the same about the right-hand side.

To proceed, we need to notice an important division between two projects. Are we trying to understand the nature of evaluative judgement? Or are we simply concerned to 'give a truth condition' for the evaluative predicates, 'X is good/right/justifiable'? Here is an illustration of the difference. Suppose we look at the verdict that a play is boring. What does this mean? We might offer:

X is boring $\equiv$ X is such as to elicit the judgement that it is boring ⌉ from most of us under normal conditions. ⌋

This might be right, and it looks to be in the right ball-park. And we could learn something about the truth conditions of 'boring' by being told that the conditions governing its application are that X is boring $\equiv$ most of us judge it boring under normal conditions. That this is a substantive claim is proved by its actually being false (normal conditions might be the noisy crowded theatrical milieu hostile to realizing that X is not at all boring, but imaginative and demanding).[25]

On the other hand, the proposal is of no use if we wanted to understand what it is to judge something boring. If, for instance, we found being bored a strange human reaction worth investigating

---

25 See also Mark Johnston, 'Dispositional Theories of Value', *Proceedings of the Aristotelian Society*, supp. vol. 63 (1989), 147–8.

philosophically, then the equation has done nothing to help us. It takes the judgement for granted.

You might think we could substitute the truth condition on the right-hand side and then understand both the truth condition and the judgement. But this cannot be done. We would get:

> X is boring ≡ X is such as to elicit the judgement that it is such as to elicit the judgement that it is such as to . . .

We could never exit from the loop.

With ethics we want to understand the truth condition, but we also want to understand ourselves as agents who think in terms of values and obligations, duties and rights. So the 'echo', to adopt a useful term of Richard Holton's, when the judgement is taken for granted, looks like a disqualification.[26]

But of course a response-dependent theorist can introduce other responses: desires or attitudes understood in other ways, or even taken as primitive for the purpose of understanding values. So we can waive this regress problem at this juncture. The response-dependence theorist is able to plug in the best available account of the response, in terms of attitudes, dispositions, emotions, or desires. So let us suppose this is done: we shall signal the place it marks just as the [value reaction]. We still have to get beyond the problem illustrated by (I) and (M).

The problem suggested above is one of navigating between two disasters that I call Scylla and Charybdis. Scylla is that we falsify the kind of judgement made by saying 'X is good', representing it as an empirical, sociological, remark. Charybdis is that we get this right, but at the cost of making the same kind of judgement at some place within the right-hand side, and thereby forfeiting the claim to advance, just as we do if we stop with (I) or (M).

Scylla then is that we go naturalistic or empirical; Charybdis that we make an ethical judgement on the right-hand side, and thereby fail to advance the interesting philosophical project of understanding the kind of judgement it is. Contrast:

> X is good ≡ X is such as to elicit desires from us as we actually are, when we come across it.

> X is good ≡ X is such as to elicit desires from good people when they come across it.

---

[26] Richard Holton, 'Intentions, Response-Dependence and Immunity from Error', in Peter Menzies, ed., *Response-Dependent Concepts* (Canberra: Philosophy Program, Research School of Social Sciences, 1993).

The first, considered as an attempt to understand ethical judgement, must be deemed to fail, because it only gives us an equation with a natural judgement about X, certifiable by empirical means. It tells us that X is something we desire, not something that is desirable. Some biconditionals like this may be true, but when they are true they have an ethical status, not a metaethical one. I might have an ethic with a simple criterion for the good. Thus a utilitarian might propose

X is good ≡ X is such as to satisfy desires

which is then debatable as a piece of ethics. But even if it stood up under that scrutiny (which it does not), it still does not help in the project of naturalizing the ethical judgement, because it is silent over what it is to see the satisfaction of desires *under the heading* of the good. The equation, taken like this, gives us a piece of ethics, but tells us nothing about what it is to think in ethical terms.

Whatever natural fix we make on [P], [C], and [R] it will be quite possible to doubt or deny that the people or circumstances or reaction so fixed are the *appropriate* ones. Suppose, for example, we privilege some group, and some conditions:

X is good/right/justifiable ≡ X tends to elicit a favourable reaction from middle-class professors of divinity in conditions in which they have cleared their minds and learned the facts.

Fairly obviously this is a terrible shot at saying what the left-hand side *means*, even if it reflects our actual procedures (imagine a Scottish university in the last century). Anyone putting it forward shows that he or she privileges professors of divinity with cleared and informed minds. But it is an open question whether she is right to do so. And even if she were right, it would be purely because as a matter of fact such people judge the good rightly. It is impossible to believe that this tells us anything about the property or concept of goodness. We might also notice that the truth condition cannot itself be the one in terms of which the professors of divinity think. They have to go through an exercise of evaluation which is not exhaustively concerned with predicting or describing their own responses.[27] Thus Scylla.

Scylla ensnares us if on the right-hand side we stick with *descriptions* of things and their powers to elicit responses from us or from some group, rather than *evaluations* of them. Evaluative judgements are *verdicts* rather than hypotheses about the suspected reactions of

---

[27] I return to this in Chapter 9.

some group (even our own group) under some putative circumstances. If I am asked whether the picture was beautiful or the play interesting, I dissemble if I say that it was *because* I hypothesize that most people in such-and-such circumstances find it so, although I personally couldn't stand it.[28] What is expected is that I give my own verdict. 'Yes, it was fascinating' expresses how I found it. My verdict can be challenged of course, but the challenge is not itself a different hypothesis about [P] and [C], but an attempt to show that my feeling was unwarranted, and that I ought not to have found it beautiful or fascinating. Notice too that if I then retreat to say (huffily, as it might be), 'Well, *I* thought it was fascinating,' I am not retreating to saying that *my* hypothesis was that it was such as to elicit [R] from some group [P] in some circumstances [C]. I am repeating my own verdict or expressing my own reaction, standing within an evaluative perspective, rather than describing one from without.

We have here a lack of harmony between the reaction and the things that make true the biconditional elaborated upon it. The logical space I enter when I make my verdict is not that of an empirical hypothesis about the reactions of some identifiable group of people. Kant was very clear about this. Taking the case of aesthetic judgement, or the judgement of beauty or judgement of taste, he asserts that this does not 'postulate' the agreement of everyone, but 'imputes' it, or 'exacts it from everyone else as necessary'.[29] 'The assertion is not that everyone *will* fall in with our judgement, but that everyone *ought* to agree with it.'[30]

We have, of course, already met cases where evaluative terms go 'dead', and are used more as sociological remarks retailing the general opinion. But this use is parasitic upon the practice of actually making evaluations out of our own mouths.

Kant's insight is confirmed by another phenomenon that is prominent in these cases. I may know empirically that X is such as to elicit [R] from [P] in [C], but because I have no experience of X, I cannot without misrepresentation answer the question 'Is X beautiful/boring/fascinating . . .?' I can only answer that other people think so, or that I am longing to see it. I cannot say *tout court* that it was one or the other without giving an overwhelming impression that I have myself

---

[28] The ambivalence illustrated by Jane Fairfax (see Chapter 3, above) shows that this might need qualification, but not in a direction that affects the issues here.

[29] Immanuel Kant, *The Critique of Judgement*, trans. James Meredith (Oxford: Oxford University Press, 1952), 52, 59.

[30] Ibid. 84.

been in a position to make a judgement, and have made it. This is highly mysterious on the hypothesis that the judgement functions as a straight description of the reactions of an identified group in identified circumstances. I can say, categorically and in full authority, that something is poisonous, if I know that it is such as to poison normal people in normal circumstances, without having myself taken it. Interestingly Wittgenstein makes the identical point even about colour judgements:

If someone asks me: 'What colour is this book?' and I reply: 'It's green'—might I as well have given the answer: 'The generality of English-speaking people call that "green"'?

Might he not ask: 'And what do *you* call it?' For he wanted to get my reaction.[31]

As we have seen with (I) and (M), a normative element can be overtly included on the right-hand side:

(O) X is $\phi \equiv X$ is such that [*P*] in [*C*] ought to give [*R*]

And typically this is right enough as far as it goes. A thing is boring ≡ people ought to be bored by it. But now Charybdis threatens. The right-hand side is itself a straightforward evaluation, so all we have is an equation between two similar linguistic forms for doing the same thing. The right-hand side is another example of the kind of judgement we might have been hoping to understand. For Kant, concerned with the judgement of taste, the salient problem was how there *could be* such a judgement, when aesthetics had to do more with felt pleasure than with applying a concept according to a rule. And Kant's problem resurfaces in the modern world of ethics, for there are people who deny that the reactions associated with evaluation can withstand the kind of understanding that a Humean, or equally a response-dependent theory, brings to them. They are wrong, but their wrongness is not shown by contemplating this kind of 'truth condition'. If we bear Kant's standard in mind, proposals like (O), or (I), or (M) will not enchant us for long.

What is done in these proposals is to equate one ethical judgement with another: it takes not observation but ethical judgement to determine whether something is such as to elicit desires from good people, since you have to judge who are the good people. Of course, in principle an advance *within* ethics could come about this way, since it

[31] Ludwig Wittgenstein, *Remarks on the Foundations of Mathematics* (Oxford: Blackwell, 1964), II. 72, p. 96.

might be somehow easier to judge who are the good people than it appears to be to judge X's. But this will not be an advance in our understanding of ethical judgement per se. It would be a strictly local advance in first-order moral theory.

The most ingenious attempt known to me to steer between Scylla and Charybdis is called the Canberra plan, advocated by Philip Pettit, Michael Smith, and Frank Jackson, in a number of papers.[32] The Canberra plan hopes to navigate between Scylla and Charybdis by listing the commonplaces or 'platitudes' associated with an evaluative term: platitudes being expressions of possibly tacit inferential or other dispositions that would be expected of everyone competent with the term. In this sense, what goes in on the right is intended to be associated a priori with the use of the evaluation, in that it can be read off from the behaviour of those competent with it. And for the Canberra planner quite a lot can be so read off. Considering the judgement that an arrangement is fair, for example, Jackson and Pettit say: 'That something is fair means that conditions of the kind registered in the following illustrative commonplaces are fulfilled'—and they then present:

1. Commonplaces about application (here we would find paradigm fair procedures and arrangements, such as arrangements that informed rational contractors could agree upon);
2. . . . about truth conditions (here the main listing is that the fairness of an arrangement supervenes upon other descriptions of it);
3. . . . about justification (fairness in an arrangement justifies preferring it or selecting it, other things being equal);
4. . . . about justificatory power (here is cited the place of fairness in a ladder of considerations, where it is important, but not always overwhelming);
5. . . . about motivation (anyone who believes one option only to be fair will prefer it, other things being equal);
6. . . . about motivational power (the place of this motivation in a ladder of considerations—it is strong, but can be overriden);
7. . . . about the connection of fairness to virtue. The fact that something is fair is likely to be more salient to the virtuous.[33]

---

[32] The title was invented by Huw Price; the point is that Canberra, where these authors work, was carefully planned as a rational city by the architect Burleigh Griffin in the first part of the century. See Frank Jackson and Philip Pettit, 'Moral Functionalism and Moral Motivation', *Philosophical Quarterly*, 45 (1995), 20–40.

[33] Ibid. 22–3.

Obviously, the collection is quite heterogeneous. For example, some of the commonplaces are supposed to pertain directly to the content of what is judged. Others are more metatheoretical, talking about the natural or likely consequences of making the judgement. That is, the commonplace that judgements of fairness motivates is apparently a remark about what the judgement does, rather than an attack on the problem of what is its content that it manages to do it. Remember Kant's problem, again: by Kant's standards, or indeed those of any non-cognitivist, an approach to the judgement of beauty that said 'being beautiful is that truth about an object (or, beauty is that property of objects) such that to apprehend it makes you motivated to pursue it' would simply slide by the major philosophical problem, which is how there *could be* such a truth or such a property.

What, in the light of all the platitudes, does it mean to say that something is fair? The term on this account gets its meaning holistically. There is a network of moral terms (fair, just, virtuous, . . .) and each member of the network is given its meaning partly by its connections with others. Jackson and Pettit make a number of claims about this in the first paragraph of their introduction.[34] The first is that 'the moral terms are specified by their role in received moral theory— folk moral theory'. Second, folk moral theory has a 'purely descriptive content'. Hence, apparently, 'moral terms are reducible to descriptive terms, at least in principle, but the reduction involved is holistic, not atomistic'. 'The content of any one claim is fixed only so far as the contents of others are fixed simultaneously.'

There seem to be two rather different concerns here. One is with establishing a holism. The other is with establishing a kind of descriptivism, which involves bringing moral judgements or concepts down to earth by identifying them with natural or descriptive judgements or concepts, thereby, of course, risking the wrath of Scylla. But how do the concerns for holism and naturalism relate? It is not at all clear. To fix our thoughts, I shall begin by listing four kinds of problem that already seem prominent.

(1) As already remarked, remembering Kant, the platitude that moral judgements motivate is a dangerous element in a theory that aims at showing that their content is purely descriptive. For Kant, the point is that it is not an accident that the judgement of taste connects with pleasure, and no more that ethical judgements motivate: ethics, as I have already explained, is *essentially* practical. But then the problem is

[34] Ibid. 24.

how there can be a purely descriptive content that is at the same time essentially practical—one that cannot, as we might say, be apprehended in general just with a shrug (this is the problem McDowell properly faced, and heroically met, by the denial of eighteenth-century psychology). If they 'just happened' to motivate us, in the same way that discovery that the bedroom is yellow might just happen to motivate someone to change it, this would be fine, but that is not the way it is.

(2) In any case, do the commonplaces encourage us to believe that folk theory 'has a purely descriptive content', or identifies a purely descriptive content for any ethical term? At least three of the families of platitudes (3, 4, and 7) are *overtly* moralistic in tone: they describe fairness in terms of what it justifies, or whether good people notice it. Others, while not overtly moralistic, will only be accepted by people who have a certain practical stance: these are the commonplaces of application. 'Giving boys and girls identical educations' is, in my view, a paradigm instance of fairness. But it wasn't (and, unfortunately, isn't) always so regarded. According to the authors of the Calvinist Westminster Confession of 1648, 'others did He appoint for eternal condemnation, according to his most free, just and Holy Will'. This strikes the authors as fine, but seems to many of us as a paradigm of injustice. Coming to hold that one thing or another is fair involves a moral change, and in so far as the commonplaces are in this way evaluative, they leave it most obscure why folk theory can be said to have a 'purely descriptive content'.

(3) Following on from this, we must raise the question of how many of the platitudes are really good candidates for a prioricity. In Jackson and Pettit's work this is extremely important. For Canberra planners, the work divides like this: philosophers can work out the a priori commitments of a certain concept. But then it is up to the world, and its investigators, to determine which properties fill the role specified by the content. The part we are engaged upon is the analysis of the judgement that something is fair. There may be a further chapter to be written about what properties 'realize' that role. It is as if we write a job description, and then other things determine who best satisfies it, if anyone does.

Consider, for instance, thoughts about the place of fairness on a 'ladder of justification'. Fairness is important, but not too important: 'Better to be unfair than allow someone innocent to perish', for example. Well, I hold that, and I expect most people do too. But some people don't: *fit justitia et ruat caelum* (let justice be done though the heavens fall), they say; desperately caring that they never commit injustice or unfairness, and resignedly putting up with the thought that they may thereby be about to allow innocent people to perish. With other 'thick' terms the point would be more obvious. It is clearly morally contentious whether, for instance, the fact that an action indicated courage justifies us in admiring it, just as it is morally contentious whether the fact that an action is lewd justifies us in condemning it.

In fact, if you strip out the commitments that seem indicative of a moral point of view, I think you are left only with the motivational metatheoretical platitude, that perception of fairness tends to motivate people. Which I think is true. But it is not a way of showing how the judgement has a content or truth-condition that is itself magnetic.

At first sight, points like the ones I just made—the extent to which the platitudes are shot through with moral claims—seem to stand in the way of a 'reduction to descriptive terms'. But perhaps holism gallops in to the rescue. The obstacle seems daunting because either the platitudes contain terms like 'should motivate' or 'justifies', or, even when that is not true, they are only acceptable to those of a certain moral persuasion. But, goes the promise, repeat the exercise round the circle and eventually we are in a position to locate 'descriptive properties' associated with the role of each moral term (Jackson and Pettit talk in their next paragraph of 'the descriptive property associated with the rightness role'). My fourth query, therefore, is:

(4) Whether this promise can ever be made good. For very few terms are needed to generate all the ethics we need. Perhaps 'right' and 'good' are needed, or we might try to get by with the one term, such as 'is a reason for' or 'is justifiable': X is good means that there is reason for doing X or promoting X or admiring X, or that these things are justifiable; X is right or obligatory means that there is reason for doing X and no reason for doing anything else, or that nothing other than X is justifiable; X is impermissible means that it is right to forbid X; and so on. Examples like 'fair' get treated as (roughly) 'according to procedures that can be agreed to from a common point of view, and on that account justifiable'; 'courageous' means 'more able to face difficulty or danger than it would be justifiable to require'; and so on. What is evaluatively interesting about these 'thick' terms gets thrown back on the general moral role of 'justifiable'. Note that such an account predicts the phenomenon that there may be no telling to what we apply the specific 'thick' terms, for anyone who cannot share, or at least understand

[margin note: (4) can get to descriptive?]

or simulate, our attitudes or the boundaries we find important. Because they won't know what the justifiable way is. On such an account there simply doesn't exist a rich tangle of 'thick' terms, with individual tentacles stretching out towards the natural or descriptive, that serve to fix the content of 'justifiable' in descriptive terms.

The Scylla/Charybdis problem applied to response-dependent approaches to the content of evaluative remarks is this. Is judging X to be fair saying that it does elicit some response from us?—but that way lies Scylla. Is it saying that it *justifies* such a response?—but that way lies Charybdis. Jackson and Pettit ingeniously negotiate the trap by providing a lot of both: some statements about what responses are elicited by the judgement (the metatheoretical side, in which the judgement's typical effects are noted), others about what arrangements justify description as fair. So we are, as it were, tossed from side to side of the strait guarded by Scylla and Charybdis. But that is not the same as a straight passage through it.

There is a related way in which response-dependent theories can be developed, best illustrated in the work of Michael Smith. Smith's account works with 'desire' as the response in question, and hopes to tell us when it is appropriate to use this response as certifying true values, just as a selection of what counts as 'normal' or 'standard' in the case of colour should tell us when seeing something as red is a certification that it is indeed red. It is so when it is normal people in standard circumstances who see things as red. Smith applies his account to the judgement that it is desirable for an agent to perform ϕ in circumstances C:

> ϕ-ing in C is desirable $\equiv$ if we were fully rational, we would desire to ϕ in C.[35]

This abbreviates a slightly longer account in terms of what our fully rational selves would have our everyday selves (with their given freight of interests and desires) do. But the abbreviation is harmless for present purposes, and I discuss the full account in Chapter 8. Like other Canberra planners, Smith takes it that the task of an analysis like this is to 'make explicit what we otherwise knew at best only implicitly in virtue of being master of evaluative concepts'. The mention of 'fully rational' in the analysis thus serves to label or summarize procedures whereby we sift desires into those that are, and those that are not, taken to be indicative, or indeed in a sense constitutive, of what is

---

[35] This formulation is from Michael Smith, 'Response Dependence without Reduction', *European Review of Philosophy* (1997).

[margin annotations: "sum — description & false or normative & true" next to the Scylla/Charybdis paragraph; "MS" next to the indented formula]

desirable. Smith believes that when enough a priori 'platitudes' about processes of sifting desires into the good and the bad are added, he can escape the dilemma of Scylla and Charybdis. Having seen the difficulties that beset Jackson and Pettit, we will be alert to noticing whether this claim is made good mainly by lurching from one side of the straits to the other. Or more immediately, whether it is made good by the time-honoured nautical device of hoisting misleading colours, which in this case is the norm of rationality.

We certainly talk about rising to our better selves. And there are already good words for the imagined end of that process: 'ideal' or 'perfect'. Why isn't the desirable that which, if we were perfect, we would desire to do, or, as (I) had it, that which our ideal selves would have us do? Certainly, if there were a failure of harmony between what our ideal selves would have us do, and what our fully rational selves would have us do, one would think ethics would need to go with the ideal. And this seems to be a real threat. Suppose, for example, fully rational selves maintain serenity by having no desires at all: they have achieved Stoic serenity or Buddhist Nirvana, and learned the folly of all human struggle. Then there is nothing they would have us do, for they would have no preference for whether we do one thing or another. But that (I would say) just shows that this is not the standpoint from which things are to be assessed as desirable or not.

'Fully rational' in Smith's work is a very slippery fish. It seems to face in at least three different directions:

(1) It is just a variant of 'ideal' or 'perfect': free of any flaw or defect. By most moral standards Stoics and Buddhists would not count, because they are insufficiently this-and-that: insufficiently sympathetic, or concerned, or caring, for example.

(2) It is a description, in natural terms for psychologies of a specific kind. Smith often provides this description of the rational self: it is fully informed, and has 'a maximally unified and coherent desire set' (I shall call psychologies of which this is true, MUCK: having a desire set of a Maximally Unified and Coherent Kind).

(3) It insinuates a different set of norms from moral norms, namely those of rationality, which can be used to underpin moral norms.

The first option falls of course straight into Charybdis. Certainly when I respond to something as desirable, I can express that by saying that from an ideal point of view it would be desired, or that my ideal self would desire it. This is just an ethical paraphrase.

Option (2) looks a little more promising. But how does it avoid the jaws of Scylla? There is such a thing as the struggle for 'unity and coherence' in desires: the struggle to attain what Rawls called 'reflective equilibrium'. Although, actually, there is also a countercurrent: we can well understand, and perhaps even silently sympathize with, the agent who wanted to be faithfully married, but to several different women.[36] But then isn't Smith just presenting something as valuable, along the lines of 'X is good $\equiv X$ maximizes happiness', except that here it is 'X is good $\equiv X$ is desired by those who desire as their MUCK selves advise or wish?' And then, even if we can fix on MUCK as a description that applies to some psychologies and not others (which is by no means obvious), it would seem that Moore's open question argument will strike. It is one thing to allow that something would be recommended by a MUCK overseer, and another to value it. It is not too clear what is good about MUCK, or bad about variations on it. After all, for all we know, Stoics and Buddhists have MUCK psychologies, but in my eyes that disqualifies them from giving advice to anyone. Looking at the human race, one might have a nasty suspicion that the MUCK advice might be to go jump in a lake, whatever we happen to want.

I discuss option (3) in Chapters 7 and 8, in connection with Kantian approaches to practical reason. For the moment we can leave it with these remarks. One might think Smith could avoid the objection from Buddhism or Stoicism by pointing that in fact we all start somewhere: we start with actual here-and-now desires, so the process of obtaining equilibrium should not be seen even potentially as a process of removing desires in the interest only of coherence and unity (things obtained more easily the less you want). But in fact this path is not open to him. For he thinks that all rational selves coincide. Actual human differences are bleached out by the processes that lead to ideal rationality. It does not matter where you start from, the fully rational *you* is identical with all other fully rational selves. So there is just the fully rational self, or, as we might better put it, the one rational standpoint. And then it is a real threat whether anything at all is recommended from this standpoint. What does an agent occupying it care about—and should we care about that, whatever it is, as well? The rational standpoint is like the view from nowhere, the God's-eye point of view. And we know that God's nature is witless and heartless in one sense, so perhaps it is in the other.

Response-dependent accounts of value terms can take many forms,

---

[36] One reason why I do not think 'desire' is a good response to work with is that evaluation is an activity that imposes norms of consistency whereas, in their less practical manifestations, desires can be faultlessly inconsistent. It is only when we come to do something about them that we have to tidy them up.

and given the size of the flotilla sailing through the straits, it may be optimistic for me to think that Scylla and Charybdis will claim all of them. But I believe this chapter has established that they share a natural infirmity. It can best be summed up by saying that they conflate speaking from within a moral perspective, and describing truths about those who speak from within it. And that is changing the subject (Scylla), unless of course it is evaluating the speakers, or in other words doing more of the same kind of thing we were trying to understand to begin with (Charybdis).

6. CORNELL REALISM

The final approach I shall mention here is loosely described as 'realism', and often thought of as opposed, therefore, to 'anti-realism', or to 'non-cognitivism'—the label I have agreed, for the moment, to accept for my own view. It is thought to deserve this title because it seizes a certain doctrine, and regards this as characteristic of ethical realism. The doctrine is that ethical predicates refer to real natural properties of things.

This sounds at first like the naturalism that, I urged, is refuted by Moore's open question argument. But Cornell realism deflects this criticism by deploying a distinction drawn from Putnam and Kripke. It urges that we can see the property of goodness (say) as identical with the property of creating happiness (for example), without identifying the proposition or thought that something is good with the thought that it creates happiness. Moore may have been right to insist on separating the thought that something is good from the thought that it creates happiness. But it does not follow that the properties are distinct. There is a distinction, in other words, between *properties* and *concepts*, and different concepts can be expressed by predicates that nevertheless refer to the same properties. But since the predicate 'is good' refers to natural properties, this is enough to locate a 'truth condition' for sentences containing it. And it is enough to maintain each of naturalism, for the properties involved are natural ones, realism, for they are real enough, and cognitivism, for we know about them.

There is something unnerving about so much being delivered by so little. Does the distinction between properties and concepts deliver so much so swiftly? I think not. Reflect back upon the teenage users of 'fat↓'. Everything suggested about 'good' can be echoed here, telling us that this term refers to a quite natural property of size and bodily constitution. Are we to conclude: hence realism, naturalism, and cognitivism? Is it purely a cognitive matter whether someone is fat↓? Surely not. What has been ignored is the particular take on size and bodily constitution exhibited by the teenagers. But it is this peculiar take that puts us in the sphere of evaluation at all. The teenagers are not distinguished by a special cognitive gift, a special piece of knowledge. They are distinguished by a special reaction or attitude or emotional stance towards fat people.

Realism, naturalism, and cognitivism are terms of art that philosophers can define pretty much at will. But in the theory of ethics they hold out a promise. The promise is one of understanding the authority of ethics (model it upon the authority carried by true natural descriptions of the world) and therefore the appearance that something objective is at stake in ethical dispute, such that, in favourable circumstances, one side might be shown to be right. But now we see that none of this is delivered by the suggestion that evaluative predicates refer to natural properties. For none of this is in place in the 'fat↓' example. We are shown no way of proving that the fat↓ists are wrong. We are shown no authority for their position or that of their opponents. We are shown no special cognition involved: indeed in this example we are shown that there is none.

Consider a different case. Suppose in some business community the standards are fixed. A good decision is one made to maximize expected profit, and that is all. Is it in order to say that, in their mouths, 'good', applied to business decisions, simply means or represents or refers to maximization of expected profit? Semantic terms like 'means' and 'refers' are terms of art, and we might deploy them so that this is the right thing to say. But if we do so, we must not conceal the distinctive fact about the community. This is not that it refers to this property, but that it uses it precisely as a standard of evaluation. It is the practical role the property is being given that brings us into the domain of evaluation, and eventually of ethics.

There is also a major asymmetry between such a case of 'reference' and others. In normal cases reference connects intimately with truth. If a term 'X' in someone's mouth refers to X and 'P' refers to the property P, and she says 'X is P', then she speaks truly if and only if X has the property P. But if I have different standards from the business community, I will not allow that they speak truly, when they say 'X is good' if and only if X has the property of maximizing profit. In cases where the standards come apart (it maximizes profit to tread on the widow and orphan) I deny it. So I should not be saying that they refer to maximization of profit. To conform to the connection between reference and truth, I must see them as referring to whichever properties I myself regard as standards for good decisions. This can be extremely odd if, for instance, they have never heard of those properties, or cannot be brought to understand what they are.

We might swallow this oddity, or we might heroically abandon the link between reference and truth. If we did, it might be permissible, at the end of the day, to throw in the idea that evaluative predicates refer to whatever natural properties are held to justify the evaluation. We might hold that the businessmen refer to maximization of profit when they call a decision the best or right decision. We might be especially inclined to do this if we can thicken up a convincing natural relation between such a property and our valuations. For example, we might hope for the kind of story told by Aristotle, in which human life has a *telos* or natural goal, and human evaluations concern only how well that goal is being promoted. We might think we can make such a story good in evolutionary terms, describing what is adaptive for human beings. We might further think that our habits of valuation are themselves adapted to pick out and encourage these properties of flourishing. If we thought all this (the difficulties are formidable) we might think that valuations exist for the purpose of picking out this set of natural properties, and that this bolsters their claim to refer to them.[37]

Such a story might be told about the business community and maximization of profit, or for that matter about teenage denigration of fat. But it is optional, and it carries the (large) cost that people become interpreted as sometimes referring to a property with a predicate, applying the predicate to something that has the property, but be said (by others who do not share their standards) to be speaking falsely. And it should not disguise the truth that the reference to a property is one thing, and the evaluation of it quite another. What is needed, therefore, is not the suggestion that evaluative predicates refer to whatever properties ground the values. We need to understand the special take on those properties had by those who value them one way or another. Until we have a theory of that, we do not understand anything of ethical thought, the content of the ethical proposition, its motivational power, its authority, and the question of whether disputes involving different valuations are cognitive disputes or something else. All these are better understood by expressivism than by the approaches considered in this chapter.

---

[37] The expressivist Allan Gibbard is somewhat more optimistic than I am about the possibility of such a story.

5

Looking Out for Yourself

The economy of nature is competitive from beginning to end. Understand that economy, and how it works, and the underlying reasons for social phenomena are manifest. They are the means by which one organism gains some advantage to the detriment of another. No hint of genuine charity ameliorates our vision of society, once sentimentalism has been laid aside. What passes for co-operation turns out to be a mixture of opportunism and exploitation. The impulses that lead one animal to sacrifice himself for another turn out to have their ultimate rationale in gaining advantage over a third; and acts 'for the good' of one society turn out to be performed to the detriment of the rest. Where it is in his own interest, every organism may reasonably be expected to aid his fellows. Where he has no alternative, he submits to the yoke of communal servitude. Yet given a full chance to act in his own interest, nothing but expediency will restrain him from brutalizing, from maiming, from murdering—his brother, his mate, his parent or his child. Scratch an 'altruist', and watch a 'hypocrite' bleed.

M. T. Ghiselin, *The Economy of Nature and the Evolution of Sex*

1. EMOTIONS AND DECISIONS

In this chapter we begin to explore the structure of human motivation. This is the question of the categories we need in order to grasp the way in which our awareness of the world and our situation in it issues in behaviour and action. We have already begun to square up to the looming issues of Dionysus and Apollo, emotion and reason. But first we need to think accurately about the actual ways we are motivated. Are we always, for instance, as the quotation in the epigraph claims, self-interested, or ought we to be? Or do our desires always involve ourselves in some more subtle way? Are our real concerns masked by faked conformity to the ways people are supposed to be, so that we are typically self-deceived? Does our biological nature condemn us to some concerns, and forbid us others?

Suppose, then, we take a case in which we are uncertain about what to do. The issue, say, is whether to get rid of the garden and sell the land. Various considerations present themselves. We could make some money that way. We could take more holidays without the garden: it takes up too much time. But Uncle George, God rest his soul, was so fond of it. There are too few green spaces left in this part of the country. The neighbours wouldn't approve. Actually, I remember promising father that we wouldn't sell it. It looks lovely in the spring. Some friends use the apples to make the most delicious cider. And so on and so on. These considerations come to mind, perhaps unbidden. As considerations they represent features of the situation we care about. The considerations that come to mind are those aspects of the situation about which we think as we deliberate. They are sometimes called 'intentional' contents, meaning simply things that come to mind, things that we care about, aspects of the situation that present themselves as reasons for or against action.

These contents are sometimes thought of as intentional objects of *desire*. But this is dangerous. Sometimes we act not so much in ways that we want to act, but in ways we feel we have to act. We are, as it were, *resigned* to acting in some way, rather than actively wanting to do so. Occupying some role, such as father or mother, we may be resigned to pursuing the conventional daily round. Being dutiful, we may feel *bound* to do various things. It is not so much that we want to go to the office or wash the dishes, but it has to be done, and our role is that of doing it, or perhaps it is our duty to do it. Common sense tells us that we do not always do what we most want to do. On the other hand, once any consideration has an effect on our dispositions to act, then we have a subject who can be described as *caring* about it—caring about preserving George's garden, or making money, or keeping the promise to father, or earning a living, or doing the dishes. The considerations that enter our reasoning are the things we care about. They could be called our interests, but sometimes the things we care about oppose our interests in another sense of that term. I may care about getting even with the boss, even while I recognize that the project is self-destructive. I may care about getting revenge, even if I perish in the attempt. I shall call the things that matter to us our *concerns*. Concerns at this stage may be backward-looking, forward-looking, self-centred, not self-centred, moral, non-moral. They may nag us and badger us, and when we reflect on them they may be causes of pride or shame or neither. The phenomenology of deliberation is one of some such jumble, with our concerns operating, consciously or otherwise, in their varying strengths, and eventually a decision bubbles up.

Suppose, now, somebody says that everyone does what they most want to do. There is a boring sense in which this is wrong: I most want to watch the game, but I am resigned to doing the dishes. But there is a more interesting sense in which it has a point. If some third person is to understand why I am doing the dishes when I want to watch the game, then they must find the aspect of doing the dishes that concerns me: my concern to fill my role as dutiful husband, or to get them out of the way before they smell, or whatever. They have to see what it was that I thought about the situation that makes doing the dishes the option that I choose. Furthermore, since doing the dishes beats watching the game, the concern has to be regarded as stronger, at least at this time and on this occasion, than the desire to watch the game. If the third person draws a blank here, then they are left saying that I do the dishes for no reason. It is, as it were, an accidental happening, perhaps more like a reflex than an action that can be explained in terms of my beliefs and my motivations. In this 'thin' sense it is true that we have to interpret people so that everyone does what they are most drawn to doing (and there is reason to say that the way in which we have to *interpret* people is the way that, psychologically, they actually *are*—see Chapter 3). But although this marks a fact about the explanation of action, it puts no limit on the aspects of situations that *do* draw us, with more or less strength, into particular actions. It leaves the heterogeneous nature of human motivations untouched. It merely tells us that, as a matter of accounting, if we think someone acted for some reason and in the face of other reasons for acting another way, then that reason should be regarded as having had more significance at the time. If the balance went down that way, then that is the side that had the more weight on it. Our actions reveal what most concerns us, at the time.

So far I have equated concerns with those things that affect us when we bring them to mind. But we should not rule out self-deception and lack of self-knowledge. A feature of a situation may be influencing us although we do not realize it. From the agent's point of view the motivational power and direction of a consideration may not even be recognized. We often do not know why certain choices are just not on, and others so strangely attractive. Sometimes we do not even know what the direction of a consideration is. Suppose someone has the offer of a job, in a place that takes her to live close to an old friend or family member. This may clearly bother her, without it being clear whether it is working for or against the decision. It is a significant factor, but it need not be clear whether it pulls for or against. It opens up too many possibilities, and perhaps she does not know whether they will pan out well or badly. Perhaps she only knows that the consideration has increased the stakes: she fears it is going to turn out very well or very badly, but has no idea which. This may be why she is disturbed. Even when she takes the job, she may not know whether she took it in spite of the old acquaintance, or because of him or her. And even when we know the direction of a consideration, we may not realize its strength, or the extent of its power over other considerations. Sometimes we surprise ourselves, and it is often only in retrospect, when a course of action has settled down, that we can hit upon a story about what was influencing us, according to which our eventual decision made good sense.[1] We ourselves sometimes have to construct a retrospective story: 'I suppose what must have been bothering me was that . . .'

These reflections have been relatively a priori. That is, there is the question of how an agent thinks of a situation, and there is the question of how important the features of it are to her, with intentional action seen as the upshot of the features that she notices, and the degrees of importance they have. The rule that the *strongest concern wins* represents a piece of book-keeping: it simply means that we interpret the considerations that do in fact win as those that are the strongest. But there is evidence from empirical studies that can be used to amplify this picture by bringing in empirical facts about the role our emotions play in decision-making. In his fascinating study the neuroscientist Antonio Damasio described the structures of the body and brain that subserve decision-making, and the striking consequences when they go wrong.[2] Damasio presents patients whose capacities for attention, whose intelligence, memory, abilities to hold several things in mind at once, social knowledge, moral reasoning, inferential or logical abilities, and language, are quite intact, yet whose capacity to live their lives in any sensible way is virtually zero. What has been lost is the application of such knowledge, in the formation of emotional affect, and thence in decision-making. So such a subject can say which of two alternatives is better, what the consequences of one or another would be, and can select and register (verbally) those aspects of a situation that people count as important considerations. But all this fails to translate into action. Such patients behave in hopelessly inappropriate ways. They fail to execute simple tasks, they get sidetracked, they cause social havoc, and are incapable of elementary organization in their own lives. The most famous example of the type was the nineteenth-century railway worker Phineas Gage, whose forebrain was penetrated by an iron rod in an accident with explosives. The horrendous damage to the front of the brain (the ventromedial region of

---

[1] Bernard Williams, *Shame and Necessity*, 44–6.
[2] Antonio Damasio, *Descartes' Error* (New York: Putnam, 1994).

the prefrontal cortices) left Gage, in the words of his contemporary physician:

fitful, irreverent, indulging at times in the grossest profanity which was not previously his custom, manifesting but little deference for his fellows, impatient of restraint or advice when it conflicts with his desires, at times pertinaciously obstinate, yet capricious and vacillating, devising many plans of future operation, which are no sooner arranged than they are abandoned . . .[3]

The reason for the inability to function normally—although, of course, elements in the pattern are shown by all of us, some of the time—seems to be that these patients have lost any normal associations between representing aspects of a situation, and the stable onset of 'affect' or emotion. Scenes which would excite positive or negative emotions in normal people may leave such patients entirely cold. They do not become excited at the prospect of gain, or fearful at the prospect of loss. In these emotional lives, everything has either disappeared, or at least become unstable.[4] Damasio describes how their representations are not 'somatically marked', or in other words how things like 'unpleasant gut feelings' or other bodily expressed emotional changes fail to occur when, in normal people, they would.[5] When there is entire absence of affect we have a flat decision-making landscape: one in which no option reliably generates any more emotionally marked attraction or avoidance than any other. In some patients there is little or no emotional output. In others, such as Gage, some associations between awareness and emotion seem to be there, but unstable, transient, and frequently absurd.

While the empirical facts seem to be clear enough, their interpretation is not so obvious. The idea is that a situation is somatically marked when we have pleasant or unpleasant bodily responses, such as those associated with fear or anger, as we think of the situation. And it is clear that the basic emotions of anger, fear, disgust, sadness, and happiness or joy can be thought of as the upshot of fairly specific 'affect programs' subserved by the limbic system in the brain. The systems responsible for them are homologous with similar systems found in other mammals, and especially primates.[6] Such systems work invol-

[marginal handwritten note: for problem with decisions?]

---

[3] Ibid. 8.

[4] Arguably Damasio is a little insensitive to this distinction. He makes it sound as though Gage, and particularly another patient, Eliot, have lost all emotion or affect, whereas at least on the surface the problem is not this. The problem is that their emotions show no predictability or stability, so that 'affect' lights at random on different courses of action.   [5] Damasio, *Descartes' Error*, 173.

[6] This means that primate systems are not only analogous in operation to ours, but are their evolutionary ancestors.

untarily. They take as input a stimulus, which may or may not be conscious, and deliver a syndrome of changes as output, including typical facial expressions and changes in the autonomic nervous system, such as the thumping heart, elevated adrenalin, and constricted gut characteristic of fear. The operation of this system may be 'passive' in the precise sense that it operates without control by higher-order cerebral processes. We may be, and often are, unaware of what sets it off, although we will be conscious of the resulting anger or fear. In this respect we are often opaque to ourselves. But saying that such a system operates without this higher-order control is not implying that it is always immune to such control. Sometimes it is indeed immune. In Hume's famous example a man suspended in a cage over a precipice may be very afraid, although he knows at one level that he is perfectly safe.[7] The system does its work regardless. But sometimes we can control our fear, and the panic subsides.

The apparent disadvantage of the automatic nature of the operation is of course outweighed by the benefit of speed. It is evolutionarily advantageous to be very quick at preparing for flight or fight, or at avoiding noxious substances, even if the system that makes us quick to do so delivers a fair number of 'false positives'.[8]

Saying that a system may operate relatively independently of higher-order cognitive functioning is not denying that the input side may develop differently in different environments, or be trained differently in different societies. Very few kinds of cue may be available to trigger emotional responses in the youngest children. Features such as the smile or frown of the caregiver may be examples. But they learn by experience and by imitation of others. A single experience of a burn or a shock is enough to bring children to fear what burned or shocked them, and a little awareness of what elicits fear from others infects them with similar aversion.

The passivity of other emotions, or perhaps we should say emotional states, are plausibly claimed to involve more complex layers of design. Thus there are emotional states whose social point is that they are treated as 'passive', although it is plausible to see unconscious motivation in the people who get themselves into them, and unconscious collaboration in those who treat them as out of control.[9] The

---

[7] *Treatise*, I. iii. 13, p. 148.

[8] Peter Godfrey-Smith, 'Signal, Decision, Action', *Journal of Philosophy*, 88 (1991), 709–22.

[9] See Paul Griffiths, *What Emotions Really Are* (Chicago, Ill.: University of Chicago Press, 1997), ch. 6.

alleged or imputed passivity becomes an excuse for the abnormal behaviour or the absence of conformity to usual social norms. It may enable a person to retain his respect or honour under stress, and the society in turn may want to settle for that upshot. We even get the apparently paradoxical phenomenon of people who obviously 'work themselves up' into such states: deliberately aiming for a state at which they can excuse themselves as having been overcome by emotion.[10]

Basic affect programs operate rather like a reflex, producing stereotypical changes in the face and body. They account for immediate, phenomenologically salient emotions, and indeed invite the addition made in the James–Lange theory of emotions, which is that the characteristic 'feel' of emotions consists in a perception of the abnormal bodily states of arousal or depression. But basic affect programs seem not so central to higher cognitive emotions such as envy or jealousy, or long-term syndromes of emotion, such as cold calculated anger, or even grieving or being in love. In his recent book, Paul Griffiths suggests that these differ from Damasio's primary emotions in four important ways.[11] First, they are more flexible on the input side, not elicited by any specific kinds of functional situations, in the way that fear is elicited by apprehended danger, or anger by obstacles and challenges. Second, they are sustained through time, unlike the muscular and physiological effects of the affect programs. Third, they do not have stereotypical outputs, such as distinctive facial expressions or states of physiological arousal. And, finally, they are integrated with other conscious processes, and can lead to long-term plans of action, rather than triggering reflex-like responses. This leads Griffiths to propose a division: the folk concept of emotion pulls together two entirely different systems, which there is no reason for cognitive science to treat as any kind of unity. Griffiths suggests that the best account of the higher cognitive emotions should simply treat them as 'irruptive motivational states': states 'which interfere with the smooth unfolding of plans designed to secure our long-term goals'. There may be good game-theoretic reasons for us to be subject to such states, but they remain irrational in the classical economic sense. Cognitive theory, however, should find no single natural kind common to both the primary emotions of the affect program and these more complex states.

---

[10] In his treatment of this Griffiths suggests that in these cases the practice could not survive general awareness of its own nature as a social construct. It would be a case of us 'seeing through' a pretence, and the pretence then cannot continue. I am not so sure: people can be well aware of the artificial and constructed nature of emotions connected with, say, 'fine' displays of fashion and etiquette, yet continue their attachments just the same. [11] Griffiths, *What Emotions Really Are,* 102.

My objection to this is partly conceptual and partly empirical. Conceptually, the picture of higher emotions as simply disruptive motivational states ignores the extent to which our attachment to our 'long-term goals' is itself an emotional state. The person who has a driving concern for his future financial status or future health is not different from the person who wants to do down his neighbour, in that the latter is emotional and he is not. He has different concerns, but they equally engage his emotions. It is even likely, and according to some theorists inevitable, that those concerns will themselves involve overt emotions, such as pride or vanity: if theorists such as Mandeville and Adam Smith are right, once we are beyond a basic level of sustenance, the reason anyone cares so deeply about financial status is that they care deeply about status.[12] And even if they are not right, the concern will involve such things as fear of failure or anger at obstacles. Seeing long-term interest as 'unemotional', whereas other things are emotional, is in fact mobilizing the negative connotations of 'emotional': it is like Cold War warriors saying that dissidents revealing the bad effects of nuclear explosions on people are arguing 'emotionally'— whereas they themselves, painting the lurid evils of the enemy, are arguing 'rationally'.

Empirically, the suggestion that we simply split the operation of the affect program from 'higher cognitive emotions' seems to ignore the most fascinating result of Damasio's work, which is the extent to which 'higher-order' decision-making has to harness the limbic system in order to work at all. The clinical evidence is that when the primitive system is disrupted, then the higher-order decision-making system collapses with it. Unless the outcomes of action that the cognitive system can identify come 'somatically marked', the decision-making system malfunctions. The whole point is that there is no dualism, in which the one floats free of the other. And in the light of that, if we look again at the four reasons for separating the higher-order cognitive emotions from the others, then I think we can see that they are not at all compelling. These points are quite compatible with seeing the long-term, culturally variable states as essentially dispositions whose manifestations are particular patterns (and blends) of occurrences of the primary emotions. Thus a jealous person is prone to occurrences of anger, fear, and sadness elicited by perceivings or memories or even imaginings

---

[12] Bernard Mandeville, *The Fable of the Bees*, ed. F. B. Kaye (Oxford: Oxford University Press, 1924), note N; Adam Smith, *The Theory of Moral Sentiments*, ed. D. D. Raphael and A. L. Macfie (Oxford: Oxford University Press, 1976), I. iii. 2. 1, p. 50. The emotional side of financial concerns is explored in James Buchan, *Frozen Desire: An Inquiry into the Meaning of Money* (London: Picador, 1996).

that represent the rival attentions of the beloved. But this is just what Damasio means by saying that representations of events of that kind have become 'somatically marked'. And if they hadn't, and the agent could think about, or look with perfect equanimity on, such scenes, then he or she is not jealous. It is not even clear that in cases like this the input and output are less stereotypical than in the case of primitive fear or anger, remembering the amount of learning and development that has to lie behind a child's coming to perceive the 'right' things as fearful or threatening. Of course, there may be a further layer of acculturation as well, on top of the stereotypical output. Different cultures will have different norms for appropriate expressions of such an emotion, including its suppression, but that is true also of basic anger or fear, happiness or sadness. For example, Japanese apparently show facial behaviour characteristic of negative emotions which are almost instantly suppressed in the presence of authority figures, and replaced by a polite smile.[13] A correct English expression of grief would scarcely do in the Middle East.

Again, a person of cold calculating anger, bent on a long-term project of revenge, may not often bare his teeth or clench his fists involuntarily. But if it is genuinely anger, rather than dispassionate malice, for instance, then there will be a disposition to those kinds of output if the circumstances are right. Learning that his enemy has escaped his plot, or scored yet another triumph, his heart pounds, he grinds his teeth, vents his spleen on his family, and so on.

But emotional states are not simply perceptions of bodily arousals and changes, as, for instance, feeling sick may be thought to be. Their essence includes directedness: unlike moods, emotions have objects.[14] To integrate the directedness of emotion with the neurophysiological facts, we must suppose that our visceral arousals are not merely 'perceived' but play a part in determining what attracts and repels us or what we become inclined to do.

It would be tempting to say that if the thought of an object causes such responses, then this is what it is for it to be the object of an emotion. But this is not quite right. I may think of you and become angry. But it does not follow that it is you I am angry at. Thinking of you may remind me of the party where I met you, and this may make me angry

---

[13] Griffiths, *What Emotions Really Are*, 53.

[14] This is emphasized by almost all philosophical writing on emotion; perhaps the last theorist to ignore it was William James, and even he backed away from the view that emotions simply denote feelings of excitement and bodily arousal. For discussion, see Robert M. Gordon, *The Structure of Emotions* (Cambridge: Cambridge University Press, 1987), 93.

for some quite different reason. Or, thinking of you may make me depressed. A lethargy of body and spirit may come upon me. But it need not be you that I am depressed about. It is not the fact that you cause my anger or depression, however directly or indirectly, that makes it true that I am angry or depressed at you. What does make it you that I am angry with is the fact that my anger is directed at you, or in other words that I would be inclined to vent it upon you or to blame you for something, at least in the absence of other inhibitory mechanisms. When Damasio talks of 'juxtaposing' a somatic marker with the representation of a situation, what he has in mind is this functionally active juxtaposition, whereby the marker comes to operate either as an 'alarm bell' warning us off the situation, or a 'beacon of incentive' encouraging us towards it.[15]

So, our emotions do not, as it were, finish with a consciousness of bodily and visceral states. Instead, these somatic markers function as 'biasing devices'. Eventually they translate into ticks and crosses on options about which we deliberate, and features of situations that we think about. What patients like Gage show is that without such markers, and the arousal of emotion or feeling to which they can give rise, no amount of information (or reasoning or inferring) is more salient than any other: the decision-making landscape remains boringly flat, for none of it *matters*. We are back with Hamlet and Jacques again. Without emotions the will is rudderless. So we can see our cognitive relations with the world, our capacity to represent it as being one way or another, as tied in partnership with the mechanisms of emotion and of affect that turn the input into output. Our emotional dispositions and our representations act together to issue in action, with neither apparently able to achieve its results without the other.

The neurological evidence clearly suggests two separate faculties or modules working in partnership. We can separate two distinct properties of an agent: the way she represents things as being, and what effects those ways have on her conduct. She may represent things in just that way because of somatic markers directing her to find some features important, and directing her to ignore others. These markers may in turn have the place they do because of previous experience and previous pains and pleasures. But the role of memory, experience, and emotion can be distinguished none the less. Patients such as Gage show the split most dramatically: by seeing what happens when things go wrong we can marvel at the harmonies involved when things work right.

---

[15] Damasio, *Descartes' Error*, 174.

Reason affects decisions by engaging with our structure of concerns. Reason presents aspects of situations that are of concern to us. Learning that the liquid is benzene rather than water, I lose any desire to drink it. Reasoning can even alter our concerns. It does this by engaging yet further concerns which we then mobilize to suppress some concerns, or encourage others. Some may come with a fixed emotional impact or affect: that we can make money selling the garden may recurrently present itself as a consideration that excites us in favour of the course of action; that Uncle George loved the garden may start with a negative affect as we consider selling it, but we may on further reflection be able to neutralize that affect by drawing on other considerations: Uncle George was an awful sentimentalist, after all. Sometimes we cannot do this: a consideration may continue to produce its affect, even when we wish it wouldn't or deceive ourselves into thinking that we have neutralized it. Reason and experience may also show us that what we cared about was delusive (would not bring the happiness we thought it would) or that our concern was based on other misunderstandings or cognitive errors. Once they do this, our concerns can change.

In the case of the garden, the aspects that come to mind are somatically marked: they are associated with positive or negative affects. But they form something of a jumble. To bring more system into the process we might suggest that the surface considerations are only the end product of some deeper process of reasoning. Suppose I keep returning to the fact that Uncle George would not have liked it. The suggestion is that this represents a more protracted train of thought, perhaps something like: Uncle George would not have liked it; it is good that we respect the likes and dislikes of others; hence it is good that I respect Uncle George's wishes. Evidence that something more systematic lies behind the surface jumble comes from the fact that if we are challenged ('Why care so much about Uncle George? He is dead') we will try to justify the affect by placing it in a wider context, trying to defend it as a coherent part of our stance towards the world, not just a fetish. Not being able to do that may result in a change of relationship between the feature and its impact: at the limit, it may stop mattering to us altogether whether Uncle George would have wished it or not. Naturally, some such changes may improve us, and others will do the reverse.

If considerations remain heterogeneous, each with its own contribution of affect, the eventual decision seems to pop out of nowhere. This is indeed how it feels. Hobbes memorably described the will as the last appetite in deliberating, and his view may seem to accord with the feeling we have when, after a train of deliberations, we just find ourselves finally inclined to one thing or another.[16] But it is not so much that the arrival of a choice is the same as the arrival of the last 'appetite' or characterization of the situation as desirable or undesirable in some respect. When the will is activated, our inclinations take the form of actual actions or at least the formation of decisions and intentions to act. This is not the same as the arrival of a final consideration. It is a resolution of the problem rather than another contribution to it. With desires and concerns the bow is bent, but with intention and decision the arrow is sped. Hobbes's point, presumably, is that the direction in which it is sped is the last one towards which the bow was bent.

To inject some system, we may want to interpret the process of deliberation as one of accounting: adding and subtracting affects in some common currency, until eventually a balance is achieved. I have already said that we will interpret people whom we regard as acting for reasons as if whatever they decide to do matters most to them at the time. We can impose a kind of unconscious calculus of weights of affect. Sometimes, but fairly seldom, we consciously perform a process something like this, going through a cost-benefit analysis which determines a solution. But often we do not, and cannot, and there is usually something absurdly artificial about the process of drawing up a list and commensurating the considerations. It is like filling in some silly questionnaire—'twenty ways of measuring the success of your marriage'—or reading an airport book on management technique—'fifteen ways to rate your job'. There is always the suspicion that any such project is in fact a pantomime, perhaps disguising the extent to which the decision has already in fact been taken. We should notice as well that cost-benefit analysis does not supplant the emotional basis of decision-making, but at best systematizes it. For it is only in so far as some outcomes attract us and others do not that we are actually treating them as real costs and benefits at all. In the world of Damasio's patients, the intellectual exercise of entering something as a cost or benefit is detached from its normal association with emotional affect, and has no impact on decision-making. So compared to its normal counterpart it remains a piece of play-acting.

In Chapters 7 and 8 we confront one way in which the scene so far has been complicated by moral philosophers. This is through the introduction of the spurious figure that I shall call the Kantian Captain. But

---

[16] Thomas Hobbes, *Leviathan*, ed. John Gaskin (Oxford: Oxford University Press, 1996), 1. 6.

in the culture at large, as opposed to professional philosophy, far the most important attempt to see system in the jumble of surface considerations derives them from some fundamental stock of motivations. And of these, the most famous, the darling of biologists, businessmen, and cynics alike, is the idea that underneath the surface lies the ruthless pursuit of self-interest. Beneath the surface diversities of desire and emotion lie the hidden selfish mechanisms. Scratch any other consideration, and underneath is revealed the ceaseless concern for the self.

2. ECONOMIC MAN[17]

Here is a characterization of the 'rational actor' of central, orthodox economic theory, and political and social science:

1. Actors pursue goals
2. These goals reflect the actor's perceived self-interest
3. Behavior results from a process that involves, or functions as if it entails conscious choice
4. The individual is the basic agent in society
5. Actors have preferences that are consistent and stable
6. If given options, actors will choose the alternative with the highest expected utility
7. Actors possess extensive information on both the available alternatives and the likely consequences of their choices.[18]

The human being as painted by this theory is *homo economicus* or economic man. Economic man is supposed to conduct deliberation in a specific way. He (or she, for *homo* covers both sexes) always acts with his or her own interest in mind. In the more formal jargon, his single-minded principle is that of maximizing his expected utility: of getting the most, for himself, that can be expected by any course of action he could take. Economic man is usually presented as a paradigm of rationality rather than a moral paradigm. In fact, his nature can easily seem opposed to morality, which would demand at a minimum some kind of concern for others. Indeed one of the classics of British moral philosophy, Henry Sidgwick's *Methods of Ethics*, is structured around the unsuccessful attempt to circumvent the oppositions between ego-

[17] Some of the material that follows is presented in my 'Trust, Co-operation and Human Psychology', in Margaret Levi and Valerie Braithwaite, eds., *Trust and Governance* (New York: Russell Sage Foundation, 1998).

[18] Kristen Renwick Monroe with Kristen Hill Maher, 'Psychology and Rational Actor Theory', *Political Psychology*, 16 (1995), 1–21.

ism and ethics. But of course the self-interested rationality of *homo economicus* also attracts devotion of a moral kind. Enthusiasts in the nineteenth century and, as the notorious quotation at the head of this chapter shows, in our own time as well, have no trouble painting opposition to the principle as impractical, unworldly, a mark of unfitness, a non-adaptive and sickly aberration, a stigma. Rational self-interest is deep in our image as the goal we are to pursue. And there is something reassuringly empirical and down to earth (earlier critics would have said, English) about expected utility. The principle has a realistic ring about it: don't expect too much from people. Look for their interests, even if they are disguised by what they say they want. And, after all, practical politics is largely a matter of appealing to what people perceive to be their own interests.

Yet elementary questions about what is intended are enough to raise doubts about the principle that rational persons always act on the principle of maximizing their own expected utility. What does it mean? Indeed, is there anything for it to mean? When we are sure what it means, are we sure that there is anything uniquely rational about it, and what is the force of the word 'rational' here? Are we dealing with a human universal, characteristic of us simply through our species-wide natures, or with a very specific cultural self-image: the ideology of 'possessive individualism' or Western capitalism? Why is it advisable to maximize our expected utility? What are we like if we do so, or if we do not?

Here are three possibilities about the status of the principle:

(1) The thesis, if true, is an empirical truth, describing ourselves as we are. So taken, it issues in specific *predictions*. Since it is true of us, we will do some things and avoid others; had the principle not been true of us, we would have done otherwise.

(2) The thesis, if true, is a normative truth, describing ourselves as we ought to be. It does not issue in predictions, but in *recommendations*. It is a rule of conduct, like, for example, 'never give a sucker an even break'.

(3) The thesis, if true, is analytic or definitional. It is a principle or grid for imposing interpretation: a mathematical structure, designed to render processes of deliberation mathematically tractable, whatever those processes are. As such it issues in neither predictions nor recommendations.

Many people think the truth lies in (1) or (2), or somewhere joining them, saying that we are to some extent like *homo economicus*, and by authoritative criteria of rationality, this is how we ought to be. We should, as it were, thank God that we have that motivational cast, just as we might thank God that we are English, or whatever. Equally, critics of the theory may attack its empirical basis, or its moral credentials, or both. Perhaps to a large extent we are not like that, and should thank our lucky stars for it. Critics from a feminist perspective, for example, often suppose that the theory insinuates a false, patriarchal ideal—that is, an ideal that is at least false of women, and arguably to their credit. On this kind of view, the rational actor is self-directed, self-assertive, opportunistic, aggressive in pursuing his interests, independent, uncaring, calculating: a nightmare Machiavellian figure projected over the entire sphere of human relations.[19] But then the theory becomes empirically false, for these are traits that not all of us exhibit all of the time. And it becomes morally obnoxious, for these are not traits we exhibit when we are putting our best foot forward. But before condemning the theory so roundly, I should like to consider more carefully what the theory strictly means—although that is not to say that these critics were misguided in highlighting the tawdry vision it has stood for in practice.

It may be that the truth lies in (3), a less familiar option already foreshadowed in the remarks in Chapter 3 and the first section of this chapter, and that I explain at greater length in the next chapter. Of course, it is tempting, and writers have fallen into the temptation, to want to preserve some empirical content, and some normative bite, for the theory while comfortably enjoying the security of the third option. Defend it as a tautology, but deploy it as an empirical insight or recommendation. This melancholy combination is sufficiently entrenched in the area to deserve a name. While saluting noble exceptions we might call it the economist's fallacy. Philosophers however are not wholly innocent of the economist's fallacy. Here is John Stuart Mill:

And now to decide whether this is really so; whether mankind do desire nothing for itself but that which is a pleasure to them, or of which the absence is a pain: we have evidently arrived at a question of fact and experience, dependent, like all similar questions, upon evidence . . . I believe that these sources of evidence, impartially consulted, will declare that desiring a thing and finding it pleasant, aversion to it and thinking of it as painful, are phenomena

---

[19] The papers collected in Marianne Ferber and Julie Nelson, eds., *Beyond Economic Man* (Chicago, Ill.: University of Chicago Press, 1992), include many such criticisms. Kristin Luker, *Taking Chances: Abortion and the Decision not to Contracept* (Berkeley, Calif.: University of California Press, 1975) provides a compelling study of how to understand womens' contraceptive decisions that would be easy to dismiss as 'irrational'.

entirely inseparable, or rather two parts of the same phenomenon . . . that to think of an object as desirable (unless for the sake of its consequences) and to think of it as pleasant, are one and the same thing; and that to desire anything, except in proportion as the idea of it is pleasant, is a physical and metaphysical impossibility. [20]

Here Mill starts by telling us that he is dealing with an empirical question of what people do in fact desire. The thesis is that they desire 'nothing for itself but that which is a pleasure to them'. Arguing that this thesis is true, Mill substitutes an equation between thinking of an object as desirable and thinking of it as pleasant. He then transforms this into the thesis that it is physically and metaphysically impossible to desire anything except in proportion as the idea of it is pleasant. But the substitution and transformation takes him much further than he realizes from the original question. There may be a sense in which desiring something implies thinking of it as pleasant. If I desire the death of the infidel, I may think it pleasant that the infidel die. If I desire the survival of the whales, I think it pleasant that whales survive. But this is not relevant to the empirical question with which Mill starts out, that is, whether people only desire their own happiness or pleasure. The fact that I think of the survival of the whales as pleasant does not even imply that I think it will be pleasant *for me*. I might expect to be dead before the survival of the whales or the death of the infidel is secured. And it does not suggest that it is not really their survival, but only my own pleasure, that I desire. All we are told is that in desiring such things I must be thinking of them in a pleasant or favourable light. But it does not follow, and is not true, that it is my own pleasure or happiness that I thereby desire. Curiously enough, Mill could have learned to avoid this mistake from a philosopher who wrote just over a century before him, Joseph Butler, whose exposition we now consider.

3. THE EMPIRICAL CLAIM: BUTLER ON DESIRE AND INTEREST

The theory is that when we act, we act out of self-love, or self-interest. Sometimes, more fashionably, the idea is that we only ever act out of what is in the interests of our genes, but I shall consider the more traditional view first. This view goes under the heading of *psychological*

---

[20] John Stuart Mill, *Utilitarianism*, ch. IV.

egoism. It has a tremendous emotional power. If we believe it, we know the world, we are nobody's fool. We are not taken in by cant and hypocrisy; like conspiracy theorists, we have penetrated below the surface; like Freud finding sex everywhere or Marx finding economics everywhere, we see the real face of human beings behind the mask.

It is true that the view is not very popular among philosophers, but everyone acknowledges that it is one of those hardy perennials that never die, however thoroughly philosophers believe they have dug up their roots. The standard attempt to dig them up is due to Bishop Butler, and has been accepted and repeated in various forms by Bradley, Sidgwick, Broad, and many others. Butler begins with a powerful a priori point: even if there is a principle of self-interest, it has to be true that as well as acting on it in the abstract, we aim at particular external things. We want, on occasions, drink, food, warmth, exercise, and so on. These, the psychological egoist says, are desired as a means to our happiness or ease or content; it is in his interest that these particular desires are met, and it is because it is in his interests that the desires exist. But at any rate, says Butler,

> that all particular appetites and passions are towards *external things themselves*, distinct from the *pleasure arising from them*, is manifested from hence; that there could not be this pleasure, were it not for that prior suitableness between the object and the passion: there could be no enjoyment or delight from one thing more than another, from eating food more than from swallowing a stone, if there were not an affection or appetite to one thing more than another.[21]

The point being that we have to admit that we have a desire *for* the water or food or whatever, since were it not so, there would be no 'pleasure' arising from satisfaction of the desire. The desire for water or food Butler calls a particular affection, and his first point is to distinguish having such a particular affection from having an interest in the 'pleasure arising' from its fulfilment.

What Butler is doing is forcing the distinction between:

(1) The object of my 'particular' desire, which might equally be for water, food, or the happiness of my neighbour (or for anything else: the continuation of the whales, or the destruction of my enemy, or the triumph of the Party, or the death of the infidel)

---

[21] Joseph Butler, *Fifteen Sermons Preached at the Rolls Chapel*, ed. D. Matthews (London: Bell & Sons, 1953), Sermon XI, 167. The sermons were delivered in 1726, so credit should also be given to Frances Hutcheson, *An Inquiry into the Original of our Ideas of Beauty and Virtue* (London: 1725; 4th edn., reprinted by Gregg International, 1969). The second part of this (*An Inquiry concerning Moral Good and Evil*) is a sustained attack on Hobbes and Mandeville, making many of the same points as Butler.

on the one hand, and:

(2) The pleasure that will accrue to me upon the satisfaction of that desire

on the other hand. Inevitably the pleasure mentioned in (2) is my pleasure, because it is my desire that we are talking about. But, Butler argues, we should not conclude from that fact alone that the *principle* of my action is always self-love:

And if, because every particular affection is a man's own, and the pleasure arising from its gratification his own pleasure, or pleasure to himself, such particular affection must be called self-love; according to this way of speaking, no creature whatever can possibly act but merely from self-love, and every action and every affection whatever is to be resolved up into this one principle. But then this is not the language of mankind, or, if it were, we should want words to express the difference, between the principle of an action, proceeding from cool consideration that it will be to my own advantage; and an action, suppose of revenge or of friendship, by which a man runs upon certain ruin, to do evil or good to another.[22]

This is an exposure of Mill's fallacy. That is, the tautology that the pleasure mentioned in (2) is my pleasure does not at all entail that my actions have any such state as their object. The fallacy turns on ambiguity in English constructions with the word 'pleasant'. If I am concerned for the survival of the whales, we might say that I find their survival pleasant to contemplate, and by confusion we might go on to suppose that this identifies a pleasure for the sake of which I am campaigning. This was Mill's mistake.

Why is this a confusion? We may enter a small complication, before returning to expand Butler's main point. Not all desires seem to bring 'pleasure' upon being gratified. I may want to go for a run, not because I find it enjoyable or expect it to be pleasant, but because I believe it is good for my health, and I want to be healthy. Or, I might have a sudden craving for some special food, even though I don't much like its taste, and don't expect to get much pleasure from eating it. Psychologists sometimes talk of satisfaction of desire in terms of release of tension rather than onset of pleasure. The idea is that being in the state of desire is rather like being under pressure, and the change in the self that comes with gratifying the desire is the release of the pressure. It is not clear that this is even true empirically: if I pass a newsvendor and decide I want a paper, I don't feel under pressure, and I don't feel a release from pressure when I have bought it. Still less,

---

[22] Butler, *Fifteen Sermons*, Sermon XI, 168–9.

when I have bought it, am I likely to feel rapturous, or exalted, or euphoric; I am not likely to savour the moment, or revel in the good feeling. I simply wanted a paper, and got it. I gratified a particular passion, and that is all.

Still, the theorist may say, what happened was that there was a pressure, and now it is gone. We may speak like this if we wish, but notice that it is quite wrong to infer that what I wanted was release from the pressure. 'I want a paper' and 'I want to be released from the pressure of wanting a paper' are two quite different things. It is not just that in wanting the paper I may be unaware of anything that deserves calling a pressure. But more importantly, even if I began to recognize the pressure, it is still true that in wanting a paper I only want to be released from the pressure in one specific way—namely, by obtaining a paper. If someone hurled me onto a couch and psychoanalysed me out of my desire, and thereby release me from the pressure, I would not have got what I wanted—that is, a paper.

I might be satisfied with this way of removing the desire, but only if at some level I did not really 'identify' with the desire. If I felt that it was an obsession, or a kind of external imposition, I might be happy to have it removed surgically, as it were. So, for example, a person might want release from sexual desire, and if that could be procured by taking bromine or some pacifying hormone, then that would suit them fine. But most people subject to sexual desire would not at all want that way to peace. They want the natural expression of sexual desire, which is sex.[23]

For a further example, imagine someone bent upon revenge. She wants to destroy her enemy. Suppose someone redescribes her as wanting release from the pressure of desiring revenge. Here are ways of doing that: give her a pill that wipes out memory of her wrongs. Or, give her a false report that her enemy has been destroyed. These ways give her peace of mind. But do they get her what she wants? Suppose you are her henchman, and she orders you to destroy the enemy. You come back and slip her the pill, or manufacture the false report. Imagine the deception comes out: could you defend yourself by saying 'I only got you what you wanted'? Hardly. If I want the destruction of my enemy, or the health and happiness of my children, I don't want to live in a fool's paradise, in which I believe wrongly that my enemy has been destroyed or my children live in health and happiness. I want

---

[23] Wittgenstein, *Investigations*, § 440: 'Saying "I should like an apple" does not mean: I believe an apple will quell my feeling of nonsatisfaction. *This* proposition is not an expression of a wish, but of nonsatisfaction.'

these things to be *really* so. My own states of mind are incidental. Of course, normally I would also like to know that my enemy is destroyed, or that my children thrive. But if it comes to a choice, the combinations of {my enemy being destroyed; my not knowing about it} , or {my children thriving, my not knowing about it} beat {my enemy not being destroyed; my falsely believing that he has been} or {my children not thriving; my believing that they are}. The peace of mind is incidental; it is not that which I order my henchmen to bring about, and it is not what I normally want.

There are certainly special cases in which my own state of mind is what I aim at, but these are interesting precisely because they are different. Suppose someone gives some money to a charity, apparently wanting to help the children of the Third World. Suppose it then comes out that the money all goes to corrupt administrators of the charity. If the person is irritated not so much at the administrators, but rather at the reporter who breaks the story, we could suspect that really they didn't care about the children, but about their own virtue or their own self-satisfaction. Such a person may 'shoot the messenger', getting annoyed at the existence of reports that destroy their peace of mind, in cases where they didn't mind living in a fool's paradise. But such cases are empirically different. They are interesting because they go along with detectable (and often, rather embarrassing) syndromes of behaviour. They are cases where our real motivations are revealed, to our discredit, to have been less glorious than we presented them as being. But because they are special, they cannot be turned into a universal theory of human nature. If I gave money to help my children thrive, I would certainly want to be told if the money never reached them. I would want to shoot the post office, not the messenger who tells me that the post office failed to deliver.

Egoism rightly notices that there is a subjective change: a change from a state of desire to one of fulfilment. This is the change occurring when the subject has a desire gratified. Then the present suggestion of the egoist is that this change, whether we describe it in terms of a pleasure, or release of a pressure, or in some other way, is always the true object of desire. But Butler's a priori point is that this cannot possibly be true. For this change from 'having a desire to having no desire' can only itself be a *parasitic* object of desire. It is a change that presupposes a preceding desire—what Butler calls the particular appetite or passion, such as the desire for the paper or the well-being of my children in these examples—that is gratified or goes away. The desire to 'be someone who has his desires gone' is a second-order desire: it presupposes others. The egoist simply cannot pretend that the second-order desire is all that there is. The same point applies to 'desiring to have my interests served': this, too, presupposes that I have interests, which in effect means concerns and desires, which are independently specified. We might say that these particular desires 'make up' my own interest, in the sense that any third party who is concerned for my interest would have to ensure that those are the desires that are satisfied. But my own interest or my own desire cannot be my primary object of concern.

So we must distinguish between these other specific desires and concerns, on the one hand, and the principle of self-interest proper: 'the principle of an action, proceeding from cool consideration that it will be to my own advantage'. But when we do that we immediately see the contingent but incontestable point that this principle is in fact often notably absent from our deliberations. Seeking revenge, perhaps I 'run upon certain ruin' to do harm to my enemy. Here the object of my particular desire is my enemy's harm. I do not act for the sake of my own pleasure, nor, obviously for the sake of my own ruin. I concentrate my efforts on my enemy. Such examples exist, empirically, and they seem to be enough to refute any psychological egoist who believes that self-interest is *always* one of our objects, even if Butler has shown that it cannot be the only one. Butler shrewdly offers us the bad case as well as the good, presumably since the example of malice or revenge is perhaps more apt to appeal to the cynic, who prides himself on detecting self-interest under the bland mask of goodness.

Once we correctly distinguish between the particular affections and the principle of self-interest, we see as well that there is no essential opposition between altruism and this principle. As Butler puts it:

> Every particular affection, even the love of our neighbour, is as really our own affection, as self-love; and the pleasure arising from its gratification is as much my own pleasure as the pleasure self-love would have, from knowing I myself should be happy some time hence, would be my own pleasure.[24]

Concern for my neighbour's good is just that—a concern. It is no more opposed to my own interest than resentment, or ambition, or concern for an inanimate object or a pet. I may be someone who will not be truly happy unless my neighbour is so as well, in which case my own self-interest would require me to work for my neighbour's happiness. Butler rightly remarks that finding a direct opposition between a principle of self-love and a principle of altruism derives from thinking of a cash transaction: if my neighbour gets the money, I do not; if I get it, he

---

[24] Butler, *Fifteen Sermons*, Sermon XI, 168.

does not, and I may have to choose one outcome over the other. Obviously we do have bargaining relationships like this, and perhaps too much of our social life is perceived in terms of them. But not all relationships are 'zero sum' (so if I win, you lose, and vice versa). A person might share goods within a group even when the goods involved are scarce; their perception of their real use and advantage may be so thoroughly identified with that of those who bear the kinship relation to them. Whether people are like that is a contingent fact: some are more benevolent or charitable, or locked into sharing relationships, than others. In the abstract Butler's point is undeniable: there is no more competition between benevolence and self-interest than, in those who are malicious, there is competition between malice and self-interest, or in those who are ambitious, competition between ambition and self-interest. Any such concern may be one of the particular (first-order) concerns whose satisfaction goes to making up our own self-interest. It is this no-competition thesis that is the lynch-pin of any correct understanding of motivation at this point.

In our generation there has been a permanent condition of pessimism about human interpretation, in two ways. First, behind the apparent wants and desires that people seem to have, we think there lurk the dark forces of the unconscious. Second, when it comes to describing what someone really wanted, or believed, or intended, we feel we have no moorings: almost anything goes. Freud is of course the paradigm figure behind the first belief, and in his practice he probably inspires the second belief as well, since if you can swallow Freudian interpretations of many things, there is little reason to strain at others. So it is refreshing to remind ourselves of demonstrations that, in the theory of interpretation, it is just not true that anything goes. Butler provides a paradigmatic example of one kind of way of doing this. Hobbes had proposed that pity is 'imagination or fiction of future calamity to ourselves proceeding from the sense of another man's present calamity'.[25] Butler rebuts this with the following points. First, if this were so, being compassionate and being fearful would be the same thing, but everybody recognizes that they are not. Second, compassion is regarded as a virtue. If Hobbes were right, how would it be that a compassionate man is regarded as especially deserving our kindness, if he himself falls into distress? 'Is fear, then, or cowardice, so great a recommendation to the favour of the bulk of mankind?' Third, Hobbes

---

[25] Hobbes, *The Elements of Law*, Pt. II: *Human Nature*, ed. Douglas Gaskin (Oxford: Oxford University Press, 1994), ch. 9, § 5.

himself goes on to ask why we pity our friends in distress more than others. But, says Butler, if the question is why we are more fearful for ourselves when we see friends than others in distress, the fact may be doubted (and in any case is plainly not the same as the fact to be accounted for). A friend under a bus is not a better sign of our danger than anyone else under a bus. Fourth:

Suppose a person to be in real danger, and by some means or other to have forgot it; any trifling accident, any sound might alarm him, recall the danger to his remembrance, and renew his fear: but it is almost too grossly ridiculous . . . to speak of that sound or accident as an object of compassion; and yet, according to Mr. Hobbes, our greatest friend in distress is no more to us, no more the object of compassion, or of any affection in our heart; neither the one nor the other raises any emotion in our mind, but only the thoughts of our liableness to calamity, and the fear of it; and both equally do this.[26]

It is hard to imagine a more complete refutation of a psychological stab in the dark. Yet Hobbes's view is no more implausible, at first sight, than many other such suggestions, and Butler's destruction of it shows us how to decide them. That is, we ask whether the empirical predictions you would expect from the suggestion are in fact borne out. In the cast of strained reinterpretations, taking us far from the surface appearances, they frequently are not.

4. THE SELF AND BIOLOGY

I mentioned at the outset the appeal of psychological egoism to those who pride themselves as realists. Have they any answer to Butler? The leading recent source for such approaches has been the synthesis of evolutionary theory and social theory known as sociobiology. The quotation at the head of this chapter is more florid than most, but not different in spirit. Ever since Darwin there has been a strong tendency to interpret the theory of evolution in terms of a ruthless selfish battle for survival. In the nineteenth century, 'inferior' or 'primitive' races and classes were interpreted as being the losers in this inevitable struggle, and this in turn justified the winners continuing the struggle as aggressively as they could. Capitalists like Rockefeller and Carnegie could regard any proposal to limit the operations of the free market as a kind of fantastical attempt to interfere with the very processes of history and nature. The chosen people no longer have the mark of God on them,

---

[26] Butler, *Fifteen Sermons*, Sermon V, 'Upon Compassion', 85.

but the mark of the future. So the only honest course is to unmask altruism for what it is, and get on with the struggle.

The confusion here is almost as prevalent as Mill's fallacy. Popular or vulgar sociobiology trades on sliding effortlessly from evolutionary *explanation* to evolutionarily inspired *redescription* of the phenomena to be explained. The metaphors with which biological fact is often presented consistently oil this slide. For example, in his book *The Selfish Gene* (which is far more sophisticated than much writing in the same genre), Richard Dawkins wages a constant battle against the implications that his title suggests: the view that since our genes are 'ruthlessly selfish', so must human beings themselves be.[27] The trouble he describes is that 'if you wish, as I do, to build a society in which individuals co-operate generously and unselfishly towards a common good, you can expect little help from biological nature'. So he invokes an is/ought gap, and counsels: 'let us try to *teach* generosity and altruism because we are born selfish'. What is not thereby explained is how it can be more than spitting in the wind to try to teach generosity and altruism if that is how we are born. You cannot, after all, teach people to change their height or the colour of their skin. Later on, after discussing the benefit of co-operative strategies, Dawkins speculates that perhaps 'we have the power to defy the selfish genes of our birth' or 'rebel against the tyranny of the selfish replicators'. But it is more than a little hard to understand how a creature made in accordance with instructions provided by his or her DNA can then defy his or her DNA.

The problem is not helped by the way Dawkins later characterizes the 'nurture' side of the nature versus nurture debate, in terms of opposition to 'genetic determinism':

If genes really turn out to be totally irrelevant to the determination of modern human behaviour, if we really are unique among animals in this respect, it is, at the very least, still interesting to inquire about the rule to which we have so recently become the exception.

Dawkins here presents the opposition as believing that genes are 'totally irrelevant' to the determination of modern human behaviour. But of course nobody believes that. Genetic instructions determine the kind of brain I have. The brain at the very least puts limits on the kinds of behaviour I can choose. It may even make some kinds of desire inevitable, in the way that lack of nutrition makes hunger inevitable, or lack of liquid, thirst. But it is then a matter of empirical social

---

[27] *The Selfish Gene* (Oxford: Oxford University Press, 1976, revised edn. 1989). The quotations are from pp. 200–1 of the 1989 edition.

observation (anthropology, not biology) to what extent this is true, and fortunately the overall results suggest massive flexibility rather than genetic determination. Dawkins's picture at this point is one of ruthlessly selfish genes, hence selfish people, and hence the counsel of teaching altruism, but with the strong implication that doing so makes sense only if human beings can, by some transcendental miracle, attain a position that no other organism can match, in which their genes are 'totally irrelevant' to their behaviour.

But all this is unnecessary. First, we should get rid of the title *The Selfish Gene*. As Dawkins knows, genes are not literally ruthlessly selfish. They have no brains. They have no way of representing choices to themselves, no way of choosing one future over another, no cognitive activity of any kind at all. They are no more ruthlessly selfish than a blackberry bush is selfish if it takes over a garden or a rose is polite as it yields up its place. A gene cannot sit and plan and evaluate and choose future outcomes in terms of which ones are good for its numbers. All it can do is replicate, and sometimes its replications will survive and sometimes they will not. All that bits of DNA have are different chances of becoming extinct in different environments, depending on the different reproductive profiles of the creatures that have them. Some will proliferate more than others. But of course there is no purpose in any of that, any more than there is to the number of sunspots next month.

Some genes may proliferate because the creatures that have them are 'ruthlessly selfish'. Others may do so because the creatures that have them are altruistic and concerned for all the members of their species, or just their tribe, or just their kin, or just their children. In some species, some kinds of genetic material get most efficiently passed to the future because some of the creatures that possess them are sterile.[28]

But Dawkins is following a long tradition in implying that biology carries simple messages for understanding the sociology and psychology of human beings. For over a century it has been quite orthodox to use the language of classical economics to describe the order of nature (this fact about Darwinism was immediately noticed by Marx).[29] Thus it raises no eyebrows if you put the pure facts about probability and numbers in terms of 'competing' genes in universal 'struggle', each 'aiming' at 'maximizing' reproductive 'successes and failures'. In fact,

---

[28] W. D. Hamilton, 'The Genetical Evolution of Social Behaviour', *Journal of Theoretical Biology*, 7 (1964), 1–52.

[29] Alfred Schmidt, *The Concept of Nature in Marx* (London: NLB, 1971), 46.

it is quite difficult to think of a neutral term, such as 'reproductive pro-files', to describe the different amount or proportion of genetic mater-ial of any particular kind in a future generation, without invoking the language of competition and success. It would be extremely naive to regard this universal anthropomorphism as harmless. The metaphors determine our interpretation of nature in terms of classical economic competition; the interpretation of nature then feeds back to determine our interpretation of ourselves. Of course, biologists would be quick to protest that the use of economic language is only intended figuratively, but language has a way of taking over our intentions. Let us say that the biologist's fallacy (again, of course, there are many honourable, clear-headed biologists who are not guilty) is that of inferring the 'true' psychology of the person from the fact that his or her genes have proved good at replicating over time. Nobody would be stupid enough to commit this fallacy outright, were the transition not already prepared by the economic interpretation of purposeless natural events.

But suppose for the moment we let pass the rhetoric of the selfish gene. Would it follow that the creature which possesses them is 'born selfish'? Of course our desires and concerns exist only because of our biological natures, working themselves out in different physical, eco-nomic, and social environments. And we can certainly try to under-stand our biological natures in terms of the evolution of animals with specific kinds of genetic material. But a claim in those terms is not one about what we are 'really' like or what we 'really' or at bottom desire. Nothing whatsoever follows about the nature of the animal possessing the gene.

This point does not depend on the unscientific belief that 'genes are "totally irrelevant" to the determination of modern human behavi-our'. An animal might be born with an innate disposition to many kinds of affective response to others. If it is as complex as humans, it is probably genetically endowed with a plastic second-order disposition to form different affective responses of various kinds in various social environments. Thus, by a very close analogy, we as human beings are born with a strong disposition to learn Chinese if as infants we are sur-rounded by Chinese speakers, or Arabic if we are surrounded by Arabic speakers. Genetics is not irrelevant to the skill we have in learn-ing a language. But nor does it determine, independently of environ-ment, which language we learn. What our biological endowment gives us is a disposition to fit in with the linguistic dispositions of those around us, or in other words, a second-order disposition. A human being might similarly be born with a disposition to form the desire to help others if it finds itself in a helpful environment, and to aggression if it finds itself in an aggressive environment. It might be born with a quick disposition to fit into the kinship patterns of its group, whatever those might be (the comparison with language is very close here). Or, it might be born only with a third-order disposition to form such a second-order disposition to mimic the social environment unless yet other interfering factors click in. It is also worth remarking that genetic theory does not even insist that if we are born with such plastic dispositions, this is because they will have been selected for in competition with different natures which have been less successful. For not every feature that we are born with is an adaptation to which the theory of evolution automatically applies.[30]

At the risk of sounding simplistic, we might say that the biologists' fallacy is the inference from:

(a) a gene which leads to members of a species having a characteristic Y is good (or better than others) at replicating itself in such-and-such an environment: this plausibly explains the evolution of such a species in which members have such a characteristic.

to:

(b) Human beings are to be interpreted as consciously or unconsciously pursuing their genetic success (the survival of themselves, their children, their relations, their tribe or their species) when they exhibit characteristic Y.

It may be unkind to talk of fallacy, for reputable evolutionary psychology will not infer (b) from (a), but rather postulate psychological mechanisms of the (b) form as predicted upshots of adaptive histories of the (a) form. But, unfortunately, many of the locutions in use waver between the two and thence lubricate a much more confident and unguarded inference. Consider, for instance, the idea that we go to the help of other people in distress in order to impress them (directly) and others (indirectly) with our dependability and so maximize the chance of profitable reciprocal relations with them in the future.[31] This could mean, in accordance with (a), that in a suitable population, disposed to reciprocal aid, the distress-helping behaviour provides an environment in which genes replicate; this explains the evolution of the species or of groups or individuals within groups who have the trait. This

---

[30] Numerous essays counseling caution in interpreting just any old feature of an organism as an adaptation are found in the essays of Stephen Jay Gould, in such collections as *Bully for Brontosaurus* (New York: Norton, 1991).

[31] Robert Trivers, 'The Evolution of Reciprocal Altruism', *Quarterly Review of Biology*, 46 (1971), 35–57.

could be a geneticist's theory of how it comes about that animals (or plants or people) aid one another in distress. It may be true, although specific stories of the kind would require specific historical implementations, for instance postulating long histories of tribal structures with particular internal and external relations. But it could mean, in accordance with (b), that any one of us aids distress 'in order to impress others with our dependability', or in other words that this is our conscious or unconscious purpose or plan. As a remark about human psychology, this seems just false, and is shown to be so in effect by the method Butler uses against Hobbes. For example, if it were so we would predict that people would go to the aid of others more readily when there are other people about to be impressed. In fact, if anything the reverse seems to be the case.[32] It should be noted that this methodology applies even if the psychology inferred is supposed to be deeply unconscious. For reputable use of the notion of an unconscious desire or motive requires seeing the subject as acting according to a pattern: acting 'as if' they desired whatever they are interpreted as unconsciously desiring. This is where the interpretation earns its living. But this means that it can be assessed by looking at the patterns of behaviour, and in this kind of example they are not the patterns we find.

For a more obvious example of the fallacy, consider the idea that homosexuality is a way of helping your brothers and sisters to raise more children.[33] As a remark about the explanation of homosexuality as a trait, this is one thing. Homosexuality does presumably tend to take the individual and his or her partners out of the reproductive scene; it thereby has the potential to assist genetic relatives, by ensuring that they have fewer competitors; whether this explains its existence is then up for empirical debate.[34] As a remark about human conscious or unconscious psychology it is of course crazy, and especially tough on those homosexuals who might be supposed unconsciously to have the project of helping their siblings and nephews and nieces, although in fact they know they have no such relations. Amusingly, if we could get to the psychology from the genetics, then we should with equal plausibility predict the reverse of homophobia. Male heterosexuals should especially cherish those who opt out of the

[32] Bibb Latané and J. M. Darley, *The Unresponsive Bystander: Why Doesn't He Help?* (New York: Russell Sage Foundation, 1970).

[33] The suggestion comes from Robert Trivers, *Social Evolution* (Menlo Park, Calif.: Benjamin/Cummings, 1985), 198.

[34] For what it is worth, I would myself be extremely surprised if it does. The suggestion is satisfyingly mocked in Steven Rose, Leon J. Kamin, and R. C. Lewontin, *Not in Our Genes* (Harmondsworth, Middlesex: Penguin Books, 1984).

reproductive competition, both releasing more potential partners for the raging genetic engine within the rest of us, and leaving a less competitive field for our own progeny to grow in. But I don't think that anyone supposes that *this* prediction is borne out, so that the attitudes of the most phobic brigadier or Senator are really hypocritical, and all the time within there lies a tolerant, gay-loving liberal.

Perhaps the clearest instance of the fallacy is the belief that genetic theory 'shows' that we all have a ruthless, burning desire to perpetuate our genes. Once more, it is obvious that many people obviously have no such desire—sincere celibates, for example, or dual-income-no-kids couples who intend to keep it that way—and in any event you can only desire what you can conceive, and the object of such a desire is quite literally unintelligible to most of the human race, and was to all of it until late in the twentieth century. In fact, concern about our genes is incredibly faint: few of us in the First World can be persuaded to give up exuding even a little of our five tons of hydrocarbons per annum by the thought that our grandchildren's grandchildren will have a harder time if we don't. If the idea is the different one that you desire to have as many children as biologically possible, then, again, it is just false: most of us would be horrified at the idea, and (as Godwin pointed out against Malthus in the early nineteenth century) the greater their economic freedom the less people are inclined to breed to anything near their biological limit. In fact, anthropology shows that a remarkably delicate and variable set of norms determine what is regarded as appropriate child-bearing in different societies. The actual ethnographic record suggests

that there is not a single system of marriage, postmarital residence, family organization, interpersonal kinship or common descent in human societies that does not set up a different calculus of relationship and social action than is indicated by the principles of kin selection. [35]

In so far as sociobiology depends upon predicting that the traits in the human phenotype (the characteristics people actually have) are an expression, albeit unconscious, of a deep structure of concern for the reproduction of our own genetic material, it is deeply unpromising.

It is possible to think that society somehow 'distorts' or suppresses a fundamental human psychology, replacing our true Darwinian goals with socially manipulated masks that disguise them. This is the implication of the quotation from Ghiselin at the head of this chapter. It is

[35] Marshall Sahlins, *The Use and Abuse of Biology* (Ann Arbor, Mich.: University of Michigan Press, 1976), 26.

also the claim that what is 'natural' about human nature is to be seen by imagining people as lone individuals outside society. This is another part of the ideology of competitive individualism, no more likely to be true than the belief that human nature is best expressed in people who grow up without human bonding or parental love, or perhaps even in the wild. By those standards our capacity for language would be demoted as 'unnatural', since it only manifests itself if we are raised in a linguistic community. Another test would be to turn to developmental psychology to see whether this confirms the picture of the ruthless infant, so barely restrained, according to the epigraph above, from 'brutalizing, from maiming, from murdering—his brother, his mate, his parent or his child', gradually socialized into something more tolerable. But as many parents know, and as psychologists painstakingly find, nothing actually observed encourages us to think this way. On the contrary, toddlers are frequently friendly, naturally sympathetic to the pleasure or distress of others, co-operative, and delightfully quick with mutual help and reciprocation of services.[36] It takes culture to brutalize them.

To repeat, then: if genetic theory is to be genuinely explanatory of human behaviour and desire, it must not start by distorting what is to be explained, and distorting its description of what is to do the explaining, by importing unjustified psychological conceptions from the outset. Only once we are clear what people are in fact like, can we try various combinations of nature and nurture to explain how they get to be like that. The possibility of light and progress is certainly there, but so is the fog of misinterpretation.

The fog makes it easier to believe that there are moral and political messages to be derived from the synthesis of genetic theory and sociology. First let us put one weak charge against such an enterprise out of the way. Does such a suggestion inevitably commit the supposed sin of inferring an 'ought' from an 'is'? In principle, no. Facts about human nature are a perfectly proper part of the input to any ethical reflection, and biological constraints on human nature are among those that we are right to notice. Keeping prisoners in the cold, or the dark, or deprived of sleep, or fed on rotten meat, is abominable because of our biological need for warmth, light, sleep, and a proper diet. If we had other natures, like polar bears or cockroaches, it might not be so bad.

In practice, however, the discipline has not been so innocent. The anthropomorphizing of the gene, and the inference to what we are

---

[36] Irenaus Eibl-Eibesfeldt, *Human Ethology* (New York: De Gruyter, 1989).

'really' like, readily yield a picture of biological limits on social organization which provides a spurious rationale for moral and political
counsels, just as it did in the nineteenth century. Usually, of course,
these are counsels of a conservative kind, justifying the economic and
cultural meanings that were first read into genetics, and then back out
of it. For example, if it were not for the overwhelming anthropological
evidence to the contrary, we might interpret the mathematics of genetic replication to show that people are bound to be more concerned
for their blood relations than for anyone else, and think of that as a
boundary on possible human societies. But in fact there is no such
boundary, because people are not as the theory is taken to predict them
as being.

To take another example, there is a widespread belief, at least
amongst men, that sociobiology shows that it is 'natural' for men to be
promiscuous (and perhaps aggressive), females faithful (and caring
and home-loving), and that this is somehow guaranteed by our biologically asymmetric roles in the production of children. Now it should
be said at once that this story is simplistic even in evolutionary terms.
A more realistic model would need to take into account both male and
female 'strategies' for ensuring replication of their individual genes.
Suppose we start off as the conventional story wishes, with a population of males of limited nurturing impulses, but active would-be
'sperm-spreaders', and females of less promiscuous bent, who are
would-be 'nurturers'. Then it is easy to see how it might change.
Females may be able to detect males less concerned with spreading
and more with nurturing, and by selecting them as mates ensure that
this becomes a successful trait in males. Males may be more attracted
to less nurturing and more spreading females, and that may enable
such females to harness the energies of males most successful in other
dimensions, and have their genes replicate more successfully than
their stay-at-home sisters. Some of each sex might develop who
deceive the others about their real spreading or nurturing tendencies;
evolution would then start to favour any who are good at detecting
deception, and so on. There is no reason at all to predict that the conscious or unconscious psychology would stay as it started.[37] To find
out what is actually true of human beings here and now, we have to
look to the anthropological evidence. And for humans, once more, the
variation in culturally acceptable practice shows only the same kinds
of plasticity already mentioned, working themselves out in a variety

---

[37] I am indebted here to conversation with Amy Ihlan.

of cultural settings. And then it is up to us to campaign for whichever realization of this plasticity commends itself to us. Culture matters.

None of this should be interpreted in terms of undue optimism about the human animal. Self-centred reinterpretations of behaviour can earn their keep: renunciations turn out to be driven by pride, apparent altruism can be driven by self-importance, meekness by resentment, morality by hatred. But to earn their keep they must be applied to particular cases, and kept on a tight empirical leash. We need to see that by their means the pattern of action is better explained, or predicted, or made sense of. There will be cases and cases, but there is no reason to expect a grand unifying theory, revealing one desire or kind of desire under any and every pattern.

When reinterpretations of ourselves are taken seriously, they not only have power to change our view of others for the worse, but even more power to change our own self-definition, so that we start to live up to them. Believing that all men are mortal does not change my chance of immortality. But believing that all other-directed concern is hypocritical, or that all human transactions are ones of economic exchange, or that everyone is really treacherous or selfish, will alter me much for the worse. And people are subject to the curious combination that while our desires are in this way plastic, once they are settled we are apt to take ourselves for the rule, and suppose that however much they protest, others are like us too. It is in general true that people who care about a narrow range of objects find it hard to credit others who care about more: witness the vulgar belief that people who profess to like high culture are hypocrites.

5. SELF-REGARDING VERSUS SELF-REFERENTIAL DESIRE

Can psychological egoism be refurbished? The best way of trying to do so is to invoke a distinction first introduced by C. D. Broad. Broad enumerates a number of desires which 'might reasonably be called "egoistic" in one sense or another': desire for self-preservation, for one's own happiness, for being a person of a certain kind, for self-respect, for property, for self-assertion, for the notice, respect, and love of others.[38] But he also notices that we have desires which are concerned primarily not with ourselves, but with other things or persons; nevertheless

[38] C. D. Broad, 'Egoism as a Theory of Human Motives', in *Broad's Critical Essays in Moral Philosophy*, ed. D. R. Cheney (London: Allen & Unwin, 1971), 248.

these desires 'either would not exist at all or would be very much weaker or would take a different form if it were not for the fact that those things or persons already stand in certain relations to oneself'. These relations to ourselves are what he calls 'egoistic motive stimulants'. It is because *I* own a house that I seek its improvement, because they are *my* children that I desire their well-being, because it is *my* institution that I want it to flourish, and so on. Broad classifies desires which have this kind of underlying cause as other-regarding, but self-referential. Butler's example of the desire for revenge is a clear case: what I desire is the destruction of my enemy, but the reason I desire it is some relationship he bears to myself.

Broad remains agnostic whether all other-regarding desires are self-referential. But it is plausible to suppose that in a very weak sense they have to be. First a thing has to bear some relation to an agent in order to figure in her decision-making: it is only because the infant sees her mother that she is motivated to smile at her, or only because I have heard of the plight of the whales that I am motivated to help to save them. What we do not get from this, however, is that all other-regarding desires are self-referential in a stronger sense, in which their motivational power derives from some conception of a personal, private interest.

An interesting example of a theory in which all desires are self-referential in the weak sense is that of David Lewis. Lewis's 'modal realism' is the doctrine that 'there are other worlds that are other ways': when we talk of a way things might have been, we are talking of a world in which things are that way, albeit a world causally and spatially insulated from our own.[39] These other worlds really exist, only they are not the actual world. One objection made to this profligate doctrine is that it makes no sense of practical reasoning: why bother to save the whales, if whatever we do the sum of whales across the entire universe of possible worlds remains the same? That is, there is a possible world in which whales continue, and one in which they die out: what is the urgency in making sure that the first of these is our world, the actual world? From a truly objective point of view (God's point of view, as it were) this makes no difference at all, for the sum of goods and evils across the totality of possible worlds is just the same, and cannot be other than it is.

Lewis's response is in effect that just because of that, there is no point in working up a 'concern' about the state of reality as a whole.

---

[39] David Lewis, *The Plurality of Worlds* (Oxford: Blackwell, 1986), 2.

Our concerns must confine themselves to what we cause and prevent, and how things are with our world and our 'worldmates'. It is because the surrounding are *ours* that we are and should be concerned with them, and only them: extending our family concerns to the whole actual world is quite universalistic enough.[40] In this sense, all my sensible desire and practical concern has to be for things because of their relationship with me.

As Broad notes, psychological egoism is much diluted if it turns into the thesis that all desire is self-referential in this weak sense. For that is compatible with the desire being other-directed from top to bottom. The person who is bent on the survival of the whales is bent on it because the whales bear some relationship to him (in Lewis's case, the relationship merely of belonging to the same world, or perhaps of being in causal connection with him), but this does not license us to reinterpret him as not 'really' concerned about the whales at all. Indeed, the weak doctrine teeters on triviality: as already said, I am only aware of the whales in the first place because they bear some (causal) relationship to me. This is not the doctrine that there is some hidden concern for pleasure or power or private experiences. The life of self-sacrifice, or the choice of the deliberate martyr, or deep concern about the state of the world after you are dead such as is exhibited in concern for the proper execution of your will, all remain perfectly good examples of other-regarding desires. You may be concerned about them because you are concerned that *you* cause this or that, or because your actions affect people and things in *your* world, but this is not the revelation of hidden, selfish motivation.

There is room, however, for a more subtle and plausible version of egoism here. Consider again the case of revenge. Agreeing with Butler that we are not 'really' pursuing private gain, and that we do really want the death of the enemy, we can remark that nevertheless there is something recognizably selfish in the motive. The force behind the action is an 'ego stimulant'. Here, my involvement does not just put me in an epistemological position (if I did not know about something, I could not be concerned about it). Rather, it is because of some genuinely egoistic concern of mine, such as restoring my own honour, or avenging the insult to me or mine, that the man is my enemy and I seek his destruction. Again, consider the good worker, patiently fighting for the future of the whales. This fills her thoughts; there is no self-interest anywhere on the scene. But now suppose she does not get elected to be secretary of the Save-the-Whales society, whereas a rival

---

[40] Ibid. 128.

does. And suppose that upon this, her interest in the whales diminishes markedly, or evaporates. What seems to have happened was that her role in the society gives her something for herself—dignity, respect, a feeling of being needed—and when these are withdrawn, her overt interest disappears. And in this case too we might talk of unconscious selfish motivation. For a final example, it is a cliché that romantic love is at bottom selfish, meaning that at some level to the lover it is his or her own self-esteem or pleasure or happiness or stability that matters far more than the welfare of the beloved. A lover may (typically even) be far less badly affected by the misfortune or death of the beloved than by supposing that he is too friendly with someone else.

This undoubtedly shows a way in which a large range of apparently other-regarding motivation can be seen to be, at bottom, selfish. How much? The question is ancient, and the answer not obvious. The methodology is to find that a change in disposition occurs when the agent is no longer getting something from pursuing the apparently disinterested concern, and then this change of disposition suggests that the motivational force, the 'steam' behind the original pursuit, was more self-involving than it seemed. Sometimes this inference seems reasonable, but sometimes it is not. After all, pursuing most concerns depends upon a background of stable life-support. If I become hungry, my concern for the whales may take a back seat to my concern to get food, but this change of disposition scarcely shows that the original concern was somehow self-involving. If my physical or mental well-being is disturbed, then my wider concerns will begin to diminish, but that does not justify a reinterpretation according to which they were only superficial guises for self-interest in the first place. Perhaps the worker was genuinely concerned for the whales, but the concern began to wither when her personal problems became too severe. A well-run charity will want to make sure that sufficient support systems are in place to sustain the concern.

Furthermore, before we relapse too far into cynicism, we should reflect that while a charity worker may behave as described, she also may not. People *can* continue to work for the whales although the society fails to promote them, or care more about the lover's misfortune than about his or her fidelity. All we get is the prospect of extending a conception of egoism to cover more cases of apparently disinterested motivations, but we do not get a recipe for undermining the latter category entirely.

It may be useful here to compare the case of emotional arousal by representations of scenes, in plays or novels. Overtly I may be 'lost' in a play or a novel, and I am not thinking of myself when I weep for

Ophelia, or become irritated with Hamlet. But it is because I share a common humanity, with common vulnerabilities and defects, that I so respond. The crude way of interpreting that fact in egoistic terms was Hobbes's, refuted above by Butler, whereby sympathy with Ophelia is interpreted in terms of fear of getting into her position. This cannot be sustained. But there may be a more subtle way, in which concerns for the ego are, indirectly, responsible for the capacity to sympathize with Ophelia. There could be a link like this: the child's emotions are trained by reward and punishment; it is because of the egoistic concern to gain the one and avoid the other that the child practices emotional responses, and ends up as an adult weeping for Ophelia, without any thought of herself. The point remains that any such story (quite apart from being highly speculative, of course) is diachronic, not synchronic. It is only explaining how people *come to be* other-regarding. It is not a device for *reinterpreting* what they end up like, but only a story about how they *get to be* like that. In the same way the person of principle, say, who could not bring herself to tell a lie or break a promise, may have been trained to be like that by a process of sticks and carrots. But that does not undermine the fact that she is, now, like that, regardless of present sticks and carrots.

6. OUGHT WE TO BE SELFISH?

The recommendation is that we should always act on the principle of maximizing our own expected utility. And for the purpose of this section we are taking this as a specific, realizable, empirical goal. Following the recommendation is a success that can be achieved by some and failed by others. The suspicion that, on the contrary, the recommendation is empty is the subject of the next chapter. So for the moment we continue to interpret it as Butler does, always to follow 'the principle of an action, proceeding from cool consideration that it will be to my own advantage'.

Butler asks what following this recommendation has to do with actually achieving happiness. We might be very concerned to act from the principle of self-love, but quite fail to achieve happiness, either because we mistake our private good, or more interestingly because the concern suffocates others. In fact this is frequently so:

Disengagement is absolutely necessary to enjoyment: and a person may have so steady and fixed an eye upon his own interest, whatever he places it in, as may hinder him from attending to many gratifications within his reach, which others have their minds *free* and *open* to . . . immoderate self-love does very ill consult its own interest, and how much soever a paradox it may appear, it is certainly true, that even from self-love we should endeavour to get over all inordinate regard to, and consideration of, ourselves.[41]

The paradox Butler refers to is sometimes called the paradox of hedonism, that typically you can only be happy when you forget about being concerned with your own happiness. It is not of course a true paradox, but a reminder that some goods can only be obtained indirectly: perhaps you can only play stylishly when you forget about style, and you can obviously only act spontaneously when you forget about spontaneity. Immoderate self-love is here a restless, permanent concern with our own well-being: a voice forever asking us whether we are truly happy now, or are best consulting our future interests by doing whatever we are doing. Unless this voice is sometimes silenced we cannot get on with it and enjoy ourselves. We cannot immerse ourselves in our pleasures if we are forever testing the waters. Far from being a source of happiness, this voice utterly destroys it.

Butler is not arguing that we should always try to banish the voice of prudence. As a good Aristotelian, he thinks there is a mean: there is a time to look to our future interests, and a time to immerse ourselves in our particular concerns. It is *immoderate* self-love that ill consults its own interest. Sometimes certainly, the advice to think less of others and more of ourselves is sound advice, just as the advice to think less of our pets or our porcelain collection and more of our health or wealth, or less of today and more of tomorrow, is sometimes sound advice. But not always: if I have finally got free of the cares of work, and without other cares look forward to immersing myself in my porcelain collection, the advice to forget my porcelain and look after myself is scarcely intelligible. It is then only by attending to my porcelain that I can look after myself.

So now consider someone advancing the principle that we should always act on the principle of maximizing our own expected utility as a *recommendation*, the second interpretation of the principle that was offered. Why should we listen to the recommendation? The paradox of hedonism shows that always listening to it is not at all apt to promote our own happiness. While this concern engrosses us, we (literally) cannot forget ourselves; and while we cannot forget ourselves life itself escapes us. Is this a recommendation we would drum into our children? Would we reprove their spontaneity in the name of perpetual care? On the grounds of their own interest?

[41] Butler, *Fifteen Sermons*, Sermon IX, 171.

Remembering Butler's 'no-competition' thesis, we can now offer two different kinds of case. Suppose first that a person's package of first-order concerns includes concern for the good of others. Then whose good is served by the recommendation? Not the neighbour's, for her good is already an object of concern to the agent, and it is unlikely to be better furthered by asking the same agent to take his eye off it, and reflect upon himself more. Not the agent's, unless it is indeed one of those cases where he is sacrificing his own good to that of others, and that case cannot be generalized. The agent and his neighbour may best be left to pursue their benevolent aims unencumbered by thoughts of themselves, in which case neither benevolence nor self-interest underwrites the recommendation.

Might the recommendation be made in the name of reason? Of course, if Hume's thesis that reason is the slave of the passions is taken as it should be, this authority is spurious. But even without relying on that, it is hard to see what could be meant. For how is someone happily immersed in a particular concern—be it their porcelain, or pets, or ambition, or the welfare or destruction of others—less reasonable than someone who stands back to survey the total package of their own interests? The second concern, all right in its place but destructive of happiness when it is indulged immoderately, is just another concern. It has no more, nor less, to do with reason than any other.

Now consider the other version, in which the agent's concerns exclude the interests of others. Here it does not matter, unless incidentally, to the neighbour, whether the agent acts with his own concerns in his mind's eye or not: either way, the neighbour is not getting any attention. As for the agent, the paradox hovers just as much in this case as in the other: his inability to forget himself prohibits whatever pleasures he can only gain by losing himself in them. So he has no general reason to refrain from forgetting himself on many occasions. And finally, rationality as such is as silent here as in the other version.

The advocate of self-interest may now protest that he wanted all along a different interpretation of the principle. You have gained this victory, he will say, by insisting on Butler's reading of what he intends, namely always acting on 'the principle of an action, proceeding from cool consideration that it will be to my own advantage'. But, he may protest, what he really advocates is something more simple, not second-order, and not self-conscious. His advice is intended in something like this sense: limit your concerns to yourself and your family. Don't concern yourself with the wider picture, or turn yourself into a 'servant of the world'. The advice is not intended to put 'consideration of your own interest' in competition with your first-order concerns, but only to delimit the content of those first-order concerns: roughly, to constrict them to things, situations, and events in which you yourself are immediately involved. Cultivate your own garden; leave other people to look after theirs.

This is advice, certainly, and on occasion it might be quite good advice: don't be a busybody, take better care of yourself. But it is hard to see it as more than occasionally applicable. Sometimes we dissipate our energies by bothering too much about other people. But sometimes the situation of others demands more generous concern. Suppose, for instance, there is distress or oppression that we could do something to alleviate. Then in whose name is the advice to turn aside and cultivate our own gardens given? Generosity and humanity cannot give it. Self-interest cannot give it, for as we have seen, making the betterment of others my own concern accords as well with self-interest as anything else (the no-competition thesis). And reason is surely silent: the person working for famine relief or the abolition of slavery is at least as reasonable as the person who is not. There was nothing wrong with the Good Samaritan's head.

The advice to limit our concerns might go along with the happy belief in an 'invisible hand' or mechanism by which a number of independent agents, each acting on their own narrow concerns, in fact maximize the social good, so that each does as well or better than if he had acted with the general interest in mind. This mechanism is the great buttress to free markets and laissez-faire capitalism. Unfortunately, as we soon see, there are situations in which instead of an invisible hand there is an invisible boot, ensuring that the same agents do worse than they would under a more generous regime of concern for each other.

So far, then, we have no empirical thesis of psychological egoism worth taking seriously, and no recommendation either.

6

Game Theory and Rational Choice

There is, I admit, the obligation of the Treaty . . . but I am not able to subscribe to the doctrine of those who have held in this House what plainly
amounts to an assertion, that the simple fact of the existence of a guarantee is binding on every party to it, irrespectively altogether of the particular position in which it may find itself at the time when the occasion
for acting on the guarantee arises.

W. E. Gladstone[1]

1. UTILITIES, PREFERENCES, AND CHOICES

The third interpretation of the principle of maximizing expected utility that I distinguished in the last chapter said that it was definitional:
a grid imposed upon the process of interpreting others. It is this that
we now turn to explore.[2] What I shall do is to introduce the bones of
the classical analysis due to F. P. Ramsey.[3]

We have just learned from Bishop Butler that it is not at all true that
people act so as to maximize the intensity or duration of some state of
themselves. They do not even always act with their own interests in
mind, where these interests are construed as states of themselves. Nor
would we want them to do so. So we could conclude that the principle
of acting to maximize expected utility has been exploded as empirically and normatively bogus. But suppose instead we interpret
utility and interests differently. We have already foreshadowed the

---

[1] Hansard, 10 August 1870. I owe the reference to Keith Wilson, ed., *Decisions for War
1914* (New York: St Martin's Press, 1995), 189. Gladstone cites as like-minded authorities Lords Aberdeen and Palmerston.

[2] This chapter recapitulates and also elaborates some of the dialogue from my
'Practical Tortoise Raising'.

[3] 'Truth and Probability', reprinted in *Foundations: Essays in Philosophy, Logic,
Mathematics and Economics*, ed. D. H. Mellor (Atlantic Highlands, N.J.: Humanities
Press, 1978), 58–100. Mellor's Introduction gives a pithy, and accurate, description of
Ramsey's contribution as what later came to be known as functionalism in the philo-
sophy of mind.

difference. We saw in Chapters 3 and 5 that we interpret people as having an interest in some object when that object figures in their decision-making. We are here talking of Butler's 'particular appetites', which are directed to a whole variety of things, so objects, interests, and concerns here include states that are not states of the subject: the survival of the whales, or the relief of the famine, or the death of the blasphemer. It is this kind of interest that is to matter. In the apt phrase of David Gauthier, 'it is not interests in the self, that take oneself as object, but interests of the self, held by oneself as subject, that provide the basis for rational choice and action'.[4]

Now this does not by itself give us any conception of the 'sum' of an agent's concerns, for you cannot add, for instance, the fate of the whales and the death of the infidel. Yet someone may be concerned about each of these. So no conception of an agent's overall utility seems to arise. But what we do have are agents who are concerned about various things, and who prefer various outcomes to others. An agent may care more about the fate of the whales than about the death of the infidel, and this asymmetry could show itself in her choices and actions. The brilliant idea on which the theory of rational choice rests (officially) is that we can *reverse* our reading of the principle that rational agents act so as to maximize utility. Instead of this being a specific principle, with 'utility' a particular kind of goal, we see utility itself as a construct from mathematically tractable ways of handling their concerns. We see where peoples' utilities lie by seeing what they care about.

Ramsey saw that, given very weak assumptions, an agent with an ordering of preferences over each of some set of options can be represented as if she had attached measurable 'values', called utilities, to those options.[5] The provision of a scale is just like that of providing numerical measures for weights, given only the results from a balance. A balance is simply an empirical determination of when one object weighs at least as much as another. An element has at least as great a weight as another if and only if the other does not outweigh it, which is to tip the balance against it. So the results of tests for whether one object is at least as heavy as another can be presented numerically, with

[4] David Gauthier, *Morals by Agreement* (Oxford: Oxford University Press, 1986), 7.

[5] For other presentations see J. von Neumann and O. Morgenstern, *The Theory of Games and Economic Behavior* (Princeton, N.J: Princeton University Press, 1944); David Gauthier, *Morals by Agreement*, chs. 1 and 2; Ken Binmore, *Game Theory and the Social Contract*, vol. i (Cambridge, Mass.: MIT Press, 1994); David M. Kreps, *Game Theory and Economic Modelling* (Oxford: Oxford University Press, 1990); Robyn M. Dawes, *Rational Choice in an Uncertain World* (Orlando, Fla.: Harcourt, Brace, 1988), 154 ff.

the numbers representing weights of the objects in the set. Similarly, then we can say that if *a* is preferred to *b*, and *b* to *c*, *a* has (arbitrarily) three units of utility to the agent, *b* has 2, and *c* has 1. More accurately, the value of an option is equated with its *expected* utility, since an option's actual utility to an agent may be discounted by a probability factor. Ramsey provided the basic way of solving for both expectations and utilities, given an agent disposed to make sufficient choices amongst options. In the standard development, for instance, an agent might be offered choices between one outcome and only the chance of another, and behaviour over a series of such choices can give a measure of how much one outcome is preferred to another. An agent might just prefer a 50 per cent chance of *b* to certain *a*, but also prefer a 10 per cent chance of *c* to certain *b*, in which case she prefers *c* to *b* more than she prefers *b* to *a*. For she jumps at even a faint chance of *c* instead of *b*, whereas it takes a good chance of *b* for her to prefer the gamble to certain *a*. The numbers to be attached to her utilities for *a*, *b*, and *c* will represent that difference.

So if we have preferences across choices in a set, we can represent their utilities numerically. But what corresponds to the empirical results from the balance, telling us when *a* is preferred to *b*? The obvious answer is that you see what an agent prefers by seeing what she chooses, or what she would choose under conditions designed to minimize interfering factors or 'noise'.[6] True preferences are those that are revealed by decisions. It is, after all, a truism that to know what you or anyone else wants, see what you or anyone else chooses, or would choose given suitable options. To know that you prefer oil to butter, you see whether you choose it, at least when nothing further hangs on the decision. It is, however, quite a long road from simple choice behaviour, as it might be witnessed by a camera, to an interpretation of an agent's preferences. We need to know how the agent thinks of the situation, that is, the beliefs they have about what they are doing and causing. In particular we will need to distinguish between what an agent *chooses* and what she *prefers* when preference relates to aspects of a situation beyond her control. She may prefer some upshot to others, but choose differently because she does not expect that upshot to be realized. This distinction becomes important in strategic problems and games, where an agent conforms her move to safeguard her situation in the light of what she expects others to do, and this may be very different from aiming at the outcome she would actually regard as best.

---

[6] This answer was initially defended in the work of the economist P. A. Samuelson, *Foundations of Economic Analysis* (Cambridge, Mass.: Harvard University Press, 1947).

Meanwhile, putting the two foundation stones of the theory of rational choice together, we have:

> (*Util*) A utility function is defined such that the expected utility of *a* is at least as great as that of *b* if and only if *a* is weakly preferred to *b* (i.e. preferred to *b*, or at least as much as *b*). Such a function can be defined over a set of options if preference satisfies two consistency conditions: for all outcomes *a*, *b* either *a* is weakly preferred to *b*, or *b* to *a* (totality), and if *a* is weakly preferred to *b*, and *b* to *c*, then *a* is weakly preferred to *c* (transitivity).

> (*Revpref*) Choice behaviour is primitive. If a player makes choices, then he or she is making choices as though he were equipped with a preference relation which has that choice preferred to others, in the light of what else he believes about the situation. An eligible agent is always interpretable as though he were seeking to further a preference.

The first part of the approach makes utilities 'logical constructions' out of preferences, while the second makes preferences logical constructions out choices, given beliefs.

Util and *Revpref* apply to anyone with consistent, transitive preferences over a set of options. We can call such persons eligible persons. It is extremely important not to confuse the issue by calling them rational, as is frequently done, because this perpetuates the illusion that we are talking about special sorts of person, or giving *recommendations* in the name of reason. Whereas all we can say so far is that an ineligible person would simply be someone who cannot be interpreted in terms of utilities, so far as the set of options in play is concerned. Similarly, if a balance cannot weigh some element in a set of objects, or if it weighs $a > b$, and $b > c$, but $c > a$, then it cannot deliver a set of weights defined over the set. This makes it a bad balance, but it may be useful for other purposes, such as introducing philosophy of science to students, or confusing an enemy.

Putting *Util* and *Revpref* together means that we can always interpret any eligible agent as if they were seeking to maximize expected utility. This would have been surprising, if we had not gone through the two preceding interpretations of the principle of rational choice in the last chapter. It was their failure that led us to look more closely for a genuine conception of the concerns of an agent (their particular appetites, in Butler's terms) and the problem of defining a conception of their utility that is consistent with that notion. *Util* and *Revpref* deliver what is wanted, and we shall see that it is very doubtful whether any other approach could do so.

Do the principles make it analytic that anybody can be interpreted as pursuing their own utility? Not quite, because you can forfeit eligibility. It is appropriate to compare the methodology of interpretation used in Chapter 4, to determine the content of propositions from the inferential habits of agents. Logic imposes a similar grid, in the sense that it is only if agent's inferential patterns are isomorphic with the deductive relationships amongst propositions that we can interpret them as thinking in terms of those propositions. It might sound as though this makes it impossible for anybody to hold a contradiction, or flout any sufficiently elementary logical law. But the interpretational strategy is not quite as charitable as that. If enough else is true of an agent to suggest that she must by one statement mean 'p' and must by another statement mean 'not-p' and she is sincere in asserting both, then we do not automatically reinterpret to preserve her logicality. Similarly, given enough chaos in an agent's dispositions to choose, then Ramsey's grid becomes inapplicable. But, as the discussion of interpretation in Chapter 4 suggests, the case is necessarily exceptional. Even chaos can be interpreted: perhaps one of the agent's concerns, and hence a source of their utility, is to display a charming unpredictability.

We should now pause to disarm two possible objections to *Util* and *Revpref*. One thing that disturbs some economists is that utility, as here defined, need have nothing to do with an agent's welfare, nor with their personal economic gain. We need only remember Butler's man who runs upon certain ruin in order to revenge himself on his enemy. He prefers revenge, hence revenge has a higher expected utility. But his welfare is predictably diminished. Amartya Sen, for example, finds this troubling.[7] Sen believes that this undermines the authority of an approach based on *Util*. But it should not do so. 'Welfare' implies a specific empirical aim, and takes us back to the dialogue of the last chapter: we will get no authoritative conception of a rational or even an admirable agent as one who is wrapped up in her own welfare. Choice by contrast is truly the upshot of whatever the player cares about, and all we have is a conception of utility derived entirely from choice. We certainly cannot criticize either axiom by reminding ourselves of the heterogeneous nature of desire, for they are designed precisely in order

---

[7] Amartya Sen, *Choice, Welfare and Measurement* (Cambridge, Mass.: MIT Press, 1982), esp. the essays collected in Pt. I.

to cope with that nature. An agent, for instance, who prefers revenge to life or liberty attaches a higher expected utility to revenge. This is now definition, not doctrine.

The same caveats apply if we start to contrast preference with principle or with conscience, as Sen also does. There is certainly a vernacular distinction here, for we talk of being obliged to do what we do not prefer to do. But preference, revealed by choice, may include the preference for acting on any specific principle: the preference to keep a promise, or keep a vow to God, or to avoid the gaze of the man within, or the preference to do one's bit, or the preference for being the man who bought the Brooklyn Bridge, rather than the man who sold it. The better way to describe the 'conflict' between a narrow sense of preference and what happens when principle is introduced is to say that sometimes we are obliged to do what we would not otherwise have preferred to do; but this leaves it open that now, in the presence of the obligation, our preference is actually that we conform to the requirements of obligation or duty. The counterfactual preference that we would have had, had we not made the promise, or felt obliged to co-operate, or whatever it is, is not our all-things-considered preference: our strongest concern. As we saw in the last chapter, there is an element of regimentation here. We sometimes choose things because we think of ourselves as having to do so, rather than wanting to do so. The view that preferences are revealed by decisions accommodates such cases by saying that your choice then reveals that you prefer to fulfil your role, or do your duty, or follow your principles. If a choice is apparently unmotivated, like the destructive behaviour of a child in a tantrum, then we say that it reveals that the agent prefers to be a nuisance, or make a scene. If the agent's behaviour is sufficiently random to defy interpretation then he is ineligible, and cannot be understood in terms of preferences and beliefs.

Still, the word 'preference' disguises where we are. It tempts us towards thinking of desires with narrow and perhaps hedonistic objects. By contrast, it is common to think of values as things of greater weight and dignity: as we described in Chapter 3, values come in the region of what we are set on preferring, or prefer to prefer, or what we fail to prefer only at some cost. If this bothers us, it would be better to substitute a word like 'concerns' or 'aims'. In a decision-theoretic situation, a higher number attached to the utility of a choice represents the extent to which the agent is concerned about it, or the strength of purpose with which she aims at it. And by *Revpref* this in turn is measured simply by the extent to which she inclines towards it. Principles and values just give us some of the things that we are concerned about:

keeping promises, or telling the truth, or stoning the unfaithful. We could substitute for *Revpref* a principle *Revconc*:

> (*Revconc*) Choice behaviour is primitive. If a player makes choices, then he or she is making choices as though he were equipped with a concern relation which has his concerns better met by that choice than others, in the light of what else he believes about the situation. An eligible agent is always interpretable as though he were seeking to do what most concerns him.

I shall continue to talk of preference since it is entrenched in the literature. But *Revconc* represents the true situation better.

We now have all the ingredients for the third, tautologous or mathematically imposed way of reading the principle of maximizing expected utility. *Homo economicus* is now not a special kind of agent, but *any agent at all* described in terms of concerns and utility. Ramsey's approach gives us a kind of grid within which to place our understanding of agents. In fulfiling this role it does not issue recommendations or norms, or give advice in the name of 'reason'. The framework by itself issues no empirical predictions, nor any normative recommendations. Why not? No empirical predictions, because nothing an agent does is inconsistent with it. The agent who ignores his own welfare is as much 'maximizing utility' when he indulges his revenge as the one who swallows his vengeful feelings and goes about cultivating his bank balance. If you did it, that just shows where your concerns lay, and, perhaps in retrospect, that you attached more expected utility to doing it than doing the other thing. More surprisingly, it seems that the approach issues no recommendations, because a recommendation is something you can succeed in following, or in disobeying. But under the present suggestions, nothing you do would count as acting not to maximize expected utility. As Wittgenstein might have said, anything you do would equally accord with the advice, and that means that no advice was given.

This last claim may look to be a little too strong.[8] We can return to the question of whether logic has any normative bite, given its similar status as an interpretative grid.[9] We want to say both that interpretation must represent its subjects as obedient to logic, and that this obedience should play a role in their system of normative governance: should dictate their inferential habits from within. Can we similarly

---

[8] I am indebted here to discussions with Eric Cave.

[9] See, for instance, W. V. Quine, *Philosophy of Logic* (Englewood Cliffs, N.J.: Prentice-Hall, 1970), 80–5.

say that obedience to the norms of expected utility theory is an interpretative grid, but also something to which a subject should conform his or her deliberations? Up to a point. A subject may, from within the deliberative perspective, be fairly clear about his concerns. And a decision theorist may be able to say that with those concerns, in such-and-such an environment, such-and-such a policy is the correct one to follow. What is not thereby given is what to say if the agent does something else: whether this illustrates 'irrationality', or mere lack of awareness of the totality of operating concerns. We shall see more of this in what follows.

2. BLACKMAILERS AND CENTIPEDES

So what goes on when we apply the mathematical apparatus to the kind of decision problems that arise? For game theorists certainly give advice, indeed conflicting advice, yet we just came close to suggesting that any such pretension must be based on confusion.

To sort this out, and indeed to bring us back to ethics, we need to distinguish between what I shall call an empirical situation or an empirical game, and the theoretical situation, or *interpreted* game. The empirical situation is described in empirical terms: if someone makes such-and-such a choice, then they will receive so many dollars, or so many years in prison, for example, according to the move the other player makes. But describing a problem in these terms is not describing it in the terms in which an agent necessarily sees his or her situation. They may not care about dollars, they may even not care about years in prison. They may also care about such things as how the dollars were gained, or how the years in prison were avoided. In fact, if we think of an 'option' in a concrete situation, then there is no limit to the number of features that, potentially, might engage someone's concerns. Imagine someone choosing to stay at home, rather than go to the Alps. What attracted or repelled him? Was it: staying at home, being in London when it is relatively empty, staying-at-home-with-Aunt-Mary, staying-near-Jane-and-not-having-to-face-the-channel-crossing . . . or whatever, for an indefinitely large number of possible qualifications and riders?

It is now widely recognized that in the application of decision theory, interpretation is critical. For example, John Broome presented a plausible case in which, when offered pairwise options, someone shows intransitivity, and hence is apparently bound to seem irrational.[10] Offered a choice between going to Rome and hiking in the Alps, Maurice prefers Rome ($R > A$). Offered a choice between going to Rome and staying at home, he would stay at home ($H > R$). Transitivity requires that $H > A$. But, alas, offered a choice between staying at home and going to the Alps, Maurice would go to the Alps. This is classic intransitivity of preferences, and would equally classically be a hallmark of irrationality (in our terms, we would say that Maurice is ineligible, or has no defined preferences over this set of options). But suppose we can interpret Maurice as follows. Rome beats the Alps in a straight choice, because the Alps are frightening, and the alternative is interesting enough. Home beats Rome in a straight choice, because although Rome is interesting, home is comfortable. But if the options are home or the Alps, it would be cowardly to avoid the challenge: to allow comfort to overcome the frisson of danger is unmanly (note that there was nothing cowardly about preferring Rome to the Alps: the interest of museums defends against any incipient charge of cowardice). In other words, different contexts of choice must be taken into account. A sufficiently fine-grained description of Maurice's practical thinking reveals nothing irrational at all. Home-when-the-alternative-is-the-Alps represents one object of concern, and one that does not appeal to Maurice as much as Home-when-the-alternative-is-Rome. 'Outcomes' as objects of concern are more fine-grained than outcomes thought of as identified empirical states, and they come identified by particular complexes of potentially important properties.

But what is right is that Maurice as so far described has no answer to the question of which of the three he prefers when *all three* are on the table. We have only given him pairwise preferences. If we sought to infer his 'all three' preferences from that, there would be inconsistent ways of doing it. But that would be our fault (for trying to do such a thing) rather than Maurice's (for being in a state from which it cannot be done). Maurice would need to confront the question only if and when it comes up, and then indeed he has to change in some way before selecting one option as best overall. But there is nothing irrational or defective about a Maurice who simply puts aside the question of what he would do if all three came up. Perhaps, indeed, he knows that they will not, for instance because his climbing and museum-going partner will have already limited the options before him.

Obviously we need to know something about the agent's pattern of concerns to select one conceptualization of the situation, and say that

---

[10] John Broome, *Weighing Goods* (Oxford: Blackwell, 1991), 100–2.

he preferred this to the other decision, also conceptualized in terms of features that mattered. There can arise here a kind of circularity in the theory of interpretation. If we start with raw behaviour, as registered by a camera or a choreographer, we do not know which features of the situation are part of the agent's decision-making representation of it. We don't know what he understood or believed about the situation, and the consequences of different actions. But fortunately the problem of interpretation is not impenetrable. We guess at which features of situations matter by seeing the agent's raw dispositions to move and avoid; we feed back our interpretation, and learn how he sees his situation by applying our theory of which features are significant to him. In other words, there is a to-and-fro between our understanding of which features of situations in general matter to the agent, and our understanding of how he thought about the options in front of him on any concrete occasion.

To illustrate the distinction between the theoretical and the empirical situation further, consider Adam and Eve. They each face a simple choice, X or Y. If they choose X then they gain \$1 and the other gets \$0; vice versa if they choose Y. This describes the empirical situation, and it is identical for each of them. Now suppose Adam chooses X. This choice shows what he prefers, and this shows what was his expected utility: higher if he gets \$1 than if Eve does. Suppose Eve chooses Y. This shows what she prefers, and shows that her expected utility is higher if Adam gets a dollar than if she does. Maybe she is altruistic, or expects benefits from Adam in return, or hates money, or wants to score off the experimenter, or whatever.

This means that Adam and Eve were in different theoretical games or choice situations. We can write the same empirical choice for each of them:

X \$1 for me, \$0 for the other;
Y \$0 for me, \$1 for the other.

But we cannot write the same theoretical choice for each of them:

X n units of utility for me, $(n - m)$ for the other;
Y $(n - m)$ units of utility for me, m for the other.

For only Adam is in this choice situation, with positive n and positive smaller m. We *must* (by *Util* and *Revpref*) write a different matrix for Eve: one in which she gets more units of utility by choosing Y than by choosing X, since that is what she actually does. We can sum this up by saying that Adam is correctly modelled by the second, theoretical, description, but Eve is not.

Can anyone recommend Adam's choice over Eve's, or vice versa? One might like or dislike someone whose preferences go with their own monetary gain. But as it stands, Eve is just someone with one set of preferences, and Adam is someone with another, and that is all there is to it.

With the distinction between the empirical and the theoretical to hand, we can now consider more interesting decisions. Consider first the situation of Blackmail. The story is that before the situation arises Eve has committed an indiscretion. If Adam does nothing, he has $1, and Eve has $2. If he blackmails Eve and she submits, he takes one of Eve's dollars. But if she does not submit, she blows the gaff on him, revealing him as a blackmailer, but also revealing her own indiscretion: a cost of everything they have, so leaving them $0 each. It is common to describe the different options as 'hawkish' or 'doveish', the idea being that one option in each case is more aggressive, and the other less so (this is preferable to saying that one option involves 'ratting' or 'cheating', as is sometimes done, since the hawkish option need involve no defection from any previous agreement or any previous convention of behaviour).

Adam: Dove: the status quo: he has $1, Eve enjoys $2
   Hawk: he makes his threat: it moves to Eve's turn . . .
Eve: Dove: she submits, and is left with $1, Adam has $2
   Hawk: she blows the gaff, and they are each left with $0.

We can draw the choices in the diagram:

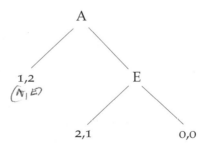

Hawkish options are to the right, doveish ones to the left. Adam's holdings are described first, Eve's second. This is the empirical situation. What should Adam do? What should Eve do?

As we should by now expect, there is no unique answer. For it depends on the theoretical game. Suppose, first, that for each of them, expected utility (measured, remember, by what they are inclined to choose) simply goes along with their own dollars. This means that they care about nothing except their own dollar holdings. Suppose, too, that each knows this about the other. Then Adam knows what will happen if it comes to Eve's turn: she will play dove, to keep $1, instead of playing hawk and moving to $0. And knowing this, Adam will play hawk, for, given that all he cares about is dollars, it would be a contradiction (by *Util* and *Revconc*) for him to stick with less utility, i.e. fewer dollars, when by a simple choice he can have more. So he will play hawk, Eve will submit, and Adam takes one of Eve's dollars.

Poor Eve. But now suppose Eve has been to a good school, which has taught her to be proud and vengeful. And suppose Adam knows this. Then Adam knows that Eve's *theoretical* situation is not represented by the dollar payoffs. Submitting and leaving Adam better off might be unthinkable to this Eve. Her preference, and hence her utility, would be to blow the gaff, even if this means running upon her own financial ruin. In terms of utilities, her play might look like this:

> *Eve*: Dove: she submits and is left with −20 units of utility overall, Adam with +5
> Hawk: she blows the gaff, and is left overall with −10, Adam with −5.

Each loses dollars in the gaff-blowing finale and the (arbitrary) negative figures simply represent that it is worse for each of them than the status quo. But Eve prefers it to losing only $1 to Adam, and having to live with the fact of having been blackmailed. That is worse for her.

In a real-life situation, Adam may know the empirical game. But he is very unlikely to know the theoretical game: in fact nobody is likely to know it until after the actions have been taken, and revealed the agents' concerns. If Adam is minded to be a blackmailer, he had better look out not to pick on vengeful and proud subjects. And if Eve is going to be a possible target for blackmail, she had better develop and even publicize a nice vengeful streak. In other words, we can reflect on the social situations in which people may find themselves, and recognize which characters will succeed and which will not in those situations. The game theorist can *only* say: be someone, or don't be someone, who is modelled as being in this or that theoretical game. What she *cannot* say is: once you are in this or that empirical game, play this or that way.

Now consider more interesting situations. One that has attracted some attention is Centipede. In this game, we imagine a known sequence of actions, either co-operative or not, taken by each player in turn. At any point a non-co-operative move breaks the sequence, and each player stops with the payoff so far. Each combined sequence of (co-operation + reciprocation) ratchets up the payoffs. But at any stage a player's co-operation is an *immediate* loss; it only recoups when the other player reciprocates.

CENTIPEDE

	1a	1e	2a	2e		98a	98e	99a	99e	
	A >	E >	A >	E	...	A >	E >	A >	E >	End
A	1	0	2	1		98	97	99	98	100
E	1	3	2	4		98	100	99	101	100

So in the diagram Adam's move at 1a takes him from 1 to 0; Eve's move at 1e takes her from 3 to 2, and so on. The classic example of this kind of structure is Hume's case where I help you get your corn in, expecting you to help me when my field, which ripens later, is ready. If we each co-operate we each do better, and we suppose that each passing season increases our wealth. But if I co-operate and you don't reciprocate I am worse off than if I hadn't bothered. Maybe I am too tired to get much of my own harvest in, and in any event your harvest being on the market depresses prices. But you are better off than if you reciprocate in return: reciprocating means hard work, and in turn you get a better price for your corn, if less of mine is harvested.[11]

If the figures measure something we care about, such as money, it seems obvious that we ought to co-operate. Each co-operative round racks up our holdings. But the classical analysis has problems with this. Under that analysis we suppose that each player knows the other is rational, each player knows the other's payoffs, and each knows that the other knows this (and so on: the structure of the game is 'common knowledge' between them). But in particular, each of them knows when the game ends (perhaps their leases have a definite term). Now consider the last round. Each knows it will be the last round. Eve's reciprocity leads her to loss: she substitutes 100 for her 101. So, she won't reciprocate. But knowing this, Adam won't co-operate on round 99. But knowing that, Eve won't co-operate just before, and so on back. The backwards induction means that truly rational players, knowing their situation and knowing that the other knows it, never start on co-operation, but would stay with their miserable holding of 1 each.[12]

This seems very odd: if you're so smart, how come you ain't rich?

---

[11] Hume, *Treatise*, III. ii. 5, p. 519.

[12] Philip Pettit and Robert Sugden, 'The Backward Induction Paradox', *Journal of Philosophy*, 86 (1989), 169–82. See also J. Sobel, 'Backward Induction Arguments: A Paradox Regained', *Philosophy of Science*, 60 (1993), 114–33; Luc Bovens, 'The Backward Induction Argument etc.', *Analysis*, 57 (1997), 179–86.

Again, the first step to a solution is to distinguish the empirical game from the theoretical game. Empirically, the set-up may be as given, if the units represent dollar holdings, for example. But what inclinations might each player plausibly have? Among other things: not being idiotic enough not to try co-operation; feeling a bit of a bounder for not reciprocating; feeling that once the pattern is established, it would be wrong to break it, and trusting the partner to feel the same. If Eve has such inclinations, and Adam can reasonably expect her to have them, and vice versa, then the pattern of reciprocation is established, and they do well.

The theoretical game need not at all share the empirical game's feature that Eve's final co-operation represents pure loss. As a real, multifaceted person, she may be proud of the pattern and loyal to it; she may not want to be the first and last to break it; she may have formed an affection for Adam as the seasons unwound; she may be going to take up a new lease and foresees that she will need co-operation either from Adam or from other people in the future. She may feel unease at the real or imagined verdict of others (this is explored further in the next chapter). Hence Adam cannot predict that she will defect even on the final round. Hence Eve cannot predict on any previous round that Adam will defect because he will expect her to defect immediately afterwards. And in fact, even if Adam does suspect that Eve will defect on the final round, he in turn might be loyal to the pattern for similar reasons, and prefer to leave with an intact sense of having done his bit.

Of course Eve may be tempted to cheat at the end, and Adam may fear this; one can well imagine them becoming uneasy as the last seasons draw on. Eve might be a bounder, and Adam may indeed wake to find that she has decamped leaving him tired out and with his harvest still to gather. But it would be strange for him to fear that outcome so much that he never risks co-operation.

At this a game theorist may well complain that we have illegitimately introduced concerns that are not represented in the game's pay-off structure. In other words, we are (arbitrarily from his point of view) specifying that the theoretical game is not like the empirical game. But if he stringently insists that the numbers do represent expected utilities, then there is nothing paradoxical or surprising in the result that the sequence never gets started. Adam expects to lose by his first action of helping Eve, for $0 < 1$. So he won't do it, period. Remember that by *Revpref* and *Util* nobody ever chooses in such a way that their expected utility is diminished by the choice. It is a matter of definition that people act so as to maximize expected utility (if they can be interpreted as acting at all in terms of the choices we are describing). If you know some agent's expected utilities, you know what they will do. If they expect loss from a choice, then they won't make it (definition, again). So indeed we don't here have a coherent description of a theoretical game that gets off the runway at all, but this is no longer surprising. Rather, if Adam really expects loss through making a first co-operative move, then this must be because he expects Eve not to co-operate back, and then he will not essay the move himself. It would be as if Eve had already posted a notice saying that under no circumstances will she ever help with Adam's harvest. And then, of course, they stay impoverished at the baseline. People might post such notices, just as real neighbours do, but not because they are especially 'rational'. They post them because they are jealous and fearful, or too short-sighted to see beyond this year's possibility of loss, too bound up with the immediate future to let the prospect of increasing prosperity in the distant future lure them.

In Blackmail, we saw that Eve needed to have gone to a good school to flourish in the world of people like Adam. Assuming that he has not been educated to find blackmail repellent, then her public nastiness alone protects her. In Centipede, the farmers need to be people with some reason for expecting each other to co-operate. They need to have and hope for a little bit of ethics. Hume was the first to recognize that the prevalence of such interdependencies is sufficient to explain the evolution of many of our social concerns. In a famous passage (talking not about mutual aid, but about abstaining from predating upon one another's property), he says:

I observe, that it will be for my interest to leave another in the possession of his goods, *provided* he will act in the same manner with regard to me. He is sensible of a like interest in the regulation of his conduct. When this common sense of interest is mutually expressed, and is known to both, it produces a suitable resolution and behaviour. And this may properly enough be called a convention or agreement betwixt us, though without the interposition of a promise; since the actions of each of us have a reference to those of the other, and are performed upon the supposition that something is to be performed on the other part. Two men who pull the oars of a boat, do it by an agreement or convention, though they have never given promises to each other. Nor is the rule concerning the stability of possession the less derived from human conventions, that it arises gradually, and acquires force by a slow progression, and by our repeated experience of the inconveniences of transgressing it. On the contrary, this experience assures us still more, that the sense of interest has become common to all our fellows, and gives us a confidence of the future regularity of their conduct: And 'tis only on the expectation of this, that our moderation and abstinence are founded. In like manner are languages gradually established by human conventions, without any promise. In like manner do gold and silver become the common measures of exchange, and are esteemed sufficient payment for what is of a hundred times their value.[13]

He was sufficiently proud of discovering this mechanism to return to it later:

Thus two men pull the oars of a boat by common convention, for common interest, without any promise or contract: thus gold and silver are made the measures of exchange: Thus speech and words and language are fixed by human convention and agreement. Whatever is advantageous to two or more persons, if all perform their part; but what loses all advantage, if only one perform, can arise from no other principle. There would otherwise be no motive for any one of them to enter into that scheme of conduct.[14]

One of Hume's major concerns in these passages is to show that the origin of this kind of co-operation does not lie in the giving of any explicit promise or the formation of a contract. The convention is a natural growth, founded originally on the hope or expectation of benefit in return. Just as various mammals go in for 'reciprocal altruism', scratching another's back if they get theirs scratched in return, without any kind of contract, so do we. We return to this point in section 5.

3. THE PRISONERS' DILEMMA

And so to the most discussed decision problem of all, the celebrated prisoner's dilemma.[15] Here again we have an empirical game and a theoretical game. But to analyse it I shall reverse the order so far adopted, and present the theoretical game first. Each player plays at the same time, knowing that the ordering of the other is the same as his or her own.

In the diagram below we are told only Adam's preferences. Adam's first preference is that he play hawk, and Eve dove. His second is that both play dove, his third is that both play hawk, and fourth that Eve plays hawk while he plays dove. We suppose that Eve is a mirror-image of Adam. Her preferences are the same as applied to her, that is, she prefers most her playing hawk and Adam playing dove, and so on down. So Adam's best outcome is her worst, and vice versa. They each

[13] *Treatise*, III. ii. 2, p. 490.

[14] *Enquiry Concerning the Principles of Morals*, App. III, p. 306.

[15] The name is due to A. W. Tucker, although the structure appears to have been discovered previously by Merrill Flood and Melvin Dresher. See Russell Hardin, *Collective Action* (Baltimore, Md.: Johns Hopkins University Press, 1982), 24.

rank <H, H> 3rd, and <D, D> 2nd. I shall call this ordering of preference, the prisoners' dilemma ordering. I shall call <H, H> War (short
for the war of all against all); <H, D> Victory (for whoever plays H);
<D, D> Co-operation, and <D, H> Ruin. So their ranking is Victory, Co-
operation, War, Ruin: <V, C, W, R>. We are, of course, not told by how
much Adam prefers one option to another. Maybe the fourth option is
truly terrible, and the first truly wonderful, but maybe not.

Adam

		H	D
Eve	H	3rd	4th
	D	1st	2nd

What will Adam do, understanding this to be the situation? Choices
are thought of at this stage as made independently, and in ignorance
of the other's choice. So it seems as though Adam must play hawk.
Here is the famous proof: the 'dominance' argument. Adam knows
that either Eve plays hawk, or she plays dove, and which she plays is
independent of anything he does. Suppose she plays hawk. Then
Adam is better off playing hawk: he gets his War instead of Ruin.
Suppose she plays dove. Then Adam is better off playing hawk: he gets
his Victory instead of Co-operation. Playing hawk therefore has
greater utility than playing dove for Adam. Mathematically its greater
expected utility than playing dove is the sum:

$$(W - R)(\text{Prob. Eve plays hawk}) + (V - C)(\text{Prob. Eve plays dove})$$

where 'W' represents the utility Adam attaches to the War outcome,
and so on for the others. The increased utility of War over Ruin is multiplied by the probability of Eve playing hawk, and the increased utility of Victory over Co-operation is multiplied by the probability of Eve
playing dove. We know this expression is positive, since otherwise we
would have got the rankings wrong. Knowing it is positive, we can
only interpret Adam as being in this theoretical situation if he chooses
the hawk option. If he were to choose the other, then by *Revconc* and

Util dove is outranking hawk in terms of utilities, in which case the sum total of his concerns is not as described in the diagram.

The same reasoning applies to Eve, and so she also plays hawk. If each knows that the other is truly described by the matrix, then there is no probability of either of them playing dove. Knowing this, the sum for Adam reduces to $(W - R)(1 + 0)$, which is just $(W - R)$.

There are empirical situations that are artificial examples of this structure, and there are social situations that are plausibly modelled by means of it.

(1) Artificial games: I put Adam and Eve in separate rooms in a laboratory, and tell them to press the red button (hawkish) or green (doveish). I make sure they know that the dollar payout is as follows, where subscripts indicate who gets what.

Adam

		Hawk	Dove
	Hawk	$1_e, 1_a$	$3_e, 0_a$
Eve			
	Dove	$0_e, 3_a$	$2_e, 2_a$

Each might prefer most of all that they get the three, and the other zero. Each has as second best that they get two each and as third best that they get one each. If this is the sum total of their concerns, each plays hawk, and gets one.

(2) In the original example of the structure, two prisoners were supposed kept apart from each other. To each of them the prosecutor offers the same option: they can confess the crime, or not. If A confesses, and E confesses, then each suffer the penalty for their crime. If A confesses and E does not, then A goes free, and E suffers an extended sentence (punished both for the crime, and for being a hard case). If each refuses to confess, then all that can happen is that each suffers a reduced sentence, say on the lesser charge of wasting police time.

(3) There are social situations in which we do not have two persons, but in which each person is similarly situated, and can be thought of as acting in the light of what 'the rest' are doing. Consider gun control. It may be best for me if I am armed and nobody else is, for I can then exert power over the others, since they are unarmed. It is worst for me if the rest are armed, and I am not, for then they can (collectively or individually) exercise power over me. If this means that I am described by the <V, C, W, R> ordering, then I will arm. If we are all like that, we all arm, even although we recognize that a world in which nobody is armed is preferable to the one we bring about in which everyone is armed.

Other social cases show essentially the same structure. Each does best of all by having more than the socially optimal number of cows on the common grazing while the others restrain themselves; each does worst if they show restraint while the others do not. The result is an overstocked and underproductive common. Each fisherman may wish that fish stocks were kept at a sustainable level. But, if he expects the others to fish for as much as they can, he cannot survive by exercising restraint himself, and if in turn the others exercise restraint, it makes it better still for him to get as much as he likes. Or, in wage bargaining, each group may do best if they get all they can while others exercise restraint; each does worst if they exercise restraint while the others get what they can; and the result is unrestrained competition which, we may realistically suppose, is economically much less good than the solution produced by general restraint.

Further situations of the same general pattern go under the heading of 'collective actions'. Here we consider a good which is 'joint in supply', meaning that consumption by one does not diminish the amount available to others, and non-excludable, meaning that nobody can be excluded from participating in it. A good defence system is the standard example. The collective action problem is that of motivating people to contribute to such goods. Everyone has a motive for 'free-riding': it goes best for them if other people contribute to providing the good, and they do not, although they then benefit from it. And even if they are loath to free-ride, they may believe that too many others will do so, so any contribution they might feel inclined to make will be wasted ('the assurance problem'). This is in fact the problem that Hume thought motivated the origins of government: in a large community it is a problem insoluble except by an external authority able to insist on contribution and attach penalties to free-riding.[16]

[16] *Treatise*, III. ii. 7, p. 538.

(4) Closely related to the previous examples is the classic description of the state of nature, as represented by Hobbes. Here there is no social order, but only the 'war of all against all', and the 'life of man, solitary, poor, nasty, brutish, and short'. The war, Hobbes explains, need not be out-and-out fighting, but any tract of time 'wherein the will to contend by battle is sufficiently known', or in other words there is no assurance of peace possible. This belligerent disposition is inevitable, while there is no civil society, for

> there are three principal causes of quarrel. First competition; secondly, diffi-
> dence; thirdly, glory.
>   The first, maketh men invade for gain; the second, for safety; and the third,
> for reputation. The first use violence, to make themselves masters of other
> men's persons, wives, children, and cattle; the second to defend them; the
> third, for trifles, as a word, a smile, a different opinion, and any other sign of
> undervalue . . .[17]

What we have in these social cases is a kind of 'invisible boot' whereby agents who are individually able to recognize that it is socially better, better for us, to get into a co-operative state (each settling for the second best) stay in the competitive or aggressive or at any rate non-cooperative state, which for each of us is third best.

If we want to avoid this we have to break the link between the *empirical* description and the *theoretical* one. How might the theoretical game look different? Just as Blackmail goes best for Eve if either Adam is too nice to start it, or fears that Eve is too nasty to put up with it, and Centipede goes best if either player is conscious of how stupid they would be not to give co-operation a go, so these empirical situations go best if each has a motive to settle for the co-operative option. This might be because of straight sympathy for the other, but that may be unlikely. Or, it might be because of identification with the common good, which means conceptualizing the situation as one of what *we* should do rather than of what *I* should do. Or, the sum of peoples' concerns may mean that they do not implement the prisoners' dilemma ranking because of reputation effects, or fear of an independent authority, or just because that is the way they like to be. Then, what is at present only the second-best outcome, co-operation, but which is the best of all socially, can glide into first place.

A prime pressure upon us to move ourselves away from having the <V, C, W, R> ordering is given by the reflection that others are very much like us. In wage bargaining, for example, it is not really very sensible to expect that my union will be the only one to press for a pay rise,

---

[17] Hobbes, *Leviathan*, ch. 13, pp. 83–4.

while all the others put up with the status quo. Suppose that A believes that E is very much like he is, and vice versa. Then each is poised to reflect that the asymmetric outcomes are to that extent unlikely. Each has no real expectation of being the victor in a <3, 0> outcome. More likely they will both be left staring at the meagre <1, 1> payoff. So each may become resigned to expecting a symmetric outcome. The extra utility attached to the asymmetric, Victory, outcome begins to seem chimerical (so the expected utility of playing Hawk also diminishes). In which case each has a motive to make sure that the symmetric outcome is the best possible. Since they prefer <2, 2>, each has motivation to put into place mechanisms to ensure it. Life is not going to go as well for them as it would do if they could become happy to aim at <2, 2> rather than struggle for the unlikely <3, 0>.

This does *not* mean that in the (theoretical) prisoners' dilemma situation it is 'rational' to co-operate. As we have seen, a situation is only properly conceptualized as a prisoners' dilemma if each agent is going *not* to co-operate. Nor does it mean that in an empirical dilemma it is uniquely rational to do one thing or the other. All it means is that each of us has a motivation to generate sufficient co-operative concerns that what would *otherwise* be theoretical dilemmas become benign, because the co-operative option appeals most to us. The solution then is to ensure that the empirical game is not the theoretical game. In other words, we try to make sure *either* that people have an expanded set of concerns, *or* that their expectation of what is to be gained or lost by their defection is changed. Something has to drive their maximum expected utility away from the hawkish option and their minimum expected utility away from the doveish one. In Hobbes's analysis of the war of all against all this is achieved by the Sovereign who can punish non-co-operative behaviour. In the case of the commons or of fisheries social pressures to self-restraint can arise and in economic behaviour people may realistically come to realize that the chance of their being the only group to benefit from unrestrained greed is vanishingly small, compared to the chance of their being glumly locked into disadvantageous competition. In the real world, perception of this is exactly what motivates us to bind ourselves to co-operative arrangements. It should seem that we can then engineer the social possibility of improvement in our situation.[18]

We can tie this to the point about how fine-grained our interpretation of a decision problem is. Socialization works by changing the way

[18] A very similar analysis is given in Duncan Macintosh, 'Preference's Progress: Rational Self-Alteration and the Rationality of Morality', *Dialogue*, 30 (1991), 3–32 . I am grateful to Eric Cave for the reference.

options are thought of. A year in prison saved or a dollar gained is one thing. A year in prison saved at the cost of reneging on an agreement, or at the cost of knowing that someone else is serving a disproportionate sentence as a result, is a different thing, and, to most of us, not nearly so attractive. A dollar gained by fraud, misrepresentation, or just disappointing someone else is not the same as a dollar gained by honest toil.

Given an empirical prisoners' dilemma, some people will co-operate, or play dove, and others will defect, or play hawk. Neither side is rational or irrational because of that. By *Util* and *Revpref* their choices reveal different expected utilities: either different preferences, or different expectations about the behaviour of the other. The one person values different things, or has different expectations, from the other. He is in a different theoretical game. Perhaps he half expected the partner to co-operate, and knows he would feel a cad if he defected all the same. Or, perhaps he half expected the partner to defect, and would feel a fool if he co-operated while that happened. In a world of nice, well-socialized people who expect others to be so too, the former psychology prevails. The world as we have it is a little mixed. There are people who jump the queue, and people who stand in line.

It is important to reflect a little at this point about what can be learned from these models. Some philosophers think very little: they point out, for instance, that no historical state such as that described by Hobbes ever existed, or that we already come to artificial prisoners' dilemmas with a full deck of social concerns. And people cannot just put into abeyance the affect that a particular representation of their situation has. A 'one-off' prisoners' dilemma is no more 'one-off' than a 'one-off' exposure to a piece of English is. We cannot undo our histories, just because we are told to do so.

Hobbes himself is clear enough that his thought experiment of the state of nature describes people who never were. He explicitly wants us to 'consider men as if but even now sprung out of the earth, and suddenly, like mushrooms, come to full maturity, without all kind of engagement with each other'.[19] But this is not, as it is sometimes presented, a weakness in his construction.[20] For there are things to be

---

[19] Thomas Hobbes, *The Citizen*, ed. B. Gert (New York: Doubleday, 1972), 205.

[20] For example, in Seyla Benhabib, 'The Generalized and the Concrete Other': 'The sphere of justice from Hobbes through Locke and Kant is regarded as the domain where independent, male heads of household transact with one another, while the domestic intimate sphere is put beyond the pale of justice and restricted to the reproductive and affective needs of the bourgeois paterfamilias', *Situating the Self* (New York: Routledge, 1992), 155.

learned from the exercise. One is the function of convention and culture, and the motivations associated with them, in warding off the invisible boot. Another is the relative plasticity of peoples' motivations and expectations. And a third is the importance of providing a soil in which they grow into the right shape, if the social good is to be promoted. If your children will face situations with the empirical structure of dilemmas, you do well to bring them up to co-operate. If you are responsible for the group, you ensure that they are co-operators; if the situation is one where evolution differentially rewards co-operation, it will have the same effect. If, however, you see yourself as placing your children in a world of hawks, you may fear that they become what Hume memorably calls the 'cullies [victims] of their integrity'.[21] They become the only people to stand in line while everybody else pushes to the front, or the only fishermen to take the sustainable amount. We return to this in section 5.

4. TOXINS, BOXES, AND REASONS

It is not uncommon to see statements like this: it is a 'tautology that a rational player will necessarily choose hawk in the prisoners' dilemma'. The idea is that given the way the matrices are set up in terms of agents' utilities, we have it that Adam's utility is higher being a hawk whatever Eve does. But that just means, by *Util*, that he prefers being a hawk, whatever Eve does. And in turn, *Revpref* determines that this is made true by the fact that he chooses to be a hawk, whatever he expects Eve to do.[22]

But we must be a good deal more careful how we state the tautology. The tautology *never* applies to empirical dilemmas. We know that people choose differently in those, and I have already sketched why they do, and why it is perfectly rational for them to do so, in so far as this means anything at all. So now, all we can say is this. Suppose Adam makes the dove choice. Then he preferred one or both of the outcomes in which he acts as a dove to the others. The question is: why might he have done that, in spite of the dollar values? And the answer is that although he knows he could get more dollars for himself by choosing hawk (whatever Eve does), this has not swayed him. Some other consideration matters. So we must construct a utility function in

---

[21] *Treatise*, III. ii. 7, p. 535.

[22] Binmore, for example, frequently stresses the tautological nature of this result: *Game Theory and the Social Contract*, i. 27, 169.

accordance with that preference, and hence he was not actually in a (theoretical) prisoners' dilemma. His decision problem was not accurately 'modelled' by the <V, C, W, R> ordering. In the theoretical game we have successfully modelled a set of players only when they have no interests (nothing they care about) that are unrepresented in the game's payoff structure. But a prisoners' dilemma is defined so that the hawkish utilities outrank the doveish ones, and that in turn simply means that the hawkish options are the ones that get chosen.

In the usual terminology the dove choice in the prisoners' dilemma is strongly dominated (that is, whatever the partner does, the player does better by choosing otherwise). Playing dove is also called 'out of equilibrium' play, for the same reason (play is out of equilibrium when a player could do better for himself by unilateral defection from it). There has been debate between those who recommend strongly dominated choices as rational, such as David Gauthier and Edward McLennen, and those who dissent.[23] Some opponents deny that 'out of equilibrium play can be sustained in the long run'.[24] But it should be apparent that this is not the best way to debate things. It is not that out of equilibrium play cannot be sustained in the long run, or needs psychologies that we have not got. All we get is that in the empirical game what looks like it can well happen and go on happening, and in the theoretical game it cannot happen at all. For in the theoretical game, if a player co-operates, that shows that he attached more expected utility to the co-operative option. Co-operating mattered to him: for whatever reason, it is something that he wanted to do. So-called countertheoretical actions do not reveal the irrationality of the players, but the impropriety of this application of the theory.

Prisoners' dilemma and the other game-theoretic structures can indeed be analysed by contrasting the narrow interest, represented by dollars or years in prison, with some wider set of concerns. Thus David Gauthier contrasts the kinds of interest you maximize, with constraints of other kinds. He wants to contrast an out-and-out maximizer with a 'constrained maximizer': someone who is 'disposed to comply with mutually advantageous moral constraints, provided he expects similar compliance from others'. His ambition is to show that this second kind of maximizer is more rational than any other. Gauthier seeks to show that people understanding the dilemma structure could first rationally set themselves to acquire a disposition to co-operate, and

---

[23] David Gauthier, *Morals by Agreement*; Edward F. McLennen, *Rationality and Dynamic Choice* (New York: Cambridge University Press, 1990).
[24] Binmore, *Game Theory and the Social Contract*, i. 175.

then rationally co-operate when the moment comes, even although *at that moment* their utility would be maximized by playing hawk. This approach rejects *Revpref* and *Util*, for utility is not indicated by choice. The constrained maximizer would do better for himself (gain more utility) by choosing other than he does. I now want to argue that Ramsey's framework, represented by *Revconc* and *Util*, should not be given up here. It gives us a better set of tools to use in understanding the situation.

All sides agree that people recognize that things go better when they co-operate. It makes sense for them to cultivate the co-operative concern in themselves and others around them. On the Ramsey account this is changing the nature of the decision. The fact that the hawk option is now perceived as non-co-operative has its own *affect*. It changes, or is set to change, the bad old <V, C, W, R> ranking. If it is properly embedded in the agent's preferences it changes what they prefer to do when the time comes. But it does not change that by making it rational for them to do what would otherwise be irrational (sacrifice utility). For Ramsey it does it by changing the way in which their utility is to be achieved in the situation in question. For normative decision theorists, such as Gauthier and his opponents, that is not so.

We can see the matter like this. Ramsey's methodology is like one that calculates back from the acceleration of a body in a direction to the resultant of the forces on it. There is therefore no space for saying that some bodies do, and others do not, accelerate in accordance with that resultant. The normative decision theorist is like someone saying that there are some bodies that do, and some that do not, act according to the resultant of the imposed forces, and the question is whether to recommend those that do, or those that do not. This of course leaves a huge task, and one which is not sufficiently appreciated. For if the resultant is not read back from the acceleration, there needs to be some other method of identifying it. Ramsey's method gives us a mathematically tractable and empirically respectable concept of utility. Given (eligible) agents, we can construct utilities. Any other way of conceptualizing it requires finding a different empirical method, and there is none that promises to deliver anything mathematically tractable. Suppose, for instance, someone with a heterogeneous set of concerns: she wants to fulfil her role as mother, keep a promise, and gain some income, but unfortunately in the situation she is in, she can only act to further one of these aims. Then if we cannot say that she is most concerned about the one that eventually sways her choice, how do we discover what she *is* most concerned about? And how do we decide whether it was 'rational' or 'irrational' for her to be motivated

[margin handwritten note: (in fact, lots of alternatives]

by something that did not most concern her? The enterprises look hopeless from the start.

The Ramsey analysis allows, of course, that people who are suscep- tible to some motivational forces are bad, or silly, or imprudent. There is no problem about drawing a line around some subset of objects of concern, and recommending their importance at the expense of others. One can even use 'irrational' as a term of abuse for persons who are swayed by factors outside the preferred subset. This is the sense in which an economist might say that someone is irrational if they care about other things than money. But this is just a normative comparison of some objects of concern with others: it fails to privilege 'rational' as a diagnostic instrument in the theory of choice.

The normative theory might be developed like that. There would be a subset of the motivational forces acting on an agent, and only things from that subset represent the agent's 'real' or 'filtered' concerns. It is rational to act only in the light of those real or filtered interests. But someone may fail to do this, because of other factors. Usually this is a 'bad' thing to do: such people may typically be unstable, or fickle, or imprudent, or self-destructive. Sometimes, however, it can be a 'good' thing to do, because so doing enables people to gain the benefits of co- operation. Then some people (Gauthier) recommends the resulting choices as rational. Others say they remain irrational (although we can be glad that sometimes people are irrational!).

It is best to consider this in connection with decision problems in which, at the moment of decision, everything seems to speak against some particular choice, yet there are benefits to being the sort of per- son who makes it. The best-known pure example of this structure is the toxin puzzle introduced by Greg Kavka.[25] Here, there is someone, the experimenter, who is very good indeed at knowing my intentions. He promises me a very substantial reward, which I will get on Monday only if I genuinely intend on Monday to drink on Wednesday a toxin that induces unpleasant nausea or mild illness. I know (and he knows I know, and so on) that on Wednesday there will be absolutely no reason for doing this, and there will be some reason against doing it,

---

[25] Gregory Kavka, 'The Toxin Puzzle', *Analysis*, 43 (1983), 33–6. The case may offend people who dislike far-fetched examples. But the structure is used to cast light on situ- ations of deterrence, where something is gained by threatening to do something for which there will be no reason when the time comes. The standard example is to threaten 'mutually assured destruction', that is, to retaliate against a first nuclear strike. Here it is important that the enemy believe that this is what you will do and so stay their hand. But if their missiles are on their way, there is no very compelling reason to destroy the other side, since it makes no difference to you and is worse for them. But real cases like this always introduce extraneous factors.

since the toxin is unpleasant. It is important here that there is apparently going to be *no* reason for drinking the toxin on Wednesday. It is not, for instance, that failing to drink it would be non-co-operative, or would disappoint some trust (we can even specify that nobody else, including the experimenter, will know whether I drank the toxin or not). The experimenter gives me a motive to form an intention to do something which there will *only* be reason not to do. Can I form that intention? And if I do so, am I irrational? If I do so, and then carry it out on Wednesday, am I doubly irrational? These questions seem to make sense, and, it may be suggested, they reveal the space for normative decision theory that the analysis so far seems to have closed off.

If the toxin offer is an often-repeated event, then, given that the reward is substantial enough, I have a motivation to become the sort of person who can form the intention to do something when I know that when the time comes there will only seem to be reason against doing it. To see if this is possible, we need to think a little about forming intentions. Following Bratman, I think we should say that to form an intention is (i) to become disposed to perform an action, and (ii) to be disposed to sustain that disposition (roughly, by regarding the matter as closed, refusing to reopen argument).[26] This second clause answers to the thought that if a matter is still regarded as open, then really no decision has been taken, whatever words have been used. The experimenter is very, very good, we are supposing, at telling whether both these dispositions have been formed. I cannot deceive him, by pretending that the matter is closed when in my mind it is not. Then what I want to be is someone who, on hearing of the reward, forms both these dispositions. I need to be the kind of person who can say to myself that I shall do it, and I need to be the kind of person who will refuse to reconsider. Now this is not an easy thing to do, and for some of us may be impossible. That is because the second disposition, to refuse to reopen the question, is bound to be threatened by the awareness that, on Tuesday, it will be known that *everything* points against performing the action.

But does everything point against it? To succeed in forming the intention you should cultivate the disposition to think, on Tuesday, things like this: 'I said to myself I would do it, so I shall do it.' The question is closed in so far as you actively reject thoughts that reopen it. This means that you need to have an attitude to your own decisions rather like the attitude people of principle have to past promises: they

[26] Michael Bratman, *Intention, Plans, and Practical Reason* (Cambridge Mass.: Harvard University Press, 1987).

just finish the issue. The people who get the reward are those who can adopt this deontological attitude towards their own formed dispositions. Undoubtedly some of us are better at this than others. In childhood, some people set themselves vows, like not walking on a crack in the pavement on the way to school, and some take these rituals very seriously and others take them more lightly. Suppose someone is good at it. Then the right question is not whether they are 'rational' or 'irrational'. Normally, a deontological attitude to one's own past decisions is pretty foolish: breaking a vow made to oneself not to walk on cracks in the pavement should not be regarded as a tragedy. Being set not to reconsider can be pig-headed and stubborn. But in the surprising circumstances of the toxin puzzle, it is extremely useful. Someone who can take an initial disposition to accept the reward as 'fixing' their future course of action gets the reward. When the time comes, the fact that this was his past mind-set survives to motivate him to perform the admittedly unpleasant action of taking the toxin. Such a person is not irrational, but successful. Ramsey enables us to describe his success properly: he has transformed the situation into one in which one of his concerns is to act as he decided to act. He has given himself a reason to take the toxin, and in the surprising circumstances of the puzzle, that was the best thing to do. (I return in Chapter 8 to the strange view that acts of self-legislation somehow always lie at the bottom of our normative behaviour.)

Someone might think: the rational thing to do is to form the dispositions, as described, but all the while reserve the plan of not acting according to the intention, changing your mind, when the time comes. It is indeed best if you can be like this, for you get the reward without the penalty. In other words, you would be properly disposed on Monday, but your dispositions would have changed by Wednesday. However, the problem is set up so that you cannot *plan* to be like that. Once that is your strategy, then it is no longer true on Monday that you are disposed not to reopen the issue. Hence it is not true that you succeed in intending on Monday to drink the toxin on Wednesday, for the disposition not to reopen issues is part of genuinely intending one particular action. So such a 'plan' could not succeed in its objective: it is an incoherent plan. You cannot form an intention if you also intend later to revoke it: the fact that you intend later to revoke it shows that no intention was formed. In fact, arguably, it is not only impossible to plan to be like this, but actually impossible to *be* like this: if you are fickle in this way, then it is no longer true that on Monday you are really disposed to take the toxin, and the experimenter, knowing this, will not reward you.

The toxin puzzle has the same structure as a better-known variant, Newcomb's puzzle. Here the experimenter offers you a huge reward provided that, when it becomes time to claim the huge reward, you forgo the opportunity of taking, in addition, a small reward. He is good enough at knowing whether you will forgo the opportunity and, if he knows that you won't, he won't give you the big reward. In the standard version, you can be made the offer on Monday, and on Wednesday will be presented with two boxes. If you take only the big box, it will turn out that he had put the reward there; if you take both, there will turn out to be no reward in the big box. The situation is structurally no different from the toxin puzzle, and the same result applies. You need to become the kind of person who takes one box, even if both boxes are there (even in full view), and the second contains the bit extra which you had to learn to forgo.[27] If you are successful, then your character, adapted to a world with bizarre experimenters of this kind, is the one that a rational agent would wish for. Your action is the product of a rational character. It brooks no criticism, for at the end you are the person with the big bucks. 'Two boxers', misled by a false theory of rationality, have only the small bucks.

A way of putting it is that we need to cultivate a disposition, in theses cases, not to see what would otherwise be a decision problem as an open problem any more. In the surprising circumstances in which we get rewards for it, we need to have closed off the problem, or to be blind to the temptation to advantage. Once more then there is no reason to think that any departure from Ramsey's framework is helpful. The same kind of analysis that we applied to Blackmail and Centipede applies equally well to the prisoners' dilemma and to problems such as the toxin problem. In the easier cases, Eve's good school may have protected her against Blackmail by making her something of a firework. Adam's propensity for feeling stupid at stopping at $1 and failing to pick up nearly $100 will motivate him to set Centipede in motion, and if Eve feels the same, she will continue it. Similarly in a prisoners' dilemma, someone may be moved to co-operate not just because of principle, or altruism, but just because they would feel uncomfortable with themselves if, for instance, it turned out that they had played hawk and the other dove. As I have said, you do not have to be particularly principled, nor yet altruistic, to feel that a year out of prison at the cost of someone else languishing in it is not quite the same

---

[27] I am indebted here to discussion with Eric Barnes, who pointed out that it ought to make no difference whether the big reward is actually visible, or, as in the original version of the puzzle, concealed.

as a year out of prison *tout court*. And in the toxin problem (or more realistic problems of deterrence), finding the fact that you have formed a disposition to take the toxin a sufficient reason for shutting your mind against reopening the issue, while it is normally a dogmatic and unadmirable trait, here puts the agent in the advantageous position of gaining the reward.

The decision theorist, as we have seen, is in no position to say that smart people play some special empirical strategy. Everyone eligible plays the dominant strategy. But nor is anyone in a position to say that smart people have their utilities determined solely by money values (or year-in-prison values). Decision and game theory pride themselves on silence at this point. An Eve who is sensitive to the humiliation of having been blackmailed, to the point of throwing her financial interests to the wind and denouncing Adam, is no more nor less 'smart' (rational) than an Eve who is not like that. She just has different concerns. An Adam who can't bear settling for $1 when with luck he can make $100 is different from another Adam who has no such feelings. But his difference is not to be represented as one of rationality.

There is a moral here, too, for the theory of threats and promises. We can see why threats and promises are seldom completely incredible; they can both change the game (for breaking a promise or failing to carry out a threat is something people frequently care about) and they act as signals that the game is not what the opponent might have thought it was.

What, then, of the prisoner wondering what to do, or Eve wondering how to counter the blackmail, or Adam faced with the idiocy of settling for <1, 1> in Centipede, when minimal good sense would take him up to somewhere near $100? In the empirical and social situations it may indeed be difficult to know what to do. While agents don't know, they are in effect wondering whether to place sufficient value on co-operation, or an antecedent promise, or each others' welfare, or unforeseen effects on their own reputations, or just the discomfort they find as they contemplate some of the outcomes, to co-operate. Or do they care only about the years of prison they themselves will serve, regardless of how these are obtained? Are they more frightened of being the only co-operator than they are of being the only aggressor? In Centipede, do they care about the jeers of outsiders, if they walk away with only $1? Ramsey's decision theory rightly does not say whether people do have such concerns, still less whether it is rational to have them.

It is better, then, to avoid arguing about the 'rationality' of non-maximizing choices. Accepting Ramsey's identification of mental states such as belief and preference purely by their function, and remembering the failure of any more substantive conception of maximization, we should accept that anyone eligible is 'maximizing' in the same sense exactly as anyone else who is eligible. If a person cares about a wider variety of things (e.g. being a particular kind of person, or subject to existing contracts or co-operative conventions, or is sensitive to the narrow interests of others) she may choose differently, but she is still maximizing. Constrained maximizing is simply maximizing, as indeed is everything that an eligible player ever does.[28]

For the same reasons Ramsey's framework enables us to put aside the futile business of discussing whether a person of weak will is or is not rational in favour of the more fruitful issues of interpretation and self-interpretation. Consider someone taking a decision that somehow surprises us and them. Thinking about it, I decide that one course of action is the one to take. But when the time comes, I find myself doing another. The natural response is to suppose that, perhaps as a surprise to me and others, I actually cared more about some aspect of the situation than I realized. If I behaved better than I intended, then it gives me an opportunity to learn something about myself. My sense of honour, pride, altruism, prudence, or whatever is stronger than I had realized. If I behave worse, I can similarly learn that my greed, fears, lusts, imprudence, or whatever are stronger than I had realized. To make the decision intelligible is to look back and recognize that my emotions and dispositions were not quite as I had taken them to be. It is quite useless in such a scene to invoke a blanket diagnosis of 'irrationality'. All that has happened is that the actual affects of the various considerations in play did not deliver what I expected them to deliver when the time came. If this sounds too passive (as if the agent is being blown about by potentially fickle gusts of emotion), a fuller analysis awaits us in the next two chapters.

5. THE GROWTH OF TRUST[29]

In Blackmail we also saw that there is likely to be uncertainty about which theoretical game best models the agent's empirical decision

---

[28] A good brief discussion of Gauthier and McLennen's constrained maximization is given in Brian Skyrms's introduction, *Evolution of the Social Contract* (Cambridge: Cambridge University Press, 1996), 38–40. Skyrms points out that in many situations acting to face certain loss simply because of prior commitment is most certainly not the rational thing to do, by any standards.

[29] This section draws on material presented in my 'Trust, Co-operation and Human Psychology'.

problem, or in other words what her concerns actually do include. The same may very well be true as one of the agents in Centipede makes the first handshake. They may be rebuffed. All that the framework tells us is that if they make it, then their net expectation is one of higher utility by doing so. The sum total of (probability of gain × extent of gain) – (probability of loss × extent of loss), where gain and loss are calculated including such concerns as the desire to co-operate or not to look like a fool, comes out higher than for any alternative. This is likely to be so when they are not certain to be rebuffed (so long as there is some probability of reciprocal co-operation, the expected gain if it occurs may outweigh the expected loss if it does not). And once a little trust is in place, more naturally follows, and the agents can be rational, and rich.

But would it be reasonable to expect reciprocation, even with a small degree of confidence? How does a little bit of trust get into place, in order to kick-start the process of socialization? Hobbes saw clearly that if the social landscape is bleak enough and there is no independent authority enforcing co-operation, turning aside from your own immediate advantage may just be betraying yourself to the enemy. The impossibility of making workable cease-fire agreements in situations of old hatreds like that of Croatia, Serbia, and Bosnia illustrates the point. In such situations treaties are next to meaningless, because the risk of loss incurred by (for instance) relaxing one's guard or failing to take advantage of a weakness in your enemy is too great. The plausible expectation is that if you forswear any advantage the enemy will simply use the opportunity to gain the upper hand. Any signal that one will refrain from pressing an advantage is bound to be untrustworthy, for each side will in fact press any advantage, and will expect the other side to do so similarly. 'Making a treaty' becomes only a charade entered into for the purpose of misleading the other side. Perhaps this is how statesmen think, although for many of us it is perhaps a little chilling to hear this Machiavellian view of contracts echoed by that pillar of Victorian rectitude, William Ewart Gladstone (see the epigraph to this chapter).

Similarly in the prisoners' dilemma: suppose the agents can communicate. Suppose they 'enter upon a treaty' each to play the dove option. How can this be more than a charade? Each may do it hoping the other is foolish enough to take it seriously, while he himself is clear-sighted enough to use it merely as a device for manipulating the other in the hope of generating for himself the best (hawk, dove) outcome. How does it come about that if the <V, C, W, R> ordering described the agents before the 'treaty', it does not do so afterwards?

This is the problem with thinking of agents as 'contracting' out of the war of all against all, either by forming treaties with each other, or, as in Hobbes's own scenario, voluntarily ceding power to a Sovereign (as is often pointed out, a stupid thing to do in the circumstances, since the empowered Sovereign will predictably use the power to use violence on his subjects, for the sake of gain, safety, or reputation). Indeed, thinking this way, it can seem impossible for trust, and words expressing co-operative intent, ever to get started. It is as if each morning we in our role as warlords sit down and say things that might sound like giving promises of good behaviour, and each afternoon we return to our battles. The morning performance soon loses any significance.

We can usefully think further about the problem of the war of all by using ideas explored by game-theoretically minded biologists. The question is whether a population of people in that state could be 'invaded' not in the military sense, but in the sense of being quietly superseded, by a population at least some of whom fail to prosecute the war. Either these newcomers do not attack for gain, or attack pre-emptively out of fear, or they succeed in making meaningful treaties with each other, forming co-operative confederacies. At first sight it might seem impossible that any such pacific newcomers should succeed: they merely form prey for the predatory host population. But everything will depend on the circumstances. If the war is debilitating the population sufficiently, and if the newcomers can find time to establish a sufficient bridgehead, their superior reproductive success can begin to tell. A small enclave of peaceable people can expand at the expense of a wider population of war-torn belligerents. To change the example, a non-gun-owning minority might expand over the gun-owning majority, if, as is largely true in the USA, the gun owners spend disproportionate energy fearfully using their guns on each other, and hence are set to fail in the reproductive race.[30]

Places like Bosnia show that co-operation cannot be expected, and trust cannot exist if the soil is sufficiently poisoned in advance, and that is what has happened in genuinely intractable scenes of conflict, or where the history of treaties and guarantees is sufficiently depressing. But, as Hume insists, nature never provided a scenario in which competitive or warring conflict of interest was the *only* relation between human beings. All kinds of kinship relations enable us to practice co-operation and to learn to subordinate various of our own interests to other concerns, including the welfare of others. And once co-operation

---

[30] For a lucid introduction to these ideas and their application, see Skyrms, *Evolution of the Social Contract*.

is practised, it can be extended. Since we constantly interact with others, we will be aware of the advantages to be reaped from co-operative habits. We are aware of the benefits we all derive from mutually co-operative relations. Unless his relations with Eve are already poisoned, it is well worth Adam's while making the first move in Centipede, or making the first move to show that he is co-operative if they are settled into repeated rounds of prisoners' dilemmas.

There are various definitions of trust proffered in the philosophical literature. One suggestion is this:

> trust is an attitude of optimism that the goodwill and competence of another will extend to cover the domain of our interaction with her, together with the expectation that the one trusted will be directly and favourably moved by the thought that we are counting on her.[31]

In this account, part of your motivation to do what you are trusted to do is good will, and part is that you know the other person is counting on you. These can, however, come apart, for knowing that someone is counting on me might motivate me even when I bear them no good will at all. A further motivating state is knowledge that we *accepted* the trust: it is not only that people are counting on us, but that we allowed them to do so, or even told them that they could do so.

I do not think it profitable to treat the issues here as ones of definition. One could certainly argue over whether, for instance, good will is always involved in trust. We talk comfortably enough about trusting people to do their job, for instance, although we don't suppose them motivated by good will, but only by the thought that it is their job, or even by fear of penalty if they do not perform properly. What we need to focus upon is that we grow into communities in which the mechanism of counting on people and signalling that we can be counted upon is embedded. We find that over a large spectrum of life other people can be relied upon. This is indeed one of the first things a child learns, and only later may he or she lose some innocence, and come to a sad appreciation of the things about which they cannot be relied upon. Second, children find that a signal that you can be relied upon to do something is important. It creates a motivation, and it is supposed to create a motivation: it starts us on the staircase of emotional ascent. The child grows into someone who would be wretched if she betrayed a trust, just as if she repudiated a friend. Then a decision to signal that you can be counted upon becomes part of a causal chain that is eventually responsible for the action that fulfils the trust. I want

---

[31] Karen Jones, 'Trust as an Affective Attitude', *Ethics*, 107 (1996), 4–25.

you to rely upon me to perform a task; I communicate that I will do so; I am motivated by this having happened, and perform accordingly. If I hadn't signalled to you, perhaps I would not have done it. If you know that this is a causal chain that is very likely to be in place, there becomes an element of self-fulfilment about my signal of trust, and given that you trust me, you can be sure that your trust is not misplaced. In fact, not only voluntarily signalling trustworthiness, but simply knowing that, for whatever reason, other people are relying on you to do a certain thing, can be sufficiently motivating. A part of the mechanism may be that the others show that they trust you, and part of your response may be to assure them that the trust is not misplaced. Mutual assurances generate this common knowledge. This is confirmed rather than refuted by the fact that one of the first things a fraud may want to do is to try to signal that he is trustworthy.

This is all very well, a critic might say, but how does it help to generate real co-operation either in Bosnia, or in the war of all against all, or in the prisoners' dilemma? What it provides is a social background against which inviting someone to trust you may be quite likely to work. But it does not by itself explain how efficacious agreements can be extended to cases where it is in our other interests to break them. It does not explain how to change the climate of international diplomacy, so that Gladstone's remark comes to seem shocking.

In recent years there have been a number of attempts to refurbish 'Hobbesian contractarianism'. This is the enterprise of showing that from a state of nature like that of Hobbes, rational agents could or would design collective action to avert the war of all against all. This is the first stage: the second stage is to derive consequences about political legitimacy or moral legitimacy from discovering whatever is necessary for this task to succeed. It is now generally thought that the enterprise fails at the first stage.[32]

The view I have been defending supposes that this problem, as well, is badly posed. We should not get involved with the circle-squaring task of showing that rational agents whose entire set of concerns leads to the <V, C, W, R> ordering also have concerns that can lead them to

---

[32] The seminal works are Edna Ullmann-Margalit, *The Emergence of Norms* (Oxford: Oxford University Press, 1977); Jean Hampton, *Hobbes and the Social Contract Tradition* (Cambridge: Cambridge University Press, 1986); Gregory Kavka, *Hobbesian Moral and Political Theory* (Princeton, N.J.: Princeton University Press, 1986); and David Gauthier, *Morals by Agreement*. The attempts are painstakingly surveyed in Jody Kraus, *The Limits of Hobbesian Contractarianism* (Cambridge: Cambridge University Press, 1993). See also Russell Hardin, *Collective Action*.

design a different ordering. In the prisoners' dilemma, or Hobbes's landscape, indeed no such design is available. If I know that the concerns of the other players exclude any motivation to take account of what I trust them to do, then any signal they offer that they are to be trusted is itself to be mistrusted. Again, it is as if in the Centipede set-up Eve had posted a sign saying that she would not turn aside from her own concerns to reciprocate any help given by Adam, nor indeed for any other reason.

But in real life there will be insidious causes working against this bleak scene. For many concerns affect actual agents locked into war. As the Prince says at the end of *Romeo and Juliet:*

> Where be these enemies? Capulet, Montague,
> See what a scourge is laid upon your hate,
> That heaven finds means to kill your joys with love,
> And I, for winking at your discord too
> Have lost a brace of kinsmen. All are punished.

And this, together with what went before, sufficiently works on the antagonists that Montague sets off to build a statue to Juliet, and Capulet to Romeo. Their position is not unusual: scourges are typically laid upon hate.

What is shown by Hume's and Ramsey's approach is the motivational progress whereby trust *can* be extended, perhaps slowly and inch by inch, into the territory of the war of all against all. Parties who need to coordinate can bring to their dilemmas a history of being motivated by trust, and then their signals that they are to be trusted will not be inert. We might not initially trust them all that much, but we will not have a guarantee that they are to be *mistrusted*. And trust can be extended by being practised and found to be reciprocated. In so far as each party has a motive to back down from the state of mutual competition or hostility, and each recognizes that the mechanisms of trust would provide a way to do so, then the soil is not irrevocably poisoned, and co-operation can gradually grow. There is no 'inevitability' theorem, showing that trust must evolve, but there is no 'impossibility' theorem, showing that it cannot evolve, either. What cannot be done is to contract into its evolution, for in the state of nature no such contract can be made by agents whose motivational states exclude respect for contracts. Hume thus improves on Hobbes in two respects: first by introducing the dimension of time, and second by presenting an organic growth model in place of a rational design model.

So Hobbes's problem is solved not by rationality, but organically, by the growth of habits of reliance. With this growth, given our way of describing action, comes a reconfiguration of the agents' interests. They maximize their expected utilities, now, partly by behaving in ways that trustworthy relationships demand of them. This becomes what they prefer to do. It becomes the way they do it.

It is quite consistent with what we have found so far that there is a decision for society to make, and for educators to make. Typically, a society wants the co-operative and trusting solutions. It must therefore take pains that people care about things that will generate those solutions: reputation, antecedent agreement, co-operative bonding, the welfare of others, one's own ability to portray one's conduct in ways that others can admire, and so on. There is nothing mysterious about this being in society's interests, or the interests of people as a whole, for this is the whole point of the prisoners' dilemma. Eventually, of course, giving one's word becomes not only a motivation, but a giant among motivations.

For the individual educator, the choice may, however, remain harder. Suppose I am in charge of a child's education, and I think that by suitable precept and example I can make him or her susceptible to co-operative motivations, and by others I can make him impervious to them. Which should I do, if I have only his narrow interests at heart?

In general the answer will depend on what other educators are doing. Suppose I bring Eve up to become outraged at being black-mailed. But suppose others are bringing Adam up to care exclusively about money, and suppose the payoffs are monetary in Blackmail. Adam with only this one concern may be unlikely to predict Eve's outrage, or pay serious attention to her threats (this is an example of the mechanism mentioned in the last chapter whereby those who do not possess some motivation find it incredible that others do). So in this setting Eve's narrow (financial) interests will have been hurt by her education. Maybe it would have been better to bring her up to turn the other cheek. Clearly the point generalizes. The person who confesses does badly if put in a setting of non-confessors: educators, just as much as players, may fail to coordinate, and when they do, educating someone to be a co-operator may be against their narrow interests. I may hurt my son by making him the only citizen who is disposed to graze the common at its sustainable level, when everyone else is over-grazing, or by making him the only citizen who has no gun, when everyone else has one. Perhaps to train fledgling Gladstones for the Foreign Office teachers must dismantle some of their naturally embedded respect for treaties, because that is how the international world works.

The game theorist may here cultivate a new field of action. Perhaps

we can ascend a level to talk of metagames, or choice between characters or persona. We can then ask whether it is rational to 'choose' the
persona of a hawk or a dove, or of someone prey to various motivations, and in various kinds of population various choices may be
recommended. But to whom are such recommendations addressed?
Sometimes, indeed, to the agent. If my son is going to France, I may
advise him not to queue patiently if he is waiting for something, if I
believe, rightly or wrongly, that the French ignore queues. But one
could not address such advice in general to an agent, for an agent is
going to face many and unforeseen social circumstances, and
approaching them all without minimally co-operative dispositions is
bound to wreck his or her life. Success needs society, and society needs
trust. Nor is there doubt about the advice that must be addressed in
general to educators, or those who genuinely have an influence in the
moulding of personality. It is their responsibility to make sure that the
next generation avoids the invisible boot.

Of course, there are particular social relations that are designed to
be competitive and even aggressive, although their limits are carefully
set. Economic bargaining is supposed to be carried out with individual
economic self-interest in mind. But in spite of the laments of free-mar-
keteers, society sets boundaries even here: there is a limit to the means
a party may use to get the best of a bargain. Not everything is up for
sale, and fraud, misrepresentation, reneging on contract, exploiting
monopoly power, are among the things we put off-limits.

Society particularly flexes its muscles when a selfish choice flies not
only against a co-operative option, but against a course of action that
was previously pledged. Indeed, the basic function of promise and
contract is to communicate that you accept the role of being trusted,
and as we have described, these exist precisely to generate an addi-
tional motivational pressure and sway what you will be concerned to
do. You are now vulnerable to anger and remonstrance in case of defection. But the social pressure is also there, as Hume insisted, in other
cases. Free-riding, or failing to play one's part when others are playing
theirs, is often frowned upon almost equally severely. If Eve walks
away without doing her bit in the last round of Centipede, she will
meet social hostility.

None of this makes the situations modelled as prisoners' dilemmas
go away. They are situations in which one set of concerns suggests one
course of action, and a different set of concerns suggests another. But
that is all. There is no tribunal in which those concerns are certified or
disqualified at the bar of reason. There is no such courtroom and no
such judgement.

With a better view of our dispositions and our choices in front of us, we can now turn to a further investigation of our nature as deliberating beings: our concern for the common point of view, our freedom, and our rationality as that is conceived of in the Kantian tradition.

7

The Good, the Right, and the
Common Point of View

O wad some Pow'r the giftie gie us
To see oursels as others see us!
It wad frae monie a blunder free us
An' foolish notion
Robert Burns, 'To a Louse'

1. VIBRATING IN SYMPATHY: HUME AND SMITH

We can now return to a more detailed discussion of sentiments that
actually motivate us, without being distracted by the threat of egoism,
or the misuses of rational actor theory. In particular, we can further
delimit the nature of genuinely moral sentiments. We have already
 said that guilt and shame coordinate our own attitudes to ourselves
with the possible anger or disdain of others. The classical moral philosopher who best emphasizes this is Adam Smith. Smith talks of the
voice of conscience as the voice of 'the man within the breast'. His
theory is that this voice is not a strange extra, having a divine, unnatural, and inexplicable authority over us. Rather,

The jurisdiction of the man within, is founded altogether in the desire of
praise-worthiness, and in the aversion to blame-worthiness; in the desire of
possessing those qualities, and performing those actions, which we love and
admire in other people; and in the dread of possessing those qualities, and performing those actions, which we hate and despise in other people.[1]

That is, the subject is capable of seeing his or her action in a general
light as an action that illustrates some qualities. These same qualities
arouse admiration or hatred when they are found in the actions of
other people, and we desire our own actions to be of the kind that
arouses love or admiration, and fear the reverse. In Smith, the 'impar-

---

[1] Adam Smith, *The Theory of Moral Sentiments*, III. 2. 33.

tial spectator' within the breast is a kind of symbol of this restless (and typically Calvinist) duty of self-scrutiny: indeed, there is good evidence that Robert Burns was deliberately reflecting Smith in his famous poem. Smith had written more primly of the reformation that would be unavoidable 'if we saw ourselves in the light in which others see us, or in which they would see us if they knew all'.[2]

The sensitivity Smith describes is allied to our ability to take up what Hume had previously called 'the common point of view'. Hume contrasts assessments so made with ones made purely with regard to our own interests:

When a man denominates another his enemy, his rival, his antagonist, his adversary, he is understood to speak the language of self-love, and to express sentiments, peculiar to himself, and arising from his particular circumstances and situation. But when he bestows on any man the epithets of vicious or odious or depraved, he then speaks another language, and expresses sentiments in which, he expects, all his audience are to concur with him. He must here, therefore, depart from his private and particular situation, and must chuse a point of view, common to him with others: He must move some universal principle of the human frame, and touch a string, to which all mankind have an accord and symphony. If he mean, therefore, to express, that this man possesses qualities, whose tendency is pernicious to society, he has chosen this common point of view, and has touched the principle of humanity, in which every man, in some degree, concurs. While the human heart is compounded of the same elements as at present, it will never be wholly indifferent to public good, nor entirely unaffected with the tendency of characters and manners. And though this affection of humanity may not generally be esteemed so strong as vanity or ambition, yet, being common to all men, it can alone be the foundation of morals, or of any general system of blame or praise. One man's ambition is not another's ambition; nor will the same event or object satisfy both: But the humanity of one man is the humanity of every one; and the same object touches this passion in all human creatures.[3]

Hume stresses that there is nothing unusual or special to ethics in this change of view. If my enemy does something, such as fortify a city, and does it well, on the one hand I can curse it as an obstacle to my own ambitions or my own security, but on the other hand I can also admire it as well-adapted to its purpose, strong, well-formed, and so on.[4] These are impersonal standards for good fortifications: they describe what anybody who fortifies a city is likely to want. Is it strange that we

---

[2] Ibid. III. 4. 6. The influence on Burns is described in Ian Simpson Ross, *The Life of Adam Smith* (Oxford: Oxford University Press, 1995), 166.

[3] *Enquiry Concerning the Principles of Morals*, IX. 1, pp. 272–3.

[4] *Treatise*, III. iii. 1, p. 586.

should be able to perform this feat of abstracting from our own interests in this way? Presumably not, for we need to tell *in general* what are the good features of a well-fortified city. We may want to employ the same builder, or instruct our own builder which models to imitate, or advise our children on modes of construction. To do any of these things we need the capacity to see past the impact this fortification has on our own concerns, and assess it in an impartial manner. Of course, on occasion we are so overwhelmed by personal emotion that we cannot appreciate the good points of something that stands in our way. Equally, we find it hard to recognize good qualities in those people whom we hate. But the capacity to take up the impartial point of view remains possible, even when on occasion we are unable to rise to it.

Hume's other examples include praise and blame bestowed on historical characters whose doings had no effect on me or mine; and praise bestowed on those whose characters are admirable, but whose circumstances make it impossible for them to exercise their virtues to anyone's benefits—what he calls 'virtue in rags'.[5] In each such case we abstract away from the actual potential the subject has for helping or harming us, here and now, and think only in terms of the tendency the character has, to harm or benefit those with whom it is engaged. It is with such abstraction that an ethical appreciation of a character arises.

The exact relation between Smith, on the one hand, and Hume, on the other, is not our topic, but I will venture some brief remarks. Neither author is original in stressing a duty of self-scrutiny; indeed Hume himself acknowledged the influence of the Stoics, especially Cicero, and Calvin. What is new is the stress on the social aspect, so that self-scrutiny is a matter of internalizing the gaze of others. It is sometimes suggested that Hume does not anticipate Smith's mechanism. But, although there is more stress on 'sympathy' in Hume, this is surely wrong. There is the famous peroration on pages 620–1 of the *Treatise*. But throughout Book II of the *Treatise*, especially, the mechanism is constantly at play. On page 303, Hume tells us that 'men always consider the sentiments of others in their judgment of themselves'. Then the section entitled 'Of the Love of Fame' (II. 2. xi) is wholly an exploration of the mechanisms at work whereby the opinions of others

---

[5] 'I now proceed to the second remarkable circumstance which I proposed to take notice of. Where a person is possessed of a character that in its natural tendency is beneficial to society, we esteem him virtuous, and are delighted with the view of his character, even though particular accidents prevent its operation, and incapacitate him from being serviceable to his friends and country. Virtue in rags is still virtue; and the love which it procures attends a man into a dungeon or desert, where the virtue can no longer be exerted in action, and is lost to all the world.' *Treatise*, III. iii. 1, p. 584.

has an influence on our passions. At page 365 he talks of the ways in which the minds of men are mirrors one to the other, 'not only because they reflect each others' emotions, but also because those rays of passions, sentiments and opinions may be often reverberated, and may decay away by insensible degrees', although he also goes on to describe cases in which the reverberation magnifies them. Then we might consider page 499, where Hume is talking of our uneasiness or sense of wrong at contemplating injustice perpetrated upon others, and insists that we are not only uneasy when it is others who are doing the wrong:

And though this sense, in the present case, be derived only from contemplating the actions of others, yet we fail not to extend it even to our own actions. The general rule reaches beyond those instances from which it arose; while, at the same time, we naturally sympathize with others in the sentiments they entertain of us.

Perhaps most telling is the typically Humean example on page 589:

A man will be mortified if you tell him he has a stinking breath; though it is evidently no annoyance to himself. Our fancy easily changes its situation; and, either surveying ourselves as we appear to others, or considering others as they feel themselves, we enter, by that means, into sentiments which no way belong to us, and in which nothing but sympathy is able to interest us. And this sympathy we sometimes carry so far, as even to be displeased with a quality commodious to us, merely because it displeases others, and makes us disagreeable in their eyes; though perhaps we never can have any interest in rendering ourselves agreeable to them.

We can usefully see each of Hume and Smith as suggesting a four-part process. First we love one or another quality in people when we come across it, possibly because we have been educated to do so. Then we take up the common point of view which turns love to *esteem*, assessing a trait of character as admirable or the reverse. Third, we can become aware that this is a trait that we ourselves exhibit, or do not. And fourth, when we do so we are moved to a self-satisfaction and pride, or unease and shame, corresponding to our original assessment, and imagining this assessment made of us by others. This is a kind of internal vibration in sympathy with the imagined sentiments of others. Hume constantly insists on the way our own pride resonates with the imagined esteem of others, or the way our own humility resonates with their imagined contempt.[6]

---

[6] So what is the difference between Hume and Smith? Hume himself located the key in what he described as the 'hinge' of Smith's system, namely the view that all

Hume himself has a view of the first stage as largely consequential-ist: we love character traits according to whether they render those who have them useful or agreeable to themselves and others. Smith sought to distance himself from this, preferring to call only upon the operation of sympathetic imagination, whereby we empathize or iden-tify with either agents or those acted upon by them. There is room for debate about how great this difference is. Partly, it seems designed to enable Smith to avoid what he may have regarded as a dangerous con-ventionalism that hovers around Hume's discussion of the artificial virtues of honesty and justice. Smith can call upon a direct empathetic understanding of the bad motives of the cheat or fraud, and a corre-sponding recoil. But, when asked why such motives should engender such a recoil, Hume has an answer, whereas Smith, if he is to avoid reflections on utility, would seem only able to appeal to an innate sense of propriety. Certainly the 'propriety of affection' we have for a char-acter and its virtues and vices is to be 'found nowhere but in the sym-pathetic feelings of the impartial and well-informed spectator'.[7] But if we stop there, then there is no explanation for why some kinds of char-acter and their actions are adapted to exciting pleasurable or admiring sympathetic feelings, and others the reverse. Yet this difference is the very kind of thing for which Hume offers an explanation.

However this may be, the overall mechanism is certainly natural to us. We need only reflect on the human delight in gossip, or in stories or soap operas, to realize that discussing and coordinating our reac-tions to human doings in general is a familiar, and indeed obsessive, concern. And when we are properly socialized, an awareness that our behaviour could not survive the impartial scrutiny of others is uncom-fortable, and in principle opens the gates to reform. So can we say that Hume and Smith, between them, so smoothly and quickly solve the main problem of understanding the moral sentiments?

Myself, I believe so, but there are obstacles to overcome. Hume and Smith were writing towards the end of more than a century of reflec-tion on the human tendency to care about the notice of others, and to

sympathy is agreeable, in which case, he objects, 'An Hospital would be a more enter-taining place than a Ball': Hume, letter to Smith, 28 July 1759, *Letters*, ed. J. Y. T. Greig (Oxford: Oxford University Press, 1932), i. 312. For Smith, the agreeable sensation of identity between someone else's sentiments and my own as I contemplate them imme-diately generates a notion of esteem. For Hume, rightly, this is not so. For a convincing discussion of the issues, see David Raynor, 'Hume's Abstract of Adam Smith's Theory of Moral Sentiments', *Journal of the History of Philosophy*, 22 (1984), 51–79. See also John Bricke, *Mind and Morality* (Oxford: Oxford University Press, 1996), especially ch. 4.

[7] Smith, *The Theory of Moral Sentiments*, VII. ii. 1, p. 49

care about their affection and praise and esteem. In the seventeenth century the phenomenon was noted well enough, but quite generally regretted and satirized as a competitor to true virtue. Our pride or our concern for honour leads to what Locke called the Law of Opinion or Reputation and which he also describes as the Law of Fashion.[8] Locke has no doubt about the power of this motive. He denies that there exists 'one of ten thousand, who is stiff and insensible enough, to bear up under the constant dislike and condemnation of his own Club'. He even allows that it is typically the Law of Opinion and Reputation that we appeal to when we judge the virtue and vice of things. But he recoils with horror from the idea that this Law can provide the basis for establishing a moral law. After all, in various 'clubs' men can make or keep their reputations by pretty appalling actions. It all depends on the norms of the place and time. The aristocratic norm of honour is a Law of Opinion, and it can lead to all the absurdities, and even crimes, of courtly life, and obviously leaves the aristocrat a regrettable latitude in his relations with others, such as servants, women, and tradesmen. So for Locke the Law of Opinion is something of an understudy, or even an impostor, with the true source of morality lying in the Law of God, knowable by a combination of reason and revelation. And here he is only echoing an enormous tradition of moral philosophy and theology. True virtue is only counterfeited by behaviour motivated by concern for reputation, even if, in a good enough society, that concern might lead us, fortunately, into mimicking the real thing. If in the recesses of our hearts it is concern for esteem and praise that drives us, then we have not yet become truly virtuous. This is motivation by pride or vanity, and utterly obnoxious in the Christian tradition. Even if our environment is one in which only good behaviour gains applause, still we are victims of what Milton called the 'last infirmity' of noble minds, and Pope called a 'happy frailty'.

Yet it is clear that mechanisms of praise and blame are, after all, responsible for the norms people come to internalize and respect. The child that cannot respond to a smile or a frown is cut off from human life, and we might go so far as to suggest that self-consciousness itself requires a sensitivity to the reflective gaze of others. To be self-conscious is arguably to understand oneself as a potential object of the affective attention of others. So the question is not whether caring about the reactions of others is universal, for in this sense it must be.

---

[8] *Essay*, II. xxviii. 8–14. A. O. Lovejoy marvellously details the varying estimates of our motivation by 'pride' and 'honour' in the seventeenth and eighteenth centuries in *Reflections on Human Nature* (Baltimore, Md.: Johns Hopkins University Press, 1961).

The question becomes whether we can do something to close the gap between our desire for approbation, and a love of virtue. How do we come to love the *right* traits? And how do we come to be motivated, not by the desire for applause or praise, but by the desire to *merit* that applause and praise?

There are, I believe, two key moves made in the moral tradition culminating in Hume and Smith, which serve to answer these questions. The first is to kick-start the process with a relatively optimistic picture of human nature. The second is to separate the explanatory perspective from the resulting deliberative perspective.

1. The optimism is expressed in the notion of sympathy. If we naturally sympathize with the pleasures and pains of others, then we naturally praise and encourage actions that promote pleasures and avoid pains, and dislike and discourage actions that do the reverse. This ensures some degree of humanity in our dealings with each other. Sympathy is natural, and human: it gives us the basic repugnance from aggression, cruelty, humiliation, triumphalism, and all the large and small ways in which we and our kind seek to establish ascendancy over others. It means that even if bullies have their admirers, the word is still a term of reproach.

2. The distinction of perspectives comes in realizing that while mechanisms of praise and blame may explain the shape of our motivational natures, it does not follow that desire for praise and blame figures in those structures, let alone to the exclusion of everything else. This is the distinction we saw at work in Chapter 5: a sociobiological explanation of maternal love should not take the form of supposing that the mother desires anything except the welfare of her child. Here it means that the upshot of our susceptibility to praise and blame need not be psychologies aiming at praise or blame. We are talking diachronically, whereby the praise rubs off on the action, not synchronically, where desire for praise coexists with and somehow provides the force behind our (apparent) evaluation of the action. Education has misfired in the child who grows into a person whose dominant aim remains the achievement of praise. This suggests only a second-best or even hypocritical personality, more concerned with currying the favour of others than with love of truth or virtue. The 'egoistic motive stimulant' of praise is supposed to be self-effacing. The upshot should be that we are not concerned with such goals as praise or fame at all, but are simply concerned, for instance, to do the co-operative thing, or to avoid dishonesty and injustice. In other words, we no longer have a false simulacrum of virtue, but virtue itself.

With this understood, we can see the 'Law of Opinion' not as a lamentable competitor to virtue, but as a key ingredient in the explanation of how we come to be virtuous. In fact, we might notice that with the Law of Opinion up and running, we may not need very much natural sympathy to kick-start the process. It may be that children get to sympathize deeply and widely with others as much because they are praised for showing that they do, and the emergence of this norm could then in turn be understood on a less benevolent natural basis. For instance, a little sympathy for others, coupled with a healthy regard for our own long-term interests, could give us a motive for encouraging wider sympathy, in circumstances where we imagine that this will increase reciprocal concern. But clearly some natural motivational basis has to be there to get the normative ascent started.

Of course, if things have gone wrong, and a club admires and praises selective bad behaviour, the upshot will be bad people. But that is just a plain truth. Standing within our system of norms, we can regret it or condemn it (I defer discussing the lurking bogey of relativism in this until the final chapter). As virtuous people we will beware of joining such clubs, and as political animals we will discourage their formation as best we can.

If we now revisit the quotation from Smith on p. 200, we can see the solution to something that might have troubled us. Smith starts by talking of desire for praiseworthiness and avoidance of blameworthiness, and goes on to talk of the qualities which we love and admire, or hate and despise. And it is natural to protest that, while the first motivation involves an 'ought', the second gives us only an 'is'. We want, most of the time, to be praised or blamed for qualities that *deserve* praise or blame, not just for ones that *de facto* attract it. How does Smith span the gap? We now see that the answer lies first in the natural foundation of praise and blame in sympathy, and second in the incorporation, within our motivational structures, of the gaze of the man within: a man who sees through any layers of appearance with which we may hope to extract false or undeserved praise from others. If all has gone well, the man within will only love what is lovable.

Doubts may still arise about the *authority* of the mechanisms that Hume and Smith identify. Let us consider this in connection with the requirements of truth-telling and honesty, for instance in regard to property and contracts. Suppose someone says that while he recognizes the general benefits to human beings of being able to rely upon the truthfulness, or the honesty and integrity, of others, he feels no compunction about telling lies, being dishonest, or breaking promises himself, when it is to his benefit to do so (in other words, he transfers Gladstone's attitude to international dealings into a general habit).

Similarly, he feels no compunction about avoiding his part in co-operative enterprises when these have grown up without explicit contract, but where by convention people are expected to do their bit: he is happy to be a free-rider. He might recognize that his behaviour exposes him to the anger or disdain of others if he is discovered, but he would simply regard this as a factor to be managed in a cost-benefit analysis. The advantage of a particular case of cheating or reneging would have to be calculated remembering the possible negative effects on his reputation. He therefore seems to lack any mechanism for internalizing the disdain of others, or rehearsing accusations to which he knows he may be subjected. This person lacks the voice within. His psychology is not that of the normal socialized human being, for the fact that a piece of behaviour is of the despised kind leaves him cold. It provides no motivation, on its own, to avoid any action which, all things considered, he supposes to be to his benefit.

In Hume's *Enquiry Concerning the Principles of Morals* the character is called the sensible knave:

> a sensible knave, in particular incidents, may think, that an act of iniquity or infidelity will make a considerable addition to his fortune, without causing any considerable breach in the social union and confederacy. That honesty is the best policy, may be a good general rule; but is liable to many exceptions: And he, it may, perhaps, be thought, conducts himself with most wisdom, who observes the general rule, and takes advantage of all the exceptions.[9]

The problem is that by the standard of self-interest the knave is acting perfectly rationally. He is not against social arrangements. It is just that he stands ready to exploit them when he can. If others make contracts with him, for example to abstain from some kinds of competition, he will make the contracts if it is to his advantage, and break them when that is to his advantage. If he is lucky enough to possess the ring of Gyges, making him and his infractions invisible, he can do as he likes. It would be as if he were omnipotent. The consequences of his actions never recoil upon him. (Plato rather charmingly emphasizes the possibility of going round other peoples' beds at will, although whether people make a sufficiently gratifying response when subjected to invisible, but tangible, sexual advances may perhaps be queried.)

What problem is posed by the knave? It is usually posed as that of finding a way of showing that the knave is irrational, and it is in this form that it preoccupied both Plato and Kant. The idea is to find a way of proving that if reason controlled him as it ought to, he would sacri-

---

[9] Hume, *Enquiry Concerning the Principles of Morals*, IX. 2, p. 282.

fice self-interest out of his respect for others, or perhaps for truth, property, social order, or for the moral law, or for integrity and promises.

For Hume and Smith, by contrast, the knave just lacks what we have seen Smith call 'the desire of possessing those qualities, and performing those actions, which we love and admire in other people'. In other words, his defect is not one of rationality, but just one of lacking a normal desire or source of affect. We educate people to care that they share the desires we admire, but if our education has failed then it may be too late. As Hume continues:

> I must confess, that, if a man think, that this reasoning much requires an answer, it will be a little difficult to find any, which will to him appear satisfactory and convincing. If his heart rebel not against such pernicious maxims, if he feel no reluctance to the thoughts of villainy or baseness, he has indeed lost a considerable motive to virtue; and we may expect, that his practice will be answerable to his speculation.[10]

The point being that a large part of education involves making sure that peoples' hearts do rebel against such 'pernicious maxims', and that if such education has not been effective, then it is too late to complain. What we can do is remind ourselves of the benefits of a social order based on honesty and co-operation, and we can strengthen our determination to make things difficult for those tempted to being knaves. We can exhort the knave to share our sentiments. We can try to turn up the volume of his feelings for those whom he exploits. What we cannot do is argue the knave back into upright behaviour, for if his sentiments are only activated by what he perceives as his own advantage, then we can advance no effective consideration except by appealing to his own self-interest, and on the occasions that he exploits this is not enough.

Before becoming too worried about the knave, we should reflect a little upon the scene in which he is set. We might imagine the knave embedded in a particular order of trust and co-operation, which he then exploits. This is certainly bad. But in more hostile environments, the desire to fight for advantage is not so much knavish as human. This will be so when the social order is one in which trust and co-operation have broken down or never existed, or if it is asymmetrically weighted in exploitative ways.[11]

---

[10] Ibid. 283.

[11] In India I heard a sad instance of the war of all against all, when a television company accompanied a peasant family for some time, in order to illustrate the crushing injustice of the system of money-lending under which they existed. At the end of the shoot the company paid a fee, which to the family, represented tremendous sum. When

It is at this point useful to distinguish two elements of the move to 'the common point of view' in Hume. One is that Hume believes that in assessing a character or the actions of a character, we should consider the interests of 'the person himself whose character is examined, or that of persons who have a connection with him'. That is, we assess people by considering their impact on a fairly immediate circle: friends, family, business associates, for example. This is not a move to the interests of *everybody* considered impartially, which is why it is wrong to see Hume as a utilitarian, although his ethics certainly contains consequentialist elements. Rather, in his story, virtue is assessed in terms of a functional aptitude, and the aptitude is one of bringing pleasure or utility to oneself or to those with whom one has everyday commerce. In assessing the character of Brutus, I do not take up a utilitarian, God's-eye, ideal observer standpoint and ask for the effect of Brutus's character globally. I abstract from my own position, consider the effects of that character on Brutus and those near to him, and judge accordingly. We can all do this, and doing so provides the string to which we all vibrate in sympathy.[12]

This is the first element involved in taking up a common point of view. The second is slightly different. The first element suggests that we can see Hume as an early 'communitarian', most concerned to establish and defend virtues of character in our dealings with others of our group: our family or kin, insiders, or those with whom we have social connections. But the second element is slightly different. It is essentially an ideal of *civility*: the requirement that in a conversation with others we find common ground with them. We do not simply discount their opinion, or still less stay entirely deaf to their voice. In everyday life, it may be convenient to do this. Aristotle, for example, appears to present us with characters who are in the business of listening only to people like themselves (free Greek citizens) and who find it easy to discount the interests, opinions, or concerns of others outside the charmed circle. Hume, by contrast, seems to think that we all have an interest in pursuing conversations with others: we need to avoid the 'continual contradictions' which arise if we do not do so. This ideal of civility puts pressure on purely communitarian principles. It means that we cannot rest content with relations with the outsiders

the producer then asked what the father hoped to do with it, the answer was swift and obvious: become a money-lender.

[12] Geoff Sayre-McCord, 'Why the Common Point of View isn't Ideal—And Shouldn't Be', *Social Philosophy and Policy*, 9 (1994), 202.

that we cannot see ourselves justifying to them. We shall consider the force of this need further in section 4.

We now need to bear in mind that there are different contexts for knavery. The knave so far considered is the genuine fraud or cheat or person of weak and unreliable honesty. In a well-functioning society, there will be enough social pressures to give everyone a motivation to avoid appearing like this. And the best way to ensure that people we care for will not *appear* like this is, in turn, to make sure that they *aren't* like this, and so we educate people into the virtues. The less tractable problem is unfortunately also more common. This is the 'knave' who is secure in the social virtues, but insensitive to the needs of people outside his particular circle. Such people confine their concerns to their immediate tribe or group or class or gender. Within their group, for example, they may operate roughly consequentialist moralities, but only consequences to the group matter. Such tribal or local ethics take into account effects on a limited circle, but display less concern or no concern for the effects of action upon other people, people who don't count as much or just don't count at all. Rousseau contrasts the virtue of the citizen with the virtue of a man, and so illustrates the distinction: 'amongst strangers, the Spartan was selfish, grasping, and unjust, but unselfishness, justice and harmony ruled his home life.'[13] And like Rousseau's Spartans, within the private circle people may even gain in reputation and honour by callous or fraudulent dealings with those outside it, those who have a lesser moral status.

We can now see that the quest for a foundation of ethics in 'reason' is the search for a different answer from that of Hume or Smith, one that shows that knaves of both the domestic and the Foreign-Office variety are not only unpleasant, but in some sense irrational. Can any such foundation be discovered? Before turning to that, it is good to wonder whether we actually want any such foundation. Denying identical moral status to insiders and outsiders is a way of saying that distance matters. And in our actual moral lives distance does matter. A person would be criticized as cruel or callous, inhuman and unfeeling, if he let a child starve to death on his doorstep. But the fact that the child is distant, out of sight and out of mind, excuses us, in our own eyes and those of people surrounding us. We simply cannot shoulder the burden of the entire world: it is enough if we do our bit by those

---

[13] Rousseau, *Émile: or On Education*, trans. Allan Bloom (New York: Basic Books, 1979), Bk. 1. I should say that for the moment I am lumping together callous treatment of outsiders with fraudulent or knavish treatment of them; it would be possible to insist on differences between the two. Some emerge in Sect. 3, on Kant's Dream.

with whom we are in human contact. There are moral philosophers quick to insist that this is indefensible. They use the inhumanity of the one situation to encourage us to feel guilty about the other. Such appeals can be deeply uncomfortable.[14] But must we listen to them?

2. ARISTOTLE'S WELL-BEING

One argument would be that it is actually impossible to be a successful knave. We might urge, for instance, that there is no such thing as the perfect crime: societies arrange things so that transgressors either get caught, or live in fear of getting caught, and the cost of this is sufficient to outweigh whatever benefits they may have hoped to gain by dishonesty. And we can remind ourselves of the mechanisms of exposure connected to 'one thought too many': someone on the lookout for opportunities of knavery is unlikely to be good at concealing this disposition for long, and he will then suffer for it.

Although we might wish that things were always like that, in the real world it is hard to believe that they are. On the contrary, when success is measured by ordinary standards, including not only money but social position and respect, then we have to admit that the business world is full of people who succeed by more or less dubious means, and the political world even more so. Furthermore, by these arguments we cannot advance beyond the thesis that honesty is the best policy. For however well we arrange things so that the dishonest suffer, it will always be open to us to doubt whether the cost-benefit analysis comes down that way in a particular case, and if fear of discovery is our only motive, then doubting this we will be tempted to knavish behaviour. What was wanted is respect for honesty *as such*, but all we are given is respect for it as a means to avoiding trouble with others.

In Chapter 2 we met Aristotle's more profound attempt to align good behaviour with self-interest. Aristotle had a strong sense of the many delicate elements that go to make up human well-being or *eudaimonia*. Well-being is not, as it were, a simple sensation like that arising when we are well-fed or pleasantly tired. If it were, perhaps the means to gaining it could be fairly unethical. If it were something like a state of mind that can be achieved without virtue, then the means by which we came to acquire it would be irrelevant. Aristotle rightly refused to separate the end from the activities of life. The idea is that the goal of

---

[14] Peter Singer, *How are We to Live?* (Cambridge: Cambridge University Press, 1993); Peter Unger, *Living High and Letting Die* (New York: Oxford University Press, 1996).

life is to live well, and to live well is to live ethically. Aristotle is here refusing the idea that self-interest may oppose morality, and instead giving a theory of human well-being that aligns the two. They cannot be separated, and so there is no opposition between them. The link is that well-being involves an active appreciation of our place in society, of the respect that is due to us for our doings, of successes gained and failures avoided. Nobody had a stronger sense than Aristotle of the importance attaching to the fact that it is our nature to be social beings. To achieve our natural ends, or if we like, to live healthily, when health involves the developed activity of our natural faculties, various social relationships, particularly friendships, need to be in place. But these cannot be in place where there is no trust and no integrity, nor where there is one eye cocked on the possibility of fraud or deception. Hence, only trustworthy persons can gain these benefits, and hence we all at bottom have an overriding motivation to behave so that we can always justify our conduct in our own eyes and those of others.

Aristotle's reflections have considerable force. But it is clear that they fall far short of a refutation at least of the Spartan or Foreign-Office kind of knave. The principal problem is that the social sources of self-respect Aristotle highlights are heavily contextual, or local rather than global. For while social living is natural, and solitary living may be seen as unhealthy as well as unpleasant, the poor human animal has some quite nasty natural tendencies in its relations to people not its kin. It is at least as natural to us pretty much to confine our cares to the family or tribe or other local group, as it is to expand our view to include sympathetic practical concern with everyone, however remote. Rousseau's citizen may have a delicate sense of honour and integrity within his own circle, but treat those outside it with ruthless indifference. Within his own circle this may be known, and be forgiven, or might even be a subject of admiration. The citizen's own sense of worth and self-respect is likely to simply echo that applause. The members of his club may pride themselves on doing well in a dog-eats-dog world. Conversely those who are faint-hearted enough to treat potential opponents with justice or concern may meet contempt among their own people. And, in fact, Aristotle's own moral hero, the 'great-souled man', notoriously reflects the limited concern of educated Greek opinion of the time. The admiration of his equals concerns him a great deal, but the opinions of those who are of lesser moral status—women, slaves, non-citizens, barbarians—matters not at all. In other words, Aristotle gives us no moral lever with which to shift an ordinary, socially successful, and complacent man into a more universal ethic of respect for others outside his charmed circle. To get him to treat them justly, it seems, we have to appeal to his benevolence rather than his reason. We cannot hit him with a kind of theorem of practical reasoning.

The Humean by contrast aligns self-interest and virtue by a sentimental education. The subject is brought to feel that dishonesty, or exploitation, or discounting outsiders, will not do, and it becomes then a self-standing concern of hers neither to be dishonest, nor to appear dishonest, nor to exploit nor discount outsiders. She sympathizes with the hurt or outrage of others, internalizing their voices. So she cannot be satisfied with herself if she has failed: she will feel that letting others down is also letting herself down. It is simply a fact that this education works well for many of us much of the time.

3. KANT'S DREAM

Some philosophers feel that the right respect for justice and honesty in itself has still not been achieved. They chafe at our impotence if, facing the would-be knave, we try to drum him into the ranks of the virtuous, but find nothing on which to get a purchase. The philosopher who felt the lack most acutely and who struggled the hardest to overcome it was Immanuel Kant. For Kant, motivation by means of desire was one thing, motivation by apprehension of the Moral Law a different thing, and furthermore something with absolute or 'categorical' binding force. Morality in Kant stands apart from the world of desire, and has authority over it: the voice of the man within is no kind of projection of the good or bad opinion of others, but nothing less than the voice of reason. It is reason itself that dictates respect for moral law, and this respect can be demanded of all rational beings, simply in virtue of their rationality. Furthermore, the same kind of respect is owed to all persons simply in virtue of the same rationality. Kant, like previous Buddhist, Confucian, and Christian traditions, locates the essence of ethics in two kinds of thought (which he perhaps thought of as two expressions of one thought). One is reciprocity: 'Do as you would be done by.' The other is the demand that everyone is treated as an end in themselves. Whatever exactly this means, it is clear that it is intended to exclude any kind of manipulative or deceptive relationships, and to exclude just the kind of asymmetry of moral status that arises in Aristotle or Rousseau, or the exclusion of interest of others that is indulged by the knave. When telling lies, or giving false promises, a person treats another as a 'mere means', an instrument of his own purposes, who is denied the material to exercise his or her own reason on the actual situation. And it is this denial of moral status that Kant seeks to rule out by reason alone. In practice the ethic that emerges is one centred on a number of 'pure' or unconditional duties. These are absolutely binding, and failure in them is failure to obey the injunction to treat people with appropriate respect, as ends in themselves.

I am not here primarily concerned with the nature of Kant's ethical system, but only with its claim to foundations in reason. Perhaps it is useful to compare the situation in practical reasoning with that in theoretical, deductive reasoning. Suppose we present a system of deductive logic in terms of the avoidance of contradiction (so that a set of premises $A_1 \ldots An$ yields a conclusion B if and only if it is inconsistent to suppose $A_1 \ldots An$ and not-B. That is, the result of adding the negation of B to the set generates a contradiction: a formula of the form P & not-P). What then is the justification both of our rules whereby sets of formulae are supposed to yield various conclusions, and also for the prohibition on contradictions? We can compare the knave to the annoying character in logic classes who insists on asking either why he has to allow that one thing follows from another, or who queries what is wrong with contradiction (like Whitman, perhaps he likes to think 'I am large, I contain multitudes'). In the case of deduction we can imagine four declining grades of response:

(a) We can prove to the annoying character that he is thinking contrary to reason.
(b) We can prove to our own satisfaction that the position of the annoying character is contrary to reason.
(c) We can show that if the annoying character thinks without being constrained by our principles, his thinking will be defective in some respect.
(d) All we can hope to show is people do not actually think like that.

The distinction between (a) and (b) is between <u>what you can prove to someone</u>, and <u>what you can prove about them</u>. Even if we cannot prove to the knave that he has reason to improve, we may be able to prove to ourselves that he has. Now in practical reasoning, Hume and Smith appear to be down with options (c) and (d). Their enterprise is one mainly of 'naturalized epistemology', working out the concerns we actually have, or what genuinely moves us in practical affairs, and adding their own approvals for it, generally on grounds of utility. Hume and Smith do not differ from Kant in trumpeting the virtues of reciprocity, respect, and universalizability, at least in the sense of respect for the common point of view. Where they differ is over the status of this approval. Kant requires it to be a theorem of pure practical reason, which means at least at level (b), and perhaps more ambitiously at level (a). Hume and Smith remain below.

In the case of deduction, we might wonder what the real difference would be between the enterprise of (b) and the apparently lesser investigations of (c) and (d). Most promising would be an argument along these lines. It is not just that we don't think as the annoying character does, or expect trouble if we do so. It is rather that no way of thought that fails to respect our principles—that refuses to respect validly drawn inferences or cheerfully accepts contradictions—could count as a genuine way of thought. It would lack something necessary to count as a way of reasoning at all; it could not be adapted for investigations of truth or falsehood. The annoying character may fail to face this fact, which is why (a) may be too ambitious, but it may be a fact for all that. In parallel fashion Kant may be seen as attempting to hoist us from the view that knaves are just annoying or useless, up to the realization that they are flouting authoritative, compulsory principles that are essential to practical reasoning. The goal is ambitious—how much so may be realized when we reflect that there is no assured way even of proving the same thing for elementary principles of classical logic.[15]

We have seen how for Hume or Smith the sensible knave is just a lost cause. But for Kant this is not so. He has within himself the power to see his own conduct as odious; merely in virtue of being reasonable he could recognize that his position is untenable, and in principle it is possible to prove that it is so. The norms of reason underlie the norms of ethics.

Kant's, then, is a noble dream. But is it more than a dream? In his own version, as already said, it comes trailing a highly distinctive, formal, deontological morality. And it comes with a distinctive conception of the rational agent—a metaphysics of the self. We look further at the metaphysics of deliberation in the next chapter. But what of the foundation of morals in reason? Kant's procedure is one of finding one salient description of an action that can identify its 'maxim', which means the reason for which it was done. The central injunction, then, is to 'act only on that maxim through which you can at the same time will that it should become a universal law'. A second formulation is 'act as if the maxim of your action were to become through your will a universal law of nature'.[16] The test is clearly some kind of universal-

---

[15] See, for instance, the work of Graham Priest on logics that accept contradictions, e.g. *Beyond the Limits of Thought* (Cambridge: Cambridge University Press, 1995).

[16] Immanuel Kant, *Groundwork of the Metaphysics of Morals*, trans. H. J. Paton (New York: Harper Torchbooks, 1964), § 51.

izability test: we imagine a world in which 'everyone is like that' and if the result is to be rejected, then so is the maxim and so is the action that had it as its principle.

There is something morally attractive about the formula, just as there is about the Golden Rule of do as you would be done by, or any general embargo against claiming exemptions for your own conduct from restrictions you want applied to that of others. It is the same attraction that belongs to the common point of view, or listening to the voice of the man within. It is, however, generally agreed that when it comes to identifying maxims of action, Kant himself had a frighteningly coarse set of categories. He found it easy to put extremely simple boundaries round the complex tangles of human action. For Kant, not only the first word, but the last word about a practical situation is glacially abstract: 'It was a lie'; 'He broke a promise'; 'He took my property'; 'She broke the law.'

This abstract character may make it easier to argue that you cannot consistently will that, in general, or whenever they feel like it, people lie or break promises, or steal property, or break the law. It is not wholly implausible that there is a contradiction in conceiving of a situation in which this kind of licence prevails, since the institutions of communicating facts, making promises, property ownership, and law each depend upon sufficient general compliance, without which they break down. But why identify the maxim of a particular concrete case, for instance of lying, at that level of generality? In our everyday morality, a lot may depend on the intentions of the person to whom you tell the lie or break the promise, or the ways in which the promise or statement was exacted from you, or the injustice of the laws against which you feel inclined to rebel. Neither our motivations nor our actions have a rigid, one-word, essence. When the mad axeman asks where my children are so that he may slaughter them, and I misdirect him, I need not be acting on the maxim that lying is always permissible, or permissible when you feel like it. I am at best acting on the maxim that lying is permissible when the person you confront will murder those you love if told the truth, and there is absolutely no contradiction in willing that this maxim should govern people in general. In fact, I myself would very much want to see it governing people in general.

In his second of four examples in the *Groundwork*, Kant imagines everyone following the maxim 'give promises you intend to break when it is advantageous to do so'. The idea appears to be that we have to recognize that in such a circumstance promising becomes an empty ritual. People would no longer have a healthy practice of giving and receiving promises, since there would be no reason for relying on them or expecting anyone else to do so. But if promise-making disappears, then so do both promise-keeping and promise-breaking. In this sense, there is a kind of inconsistency in imagining a world with general promiscuous intention to break promises: whatever goes on, it cannot be the intention to break promises, because there can be no promises. The same structure exists when any institution or practice depends upon general conventions of performance. Perhaps you cannot universalize a strategy of deceptive promise-making whenever it is convenient, or queue-jumping when it is convenient to be at the front, or forging money when you would like to be richer, since promises, queues, and money only exist when there are sufficient numbers of people who do not take their convenience as licensing them to break the rules. Similarly, we might suppose that the institution of giving foreign treaties would collapse if we plan to follow Gladstone's reasoning (epigraph to Chapter 6) when the time comes to stand by them. At the very least, if it were common knowledge that all the parties to a treaty were following that plan, the performance of signing the treaty would begin to seem a mere sham.

We might think that this is a nice case of pure reason determining us to reject a maxim of a particular, morally repugnant kind. But it is not quite so easy. Before being too impressed, consider other examples. It is clear that you cannot universalize a *practice* of paying off credit cards every month. The whole institution depends upon the issuing banks receiving profits from people who do not do this. Yet there is nothing wrong with using a card and *actually* paying it off every month. People who do so are prudent and respectable, perhaps to the chagrin of the banks.

So the application of the test has to be carefully circumscribed. Now Kant attends not so much to the upshot where 'everyone behaves like that', but rather to the 'maxim' of your action. So suppose we switch attention to someone *intending* to pay off his card every month. The trouble is that, equally clearly, there is nothing wrong with making this your 'maxim'. The maxim of paying off the card every month is a perfectly good one. A Kantian might try saying: the maxim of paying off the card every month is permissible, because in fact not many people are going to follow it, and the institution survives those who do. But then, compare again the most casual case, where someone intends to break a promise if he or she feels like it. Is it contradictory to imagine this intention universalized, to govern everyone, as if by a law of nature? No. For, just as with credit cards, a healthy practice of promising could in principle perfectly well survive such a general intention. It will do so provided that people seldom feel like breaking their promises. Suppose, that is, that we are so constituted that the giving of a promise reliably determines what we will feel like doing when the time comes. Having given our promise, we are disinclined to do otherwise. Then, even if as we give the promise, we intend that on the (rare) occasions when we do feel like doing otherwise we follow our inclination, we can still be in a world in which people give and receive promises. We can be so because promises remain causally powerful determinants of what we will feel like. So, statistically as it were, their expression gives us reason to rely on performance, enabling us to co-ordinate our actions in the light of those reasons, and this will be because we know how breakage leads to loss of reputation, and, as in Hume and Smith, to unease.

So, if I wake up in the abnormal frame of mind of feeling like breaking a promise, I cannot fortify myself by talk of contradiction. For there is no contradiction in imagining a world in which people give promises, but everybody who feels like I do at present breaks promises. It is just the same as with aiming to pay off the credit card every month. There is no contradiction in imagining that all those with the aim succeed, provided few enough people have the aim.

This must not be misunderstood. Obviously, everyone agrees there is something off-colour about giving a lying promise. The question is whether talk of contradiction or of a boundary set by pure reason locates it. To think so, we would need a distinction between the credit card case, and the casual or lying promise case. In this latter case it indeed seems inappropriate to shelter behind the defence that not many people feel like breaking promises they have given, so I probably won't feel like that either, so I probably won't break it after all. The Kantian reply must be that this misrepresents the necessary psychology behind promise-giving. The scope of your intention, it might be urged, must include *banishing* impulses to non-compliance. It is not just that statistically we expect them to be rare: we also presume that in giving a promise the agent intends them not to arise, or intends to suppress them if they do. This is no longer paralleled in the credit card case. I am not misleading the bank manager when I take out a credit card, if I intend to pay it off when I feel like it, and I might even tell her this.

I think this is right, as far as it goes. But what it amounts to is that the person giving a promise while intending to break it if she feels like it is in a manner lying: she is misrepresenting herself as resolved to do something when she is not in fact resolved to do it. This is bad, although it may have an excuse on occasion. But she is also, as Hume puts it, making use of a form of words that subjects her to 'the penalty of never being trusted again in case of failure'.[17] This may be slightly exaggerated, but merely imagining penalties in this area motivates us intensely, and is supposed to do so.

can break promises for significant reason

The institution of promising contains within itself a presumption that the most casual kinds of reason for breaking a promise are impermissible. It does not contain within itself a presumption that no concerns count. If emergencies arise, or it turns out that the promisee was in bad faith, or if the promise was exacted under duress, or even if the situation changes sufficiently drastically, then a promise may be broken, or at least in some way renegotiated, without fault. And I may be relieved and even somewhat *proud* of myself at having broken my word, against the grain as it were, if, in a single prisoners' dilemma, it turns out that my opponent had also chosen to break his word to me.

Sufficiently trivial reasons do not license neglect, but it is worth remembering how in practical situations the boundary between justified and unjustified neglect is often extremely flexible. If I promise my wife to bring home some bread in the evening, a whole host of things will count as acceptable excuses for non-performance. Perhaps I thought we might like to try muffins instead, or the bakery was closed and the nearest one is five miles away, or it was raining too hard, or I felt like baking myself. In fact, almost anything upscale from 'I just didn't feel like it' might do (which also shows how we might be at cross-purposes, with one party supposing that the promise is unconditional, whereas the other supposes that a host of conditions license non-performance).

Let us return to the point that anybody who gives a promise, but intends to neglect performance just if they feel like it, is deceiving his audience about his intentions. Whereas I am not deceiving the bank if I take out a credit card, and intend to pay it off every time I feel like it. This still doesn't tell us that the lying promiser's maxim of action is in any sense inconsistent with itself. It is not as if his springs of action are paralysed in the way in which, arguably, thought without the structures of logic is paralysed. And if this is so for cases of crimes against institutions, such as breaking promises or giving lying promises, forging, failing to pay taxes, jumping queues, all for no better reason than that one feels like it, the prospect of reading contradiction into the other three cases that Kant considers is much worse.

suicide

The first case is this. Kant valiantly tries to show that there is something against reason about suicide in the face of predicted pain or evil on the grounds that 'a system of nature by whose law the very same

---

[17] *Treatise*, III. ii. 5, p. 521.

feeling whose function is to stimulate the furtherance of life should actually destroy life would contradict itself and consequently could not subsist as a system of nature'.[18] This sounds about as sensible as finding it contradictory that the driver (whose function is to make the vehicle go) should sometimes use the brake (whose function is to make the vehicle stop). A 'system of nature' might well foster life up to a point and no further, just as it generates male mantises whose function includes serving as food for their mate.

The second illustration is the case of the lying promise. The third is *self-improv* that of someone who indolently refuses to cultivate his or her own talents. Kant admits that you can have a system of society in which this is generally how people are. He shared the eighteenth-century belief that the South Sea Islanders are like this. But a person cannot consistently will that this indolence should become 'implanted in us as such a law by a natural instinct'. For, Kant says roundly, 'as a rational being he necessarily wills that all his powers be developed, since they serve him, and are given him, for all sorts of possible ends'. This is good grandmotherly advice, no doubt. The day may come when you wished you had cultivated your talents: if you are stranded on a desert island it would be nice to have learned shipbuilding; if captured by Chinese pirates, nice to have learned Chinese. But then, such days may never come, and many of us take the gamble that they won't come all of the time, and all of us take the gamble some of the time. Furthermore, it seems clear that we have at best a hypothetical imperative: 'If you want to be fortified against a range of possible problems, cultivate your talents.' Once more, the promised connection between the categorical imperative and pure reason is missing.

The fourth example is the person who refuses to help others who are *BENEF* struggling with hardships. Kant admits that the world could go on if everybody behaved like this, but argues that a will which decided in this way would be in contradiction with itself, since 'many a situation might arise in which the man needed love and sympathy from others, and in which, by such a law of nature sprung from his own will, he would rob himself of all hope of the help he wants for himself'.[19] Once more there is a respectable argument here appealing to prudence. It is well worth reminding (for instance) right-wing ideologues that children to whose education they will not contribute may one day be asked to contribute to their old-age pensions and medical support. But again it is hard to translate this into contradiction, or conflict of a will

[18] Kant, *Groundwork of the Metaphysics of Morals*, § 53.
[19] Ibid. § 57.

with itself. Recognition that a situation could arise in which you would need others to help you might well give you pause if you were to imagine provoking everyone into behaving selfishly. But not because of any kind of contradiction, but only because either we would start being fearful for ourselves, or more likely because we have sentiments of the kind Hume and Smith celebrate, that lead us to respect the verdict our behaviour would get from the common point of view. So we will feel uncomfortable at our selfishness when we imagine how we appear from the other persons' place.[20]

Of course, we wouldn't *want* a world in which a lot of people behave badly. But the whole point is that for Kant it is not a question of what we want, for that simply reminds us of our actual desires and our attitudes to the consequences of actions, which to the Kantian provide insufficient foundation for obligation and duty. Even in the institutional cases, someone might, oddly enough, actually *want* a world in which promise-making or queues or money (or credit cards) disappear. Perhaps, like Rousseau, he thinks that civil society in which contracts are such an important element is worse than a state of nature in which happy individuals cavort around without needing to make binding arrangements with each other. Such a person might counsel random promise-breaking as a move towards his preferred state, just as an activist counsels random law-breaking as a move towards overthrow of a particular legal order. Argument then has to retreat to considering the attractions of the state that is being promoted. It may be unattractive on broadly utilitarian grounds (the idea of a world without promises surely is so), but that is no longer an argument that appeals to a kind of inconsistency or contradiction.

Although stern and absolutist, Kant's ethic is accurate about the pathology of many consciences. Someone might feel that, all things considered, it was necessary to deceive the axeman. But the fact that they lied may nag at them for all that. It ought to be unpleasant to have to lie; we do not expect someone to walk away from the situation with a blithe heart. In some ways our ordinary perceptions of the salient, morally fundamental, features of what we are doing are indeed simple, as he maintains, and as simple ethics such as the Ten Commandments illustrate. The sentimentalism of Hume or Smith has to come to terms with this feeling. Would they have to regard it as somehow regrettable? I do not think so. Moral philosophers of all kinds recognize the importance of simple, memorable, publicly communicated barriers and

---

[20] Sidgwick levels similar criticism at Kant in *The Methods of Ethics*, note to Bk. III, ch. 13.

rules. Having absorbed them we feel reluctant to trespass against them, even when reflection shows that it was right to do so. A trespass can take on an awful symbolic place in our own sense of who we are and what we have done; it can weigh on us as an irredeemable blemish in the story of our lives. But perhaps what we did had to be done, for all that. So there is no reason deriving from this dangerous, often unhealthy, aspect of our psychologies for accepting a morality of simple but absolute and unconditional one-word duties and obligations. It is harder still to believe that reason by itself enjoins them; rather they seem to be expressions of the laws of a rather simple people.

The knave 'lacks respect for the Law', or doesn't care about certain duties, but if careful enough, he may prosper. It is only if life is stable enough so that effects of reputation predominate, or if the social and political order is stable enough and overarching enough to take into account relations with everyone and not just with insiders, that he is bound to fail. Those who are victims of his lying or cheating stay silent, or powerless, or do not recognize what has been done to them. He is despicable, no doubt, but successful in his own eyes, and perhaps that of the world. But he is not on the face of it irrational: indeed, to manage his knavery effectively he must be intelligent as well as daring. In spite of Kant's dream, it is better, then, to rest content with Smith and Hume. The knave is vicious and odious. We already have the words to express our contempt: it does not add anything except rhetoric also to call him irrational.

There is a further phenomenon to mention if we are to adjudicate between the sentimentalist and the rationalist traditions. We saw that for Kant virtue is *fortitudo moralis*, or something like concern for principle or rectitude. Now it may well be that he overemphasizes this at the expense of the Humean, social virtues. But can the sentimental tradition make any room for it—and if not, is this not a serious deficiency? In our motivational systems as I have described them, what place can there be for a concern for duty or principle as such? In the story as we have it, to recognize something such as honesty as a duty or principle is indeed to be concerned about it, but not to be concerned about it *because* it is a duty or principle. Yet isn't just this concern that which separates the principled, righteous person from the rest?

These questions might be put as a prelude to scepticism about the entire quasi-realist construction of Chapter 3. They might insinuate the need to think of 'X is a duty' as a robust *fact*: one that once we notice it is supposed to motivate us, and does so if we are principled, but not otherwise. But this would be unwarranted, for the questions can be answered quite well from within the quasi-realist framework. The key will be to explain the distinctive cast of mind of the 'man of principle' without regarding him as motivated by a different set of facts from the rest of us. I should say instead that the man of principle finds a certain set of *sayings* important: important enough to conclude deliberation. We start out, let us suppose, concerned not to lie. But my concern may fall short of that of others. I might regard lying as regrettable, without supposing that it terminates discussion if we find that a course of action would involve a lie. You, on the other hand, find it shocking even to think of such a course. You say things like 'I am sorry, with me it is a principle' as a way of communicating this. It is not that you are sensitive to a new and different (Moorean) fact, when I am not. It is that once you have found an application for the terms 'duty' or 'principle', practical deliberation has stopped for you, but perhaps not for me. Whether this rectitude is admirable or simplistic and bigoted will then depend upon the case.

4. HARE'S VERSION

One of the most influential neo-Kantian defences of the power of reason in moral philosophy is that of the British moral philosopher R. M. Hare. Hare sets himself to oppose what he calls intuitionism in ethics, or the 'appeal to principles thought to be self-evident'.[21] Equally, he criticizes theories that, without invoking self-evident principles, still hope for a method of 'reflective equilibrium' whereby all our concerns are brought together into some kind of coherent shape, without it being clear in advance just which ones might have to give way to others in order of importance. In such a method, much favoured by many theorists of ethics, all principles are nudged into their final form by pressures from others, and this process of mutual accommodation eventually produces a system that commends itself to the author and supposedly to everyone. Hare's reaction is that such a method is at best apt for producing undefended dogma. He contrasts it with the need for a 'secure method of reasoning' or a way of providing 'rational moral arguments'. And this, he believes, he can provide.

The outlines of his approach are twofold. First, in line with the stress on the practical function of ethics that we have already defended, we see ethics as essentially prescriptive: a matter of telling us what to do.

[21] Hare in Douglas Seanor and N. Fotion, eds., *Hare and Critics* (Oxford: Oxford University Press, 1988), 292.

Second, however, the prescriptive function is subject to a logical constraint of universalizability. This in turn is satisfied only by some version of impersonal and impartial practical reasoning. The basic idea behind universalizability is that we strip out from moral reasoning anything that remains intrinsically apt to bias us towards our first-person, local interests. Any practical considerations that favour me or us or ours against any others, belong to egocentric reason (Hume's 'language of self-love'); only those that refer impartially to the well-being of people in general are admissible (again, reminiscent of Hume's 'common point of view'). Hare's constraint obviously bears this affinity to Hume, but also a close affinity with Kant's insistence that moral maxims are those that can consistently be willed to be universal law, determining the actions of all people.

It is crucial here to notice two different dimensions of 'universalizability'. The first is a formal notion, but the second is a substantive (and not very plausible) restriction on the content of a morality. Consider the following progression:

(1) I owe special obligations to my brother (mother, child, tribe, group, etc.);
(2) Everyone owes special obligations to her brother (mother, etc.).

The move here strips out mention of 'me'. If we use (2) to defend (1) we are appealing to a purely general principle. If (1) is expanded to define a 'communitarian' or tribal morality, or an identity politics that sharply separates duty to insiders from duty to outsiders, it can still be defended as an instance of (2): everyone, the principle says, has that duty to whomsoever is related to her as an insider.

Some versions of what is called 'particularism' in ethics may deny that we have to defend (1) by appealing to (2). They hold that particular obligations can properly be claimed to apply to me (or us, or me here now) without any implicit or tacit appeal to a general principle. They may instead appeal, as in Chapter 2, to the phenomenology of deliberation. For such a theorist, as we there put it, ethics touches ground in what I am to do, here and now in some specific situation. What others do, or what I am to do in other situations, is of less concern or no concern. A universalist (as I shall call him) holds by contrast that any proposition such as (1) requires defence from a universal principle such as (2).[22]

---

[22] This is the real debate between particularism and universalism. It is the question of whether deliberation and reflection, practical reasoning, is always a matter of bringing universal principles to bear on particular situations. This is not the question of how

But now notice the crucial fact that, although universal, (2) is still what is sometimes called agent-relative, and that I shall call *partial*. For any subject, it singles out some persons specially related to that subject, as recipients of special obligations from the subject. To apply (1) to my own case, I need to single out my brother, or mother, or tribe, or whatever, because these are the people to whom I have the special relations that, on this morality, generate special obligations. An *impartial* morality would be one that acknowledges no such special obligations, or at least none that cannot be derived in some other way from equal and symmetrical relations of obligation holding between human beings 'as such'. Kant's enlightenment morality was at least largely impartial in this sense; modern communitarianism reverts to older, potentially tribal, partial morality. Utilitarianism is impartial: in the famous formula, everyone counts for one and nobody for more than one. And we may detect a drive to impartiality in the privilege Hume gives to the common point of view: a view that is impartial between the claims of me and mine or you and yours.

It is easy to confuse the requirement of universalism—the requirement that things like (1) are defended by principles like (2)—with a requirement of impartiality. But they are very different. To remove partiality, we would need to remove the feature that to apply the principle to myself I would need to know how others stand to me, for instance as brother, or fellow-citizen, or whatever.

In spite of the authority of the Enlightenment, it may be doubted whether pure impartiality is a possible ideal. As many writers have stressed, our everyday moralities are firmly rooted in the myriad special relationships that determine the moral status others have for us: the weight we give to their claims on us. Everyone acknowledges, for example, that the fact I have given someone a promise, or the fact that she is my daughter, gives her special claims on me. Histories of intimacy, kinship, expectations, all give rise to special loyalties and ties, and all these shape our natural conceptions of how we ought to behave to each other. They tell us what to expect, where 'expect' is a morally loaded term: not to come up to the expectations is to fall short.

Hare has not seen it like this. He interprets the requirement of uni-

---

complex the universal principles themselves may be (it is the question of whether there is a universal quantifier involved, not of how complex the predicate may be over which we quantify). 'Never lie' is universal, but so is 'never lie unless . . .', provided the dots can eventually be filled in. A true particularist will deny that the dots can be filled in, and hence deny that universal principles are even implicitly involved in practical reasoning. The problem then is to give an alternative account of deliberation and reflection. I return to this in Chapter 9.

versalizability strongly enough to rule out partial moralities. He believes that the requirement by itself can be interpreted to impose a strictly impartial utilitarian ethic.

This may just have been a mistake. But it may be that Hare has simply legislated away the possibility of partial moralities. If morality, by definition, contains only universalizable principles, and if partial practical codes contain other principles, such as 'Everyone care about your countrymen, and don't care about anyone else', then by definition these are not moralities. But this is just a verbal manœuvre, for the question would be what is *wrong* with the partial codes, not whether we define the world 'morality' so as not to include them.

Thus, consider injunctions such as the following: 'Everyone should be especially concerned to cultivate his or her own garden'; 'Everyone ought to look after his or her own family first.' These have a hybrid nature. On the one hand, they are universal—after all, they are addressed to everyone. Someone promoting them may have the sensible idea that the world would go better, on the whole, if people followed them. Certainly a world goes better if everyone looks after his or her garden than it does if everyone tries to cultivate everyone's garden. So we have a general, utilitarian argument for some of these hybrid injunctions. But the world in which people are following these injunctions is one in which their own low-level practical reasonings give special weight to their own gardens or their own families, and are in this sense partial. The idea is that, when deciding whether something is an eligible moral maxim, we have to look in universal terms at the nature of the world in which everybody is subject to it (reminiscently of Kant, of course), but the injunctions that then commend themselves may have first-person asymmetries built into them.

Hare himself thus defends a two-level approach to morality in which at a critical, theoretical level maxims are accepted because of their universal (which here tends to mean, impartial, utilitarian) virtues, although the maxims themselves have a partial form. Critics are apt to worry that the upshot is unstable: how am I to know on any occasion whether I am allowed to pursue a private or restricted set of goals, or whether I should be thinking about the consequences of my actions in an impartial way? In everyday life I may suppose that my own circle and their interests are best served if I pursue some competitive or aggressive course, for example, although general utility would be better served if I did not. Which kind of thought ought to prevail? We here return to the arguments of Chapter 2. There I urged that there was nothing unstable or indefensible in someone occupying a role, such as that of a referee, while at the same time reserving a place for

consequentialist understanding of the point of his role. The consequentialist thoughts secure the value of the role, and come in at best on
rare emergency occasions to moderate his single-minded occupancy of
the role.

But consequentialist reasoning can itself be entirely partial: the
agent may only care that games are good for his inner circle, not good
for humanity or sentient life in general. Why then should a person
acknowledge the authority of the higher-level universal reasoning?
The practitioners of local moralities may shrug off the interests of discounted groups: they are not impressed by the thought that, taken
across all humans at all times, their principles have bad effects, for they
are only concerned with the restricted circle. In such a world my neighbour's weeds are his concern, my own weeds matter to me, but the
quantity of weeds in general is nobody's concern.

To focus this a little, let us consider a character whom we can call
Citizen. This is someone whose concern is wholly taken up with doing
the best for a restricted group, which we can call his Tribe. He regards
the rest of the world either with indifference, or perhaps in competitive terms, so that on the whole someone else doing badly only moves
him with the strategic reflection that perhaps now he and his Tribe can
do better as a result.

Suppose Citizen enters a conversation with someone from outside
who is competing with him for some goods. Suppose that impartial
reasoning has failed, and that the self-centred nature of Citizen's value
system has to be put on the table. So Citizen says that it is better, he
believes, that he gets the goods, just because that makes *him* better off.
Suppose his partner in the conversation reciprocates with the same
kind of reasoning. We now face the situation that Hume calls a 'contradiction'. Common ground has disappeared, and we have nothing
but the conflict of self-interest; the language these two are using is not
apt for solving the conflict, but merely expresses it. Now suppose Hare
or Hume argues, as they well might, that it is part of the point and purpose of *any* language used to express practical reasoning that it enables
conversations like this to go forward, providing a common vocabulary
in which the competing parties can frame their dispute. When one side
says 'It is good that I get the benefit', the 'It is good that . . .' pretends
to express the common point of view. But if in reality it does not,
because it means only 'It is good for me that I get the benefit', then its
apparent standing is betrayed. Each side is reduced to putting forward
their egocentric claims. The point is that if all practical language is, as
it were, used up in advancing the biased claim, conversation has come
to a halt. (Notice once more that this point is independent of how large

the Tribe, or the set of persons to whose interests Citizen gives priority, is. It is just that the smaller the set, the more often this impasse will occur.)

What we are approaching is a reason not for a possibly parochial or regrettable fact about our language or our concepts, but a more authentically logical claim about the constraints on any language apt for discussing this kind of situation—any ethical language. The idea is that we can derive the requirement of impartiality from a requirement that ethical language be suitable for mutual application in this kind of competitive situation. But we should notice that the impasse is not final. The egocentric parties can bargain with each other. They each recognize the other as an obstacle to their own claim, but it does not follow that the way round the obstacle is a version of the war of all against all. Bargaining may bring about a peaceable solution. But in such bargaining the other has the status of a nuisance, something to be bought off: there is no substitution of collective interest for personal interest. The needs or interests of the other are recognized only in so far as they need to be managed: bought off or deflected from interference with one's own needs. There is no ascent to a common point of view, but only to a desire to avoid outright war.

The difference is starkly illustrated when those whose interests we ignore cannot come to bargain. Suppose I am aware that in an actual or potential conversation with some class of beings, I will eventually have to acknowledge that my only concerns are for me and mine. My last word, as it were, is going to be something like 'because I am a Greek/a man/white/a citizen . . . *and you are not*'. Well brought up as I am, I expect to feel some discomfort here. Were we to confront our children's children, after we have used up all the planet's natural resources, we might all feel a little uncomfortable. Acknowledging partiality is not pleasant when confronted with the earnest appeal to impartial justice on behalf of those who have been excluded or discounted.

Is it a requirement of reason that I should conduct my life so that, were such a conversation to take place, I should not feel the discomfort? In the real world, people often get round the problem simply by refusing to imagine the conversation at all ('It's no use discussing with them' or even 'They wouldn't understand'). I don't anticipate being actually confronted by my remote descendants whose lives will be impoverished because I and mine squander the world's resources; if I am a Greek I can live my life without having to justify my conduct to barbarians; if white, to blacks; if male, to females.

Once more, of course, all, or almost all, moral theorists are agreed that *decent* people will not shelter behind the actual absence of the discounted group at the conversation. We ought to feel the pressure to behave as though the hypothetical tribunal, at which such groups have a voice, were a real tribunal. The argument between Hume and Smith on the one hand, and Kantians such as Hare on the other, concerns only the source of this pressure.

Citizen, like us, will know that there could be conversations in which he cannot make an appeal that his partner could be expected to share. There will be conversations in which the attempt to find a mutually agreed standpoint falters. He might know that there could easily arise circumstances in which something has to be done about that. If the persons who are discounted actually confront him with the demand for impartiality, then he faces a *political* attack on his preference for himself and his, and negotiating that attack will require something more than the response 'because it's mine'. But of course such a political challenge may never arise: in the case of the real dispossessed, or the future generations, we are safe, and their silence allows our comfort. We can press our advantage without acknowledging to ourselves or anybody else that this is what we are doing.

The second aspect of the common point of view that I distinguished in Hume was civility, or the enterprise of finding common ground from which to discuss practical issues with conversational partners.[23] In conversation we try to do better than naked egoism, and the reason is obvious: we have to appeal to concerns of the partner if we want the partner to throw himself behind whatever practical stance we are promoting. The problem here is that there are persons with whom we have no actual conversation, and this motivation for finding common ground then lapses. Adam Smith would say, and Hare would say, and I agree, that we ought not to shelter behind the *de facto* lack of representation; we *ought* to have a 'man within the breast' representing the absent people without. When we do we belong to the party of humanity. Unquestionably, the disposition to think of our relation with those who are outside the circle as if they were within it is commendable: things go better when people are like that. Someone who shelters behind not actually having to conduct the conversation is what we always knew he was: partial, selfish, perhaps a little blind; uncivil in his dealings with outsiders, defective in the finer sentiments of benevolence, or the finer feelings of justice. But why irrational?

---

[23] This kind of thought has been reinvented by Jürgen Habermas. See, for instance, *The Theory of Communicative Action*, trans. Thomas McCarthy (Boston, Mass.: Beacon Press, 1987).

One device is to try to 'catch out' Citizen with reasoning of the following kind. You, it is said, advance your concerns as reasons for
action. So you, to be consistent, must acknowledge that persons' concerns *are* reasons for action; that is, you must allow the propriety of
reasoning based on concern. But, in ignoring or discounting the concerns of others, you are in effect denying this; you are therefore caught
in a kind of inconsistency.[24]

To assess this clearly let us focus on Citizen's conversation with a
mirror-image or *doppelgänger*, another person of dominantly self-referential preferences. Citizen thinks it would be better if he got the
money, because he wants to send his child to school, let us say, and the
doppelgänger thinks it would be better if he did, so that he can send his
child to school. Now Citizen of course recognizes his *doppelgänger*'s
state of mind; he recognizes, unless he is incapable of interpreting
others at all, that his double is advocating for himself just what he,
were he in the double's position, would also be advocating for himself. And he resists it with just the same claim on behalf of himself. But
this is only saying that he recognizes universally that peoples' indexical concerns are reasons for *them*. It does not show him recognizing
that another persons' indexical concerns are reasons for *him*, nor that
they are reasons for all. In the same way a reasonably intelligent
Carolina game fan can recognize herself, in one sense, in the Duke fan.
She understands why the Duke fan takes a Duke success as a reason
for elation; she does not, as it were, regard the Duke fan as entirely
alien, or at least not because of this. (Some fans—we might call them
fanatical fans—might. They think that supporting Duke is virtually
unintelligible. But this is a syndrome with which I am not concerned,
although the psychology, and the degrees of self-deception it
involves, is not uncommon.) Yet understanding the Duke mentality
puts no pressure on a Carolina fan to absorb this concern, and herself
to take a Duke success as any kind of reason at all for elation. In fact,
in such a competitive set-up, it is just the reverse.

We might return to invoking a 'two-levels' approach here. We
might say that the intelligent fan is secure in her personal sensibility,
but that she can, if she understands these matters, retreat to a universal point of view, from which she can see that it is all right for there to
be game fans; that is, it is good for human happiness that there should
exist this kind of partiality. If she runs this argument successfully, she

[24] See, for instance, Christine Korsgaard, *The Sources of Normativity* (Cambridge:
Cambridge University Press, 1996), 142–3.

can have a stable, reflexive comfort with her own partisanship. After all, without it, the enterprise of College basketball, with all the pleasures it apparently brings, would wither. Similarly, Citizen might attain an equilibrium by reflecting that moderate doses of egoistic competition make the world go round. Both he and his double are then making perfectly proper claims; it is just unfortunate that they conflict and that one of them will lose out. But it is perfectly in order for him to make sure that it is not he who loses. My response to this is that it might be like this, and one might become comfortable with one's own partisanship through such universal and impartial reflections. But there is still no argument that it *has* to be like this: that is, no proof that it is a requirement of reason that we only indulge such partisanship as can be protected by such a reflection. Perhaps people who are *more* partisan than such reflections justify are selfish, tribal, jingoistic, small-minded, and the rest; but it is still not demonstrated that their vice is in any way akin to self-contradiction or in any way contrary to the dictates of reason.

The position I would urge can be characterized as falling between that of Hare, and that of communitarians who are entirely happy with Citizen. In his polemic against the component of ethics that he thinks of as 'morality', or roughly the deontological part of ethics that concentrates upon obligations, and also against universal consequentialism or utilitarianism, Bernard Williams can be interpreted as mounting an escape bid from the *requirement* that one's behaviour bear the impartial scrutiny. We want, as it were, to be Citizen with a good conscience. Myself, I cannot feel comfortable with this ethical recommendation. I do feel uncomfortable when I have to contemplate hypothetical conversations in which I could only present myself as unconcerned about common ground, and in which my final recourse would have to be some version of 'because it is mine'. I also feel moderately comfortable with this discomfort. I think I would become a slightly worse person if I lost it. When I contemplate those politicians in whom such sentiments appear to be unknown, I cannot feel that they are better than me, although I also cannot see how to change them by pure reason. But I wish I could change them somehow.

In real human history, one of the few bright threads is genuine concern for the plight of the dispossessed. In amongst the brutal patriotisms of tribe, nation, class, and gender there does exist a voice of humanity: the abolition of slavery, the extension of suffrage, the self-restraint that comes from not pressing the actual inequalities of power too far, are all heartening enough. We are, fortunately, susceptible to the thought that there is something blameworthy about claiming for ourselves what we would not allow to others. We want to seem fair.[25]

So I am not advocating that we diminish the importance or centrality of the drive to impartiality inherent in universal prescriptivism. I only think it important to recognize its source. The concern for common ground, like any other concern, is just that: the contingent and fragile result of our sentimental natures.

5. THE KNAVE AGAIN

In possibly the most elaborate defence of the Kantian opposition to Hume in recent years, Christine Korsgaard undertakes to show that the reason we have to go beyond Hume and Smith is metaphysical as much as moral, and derives from our conception of ourselves as deliberating agents. We discuss in the next chapter whether there is a metaphysical problem for Hume and the sentimentalist tradition in the facts of deliberation. I shall argue that Hume is actually better placed than Kant to understand the empirical distinctions that are needed. But first we must tackle the moral problem, and finish with the knave.

Korsgaard presents us with a 'slightly more attractive version' of Hume's sensible knave.[26] This is a lawyer who believes Hume's theory of the moral sentiments, and finds herself in a situation in which her deceased client has made a valid will, leaving all the money to a worthless nephew. But she can suppress this will in favour of a previous but superseded will that left the money to medical research. As with many such scenarios in moral philosophy, there is supposedly no doubt that consequential reasoning favours medical research, the nephew is irredeemable, there are no side-effects, no chance of being found out, and so on. This alone makes reflection on such cases highly unreliable, for we are not necessarily any good at taking a morality evolved for real cases and recognizing how it should be applied to magical ones (this echoes the point that we cannot just leave our natures behind, that I made about artificial prisoners' dilemma situations in the last chapter). Still, Korsgaard's concern is not to argue that the Humean lawyer will make a bad decision in such circumstances, but that she is, as it were, insufficiently *fortified* against

---

[25] Robert E. Goodin, *Motivating Political Morality* (Oxford: Blackwell, 1992).
[26] *Sources of Normativity*, 86–7.

doing so. She can reflect that she hates injustice, and that she does so because of the generally deleterious effects of actions such as the one she is contemplating. But *this* case will have no bad effects. That is how it is specified. So, says Korsgaard, 'it is almost inconceivable that believing this will have no effect on her disapproval itself'; 'Her own feeling of disapproval may seem to her to be, in this case, poorly grounded, and therefore in a sense irrational.' Korsgaard rightly says that the issue is not whether, as a matter of disposition, the lawyer may find that suppressing the will brings on too much self-hatred or humility. It is rather that she does not believe that these feelings are well-grounded: if she could cure herself of these feelings this is what she would do.

So the structure is that the Humean lawyer should approach this practical situation in one way, but common-sense morality suggests that it should be approached in another. Specifically, the Humean lawyer, even if motivated to prove the valid will, should feel unsettled—perhaps a bit of a fool, even a 'cully of her integrity'—in doing so. Whereas a Kantian lawyer would be fortified by confidence in her own rectitude. And we are invited to sympathize with the Kantian lawyer, whose principles are not undermined by reflection on their origin.

So the key question is why the Humean lawyer should wish she could cure herself of her disposition to hate injustice—the disposition that is causing her to hate it even in this case, where the injustice will do good. We might have found this question difficult had we not been through the discussions of the previous chapters, stressing the real variety of human concern, and the artificiality of attempts to reduce it all to 'self-interest' or 'utility' or indeed to any exclusively forward-looking reasoning. Hume was a master of this. He never counsels that all virtuous reasoning should be forward-looking. Indeed, one of his foremost examples of a virtue is gratitude, which is entirely backward-looking, since it is because someone *has* done you a service that you now owe them gratitude. Among the motivational states that Hume would approve of in a lawyer will be the desire to act as her role demands; respect for the wishes of the deceased; and the pride or at least peace of mind that comes of acting only in ways that stand up to public scrutiny. Hume is himself a fairly conservative thinker, and it is very far from his philosophy to counsel any grubby opportunism, or even ungrubby opportunism from benevolent motives. So why does Korsgaard nevertheless think that the Humean lawyer is insufficiently fortified against fraud?

Presumably the thought is that the lawyer should be against (sentiments favouring) the application of rules in circumstances in which the specific benefits, for whose achievement the rules are designed, will not accrue. She should wish she had a more sensitive or finely-tuned sensibility, which dislikes injustice and feels guilt at having anything to do with it in the cases where it does good, but feels no such feelings in other cases. But there is no reason to think that this represents a useful or possible ideal. The referee does not wish away his disposition to ignore the benefit to the crowd of a false line call. The police are not irrational for having a disposition to enforce speeding penalties regardless of whether the speeding was on an occasion safe, and the penalty will do more harm than good.

It is worth repeating why not. Except in philosophical fairyland it is hard to know when excessive speed is safe, but then the same is true of executing invalid wills. The methodology here is one of saying: 'Abstract from all the normal consequences, and concerns and probabilities of consequences, and consider an action X in itself. Then the Humean (or other target of the thought-experiment) gives result A, but the right result is result B.' But such a methodology is very doubtful. For a start, we may think we have abstracted from normal contexts, without actually succeeding in doing so. It is like saying: 'I want you to abstract away from the fact that you are male/female. Now . . .' You cannot obey the command just like that. Lying and executing invalid wills inspire a kind of symbolic horror, and this horror will remain even if there do exist cases where you clearly ought to lie or execute the will. There is nothing to regret about motivational features that exist and are encouraged because they themselves promote the ends of human beings, and here the pressure towards honest application of the rules is just such a feature.

The case is structurally the same as that of the referee of the game who is also capable of reflecting on the point of game-playing. There we found reason to approve of the Humean solution, that apart from emergencies, there is nothing to admire in the referee whose automatic application of the rules is disrupted by thoughts about the general good. On the contrary, since game-playing and its benefits could not exist if referees were to do this, we cannot admire a referee who does so, and no referee can expect the admiration of others if he does so himself. Of course, Hume is wise enough to realize that when the disparity between general rules and public utility becomes great enough, we do face genuine conflict, and the rules may have to give way. This is the case of Sir Francis Drake mentioned in Chapter 2. Hume's own example is the governor of the town who does not 'make any scruple of burning the suburbs, when they facilitate the approach of the enemy'.[27] This is in spite of what he elsewhere calls the 'inflexible rules necessary to support general peace and order in society'.[28] His solution is the correct one. The point is that emergencies demand emergency measures, but Korsgaard's lawyer faces no emergency, and she need not regret her sense of being governed by inflexible rules.

It is, incidentally, useful to ask what a more deontological solution to the problem of the sacrifice of the suburbs or Drake's referee would be. Should the Kantian remain staunchly on the side of the rules of property or bowls? If so, we must ask whether we would actually want someone inflexible about such a matter to govern the town or conduct the game in times of emergency. In fact, in everyday life, property rules often give way to the public good: compulsory purchase orders compel people to sell out for the sake of reservoirs, motorways, and so on.

Korsgaard may well ask what we can do about it if the lawyer does not feel happy about her obedience to the rule of law. Here we are indeed faced with the same problem as that posed by the sensible knave, and we have already met the right answer. If the lawyer is tempted to transgress, her sentiments are regrettable, and she will likely be found out, and will not be able to bear the gaze of her accusers. She may, of course, feel victimized by this, but we may or may not sympathize with such a feeling, depending on the circumstances. We have already met the state of mind of those who reject the demands of ethics, and one variety of this malaise certainly can arise at this point. We imagine here someone who has been failed by the social order: once more, the cully of his or her integrity. Perhaps alone she stands in line, respects promises and property, while all around her people doing neither profit, and profit at her expense. Someone who loses out too badly by being dutiful can easily start to feel a victim, and this bitter feeling may erode her enthusiasm for continuing to do what duty requires. People can resent what they acknowledge to be their duty, and can chafe against it, just as they can rejoice in it and take pride in their rectitude. Our emotional lives are not one-dimensional. Sometimes chafing may be quite reasonable. A person may, too late, realize that their conscience uselessly stood between them and normal good things of life, for it takes a specific social order to establish harmony between rectitude and success. Morality is, among other things, a social achievement.

---

[27] *Essays Moral, Political, and Literary,* ed. T. H. Green and T. H. Grose (London: Longman, Green, 1875), ii. 13, 'Of Passive Obedience'.
[28] *Enquiry Concerning the Principles of Morals,* Appendix 3, p. 305.

We have been looking at the robust moral standing of the ꜱꭒ𝗆
Smith/Hume mechanism whereby our purely personal concerns
become infused with respect for the common point of view. I have been
praising our susceptibility to the voice of others, while at the same time
refusing to see that susceptibility as anything other than a facet of our
sentimental natures. It has no Kantian authority, nor any authority
derived purely from the nature of moral language, nor any inevitable
tendency to align with our own good, otherwise conceived. In this
sense, it stands on its own feet.

Korsgaard presents her discussion of the sensible knave in the midst
of a prolonged explanation of how a theory derived from Kant suc-
ceeds in solving 'the normative question', where the contrasting sentimentalist tradition fails. So we now turn to ask what the normative
question is; how the Humean tradition fails to answer it; and how the
mechanisms the Kantian approach brings on succeed. We see in the
next chapter that there is room for bafflement, and then doubt, over all
three elements.

8

Self-Control, Reason, and Freedom

Goodness-against-the-grain simply made me feel mean, hypocritical and servile, so that Goodness only resulted in a weight on my conscience; a weight often heavier than if I had been Bad on purpose; and nearly as heavy, as if I had been Bad by accident.

For the most muddling thing of all was that the Badnesses you did by accident were what made you feel most guilty . . . The grown-ups pretended that it was what you did on purpose that mattered. This was, and is, quite untrue. No one ever regrets doing a Badness on purpose. For instance, if you were rude or disobedient to Miss *X*, a governess you rightly despised, you felt rather pleased with yourself afterwards . . . But if you were unkind or rude by mistake to someone you loved—Ah, then you just wished you were dead.

Gwen Raverat, Period Piece

1 . SELF-CONTROL: HUME-FRIENDLY REASON

In Chapter 2 we came across Dürer's version of Plato's famous image of the charioteer.[1] In this picture, reason, the charioteer, controls the potentially unruly horses of desire. The model sets up the classic way of thinking of ourselves as self-controlling, rational decision-makers. We are aware that in the cockpit of our emotions there are unruly forces, but with calm and care we can usually control them. Here is the classic dualism of heart and head, desire and reason, with reason in control so long as things are going well. Apollo, in the light, rules Dionysus, in the dark.

Plato's model was dramatically turned upside down by Hume. 'Reason is, and ought only to be the slave of the passions, and can never pretend to any other office than to serve and obey them.'[2] He adds provocatively that:

---

[1] Plato, *Phaedrus*, 246a–b, 253c ff.   [2] *Treatise*, II. iii. 3, p. 415.

'Tis not contrary to reason to prefer the destruction of the whole world to the scratching of my finger. 'Tis not contrary to reason for me to chuse my total ruin, to prevent the least uneasiness of an Indian or person wholly unknown to me. 'Tis as little contrary to reason to prefer even my own acknowledg'd lesser good to my greater, and have a more ardent affection for the former than the latter.[3]

Hume replaces Plato's rationalistic picture with the view that our courses are set by our passions or concerns. Reason can inform us of the facts of the case, features of the situations in which we have to act. And it can inform us which actions are likely to cause which upshots. But beyond that, it is silent. The imprudent person, or the person of unbridled lust, malevolence, or sloth is bad, of course. We may even call them unreasonable, but in a sense that Hume considers improper.[4] For, more accurately, it is not their reason that is at fault, but their passions. Even the person who apparently fails to adapt means to ends is not necessarily unreasonable. Suppose I value having or even intend to have a clear head tomorrow, and I recognize that the means to that end is to leave the party now. But I fail to do so. I act as if I prefer the outcome {stay on, dull head} to the outcome {leave now, clear head}. I prefer my lesser good. There are things wrong with me, but is my reason at fault? I am perhaps imprudent, foolish, weak-willed (but after all, I may also be good fun to be with). Perhaps if I have been talking up the value of a clear head, then I am also annoyingly fickle or inconstant, or even difficult to interpret. All these are doubtless serious defects. But, according to Hume, they are defects of will or passion rather than reason. Obviously if it happens endemically, we begin to revise the interpretation of an agent as genuinely having an end. If she does not stir herself, then what we took to be her end seems not to concern her. Perhaps it is just an idle wish, scarcely even a desire. But then the fault lies with us, the interpreters, not with her, the agent. Or, if there is a fault, it may be one of self-deception: she thinks she intends a particular end, when in fact she does not, but is resigned to not achieving it.

It is quite common to see Hume described as limiting reasoning to the 'bureaucratic' or 'instrumental' reasoning, of the kind made much of by Weber.[5] This is simply inaccurate on both counts. As described, failing to adopt means to ends may be just a defect of passion for Hume. But, in addition, thinking about ends can certainly deserve the

---

[3] *Treatise*, II. iii. 3, p. 418.

[4] As well as *Treatise*, II. iii. 3, p. 414, see III. i. 1, p. 459 and III. ii. 7, p. 536.

[5] Max Weber, *The Protestant Ethic and the Spirit of Capitalism*, trans. Talcott Parsons (London: George Allen & Unwin, 1930).

title reasoning. When we deploy some concerns in order to query or criticize others, there is nothing to stop us from describing the process as one of reasoning. Hume does not make it impossible to criticize a person's ends. I can criticize your ends by deploying my values. And I can criticize some of my own ends by deploying others. Hume would make it impossible for me to criticize an end of my own only if the end represented my *sole* object of value or desire, with everything else valued or desired as mere means to it. But we are not single-minded like that. And in so far as someone approximates to the description, then Hume seems right: they would have lost any stand-point from which to raise doubts about their goal, since it represents the only currency of evaluation they can use.

Hume's point is not a definitional one. It is not an ordinary-language point about the scope of the word 'reason'. It does not affect his thesis that we often describe people who are swayed by the wrong passions as 'unreasonable'. The word is a fairly general term of abuse. We are particularly prone to describe people who are too passionate, particularly too quick to impatience and anger, as unreasonable (the equally awful opposing vice, of coldness or emotional detachment, is not so often described this way, presumably reflecting our fear of Dionysus). But Hume is not concerned with this usage and it does not matter to him. He has a much more important point to make. In terms I introduced in Chapter 1, he really wants to distinguish defects of input from ones of processing and hence output. Reason gives us our representation of the salient features of the situation we are in, and it gives us the ability to make further deductions and inferences about that situation. Reason's office is to represent the world to us as it is. But then, how we react to that situation, and that includes how we react to it ethically, is another matter. It is a matter of a dynamic response—the formation of passions, attitudes, policies, or inten-tions—and the most clear-sighted apprehension of the situation is no guarantee that this side is functioning well. The nature of our dynamic response shows our passionate nature, or sensibility. We typically express this structure by voicing ethical remarks, saying what is to be done, or felt, or avoided.

Just as Hume's point is not an ordinary-language point, so it is not opposed to the way we frequently present practical questions in terms of what it would be reasonable to do, or even what I would do if I were reasonable. I can ask what I would do if I were more generous, or more prudent, or included more people or more sentient life in my concerns. Similarly, I can ask what I would do if I understood my situ-ation better. Ignorance and confusion impede practical decision-making. They make us worse at doing things that it would be useful or agreeable to do better. One of our proper concerns is not to act on false premises, or without thinking through the implications of what we know. We can describe this by saying that we want to act reasonably. Furthermore, one of our concerns may be to solicit the agreement of others to what we are doing. We want our behaviour to withstand scrutiny from the common point of view, and this too can be called concern for a reasonable solution.

But if we pose practical problems in terms of 'what I would do if I were reasonable' or 'what the reasonable person would do', we should not think we have thereby got *beyond* the subjection of the will to desire and passion. 'Reasonable' here stands as a label for an admired freedom from various traits—ignorance, incapacity to understand our situation, shortsightedness, lack of concern for the common point of view. Being social, and being prudent guardians of our own interests, our concerns include avoiding decisions made only because of such defects. But here 'what I would do if I were reasonable' functions like 'what I would do if I were financially acute'. It signals a consideration or set of considerations that only affect me because of a contingent profile of concerns or desires or passions. In Kantian terms, it is fitted only to deliver hypothetical imperatives, or pieces of advice that gain their status only because they are baptized as important by our desires and passions. It will be important in subsequent sections to bear in mind that there is this use of 'reason' and its allied terms, but that using it marks no defection from the sentimentalist position. To repeat, this is because the considerations that are selected as 'reasonable' in this sense are so selected precisely through an operation of desire or a contingent profile of concern. Failing to select them would itself be a defect of sentiment, and it is because we have the concerns we do that we recommend full information, due deliberation, accommodations with others, absence of immoderate passions. I shall call this the Hume-friendly use of reason.

In fact, although modern moral philosophy is apt to be written as if Hume were unique and awful in presenting this picture of practical deliberation, he is only bringing to a head a tradition well over a century old by the time he wrote. Bacon had written of how we 'need to set affection against affection and to master one by another: even as we use to hunt beast with beast and fly bird with bird'.[6] Spinoza's

---

[6] Francis Bacon, *The Advancement of Learning*, ed. G. W. Kitchin (London: J. M. Dent, 1973), 172.

Ethics is premised on the proposition that 'an affect cannot be restrained nor removed unless by an opposed and stronger affect'. Spinoza's book culminates with the trenchant proposition: 'no one rejoices in blessedness because he restrained lusts; but, on the contrary, the power of restraining lusts arises from blessedness itself.'[7] Hume does not differ from Spinoza over this, but only takes away Spinoza's supposition that the intellect alone enjoins both knowledge and love of God. And in fact, the idea that it takes a passion or 'interest' to countervail a passion was a common theme in many moral philosophers of the seventeenth and eighteenth centuries before Hume.[8]

It is appropriate to end this section with a word of warning. There is a minor industry of trying to show that anyone, even a Humean, has to allow 'means–ends rationality', but that means–ends rationality presupposes 'ends rationality'. In other words, if it is a defect of reason to fail to adopt means to ends, then it is equally a defect of reason to fail to adopt certain ends, such as prudential or moral ends. It would be a long business to assess all these arguments, but the ones known to me trade on an interesting modal fallacy. They express the view that it is rationally compulsory to obey a means–end principle, in a proposition of the form: 'If we have the end we *must* adopt the means.' They then detach the consequent, and looking at it straight ask why must we adopt some means. Only, surely, if we not only have the end, but *must* have the end. Thus, to be rational, if I intend to hit the target with the arrow I must bend the bow. But considered by itself, why must I bend the bow? Not surely just because I *happen* to intend to hit the target—if that were all there were to it, I could just give up and walk away! No, I only must bend the bow if I must hit the target. So if the means–end principle has rationally compelling credentials, or rational 'normativity', so does the end.

In this specious reasoning, 'You must take means *M* if you have end *E*' is transformed into 'If you have end *E* you must take means *M*'. English makes the second form much more natural. Now suppose you have end *E*. Then you must take means *M*. But how could it be true that you must take means *M*, considered *tout court*, unless not only do you have end *E*, but you *must* have end *E*? So the instrumental principle presupposes that end *E* has the same 'normativity' as the means/end premise from which we started.

[7] Baruch Spinoza, *Ethics*, trans. Andrew Boyle (London: J. M. Dent, 1959), 224.
[8] The best source known to me for the history of this theme is A. O. Lovejoy, *Reflections on Human Nature*.

1. □ (if intend end, intend means) ⌉ fallacy
2. if intend end □ (intend means) ⌋
3. ∴ □ (intend end)

[reasons -transmission model]

Self-Control, Reason, and Freedom   243

This is the same reasoning as occurs in the paradox of gentle murder. By it you can prove that if you murder someone you ought to murder them. The paradox arises from the true premise: you ought, if you murder someone, murder them gently. This turns into: 'If you murder someone, then you ought to murder them gently.' Suppose you murder someone. Then by the principle, it follows that you ought to murder them gently. But if you ought to murder someone gently, then you ought to murder them. So if you murder them, then you ought to murder them.

In each case the fallacy is to misplace the modal operator, or the initial 'must' of obligation or rational compulsion. This starts out with 'wide scope': you must, if you are to be rational, obey the principle that if you intend the end you intend the means. The operator is then applied only to the consequent, and the rest follows.

2. THE KANTIAN CAPTAIN

Since I shall end up finding against him, it is important to realize how appealing Kant's views about deliberation can be made to seem. By the time Kant came to be writing about ethics, there already existed a number of reasons for discontent with sentiment-based theories of ethics.[9] The first and most fundamental had been amply expressed in the natural law tradition. Moral laws necessitate. It is not up to us whether we obey them. For them to have this status, argued the natural law tradition, they must be regarded as the structures legislated by an external, law-giving authority. Disobedience must provoke penalties and punishment. Moral laws are there to constrain natural appetite, and to show it how it may be legitimately pursued. But they could not do this if they were, as the sentimentalist tradition alleges, themselves simply the creatures of appetite.

Kant thoroughly shares this view, and indeed gives it its classic expression. Desires (which, in spite of Butler, Kant insists on lumping together as all desires for personal pleasure) cannot be the source of moral obligation. 'The maxim of self-love (prudence) merely advises; the law of morality commands.'[10] Perhaps because he thinks of all desire as fundamentally the desire for pleasure, it makes little difference to Kant whether empirical desires and inclinations are generous,

[9] Kant lectured on ethics from 1756 through to 1794. The major works all came in the decade following the introduction of the 'critical philosophy' in the *Critique of Pure Reason* (1781).

[10] *Critique of Practical Reason*, § 36.

beneficent, direct at the happiness of mankind in general, or meritori-
ous in any other way. They are 'subjective' and hence cannot be the
source of commands, of 'objectively necessary' laws to which the will
of every rational agent must conform.

By the time of the eighteenth century, however, an external lawgiver, whose commands, inevitably, were mediated through a social
structure of rulers and priests, was no longer appealing. Part of the
trouble is that such external authority works by substituting sticks
and carrots for genuine respect for its laws. We come to obey either
out of hope of gain or fear of penalties. This is just another instance of
acting from desire. It is not acting from respect for the law as such.
What enables us to do better? Kant shared the natural law tradition's
sense of the independence of law from contingent desire. And he was
deeply impressed by Rousseau's sense of a community that makes its
own law, and in which the appetites of individuals are constrained by
a general will towards the good of all. Kant also took from Rousseau
the view that a life spent in pursuit of appetite was itself slavish,
directed as if from outside. True freedom demanded self-legislation or
'obedience to a law one has prescribed for oneself'.[11] Furthermore,
Kant had sowed the seed for understanding this difficult notion in his
general metaphysics, the so-called critical philosophy. In that view,
the world of mere happenstance is structured in perception by laws
that are necessary a priori. In other words, these are laws that the
mind must impose in order for experience and theory to be possible.
They are the net through which the raw manifold of experience must
pass before it becomes perception and enters consciousness. If the
mind can do this (and thus, in some sense not to be misunderstood,
create the world as we apprehend it), then it can also legislate purely
formal laws to which practical reasoning must conform (and thus, in
some sense not to be misunderstood, create moral necessity). What
are the misunderstandings? In the empirical case, believing that we
could have created otherwise and then, for instance, the solar system
would have had a different shape. In the moral case, believing that our
wills *might* have been structured otherwise, and then the moral world
would have had a different shape. Kant believed that our legislations
work at a different level from this. But each combination tries to walk
a shaky tightrope: on the one hand is our own place as creators and
legislators, but on the other hand is the insistence that what is created
or legislated is not, therefore, contingent upon us as we happen to be.

---

[11] J. J. Rousseau, *The Social Contract*, trans. Chrisopher Betts (Oxford: Oxford
University Press, 1994), I. viii. 4.

Perhaps the best way to understand the tightrope is in terms of an a priori principle structuring interpretation, as in the interpretational turn of Chapter 3. If you tell me of intelligent creatures representing a world to themselves, then, be they human or Martian or made of silicon chips, I know a priori that they structure their world in terms of stable objects in causal relations in space and time. Similarly, perhaps, if you tell me of intelligent creatures that deliberate actions, then I similarly know a priori that they structure their reasoning in terms of the 'musts' of moral law, or The Moral Law. It's a valiant effort, but the trouble is, as we saw in the last chapter, there is little reason to believe it.

Kant understands the role of sentiment in swaying the inclinations of people. The Kantian objection only stands opposed to Hume's contention that *this is all that there is*. Reason for the Kantian is not the slave of the passions, but a motivational spring of a different kind, an independent source of a fundamentally different kind of pressure. To take up an inclination and make it our own, to acknowledge it or endorse it as a 'maxim', or legislate it as a principle governing action is, for Kant, a process to be understood in a quite different way from any that Hume gives us. It is an exercise of practical reason that should be *contrasted* with acting out of sentiment or desire. How should we understand this opposition?

We can start by presenting the rival theories of deliberation in terms of the Platonic model of a person as a ship.[12] For Hume or Smith, the ship is worked by a crew, each representing a passion or inclination or sentiment, and where the ship goes is determined by the resolution of conflicting pressures among the crew. After one voice has prevailed, various things may happen to the losers: they may be thrown overboard and lost altogether, or more likely they may remain silenced just for the occasion, or they may remain sullen and mutinous, or they may continue to have at least some effect on the ship's course. Some crew members may be more stable and durable, long-serving and forceful than others. Some, such as those labelled 'prudence' and 'industry', may largely have a second-order role, to encourage or silence other, first-order crew members, such as 'sloth' or 'gluttony'. Sometimes a ship will be manned by crews that are collectively hopeless, resulting in a vessel neither agreeable nor useful to itself or others. Other ships will be harmonious and useful, through fortunate composition of their crew members: these will be crews in which the propensities are to the gay, benevolent, temperate, industrious,

---

[12] *Republic*, Bk. VI, 487e–489b.

cheerful, hopeful, resolute. Why do we say that these are more fortunate? Because our own inclinations are to the happiness of ourselves
and others, and these are the ships with which we are therefore concerned to sail in convoy.

For Kant, so the contrast goes, there is indeed the Humean crew.
But standing above them, on the quarter-deck, there is another
voice—a voice with ultimate authority and ultimate power. This is the
Captain, the will, yourself as an embodiment of pure practical reason,
detached from all desire.[13] The Captain himself is free. But he always
stands ready to stop things going wrong with the crew's handling of
the boat. Sometimes, it seems, the happiest ship will have no crew at
all, but only a Captain, for, making surprising contact with Stoic and
Buddhist thought, Kant holds that it is only with complete independence from inclinations and desires that bliss is possible:

Inclinations themselves, as sources of needs, are so far from having an
absolute value to make them desirable for their own sake that it must rather
be the universal wish of every rational being to be wholly free from them.[14]

It is indeed not clear whether these particularly blissful ships travel
anywhere, and this is a problem that was first noticed and made much
of by contemporary critics such as Hegel.[15] In fact, in the different context of arguing against the power of pure reason, Kant himself provides a beautiful image of what seems to have gone wrong:

The light dove, cleaving the air in her free flight, and feeling its resistance,
might imagine that its flight would be still easier in empty space. It was thus
that Plato left the world of the senses . . .[16]

And, we might add, it seems to be that way that Kant's ethics leaves
the world of human concerns. Certainly the Captain is no kind of pro-
tector of the rest of the crew:

Inclination, be it good-natured or otherwise, is blind and slavish; reason,
when it is a question of morality, must not play the part of mere guardian of
the inclinations, but without regard to them, as pure practical reason it must
care for its own interest to the exclusion of all else. Even the feeling of sympathy and warmhearted fellow-feeling, when preceding the consideration of
what is duty . . . is burdensome even to right-thinking persons, confusing

---

[13] *Groundwork of the Metaphysic of Morals*, § 36 (412), p. 80.

[14] Ibid. § 64 (428), p. 95. Cf. also *Critique of Practical Reason*, § 118.

[15] G. W. F. Hegel, *Phenomenology of Spirit*, trans. A. V. Miller (Oxford: Oxford University Press, 1977), 365–409.

[16] *Critique of Pure Reason*, trans. Norman Kemp Smith (London: Macmillan, 1963), Introduction, A5/B9, p. 47.

their considered maxims and creating the wish to be free from them and subject only to law-giving reason.[17]

The Captain is presented not only as the embodiment of reason but also, and equivalently for Kant, as the representative of the demands of morality. Kant thought that your status as a moral agent was entirely determined by the authority of the Captain within. The nature of the blind and slavish crew is no part of the measure, for any empirical inclination is 'burdensome'. Whether he is always so embarrassingly negative about the feelings and other important dimensions of human or Humean merits—benevolence, friendship, family ties, prudence, gaiety—is a matter of controversy among Kantians. In some versions, he maintains friendly relations with the crew, even occasionally inviting one of them up to the quarter-deck, and giving him a small moral medal or 'battle citation' for being a help to the Captain. Crew members that get moral medals might derivatively be called virtues, and ships with no other crew members on board will pursue good courses, under the masterful eye of the Captain.[18] But quite clearly you only score points in Kant's moral dimension if you do things not because it goes with the grain to do them, but rather because, since it goes against the grain, principle and conscience have stepped in to *make* you do them. For Kant moral worth measures your *rectitude*, your capacity to act on principle, or out of a sense of duty. Kant loved it, but others have doubted whether we should admire rectitude all that much.[19]

Conforming to Rousseau's picture, the Captain is himself self-legislating, his own master and slave.[20] When the Captain is in control, the ship runs freely. When he is not, it is 'heteronomous', swayed by its given desires and inclinations.

Thus the Kantian Captain. He is a peculiar figure, a dream—or nightmare—of pure, authentic self-control. He certainly appeals to our

[17] *Critique of Practical Reason*, § 118. Kant sometimes speaks less slightingly of mere inclinations, for instance when admiring the Gospel command to love your neighbour gladly, i.e. with the right passions and inclinations. Commentators differ about the relative significance of such conflicting passages.

[18] Derivatively, because, as described in Chapter 2, for Kant the essence of virtue is *fortitudo moralis*, or strength of will in conforming to the categorical imperative.

[19] Bernard Williams, 'Morality and the Emotions', in *Problems of the Self* (Cambridge: Cambridge University Press, 1973), also 'Persons, Character, and Morality', in *Moral Luck* (Cambridge: Cambridge University Press, 1981). Kantian replies include Barbara Herman, *The Practice of Moral Judgement* (Cambridge, Mass.: Harvard University Press, 1993), and Marcia W. Baron, *Kantian Ethics Almost Without Apology* (Ithaca, N.Y.: Cornell University Press, 1995).

[20] Kant, *Groundwork*, §§ 70–2 (431–3), pp. 98–100.

wish to be, ourselves, entirely the masters of our own lives, immune in all important respects from the gifts or burdens of our internal animal natures, or of our temperaments as they are formed by contingent nature, socialization, and external surrounds. Context-free, non-natural, and a complete stickler for duty, perhaps the Kantian self is nothing but the sublimation of a patriarchal, authoritarian fantasy.[21] But he is also democratic, in that each Kantian Captain is in essence identical with any other, for guidance by the Captain is the birthright not only of human beings, but of any rational creature capable of agency.

How does the presence of the Captain generate any kind of freedom? Kant thought that all events in space and time, and therefore all the events that make up a human biography, are subject to the law of causation. But the Captain, apparently, is not. True to this, the Captain is reticent to the point of being beyond scrutiny altogether. That is, we can never tell whether he is operating. When he is operating, what Kant calls the 'causality of freedom' determines our actions. But Kant held that the causality of freedom is not empirically detectable:

> The real morality of actions, their merit or guilt, even that of our own conduct, thus remains entirely hidden from us. Our imputations can refer only to the empirical character. How much of this character is ascribable to the pure effect of freedom, how much to mere nature, that is, to faults of temperament for which there is no responsibility, or to its happy constitution, can never be determined.[22]

This shows that our sheer *experience* of choice cannot be an issue between Kant and the sentimentalists, since we might feel ourselves to be deliberating and choosing with great rationality and then acting out of concern for impartial duty, yet really not be doing so. This alone makes it wrong to use the feel or phenomenology of deliberation into an argument for the Kantian picture. For all we can ever tell either from within or from without, deliberation may go on in the same way

---

[21] Important works in this groundswell of opinion against Kant include Nel Noddings, *Caring: A Feminine Approach to Ethics and Moral Education* (Berkeley, Calif.: University of California Press, 1984); Iris Marion Young, 'Impartiality and the Civic Public', in Seyla Benhabib and Drucilla Cornell, eds., *Feminism as Critique: On the Politics of Gender* (Minneapolis, Minn.: University of Minnesota Press, 1988), 60–3; Margaret Urban Walker, 'Feminism, Ethics, and the Question of Theory', *Hypatia*, 7 (1992), 23–38; Seyla Benhabib, *Situating the Self*; Joan Tronto, *Moral Boundaries* (New York: Routledge, 1993); Virginia Held, *Feminist Morality* (Chicago, Il.: University of Chicago Press, 1993); Diana Meyers, *Subjection and Subjectivity* (New York: Routledge, 1994); Annette Baier, *Moral Prejudices* (Cambridge, Mass.: Harvard University Press, 1995). Possibly the best and most focused treatment is found in Margaret Urban Walker, *Moral Understandings: A Feminist Study in Ethics* (New York: Routledge, 1998).

[22] *Critique of Pure Reason*, A551/B579, p. 475.

when the Captain is asleep, or taking a long furlough. The Kantian Captain is beyond empirical discovery. He may be a nightmare figure, but at least he is a self-effacing nightmare figure.

We have to be careful of caricature. Clearly, if Kant thought we can begin to understand the difference between acting from duty and not doing so, or acting freely and not doing so, or acting rationally and merely allowing ourselves to be swayed by our desires, by adding a kind of ghostly pure agent within the ordinary empirical agent, the theory would be just a non-starter. How are we to think of the Captain's decision-making? It would not do to think of *his* decision-making on either of these models: it is neither the upshot of a heterogeneous crew of passions, nor presumably guided by a second-order Captain within a Captain, for that would launch us on an infinite regress. So it is surely wrong to see Kant's 'noumenal' subject as a kind of Cartesian ghost within the ordinary empirical agent. Apart from anything else, in the first *Critique*, Kant argues as effectively as anybody against any such conception. So perhaps it is time to drop the metaphor of the Captain.

It is usually supposed that the right way to see Kant on agency and freedom is not as postulating a second (noumenal) ontology, but giving us two 'aspects' under which human agency may be considered, or two distinct ways of considering the phenomena of human action and choice.[23] The one way of looking at it, on this account, would in effect be that of Hume, but the other way, the one involving the noumenal, free, law-giving and law-guided self, is that proper to one's awareness of oneself as a deliberating agent. It is, if you like, the first-person deliberative stance. The difference is between thinking of oneself in an objectifying way, and trying to predict what one will do in some circumstance, just as one might predict what another will do, and really deliberating what to do. Deliberating, with the upshot being that an intention is formed, is not the same as merely predicting what one will do. When we deliberate, we bring our own values or normative appreciation of a situation to bear on a choice. And this is not the same as predicting, passively, what we will do. It is 'taking control' of what to do, and it is this aspect of control that is to the forefront of Kant's picture. So has he perhaps seized on something integral to our existence as deliberating beings?

It is difficult to see that he has. For it is not really very clear what difference this change from thinking of two things to two aspects or

---

[23] See e.g. Henry Allison, *Kant's Theory of Freedom* (Cambridge: Cambridge University Press, 1990), 3.

perspectives on the one person really makes. After all, if there is a legitimate or compulsory 'aspect' under which we are not to be thought of as Hume thinks of us, and if under this aspect there is, in addition to the sentiments, a context-free control by reason alone, then it seems that under this aspect something is indeed *added*. It is being added at least that controlling reason exists, or that there are laws which reason legislates for itself. Kant himself thought that the deliberative stance discloses something that *contradicts* what is discovered from the third personal, or objective or scientific standpoint.[24] It is not as if the viewpoints differ in the way that a view in which the factory looms larger than the chimney differs from that in which the chimney looms larger than the factory: a conflict that is merely apparent.

In fact, we shall see in the next section that Kantians who are far too sophisticated to accept the metaphor of the Captain in so many words nevertheless cheerfully retain the most pernicious element of the model, which is that of the subordinate crew passively presenting themselves to the controlling master.

3. THE FUNDAMENTAL MISTAKE ABOUT DELIBERATION

It is natural to fear that Hume's model presents the agent in too passive a light. It is as if the subject is simply a container, housing different desires and concerns, which then cause him or her to lurch off in various directions, according to their various strengths. Such an agent would *find themselves* doing this or that, but it would be hard to say that they truly *choose* to do this or that. And this seems inadequate to the inside feel, the phenomenology, of deliberation. When we deliberate, within ourselves or in conversation with others, we reason about what to do, and reject some courses (and perhaps regret any inclination towards them that we feel) and accept others. By dismantling the practical agent, making him into no more than a bundle of forces, Hume seems to leave no room for a process of acceptance or rejection of this kind. It may seem as if it is here that he denies reason its real place in practical thought. Crews are there to be governed.

Suppose, then, that Hume gives us the picture of ourselves as incurably 'heteronomous', blown around by the winds of passion, victims of forces over whose origins and power we have no control. In rebellion against this picture we might insist upon the distinction between

---

[24] *Groundwork*, § 114 (455), p. 123.

impulse and *intention*. My inclinations, it is said, merely present themselves to me; it is then up to me to take them up, to accept them or reject them, to allow them to motivate me or play a role in generating my intentions. And it is certainly true that I have in principle the power to accept or reject whatever wells up from my sentimental or passionate nature. It is I myself, regarded as the person who exercises that power, who is the true Kantian Captain. And who can deny that sometimes we ought to be so regarded? For we do exercise self-control, we do reject unbidden promptings, and sometimes at least we are restrained by principle, and put our better selves forwards.

Before thinking that we here go beyond any Hume-friendly conception of deliberation and reason, we should reflect that we distinguish *empirically* the person of prudence, temperance, self-control, far-sightedness, and altruism from the person who seems to be blown around by the winds of the moment: the person often referred to as a wanton. We can certainly recognize the difference between those crews whose deliberations give due weight to caution, to reflection, to the advice of others, and to impartial benevolence—those that belong to the 'party of mankind'—from those who excitedly dash off under the influence of any latest whim. We usually find, in conversation, that we pay attention to the views of others on what we should do, and they pay attention to our views in turn. But as we saw, for Kant the causality of freedom is never empirical. For the Kantian, these distinctions are not, as it were, where it is at. The differences between the wanton and a member of the party of mankind are distinctions within the brood of dispositions, and have nothing to do with the authoritative exercise of the moral law, nor with the true operation of autonomy.

What, then, of the charge that Humeans make the self too 'passive', itself a mere slave of the passions? We might advance this charge because of the grip of the Kantian picture, only now thinking of ourselves, as Captains, suddenly subordinate to a successfully mutinous crew. Or similarly, we might be thinking of ourselves in effect as only the shell within which desires are lodged: the ship which a possibly alien crew is working and directing. But this is wrong: the person is the totality composed of body and form, or ship and crew. The self has a practical identity, made of what it desires and values and does. The self is no more *passive* when our concerns are contending for a controlling say in our direction, than a parliament is passive when it debates a law. It is only on the model that debars desires and inclinations, however cautious, however prudent and refined, from any part in *constituting* the self that we seem passive in the face of them. In other words, once the trick of separating the Kantian self (the 'noumenal' self) from the empirical nature of the person has been played, then the self conceived of as determined by that empirical nature seems passive, and ordinary experience may seem to refute the model. But disallow the trick, and the charge of passivity falls with it.

What is true is that we 'find ourselves' with this or that concern, and if the experience is unpleasant, as when we find ourselves shamefully addicted to something, or obsessed by something or someone, or for that matter guiltily ceasing to care for things or people we once did care for, then it can feel as if we are assailed from outside, a victim of forces not of our own making. But, after all, it is *always* forces not of our own making that are responsible for who we are in the first place: in my case, they have made me into a middle-aged white male of a certain education and class: in your case, probably something not too dissimilar, by historical and global standards. Kant's aim was to present the true self, the deliberator, as free from all that. He (or she) is not an embodiment of a social view, or religion, or class, or gender, but simply of reason and morality. But nothing on this earth that makes deliberations is free of his or her natural and acquired dispositions as they do so. You, when you deliberate, are whatever you are: a person of tangled desires, conflicting attitudes to your parents, inchoate ambitions, preferences, and ideals, with an inherited ragbag of attitudes to different actions, situations, and characters. You do not manage, ever, to stand apart from all that.

Once more, the Kantian fantasy remains seductive. There is an emotional pressure to think we can transcend these given facts about ourselves. Christine Korsgaard maintains that the 'reflective structure of human consciousness' gives us a necessary distance from our desires and impulses.[25] But the claim is ambiguous, and right only in a sense which does not help the Kantian. In the sense in which it is right, it means only that one can stand back from a *particular* desire or impulse, and accept or reject its pressure on one. Certainly we can do this, in the light of other desires and concerns. What is not thereby given is that we can do it from a standpoint independent of any desire or concern: independent of a desire for our own good, or for the happiness of humanity, or respect for this or that, or the myriad other passions that make up our individual profiles of concern and care.

The phenomenology of choice certainly does not give us as a brute fact that this ever happens (so Kant was right: if we insist that it does, we are insisting on something that lies beyond the range of empirical

---

[25] Korsgaard, *The Sources of Normativity*, 92–3.

data, something transcendental). The emotional pressure to think that it does is a desire for proof: for a firm ground justifying our deliberations in terms that lie beyond contingent profiles of concern. These would be knock-down arguments, capable of appealing to all reasonable people simply in virtue of their rationality, and independent of any particular desire or interest that they happened to have. The Humean is perhaps best regarded as someone who is quite content with the realization that such ground is a mirage. There is no *necessary* object of concern. There are only the contingent profiles of desire and value. To be sure, we share enough of a common nature for it to be practically certain that we can find common ground with others when conversation about our aims arises. But to the Kantian this is not enough. She is afflicted with an overwhelming ('existential') sense of loss, a sense of resulting 'arbitrariness' or 'absurdity', when our concerns are left to stand on their own feet, and digs the ground for something else to shore them up. The Humean, here like the Aristotelian, is satisfied that appeal to nature is enough.

It is now time to unmask the first and far the most important mistake made by those who oppose the Humean tradition. This comes from equating the standpoint of deliberation with a standpoint which *surveys* or takes account of desire, and then weighs it at some other tribunal—an independent tribunal, which has to mean the tribunal of reason. Korsgaard, while allowing that some of our concerns are part of us rather than 'alien' to us, nevertheless puts the process of deliberation like this:

Although I have just been suggesting that we do make an active contribution to our practical identities and the impulses that arise from them, it remains true that at the moment of action these impulses are the incentives, the passively confronted materials upon which the active will operates, and not the agent or active will itself.[26]

Nagel similarly describes the crucial moment of deliberation:

One is suddenly in the position of judging what one ought to do, against the background of all one's desires and beliefs, in a way that does not merely flow from those desires and beliefs but operates on them . . .[27]

This crucially mistakes the process of deliberation. Typically, in deliberation what I do pay attention to are the relevant *features* of the external world: the cost of the alternatives, the quality of food, the durability of the cloth, the fact that I made a promise. I don't *also* pay

[26] Ibid. 241.
[27] Thomas Nagel, *The Last Word* (New York: Oxford University Press, 1997), 110.

attention to my own desires (or what Korsgaard here calls 'impulses': note the Dionysian implication). My own concerns and dispositions determine which features I notice and how I react to them. If I am a miser, the cost takes my attention; if I am a gourmet, the quality of the food does; if I am prudent, the durability of the cloth; if I am not a knave, the fact of the promise. If I am extravagant, or a glutton, or concerned only with my appearance today, or if I am a knave, none of these features presents itself as important. There is not typically a *second-order* process of standing back, noticing that the cost is obsessing me, and deciding to endorse that fact about myself, or alternatively deciding to try to change it. In other words, it misdescribes the deliberative stance to see it as one in which our own natures stand 'passively confronted' by the controlling Captain. On these accounts, deliberation is essentially a matter of surveying (perhaps cursing and flogging) the crew from the quarter-deck. But this is wrong. The deliberative stance is actually one of surveying the surroundings—the situation of choice and the salient features. And this survey is done in the light of our concerns, represented by the crew. Deliberation is an active engagement with the *world*, not a process of introspecting our own consciousness of it. The last thing you want to do when you are wondering when to make your dash through the traffic, or whether to move bishop to rook 5, is to take your mind off the traffic or the chessboard. In fact, this may be the last thing you *ever* want to do: consider the many ways of failing that await the poet who makes his or her own consciousness of emotion into the subject of a poem, instead of the emotion itself.

It is almost impossible to overstate the consequences of this mistake: it is the leading, characteristic mistake of a whole generation of theorists wanting to go beyond Hume. Supposing that my own desires fill the foreground of deliberation is exactly akin to supposing that my experience is my normal object of concern when I attend to features of the external world. Now this mistake in the philosophy of perception nourishes the idea of a realm of 'sense data', or immediate objects of perception, and thence leads to thinking of ourselves as spectators in an inner theatre: a Cartesian self whose relationship to perceptions is uncannily like my relation to the world, but also mysteriously unlike it, if only because it does not itself need second-order sense data. The image here would be one of 'experience' presenting passively confronted materials, which a process of reason then takes up and certifies as veridical. But experience is not to be thought of in those terms. Perception presents us with an external world, not with 'objects' that we may or may not take to be signs of what that world is like. Similarly desires are not objects which, as it were, sit passive and inert until certified by reason. When we desire, aspects of the situation present themselves as affective or attracting: we may say that desires look beyond themselves, just as perceptions do.

Making desires the *object* of deliberation, rather than features of the person determining the selection and weighing of external features, inevitably leads to postulating an inner deliberator. This is a noumenal, transcendental, self whose relationship to desires is uncannily like my relationship to the world, yet mysteriously unlike it in not itself needing second-order desires to drive it.[28]

Of course, we do scrutinize our desires, but consider what really happens when we do. I find myself wanting to go to a smart restaurant, suppose, and then confront an imagined or real critic. We can describe the critic as raising an issue about the desire, if we wish, for, kept on a tight rein, this could be harmless—a mere translation of the fact that the critic is querying something about the object of the desire. What it really means is that the critic forces further thought about the very object of desire. What is it about going to a smart restaurant that attracts me? Have I thought of what I or my family must forgo if I go there; have I thought about the reactions of others, have I really imagined what likely pleasures or pains it will bring, etc., etc.? It is the *world* that we contemplate, not our own psychologies. In the typical reflective, deliberative question, 'Is *this* more important than/consistent with/to be ignored compared with/*that*?', the demonstratives refer to aspects of the world, not desires.

When desires are thought of as *objects* of concern, all kinds of panic set in. They will appear 'arbitrary'—or absurd; they are in principle changeable (if only we were weaker, or stronger!). They cannot legislate or bind, for they can be undone. If they appear to us each and every one as a desire for our own pleasure (as they seemed to Kant) then they will also seem to make up a rather grubby, almost shameful, crew, unfit to launch any vaulting flights of moral concern. Nagel, for example, consistenly supposes that if all we have is Hume-friendly reason, this amounts to a 'debunking' of deliberative thought, or a 'displacement' of the normative by the psychological.[29] Hence the retreat to Kant. But if we remember that, properly speaking, desires are read back from our real, heterogeneous concerns, then everything looks different. There is nothing grubby about a fixed, staunch

---

[28] See also Philip Pettit and Michael Smith, 'Backgrounding Desire', *Philosophical Review*, 99 (1990), 569–92.

[29] Nagel, *The Last Word*, 108.

propensity (*not* an impulse or an incentive) to take into account the fact that I owe someone a debt of gratitude, or that I have made them a promise. There is nothing grubby about me if I have thence formed the unyielding disposition to do what gratitude or my promise requires. Nor is there anything 'arbitrary' or 'absurd' about such concerns.[30] On the contrary, they are exactly the kind of concern on which we insist. Those lacking them should expect no admiration from others, and in so far as they have a man within the breast representing those without, they will find no admiration for themselves, within themselves.

4. SELF-LEGISLATION, PRACTICAL IDENTITY, AND THE NORMATIVE QUESTION

Kant, or perhaps his translators, cannot escape responsibility for the confusion here. He is habitually presented as referring to our own desires and concerns as 'incentives', and this is exactly what they are not.[31] An incentive is a further, external aspect of a situation that, by being the object of a further desire, helps to bend the will in some direction. A desire is not an incentive. Desire is that through which we see things as incentives.

On the Kantian story, in deliberation desires are 'passively' present. They sit at a table waiting for their certificate from reason (you, the Captain), just as an incentive might literally be an object, such as a pot of money, whose status as an incentive is only generated by its being the object of desire. So what does the Captain do, in order to bestow his benediction? The story is that he performs an act of 'self-legislation', taking up and confirming a concern as a law for himself. In Korsgaard's version, this self-legislation is actually the 'source' of normativity: 'the reflective structure of human self-consciousness requires that you identify yourself with some law or principle which

---

[30] It is curious that although Michael Smith co-authored the paper above in which some of these points are on view, he nevertheless holds a semi-Kantian view about the insufficiency of actual 'arbitrary' desire to fund Moral Truth: see *The Moral Problem* (Oxford: Blackwell, 1994), 172. Smith's own position is only semi-Kantian, because he equates normative reasons with what a person's 'rational self' would desire for him, whereas for Kant morality can have no basis in what any agent, actual or hypothetical, would desire. If it did so, it would lose its 'categorical' character and become merely hypothetical, advising rather than commanding.

[31] 'Incentive' was Beck's original translation of *Triebfeder*, and he is followed e.g. by Allison. I am grateful to Jeanine Grenberg for alerting me to the dubious accuracy of the translation.

will govern your choices. It requires you to be a law to yourself. And that is the source of normativity.'[32] But this is much harder to understand than it seems. How can an act of self-legislation be the *source* of normativity? Legislation, one would have supposed, like promising, is an act possible only to those who *already* think in normative terms. Consider two schoolboys, one of whom merely resolves not to tread on the cracks in the pavement, and the other of whom makes a vow to himself not to do so. There is a fine difference between them. For instance, the first might feel the resolve relatively lightly, so feeling free to abandon it at the first convenient moment. The other might feel that by doing so he would be 'letting himself down'. But could this difference between them be understood except by imagining them already practised in a repertoire of normative concepts? Each intends not to walk on the cracks, but what then?[33]

Korsgaard's best attempt to explain the difference invokes the notion of a 'practical identity'. This, I think, is much more along the right lines: it can be interpreted in terms of the discussion of values above, in Chapter 3, locating value in those concerns that we intend to foster and to guard against threat or change. But this does not justify the language of self-legislation: it involves no act of the will, and it invokes no mysterious 'source of normativity' in such an act. We typically find ourselves with our ethical natures, our natural and acculturated sources of love and hatred, pride and humility, anger, shame, and guilt. It is romantic, existential, fancy to imagine ourselves creating them by context-free acts of pure, normatively uncontaminated choice. We discover ourselves (at the same time as we discover others) more than inventing ourselves (or others).

The mistake of taking our own concerns as our fundamental *object* of concern is also visible in innumerable complaints along the lines: 'For the Humean the only reason not to be cruel/a fraud/unjust is that we do not want to be so.' That is just not true. A reason is a feature that prompts concern, and for the Humean avoiding cruelty or fraud or injustice can be a fixed, non-negotiable prompt of concern, or, in other words, a value. For the same reason it is wrong to think that only Kant delivers categorical imperatives ('Do it—whether you want to do so or not!'), whereas Hume delivers only hypothetical imperatives ('Do

[32] Korsgaard, *The Sources of Normativity*, 102.
[33] The classic development of this kind of problem, in the easier case of promising to others rather than legislating to oneself, is *Treatise*, III. ii. 5. Hume's complaint, that on most theories the obligation attaching to promises is 'magical', is exactly the complaint to press here.

it—if you want to!'). The sentimental tradition can be as demandingly categorical as possible. A Humean can issue the injunction to avoid cruelty—whether you want to do so or not. He is forbidding a class of actions, and warning that wanting to perform them counts as no kind of excuse.

Again, it is only when desires are taken as 'objects' that we can think in terms of one big problem about normativity: 'the normative question' as Korsgaard calls it. This is presented as *the* justificatory, deliberative question, the question of the form 'Why must I do that?' which seeks justification, not explanation. Because it is a justificatory question it could not be answered satisfactorily by a Humean or other natural history that simply *explains* why we think in moral terms, for example.[34] But why suppose that there is then such a thing as *the* normative question? People ask why they must do some particular thing in all kinds of circumstance, and their concerns can only be addressed in appropriately different ways. There is no more a single normative question than, for instance, a single emotional question, 'What am I to feel?' The boy asking why he must clean his teeth is answered one way; a father wondering why he must give up some golf to be with his family is answered a different way. The person Korsgaard in fact presents, who asks whether he must protect Jews against the Nazis, is to be answered, if indeed there is a standpoint from which he can be answered, in yet another way, or ways. For even in this example, the case is not specified enough for us to know what the best approach might be. We do not know which concerns of the person might give us a toehold from which to push him towards a more generous altruism. We could also notice that *none* of these questions is appropriately answered by saying that the person asking has legislated that they must do what they are querying (really? when?). And only in the last case might talk of 'practical identity' seem appropriate, as a way of suggesting that the person could not live with himself if he failed. And this in turn may or may not be true. Yet I, looking at the juncture, may hold that he must help the Jews even when his or her practical identity would all too predictably survive betraying them. The problem here is that our practical identities are the upshot of processes of 'self-definition', and it is clearly contingent how we define ourselves. We may adopt a self-image as someone constrained by some role, which may include that of being a good businessman rather than a saint, a good citizen rather than a good person, or a good soldier rather than a moral hero. No doubt people ought not to define themselves exclu-

[34] See especially Korsgaard, *The Sources of Normativity*, 14–16.

sively in terms of such roles, but they often do, and look with satisfaction on bad behaviour that accords with them.[35]

So whence arises the illusion that there is such a thing as *the* normative question? The perspective from which it seems that there is one, and even an urgent, philosophically wrenching one, is just that which I have been attempting to expose. It is the perspective from which desires are free of normativity, in themselves alien to reason, and need taking up and certificating by some entirely distinct, independent, self-sustaining source of 'musts' if we are to think and deliberate as we should. This sustaining source has to have a story about which desires it transmutes into 'musts', and a story that gains no assistance from the presence of any other desires. No wonder it is impossible to find, and encourages the vague gesture at self-legislation.

Appreciating the objectifying mistake should make us suspicious of other writings. Consider an argument implicit in Thomas Nagel, and offered by Derek Parfit. Parfit contrasts three views of what it is rational to do.[36] One family is that of 'present-aim' theories: it is rational to do what best satisfies our present aims. Another is that of self-interest theories: it is rational to do what best promotes our lifetime interests. A third is morality: it is rational to do what best promotes everybody's interests. Parfit's strategy is to show that self-interest theories get 'squeezed' between morality and present-aim theories. The claim they have against morality is brought against them on behalf of present-aim theories. The argument is ambitious, but we should raise a simple structural question at the outset. How is one supposed to treat 'present aims' as among objects of concern, whose claims might go into a competition with others? It is one's *present* concerns that dictate how one at present *judges* any competition between various ends and aims. If you take up a critical standpoint on *some* of your present concerns, as indeed you can do, it will be in the light of *others* that you do so. People who act on their present aims are not peculiar sorts of people, less than moral, less even than prudent. They are all of us, moral and prudent included.

Objectifying our desires was the first mistake about deliberation.[37]

---

[35] Of course, identities can be carved more or less finely. Part of the pervasive melancholy of Proust arises from his belief that the self that achieves a desire is never the same as the self that had the desire.

[36] Derek Parfit, *Reasons and Persons* (Oxford: Oxford University Press, 1984), ch. 6.

[37] It may reasonably be urged that Hume is not free of the mistake of 'objectifying' desires and passions, as indeed he objectified all the contents of the mind. I think this is true. But it should also be noticed that Hume is well aware of the intentionality or

But there is a second mistake that lies behind thinking in terms of the Kantian Captain. It is the mistake, so brilliantly exposed by Schopenhauer, of confusing the absence of an experience of causation with the experience of the absence of causation.[38] Since we do not and cannot be aware of all the forces that mould our agency, we think we have knowledge of the absence of such forces. But this is the problem with the light dove again. In reality we need to recognize the inevitable existence, not of a perspective of free or rational agency, but of an absence that can easily be mistaken for it. We have here the necessary existence of a 'blindspot', or aspect of ourselves that cannot be seen, by ourselves, at the same time as we deliberate. That is, suppose I make an attempt at self-consciousness. I try to take into account facts not only about the world, but also about myself and my conative nature, as I decide what to do. I feed in the thought that I am bourgeois, or timid, or ambitious, or whatever, treating such thoughts as objective facts about myself, part of the data. I can, after all, be aware of such facts about myself, and I can even attempt to discount them. It is tempting to think that the *whole crew* is then within my purview, so, necessarily, I must be standing at a vantage-point somewhere above them. But this is the romantic, existentialist illusion. It is only the same old me doing the deciding, bourgeois, timid, and ambitious—and no doubt other things as well—and if the assemblage of facts I manage to bear in mind sways me one way or another, that too is a fact about me: another contingent and situated and moulded aspect of my sensibility or conative nature.

At the end of the decision-making process there is always some such final fact that cannot simultaneously be factored into the decision-making. For it is, as it were, the fact about me that determines how the things that *are* factored in play together; it is the conduit to

---

object-directedness of desire: 'we must consider, that it is not the present sensation alone or momentary pain or pleasure which determines the character of any passion, but the whole bent or tendency of it from the beginning to the end. One impression may be related to another, not only when their sensations are resembling, as we have all along supposed in the preceding cases, but also when their impulses or directions are similar and correspondent. This cannot take place with regard to pride and humility, because these are only pure sensations, without any direction or tendency to action. We are, therefore, to look for instances of this peculiar relation of impressions only in such affections as are attended with a certain appetite or desire, such as those of love and hatred' (*Treatise*, II. ii. 9, p. 381). Here 'pride' as a sensation is specifically contrasted with desire, an appetite that is only to be understood via its end. Hume repeats the principle on p. 385.

[38] Arthur Schopenhauer, *On the Freedom of the Will*, trans. Konstantin Kalenda (Oxford: Blackwell, 1985), 43.

decision rather than one of the things that is conducted. Of course, tomorrow, after today's decision-making has played out, I may be able to recognize today's fact about myself, and, if I am being self-conscious, let that too play a role in the decision-making of the day. But then there will be another blindspot, or another conduit that is not itself part of the content of our thoughts. We can compare the situation to looking at our own eyes in a mirror. We might see that our eyes are cloudy; but if they are, it will be with cloudy eyes that we see it.

5. RATIONAL SELVES

Philosophers are professionally wedded to the power of intelligent thought. So they find it tempting to think that there is a determinate question: what would I do if only I were fully rational, or reasonable? We have seen Hume's radical answer: nothing. That is, there is no particular choice in any situation that is characteristic of reason as such: reason determines our understanding of our situation, which means the inputs, not the way inputs are transformed into outputs. So why does the question appear to make sense? Why is there an industry not only of the rational actors of Chapter 6, but of the Kantian rational choice?

The question what I would do if I were fully rational typically introduces particular ideals. That is, I am in general aware of what makes for better or worse deliberation. As already described, I recognize various common cognitive defects: failure of memory, of knowledge, of attention to relevant factors, of balance, of foresight. So I can certainly ask what would I do if I could clear my mind of this or that defect which may stand in the way of an adequate appreciation of my situation. There is nothing wrong with these ideals in which we try to suppress our perceived cognitive inadequacies. But they do not have their status as ideals because of an *independent* source of authority, that can then be used to prop up the authority of ethics. Instead, recognizing the positions they introduce as ideal positions from which to deliberate is *itself* evaluating them, and like any evaluation it is itself an expression of an aspect of our preferences and attitudes. Thus I generally prefer and counsel decision-making made in the light of (what I regard as reasonable) marshalling of information. I find it hard to imagine a world in which decision-making is better conducted without such work. But of course the ideal is itself qualified: first of all I recognize that there are many occasions when spontaneity is more important than laborious collection of facts and reflection on

outcomes. And secondly, there are occasions where too much information itself distorts our judgement: even the fairest skin looks lumpy
and blotchy from too close up, a close acquaintance with the processes
of mastication and digestion can destroy the proper enjoyment of
food, a fond and vivid representation of how pleasant it is to be rich
may make me susceptible to bribery, and so on.[39]

Often we may seek to influence someone in the name of reason and
reflection, by trying to get them to appreciate that the goals at which
they aim will not deliver what they seem to promise (and here the full
play of imaginative intelligence comes into its own). We insist on the
false blandishments of success, or the hollow emptiness of the superficially glamorous life-style. People make themselves and others miserable through envy of the lives of others when, if they knew what
those lives were like, they would thank God that they did not have to
live them. We are here back in the domain of the poet, the novelist, and
the critic. What is needed is the intelligent use of experience and imagination, in order to generate understanding of what different kinds of
life are like, of how different kinds of character work, what the different façades conceal, which worms lie in which apples. The preferred
methods will typically be ones of comparison, making false gold
reveal itself by juxtaposing it with true, displaying the ranges and
many-dimensioned varieties of true merit and fault, true success and
failure, and the impostors that resemble them so closely. Human life
is never what it seems to be at first glance.

As we have seen, Hume's preferred ships are far from being run
without any reasoning. Reasoning is allowed to assure us of the matters of fact within which our decision is situated. Intelligence is
involved in appreciating what is really involved in our goals. Most
notably, of course, reason does assure us of the adaptation of means
to ends. But it can be used to correct our understanding of what it
would be like for ourselves or others if our aims were realized.

Once we imagine a good understanding of our situation, we can
also deploy ideals in how we think such understanding should affect
decision-making. Here we are in the domain of processing the input
to deliver the output, but we still talk of being 'reasonable' or not. For
example, asking what reason requires may insinuate social ideals:
what would I do if I were concerned to get agreement with other
people, as already discussed in section 4 of the last chapter. But here
the contrast is not really between reason and desire, but between one
set of desires informed by one set of thoughts, and another set con-

---

[39] Gibbard, *Wise Choices, Apt Feelings*; Johnston, 'Dispositional Theories of Value'.

cerned with a different view, and especially one that pays attention to the effects on others, or to Adam Smith's feature: the question of whether our own decisions are apt to appear good in their eyes. We should all throw our shoulders behind an ideal of civility, even if we understand that it has no transcendental backing.

More than that, and perhaps most familiarly of all, what Hume himself calls 'reason' may be the voice of prudence, or of far-sighted, wide concerns, as opposed to narrow concerns with the immediate future. With reason in this sense we 'correct' our sentiments in the light of wider understandings. In this sense the voice that tells me not to have another glass, or another helping, is called the voice of reason, although it is better called the voice of experience, or prudence. We appeal to reason in this sense when we want long-term consequences to be weighed against the greater imaginative appeal of short-term, imminent enjoyments. In this sense Hume himself talks of reason correcting the imaginative advantages enjoyed by the thought of imminent pleasures. But we can certainly ask why a concern for my own long-term future should be thought of as uniquely reasonable. If I am immature and spontaneous and wild and careless, may I not live better than if I am mature and cautious and calculating and careful? We do not always want to behave like the preferred customers of a Scottish insurance society. Doing so implies a concern that our life shows a certain pattern: ants rather than lilies of the field, no wild excess followed by penalty, no romantic gestures for fear of the cost, no debauch for fear of the morning. A kind of ideal, certainly, but scarcely a compulsory one, not even a very noble one, and in any case one to be evaluated, inevitably, in the light of other moral ideals and concerns.

So although in these ways we talk of what we would do if reasonable, or even of what reason requires, this gives us nothing beyond Hume-friendly reason. It does not support any vision of a haven of pure reason, sheltered from the storms of the moral seas, purely by itself sustaining some kinds of living and forbidding others. When the Romantics praise uncluttered innocence, or when W. B. Yeats writes:

> I would be—for no knowledge is worth a straw—
> Ignorant and wanton as the dawn,

we might, I suppose, shake our heads disapprovingly, but it is an ethical problem that we have to engage.[40]

In his book *The Moral Problem*, Michael Smith invokes the concept

---

[40] W. B. Yeats, 'The Dawn', from *The Wild Swans at Coole*, 1919.

of reason in order to tread a delicate tight-rope. He wants to connect what is desirable with what is actually desired, but not so as to close off the space for irrational states of mind, in which we desire what is not at all desirable, which we do, he thinks, when we are irrational. The outcome is a conception of 'normative reasons' which, he claims, is not Hume-friendly. The target of his analysis is the having of a 'normative reason'. Smith equates having a normative reason to φ with its being desirable that you φ. We met his analysis briefly in Chapter 4:

Smith

> to say that you have a 'normative reason' to φ in certain circumstances C is to say that, if we were fully rational, we would want that we φ in C. Equivalently, our 'fully rational self' would want it that we, given what we are actually like, φ in C.[41]

Now we have seen that such an equation need not trouble Hume, any more than an equation drawn in terms of 'ideal selves'. And the conception of what it is to be fully rational could be drawn in Hume-friendly terms: prudent, not over-passionate, well-informed, clear-sighted, concerned for accommodations with others, and so forth. This is a version of the MUCK psychology mentioned in Chapter 3. Things get onto this list when we are disposed in their favour, not by some other route, after which they can then judge and sway our favours. Second, and equally importantly, the Humean position is that when *we* say that it is desirable that someone φ, or that someone has a normative reason to φ, or that if they were fully rational, they would want themselves to φ, we are voicing *our* attitudes towards the person and their choice situation. We are *not* therefore simply describing the state of his or her desires. Nor are we confined to approving of what they themselves have inclinations towards. We may say that it is undesirable that they actually desire something bad, whether or not we believe that they themselves have other aims or concerns that should enable them to combat the maverick desire themselves. We are judging them, not describing them.

This connects with a somewhat obscure debate in the literature about whether a Humean can deploy a concept of 'external' reasons, allowing us to say that an agent has a reason to φ even when nothing whatever in her motivational states disposes her to show a concern for φ. A number of writers, notably Bernard Williams, have suggested that the Humean cannot permit external reasons.[42] But this debate is

41 *The Moral Problem*, 151–81, esp. p. 177.
42 Bernard William, 'Internal and External Reasons', in *Moral Luck*, 101–13.

muddled by the obvious ambiguity in 'X has a reason for φ', which may be intended as a descriptive remark about X's psychology, or a normative remark about what X ought to be responsive to, whether or not she is. The Humean can clearly make this distinction, and express commitments of either sort. Consider this ladder of possible things to say:

> The agent is motivated by a concern φ.
>
> The agent would be motivated by φ if she deliberated better from her present desires, by her own standards.
>
> The agent would be motivated by φ if she deliberated better from her present desires, by our standards.
>
> The agent should be motivated by φ, in spite of her present desires.
>
> Any agent should be motivated by φ, regardless of whatever profile of desire she actually has.
>
> φ necessarily motivates any rational creature, purely in virtue of her rationality.

The last of these certainly represents a target of Hume and Williams: they think there is no object of concern with this Kantian property. But we should clearly distinguish this from the penultimate judgement, which is of course perfectly available to a Humean, and shows something we often want to say about the incurably vicious or insensitive. Hume will not preface the penultimate judgement by 'it can be apprehended by reason alone that . . . '. But a Humean can sensibly urge that any agent *should* be motivated, say, to avoid gratuitous cruelty, regardless of what profile of desire they actually have. In saying this he deploys his own values, of course, but then what else should he be doing?

In a recent discussion Williams in effect admits as much.[43] He allows that there are many things to say about the hypothetical case of a man who ought to be nicer to his wife, but has no item in his motivational set that can give rise to the desire to be nicer to his wife. We can say 'that he is ungrateful, inconsiderate, hard, sexist, nasty, selfish, brutal, and many other disadvantageous things'. But he conceives the defender of external reasons as asking for a further, importantly different, kind of verdict: that the man has a reason to be otherwise. This suggests that, in Williams's view, Kantians and perhaps others (people who think that reasons are 'there anyway' or that we merely have to

---

[43] Bernard Williams, 'Internal Reasons and the Obscurity of Blame', in *Making Sense of Humanity* (Cambridge: Cambridge University Press, 1995), 35–45.

make ourselves 'receptive' to them) not only say the penultimate thing, but seek to invest it with a false objectivity, or false pedigree or credentials in reason or in the world. In short, they want to go beyond Hume-friendly reason, but cannot make their position coherent.

Another way of putting it makes the real issue plain. Williams allows a concept of 'reason to ϕ' which goes beyond 'ϕ is an aim of X's actual motivational set S' to 'ϕ would be an element in X's motivational set S if X deliberated excellently', where deliberating excellently covers removing ignorance. He allows this counterfactual because he believes that we all have an interest in removing ignorance. The addition only unzips something that is implicit in the original motivational set anyway. But if someone urges that we also include, within deliberating excellently, something like 'deliberating within the confines of the categorical imperative', Williams will ask whether we all do, or perhaps 'must', conceal this interest (respect for the Law) within any original motivational set. And then we are back with the old dialectic: the Kantian urges that this respect is hidden within any rational deliberating agent, and Williams and the Humeans deny it.

When it is put this way I agree with Williams. But I insist upon adding that there is a perfectly Hume-friendly use of 'external reasons' in which there are such things. For saying that is merely insisting on the propriety of the verdict that sometimes a person should be otherwise, whatever his or her actual motivational profile. It is not investing that verdict with a spurious necessity.

Returning to Michael Smith, it is now hard to see why his construction goes beyond a Hume-friendly conception of reason, as he claims it does. Hume can privilege situations in which we decide coolly, with an eye on the consequences, or on the effects on other people, and he can express this approval in any of the locutions here on offer.

Smith, however, offers four reasons for the claim that the analysis of desirability, or equally of normative reason, goes beyond Hume.[44] The first is that 'it makes normative reasons the object of our beliefs, and so allows our beliefs about normative reasons a proper causal role in the production of action'. It is not plain what is non-Humean here. For Hume does not deny that beliefs have a proper causal role in the production of action. He just insists that desires (or what I have called concerns) do so as well. But also, it is not clear that holding that a fully rational version of myself would want it that I do ϕ is purely an expres-

---

[44] *The Moral Problem*, 181.

sion of belief. For, as we have seen, selecting properties as making for full rationality is already exercising evaluative judgement, and in this represents an exercise of attitude just as much as it represents belief. Second, Smith points out that the analysis 'affords a critical perspec- 2 tive even on our underived [i.e. basic] desires, showing us why we may have reason to get rid of them'. But Hume is perfectly capable of construing the judgement that it would be desirable that someone get rid of some basic desire. If his basic desire is to wallow in the blood of others, it would be very desirable indeed. And I can take up a critical perspective on any of my own basic desires and concerns, in the light of my other basic desires and concerns. Third, Smith defends a non- 3 relative conception of normative reasons, 'so claims about our normative reasons are thus categorical rather than hypothetical in character'. Once more, though, these are terms improperly confiscated from Hume by the Kantians. As we have seen, Hume is quite capable of saying that it is categorically undesirable that someone desire to wallow in the blood of others. It is not just undesirable if the agent wants other things. It is undesirable *tout court*. Nor is it to be regarded as undesirable by an onlooker X only if X wants this or that, in the way that paying a green fee is desirable only if you want to play golf. It is to be regarded as undesirable by anyone. (If anyone is perverted enough to think of it as desirable, then away with them!) Fourth, and last, Smith believes in a kind of Kantian democracy. He 4 thinks that any agent is as well-placed as any other to answer the question, 'What is there normative reason to do?' (What is it desirable to do?) Here, I think there is a genuine departure from Hume, but not one I would recommend. Hume, like Aristotle, thinks it typically takes maturity, experience, judgement, care, imagination, and sympathy to know what it is desirable to do, and in this I think they are both right. Only the simple commandment model of ethics suggests otherwise, and as we have seen in this chapter and the last, the most impressive defence of that model is far short of convincing.

What you would do if you were reasonable is whatever a twentieth-century, middle-class, bourgeois, somewhat academic male or female with your peculiarities of concern and desire would do, knowing what is to be known about their situation, and exercising such other virtues as we wish to put into the ideal of being reasonable. There is no guarantee that what you would do would be all that good. Your profile of concerns may be slanted in various unpleasant ways. Perhaps you care too much for you and yours; perhaps you are too timid to act well, too kind to refrain from benevolent lies, too proud to submit to social necessities. Perhaps, if you became ever more rational, what you would desire for a person such as you now, actually, are would become ever more queer: perhaps you would get into a state of glorious indifference to the affairs of such lowly beings. Perhaps you would be enabled to see the world *sub specie aeternitatis*, so that nothing of the current scene matters. The point is that a nice or good or desirable profile of concerns is not simply *given* by the word 'rational'. And if it were, this would be because 'rational' has been drawn into the fold of the ethical. Even if you (reasonably) discuss and collaborate with others in your decision-making, still what appeals to you as a crowd may not be all that good. As a group you may agree on conspiracies against the others, and in your best decision-making, faults and flaws may hold their sway. And of course (given the fantastical nature of the standpoint common to all of us), what you would do if you were reasonable may not coincide with what I would do if I were reasonable. Independent norms of reason simply do not underwrite anyone's chances of good behaviour. Only their sentiments do that.

Can the Humean explain what is wrong with a ship in which the crew members pay no heed to the genuine exercises of intelligence and reason, exercises that establish the actual situation we are in, and our options, and the means, and the nature of the outcomes? Plainly, it is not well-adapted to action: the course that the victorious passion would have it steer is not one likely to achieve its satisfaction. Why should I, contemplating such a ship, regard it as inferior? Because, as already said, I can only feel satisfaction upon regarding a ship as useful or agreeable to itself or others. And a crew that steers without a look-out, and without paying attention to the way to get where it wants to go, or paying attention to what it is like where it wants to go, is none of these.

We can now retreat from the metaphysics of the self, and return to the moral message. Seen this way, Kant is promoting an ideal rather than describing a psychology. We have already seen that part of the appeal of his psychology is moral or political: it takes moral authority away from the specialist and relocates it in the breast of each individual. Kant is a great democrat. But not all the moral and political expressions of Kantianism are so attractive. If we see our fellow-human beings as each possessed of Kantian control, and only succumbing to other pressures when things are going wrong, then a dangerously optimistic politics is possible. The implication is that because our fellows are fundamentally able to guide themselves by rational restraint, then of course they *ought* to be safe with guns, or drugs, or motor cars, or sacrosanct areas of private behaviour. They have themselves all that is required for self-control and reason. The unhappily common failures, when people shoot each other, abuse drugs, drive unsafely, or brutalize their families show us only defectives who unaccountably will not listen to the voice of reason within them, and these can safely be demonized, put away, rejected as beyond the social pale. We thus combine unreasonable optimism about what people might be like, with unreasonable hatred of them when they are not like that.[45] We also fail to put into place social structures that safeguard against the inevitable failures. Both the politics and the response are premised on a fantasy. In fact, much earlier in the eighteenth century, people had worried about the way in which philosophies that elevate self-control and duty imperceptibly bring it about that violence against the self, which they celebrate as the central jewel of ethics, becomes violence against others.[46] 'Freedom' sounds good as an ideal, but rapidly turns vicious when it appears to be a perfectly simple ideal that someone has (freely) abused.

An alternative politics, more in line with the sentimentalist tradition, works not so much by individual blame, but by the social and environmental changes that grow the right fruits. It conspires with the general reservations about a moralistic culture that I voiced in the first chapter to suggest that an intelligent approach to human affairs may have less to do with the primitive mechanisms of anger, blame, and revenge, and much more to do with fostering the right kinds of situation, making the kind of world where bad behaviour becomes unmotivated anyhow. But this kind of policy is expensive, and violence is cheap.

6. REASON, RAWLS, CONTRACTS, AND LIBERALISM

In modern political and moral theory Kantianism owes its ascendancy to its association with the great classic of political philosophy, *The A Theory of Justice* by John Rawls. The construction it offers is particularly appealing in the USA, whose constitution is living testimony to many of the moral ideas that are attached to this approach. We have the

---

[45] Compare the dangerous lack of realism of the virtue tradition, broached above in Chapter 2.

[46] Adam Smith, although an admirer of the awful, austere, Stoic virtues of self-control, well recognized their connection with inhumanity and injustice. See *The Theory of Moral Sentiments*, III. I. ii. pp. 35–7. See also Hume, *Treatise*, III. iii. 4, pp. 607–8.

example of a new people forging a contract of forbearance: a constitution under which essential rights and freedoms are guaranteed, and the individual can pursue his or her own private ideals under an umbrella of guaranteed rights. The idea is of a solution to a practical problem to which all reasonable parties can agree. We have thus the embodiment of the liberal state.

Rawlsian persons can agree to a constitution which lets each of them pursue the good without hindrance in their own way. This is sometimes called the priority of the right over the good. For Kant, as we have seen, rational self-legislation must be the fountain of the necessities of right and duty, because if these derived from the promotion of the good, they would become 'external', or in other words subject to our potentially changeable and fragile desire to promote one thing or another as the good. The Rawlsian construction echoes that priority. Supposedly no specific conception of the good life is either presupposed or excluded by the idea of rational people contracting together under terms of mutual co-operation and for their mutual advantage. And we have a moral foundation that inherits the self-evident utility of our power to make exchanges that benefit each side. We have in the idea of the solution to a problem of contracting together an 'Archimedean point' of moral assessment that is not 'at the mercy, so to speak, of existing wants and interests'.[47] The political result is summed up in the formula that the liberal state is 'neutral between different conceptions of the good'. Again, the idea is to stand on the ground staked out by Kant: the ground of reason and the moral law combined. If a liberal constitution only had the authority of the good life it enables people to lead, then, it is feared, its authority crumbles. As the critic Michael Sandel puts it on behalf of the Rawlsian approach:

> If my fundamental values and final ends are to enable me, as surely they must, to evaluate and regulate my immediate wants and desires, these values and ends must have a sanction independent of the mere fact that I happen to hold them with a certain intensity. But if my conception of the good is simply the product of my immediate wants and desires, there is no reason to suppose that the critical standpoint it provides is any more worthy or valid than the desires it seeks to assess; as the product of those desires, it would be governed by the same contingencies.[48]

The previous sections already enable us to see what is going wrong

---

[47] John Rawls, *A Theory of Justice* (Cambridge, Mass.: Harvard University Press, 1972), 261.

[48] Michael Sandel, *Liberalism and the Limits of Justice* (Cambridge: Cambridge University Press, 1982), 165.

here: the objectification of concerns; the insinuation that they are 'mere' desires ('immediate'); and the idea that for the Humean it is 'the fact that I hold them' which provides my moral standard. Hence the flight to the Kantian idea of a non-contingent, transcendental stand-point of reason, a necessary source of binding authority. We are not then at the mercy of any of our brood of dispositions.

The approach sounds Apollonian, authoritative, and, not coincidentally, embedded in a long tradition of public and academic rhetoric. Unhappily, taken this way, the story is also incoherent. Liberalism itself is not exempt from the law that it takes a value to make a value. The authority of fair contract is one thing; the myth that it has a self-standing foundation in reason is something entirely different, that does no service to it. It masks the battles that need fighting, and it mistakes the distinctive historical fact about the Enlightenment. This is not that it represents the triumphal moment of reason (Reason), but that it represented the moment when people grew rightly disgusted with the factions and fanaticisms of traditional authority, and had to forge something new.

It is quite easy to see why this is so. Suppose we start with the tempting idea that a contract is fair when neither side objects to its terms. Everyone recognizes that this needs qualification. For actual contracts are inevitably as dubious, ethically, as the soil they grow in. I am poor; I need food; I will do what I can to get it; you are wealthy and powerful, so you can exact almost anything from me in return. I do not object to your terms, because I cannot afford to. You can exploit your position. If I am ignorant you can exploit my ignorance, or if I am malleable you can exploit the desires you can manipulate me into having. Even devotees of the market falter in front of examples of natives selling their land for beads, or the poor selling their organs to the rich.

So when is a contract really fair? Perhaps when neither side *reasonably* objects to its terms. A just constitution, in a famous recent formula, is made of principles which could not reasonably be rejected 'by parties who, in addition to their own personal aims, were moved by a desire to find principles that others similarly motivated could also accept'.[49] The formula again models an ideal of impartiality in terms of the possibility of a rational contract. But what does reason look for to decide whether to object to some proposed bargain? One kind of suggestion is this: would either of the contractors object if the terms

---

[49] Thomas Scanlon, 'Levels of Moral Thinking', in Seanor and Fotion, eds., *Hare and Critics*, 137.

you trade they propose were applied to them—if they didn't know in advance whether they would be the buyer or the vendor, or if their position and that of the other participant were reversed? The question is certainly pertinent, and sometimes the answer decides the question of fairness. Fairness is a virtue in contracts, and the question 'What contract would you agree if you did not know whether you were buying or selling?' is a good question, that properly focuses on it.

But it does not always give the true result. For people object to what is in fact fair, since they believe they deserve better, and people fail to object to what is unfair, because they fail to realize the worth of what they have to offer or fail to recognize the possibility of breaking the mould. Perhaps they are conditioned to servile acquiescence in an unjust economic and political order. So the question becomes whether either would *rightly* object if the terms were applied to them. But then anyone thinking in these terms needs a story about what it would be right to reject. A Muslim, for instance, in a community with a minority of Hindus, may want to offer them protection of the law only on condition they forgo some aspect of their worship. He may well recognize that the minority will object. He may even admit that he would object in their shoes. But he will not admit that they are right to object, or that he would be right to object in their shoes, for *ex hypothesi* their shoes are ones in which people are almost incurably in the wrong.

So the Achilles' heel of Scanlon's formula, and many other similar ones, is the simple dualism between 'personal aims' on the one hand and the desire for 'impartial principles to which all can agree' on the other. For as well as anything they may concede to be personal aims, people, and especially people in communities, are typically attached to particular *principles*, which may not be shared by everyone. A Hindu will not regard it as a merely personal aim that cows not be killed for meat, nor a Muslim regard it as a personal aim that the Koran be respected. Such principles guide their lives, they cannot imagine living without them, they are settled in the very core of their practical identities. This may be recognized, however clumsily, by tribunals that will excuse someone from what would otherwise be a political obligation, if it can be shown to be contrary to a principle of his or her religion. Nor is it only organized religion that deserves this respect. A principle such as vegetarianism or pacifism may be recognized as affecting a person's legal status without having to shelter behind religious authority.

Now the problem is that people may well not be willing to put such principles aside when they contemplate coming to terms with others who do not share them. And if the principles are divisive, then they will stand in the way of liberal accommodations with those on the other side of the divide. The liberal believes that they ought to be put aside enough to give space for an interest in toleration, freedom of speech and religion. Well and good: so do I. It is part of my conception of the good that people should do this: one, and more than one, of my brood of dispositions disposes me to it. But does anything else, of superior authority do so?

In *A Theory of Justice* Rawls stipulates that all such specific principles and concerns be put aside when we imagine what parties could contract into in the 'original position'. The idea is supposed to be that there is a distinctive human psychology left, if we abstract in this way from our rooted social and empirical positions; a psychology partisan to some social contracts and not others. A social arrangement that could be the object of a contract after the abstraction is made deserves calling fair or just. The feat of abstraction has bothered some commentators, and it is at least worth remarking that when I abstract from my social and empirical position, any answers I give are nevertheless ones that a middle-class white twentieth-century Englishman with a distinctive experience and history gives. But the question 'What would you choose if you were concerned for this or that, and ignorant of this or that?' is a perfectly good kind of question, even if our ability to give an authoritative answer might be fairly sketchy. In some cases the question is intelligible, pertinent to the question of fairness, and metaphysically perfectly innocent.

The real problem is not so much the feat of abstraction, as the motivational one of commanding respect for what would have been chosen in that position. 'What I would have chosen, had I been different in some specified way' is just like 'what X would choose'. Whether the answer is of any moral interest depends on whether we respect and admire X or whether we think X a broken reed: ignorant or defective in other ways. Now, Rawls's contractors leave behind specific principles: they leave behind everything except a dislike of risk, a concern for a fairly long term, and a stripped-down concern for the necessities without which life is bound to be miserable, or what Rawls calls 'primary goods'. With only these kinds of concern, and motivated to choose a constitution under which to live, a person should, Rawls argued, choose a legal and economic system closely resembling those of modern western welfare-state democracies, with a substantial budget of freedoms under the law, and a substantial welfare floor. As a liberal myself, I think that morally and politically he is roughly right. I would admire such a choice; I think I even share the rather bourgeois concern for security or 'risk aversiveness' that characterizes his hero.

But that is because I have no other independent principles that I have been asked to jettison as I think myself into the initial position. Had I been a communist, or communitarian, or a bigot, or a free-marketeer, or a Muslim, I would have had such principles. The fight for liberalism is the fight against the principles defining such positions. They are not 'personal aims', nor, to adherents, do they simply represent one conception of the good amongst others. They represent The Good, and people who do not see it are blind, and dangerous, and perhaps not to be accorded the same rights as people who do. If my world is one poisoned by old hatreds, and I am asked to jettison what I (take myself to) know about the Others and contemplate what would count as a reasonable accommodation with them, I am being asked too much. For why should I regard that position—one in which Their crimes or infirmities are unrecognized—as the position in which the right kind of arrangement with Them is made?

The liberal state is one in which certain specific freedoms are guaranteed: freedom of religion, freedom of speech, freedom from discrimination under the law, and others, including, if we are lucky, freedom from dire economic exploitation or dire financial distress. I think this is excellent. I also think that were we to live in a state of some other kind, say, one in which certain groups were systematically denied the protection of the law or the basic necessities for life, I would find it hard to look the wretched in the eye. I would hope to have a voice within representing their voices without. All I am denying is that in saying such things we, We of Reason, have one kind of authority, whereas others have only something inferior. The liberal state obviously has a definite 'conception of the good'. It protects the peoples' education, health, security, freedom under the law, their power to participate in the political process, the fact that they are not humiliated by the state, and their freedom from a variety of needs that are at particular times and places agreed to be intolerable. The specific freedoms it guarantees are themselves an embodiment of one important feature of the good, namely that in a good life one is not coerced in certain ways by one's society: not coerced in matters of religion or speech, not subject by economic necessity to the exploitative powers of others. I indeed do think it is good that people should be free of such coercion. But I don't think my view on these things lies behind and apart from any conception of the good.

Other people, unfortunately, do not want a constitution that respects such freedoms. The central problem for liberalism is to combat them. It has weapons to do so, such as J. S. Mill's classic argument that only in a free market-place of ideas is truth possible, but it gains only false security by pretending it can do this purely in the name of what it is to be a practical agent, the noumenal embodiment of reason and nothing else.

Returning to Sandel's summary of the Rawlsian formula, it is simply not true that my (present) 'conception of the good' stands apart from my 'immediate' wants and desires, at least if that means my present basket of concerns (but notice how the phrasing insinuates something transient, like a fleeting whim: something, well, mere). The phrase 'my conception of the good' refers, somewhat pompously, to the things that I value and admire and encourage and want people to aim at: mutual respect and compassion, mutual forbearance over wide spheres, reasonable aid to those in distress, let us say. The fact that currently I admire and encourage such an aim is *not* independent of my current wants and desires, for we recognize no interesting split between values and desires. If it were, it would not be a real value. It is one of the very facts that *constitute* my current basket of concerns, and our concerns are simply the things that matter to us. Remembering the concern can, on occasion, give me a standpoint from which to criticize other wants and desires: for instance, when I find myself provoked to hard-hearted rejection of someone's needs.

The only clean course is to refuse the spurious posture of neutrality. Liberalism only gains by acknowledging that *of course* it is promoting one conception of the good amongst others. But that does not make it just one more option in the shopping-basket of creeds, of no particular authority. Like any ideology, it derives, and it must derive, its authority from two sources. First, there is the excellence of the kind of life that it makes possible, and the values that such a life embodies. Second, there are the disasters it protects us from: in the case of liberalism, the disasters that happen when one politically ascendant group of humans are able to impose their own ideas on others, without the checks of the common point of view. Failing to sit in a dry dock called 'reason' is not failing to float in the seas for which moral boats are fitted.

None of this detracts from Rawls's real achievement. His construction marvellously suggests a structure: a simple set of principles that, put together, generate a particular, excellent, kind of state. Our admiration for that kind of state may well be articulated and given a defensible framework by the construction, beautifully adapted for teasing out features of the kind of society we liberals admire. To repeat, I would not choose to live anywhere else than in a state with decent freedoms and a decent welfare floor. If you would, I am in various degrees likely to be against you. But this is not because of anything specifically Kantian in the construction, nor is it about the priority of the right over the good.[50] In fact, I would urge that Rawls's invocation of the notion of a contract (and equally his invocation of Kant) is misleading and in the end dangerous: once more, not only in the study, but in the political arena. It is misleading because, as many commentators have pointed out, what is really in question is not a contract but a *choice*. The Rawlsian agent is asking herself what kind of society she would want to live in, given her risk-aversive long-term concern to safeguard her access to the primary goods, and given her concern for the freedoms which rightly make up our own sense of a good life. The trappings of a contract are idle, since behind the veil of ignorance all contractors are identical. What one can choose, all can choose, and what one cannot choose, none can choose.[51]

The reason the emphasis on contract is politically dangerous is that when the choice is redescribed in terms of entering a contract, it insinuates the idea that a society is well seen as nothing but a network of contracts. Society becomes no more than an arrangement for mutual benefit like a joint-stock company or a cartel. It is this that has inflamed 'communitarian' critics of 'liberalism', such as Sandel, Macintyre, and Taylor.[52] The issues are too complex to enter into here—indeed, they make up one of the great oppositions in European thought, between the 'morality' of the Kantians and the *Sittlichkeit*, or situated social norms that tether us to a way of life, emphasized by Hegel. But a remark may be in order. Communitarians are right to doubt the a priori defence of the Rawlsian construction: this is the point made above, in terms of the false dichotomy between principles of justice on the one hand, and merely personal aims on the other. But 'liberals' are right to mistrust the conservative and potentially static and close-minded tendencies that are concealed within naïve respect for community values. The whole point of the Enlightenment was to enlarge peoples' visions beyond and away from the closed, prejudiced, stifling, and often cruel certainties of unexamined small-town moralities.

But it may be true nevertheless that it takes a community for a person to flourish, just as it takes a shared language for them to think. And

---

[50] Rawls's subsequent work has suggested that he is sympathetic to this construal of his achievement: see 'Justice as Fairness: Political not Metaphysical', in Shlomo Avineri and Avner de-Shalit, eds., *Contractarianism and Individualism* (Oxford: Oxford University Press, 1992), 186–204; 'Kantian Constructivism in Moral Theory', in S. Darwall, A. Gibbard and P. Railton, eds., *Moral Discourse and Practice*, 247–66; and *Political Liberalism* (New York: Columbia University Press, 1993).

[51] The first critic I know who pointed this out, lecturing in Oxford in the early 1970s, was Herbert Hart.

[52] A good collection of the relevant texts is Avineri and de-Shalit, eds., *Communitarianism and Individualism*.

a community is not a thing entered into for the purpose of a mutually beneficial bargain, any more than a language is. It is not optional, as if we could back out of it when things are not going our way. It makes us who we are. Communitarians are right to emphasize this. The moral solution, however, is not to choose between Hegel and Kant, or 'communitarianism' and 'liberalism'. It is to admire and work for communities that forge their ties within the spirit of respect and forbearance that characterize liberalism. There is no opposition here, except when either side overplays its hand.

During the 1980s and 1990s, conservatives played on the rhetoric of replacing a community of 'welfare' by a community of 'opportunity': opportunity being the opportunity to manufacture and sell goods and services. This is the sense in which to take Margaret Thatcher's notorious remark that there is no such thing as society: nothing more than individual atoms furthering their interests by exchanging goods and services in market transactions.[53] But one need not invest the concept of a community with very much baggage to find this vision appalling. A child, or a pensioner, does not deserve the protections afforded by their community (including protections under the law) just in so far as they are likely to contribute something back. If this were so, any of us might suddenly find ourselves stripped of our civil rights if we had exhausted our credit, and then become too incapacitated to offer others a reasonable repayment for their support. As a student of mine once asked, discussing the advocacy of just this ideal in David Gauthier's *Morals by Agreement*, what happens if you come to the bargaining table with little or nothing to offer, for example through being handicapped?—and my unthinking reply that then you would not have a leg to stand on was not a joke. People deserve the protection of their community because they need it, not because they are likely to repay it with goods and services. A community is largely constituted by its disposition to enter into common action to meet its members' needs.[54] We do not belong to families, or enter friendships, or establish loyalties, with the proviso that when our 'self-interest' dictates, we intend to abandon them. Or, if we do, our lives will go worse, and the same is true if the

---

[53] It became common, indeed *de rigueur*, in conservative circles during the later periods of Thatcher's reign, to make light of this kind of remark and to patronize people who worried about it. In fact, the remark was quite deliberate, and a perfectly understood implication of the views of her mentors, notably the Austrian economic school centred upon F. A. Hayek. See, for example, Nick Davies, *Dark Heart: The Shocking Truth about Hidden Britain* (London: Chatto & Windus, 1997).

[54] This theme is central to Michael Walzer's book, *Spheres of Justice* (New York: Basic Books, 1983).

only notion of a community that we can muster is one of conditional co-operation so long as it is to our own benefit. Mrs Thatcher's remark was aimed to foster just this latter disposition, and consciously or otherwise the priority given to the notion of a contract in moral and political thinking supports her. Once more, an apparently minor distortion in the world of ideas reflects and encourages a major fracture in the social order outside, but also, if we are lucky, it shows us the way towards a repair.

9

Relativism, Subjectivism, Knowledge

'Why, you cannot say anything to a man with which he does not absolutely agree,' said I, 'but he flies up at you in a temper.'

They both declared that such a state of things was anti-christian.

While we were thus agreeing, what should my tongue stumble upon but a word in praise of Gambetta's moderation. The old soldier's countenance was instantly suffused with blood; with the palms of his hands he beat the table like a naughty child.

'*Comment monsieur*?' he shouted. '*Comment*? Gambetta moderate? Will you dare to justify those words?'

Robert Louis Stevenson, *Travels with a Donkey*

1. RELATIVISM IN A FIRST-ORDER ETHIC

We now, I hope, have a substantial sense of the complexities of human motivation, the strength of the sentimentalist tradition, and its capacity to explain such things as the emergence of co-operation, trust, respect for principle, and other contours of the virtuous life. But the construction of the moral proposition in Chapter 4 leaves us open to the old worry, if it is a worry, of relativism or scepticism. If this is what ethics comes to, people think, then can't it be 'invented' in different ways? And how could any one way be known to be the right one? Is debating about ethical truth like debating the real location of a rainbow?

For the relativist, the last word in moral discussion is the same as the last word in etiquette, which is only: this is how *we* do it. Relativism is permanently fascinating because it can both seem inevitable (what other last word is there?), but also undermining: if morality is no more than the relativist says, then it loses its claims to universal, authoritative application. If we have in ethics nothing but the clash of desires, attitudes, and emotions then there is something misleading about the way ethical demands present themselves to us.[1] For they present themselves as having their own independent force, as binding and inescapable. They can be demanded of others, whereas mere sentiments and desires (so people think) cannot be demanded. Relativism threatens the power and independence of ethical obligation. Perhaps ethics becomes no more than a kind of social glue. And if this is what ethics is, it seems less important. If I care more about other things than being glued to my society, what is wrong with that?

In this final chapter, I try to show that this sense of threat is an illusion. I distinguish several forms of these ancient fears, and seek to show that they can be dispelled. The quasi-realist construction of the ethical proposition gives us a complete defence. We contain within our own natures the cure for the panic.

Relativism has traditionally two main forms: first as a theory *within* ethics, and second as a theory *about* the whole territory of ethics. But most importantly, it also labels the attempt to derive ethical conclusions from metaethical reflections: to derive conclusions within ethics from thoughts about our natures as practical agents. This inference detains us in the next section. In this section I consider relativism as a theory within ethics, or in other words as a practical or first-order ethic.

In practical terms, relativism also functions in two ways. First, as a plea to confine our concerns to within a certain group: a society. Second, as a plea for more understanding and less judgement in our relationship with other societies. I shall discuss the doctrine of confinement first.

The doctrine of confinement is the view that moral demands apply only within communities, like the demands of etiquette. They prescribe how *we* behave, where we make up some social group—a family, or class, or tribe, or nation, or the practitioners of some religion. Outsiders may do things differently, but we concern ourselves only with our group. It is not that outsiders are irrelevant, for our morality may dictate the kinds of relationship we are to have with them. A good Spartan, if Rousseau was right, would maintain aggressive and deceitful relations to the outsiders, just as a good Athenian, at least in Aristotle's eyes, would ignore them as contemptible.

I have explained how with ethics we make public and coordinate our attitudes. In the light of this, one peculiar and interesting practical stance is the moral reaction that stops at the first person plural, or even the first person singular. People express themselves by saying, for

---

[1] This problem is sufficiently acute for Michael Smith to call it *the* moral problem, in his book of that title.

example, that while *we* should not eat meat (or beef, or pork, or shell-fish, or whatever) we have no opinion about what *you* should do. Or, while it is a matter of principle for *me* to visit my parents once a week, it does not matter to me whether *you* do so. Such commitments feel as if they have the same importance as moral commitments, yet they seem to fall short of being directed at others. They do not apparently take us up the emotional staircase, justifying reactions of anger against persons and groups who do not share them, and yet they present themselves as matters of principle rather than of pure whim or preference. They are certainly important in practical living; indeed, as we saw in discussing Rawls, they can be sufficiently central in peoples' lives to prevent them from respecting hypothetical choices made in abstraction from them, from behind a veil of ignorance. In fact, the most central and deeply felt practical attitudes of many people frequently consist in devotion to prohibitions and ritual duties that belong exclusively to one tribe, nation, religion, or other social group. People typically bother more with obedience to dietary laws, or such things as prescribed dress or sexual etiquette, than they do with the wider human good, or with universal duties of justice or benevolence. People who have lost their religion frequently find it impossible to transgress the dietary prohibitions they were brought up on.

We can call moralities that limit their scope to some group, first-person moralities (remembering that there is a first person plural as well as a first person singular, so such an ethic can spotlight what *I* do, or what *we* do). There is something puzzling about them, and in Chapter 7 we saw Hare, for instance, presenting an account of ethics according to which they are incoherent. It is not clear how a morality can be completely self-absorbed in this way. How could one think that one is oneself under a duty not to eat meat, although it is perfectly all right if anyone else eats it? Surely one could only be under the duty if there is something wrong about eating meat (and one doesn't want to do what it is wrong to do), but in that case there must be something wrong about other people eating meat as well. Of course, often I am not concerned about making other people conform to what I regard as their duties, any more than I am concerned to make sure that they clean their teeth or wash their hair regularly.

As we saw while discussing Hare, an ethic that is partial to some groups may be derivative from a wider, or even universal, morality. Thus one may think that everybody ought to follow the dictates of their religion; I am a Jew or Christian or Muslim or Hindu; therefore I ought to eat or dress or behave in such-and-such a way. Or, one might think that everyone ought to show special loyalty to their family, or class, or other group, and then since one has some particular people as one's own family or class or group, one must show special loyalty to them. I would then be ready to express disapproval of those who belong to a different grouping, but do not show loyalty to their group and its rules. If this is the way it works, the particular duties one finds oneself under are examples of more general duties, applying to everyone, but applied in the light of one's own particular situation of family, tribe, or other grouping. In the terminology of Chapter 7, we have a universal but partial ethic.

These stances are certainly coherent, but they are not first-person all the way down, because the particular duties one recognizes oneself to be under are derivative from universal duties, that apply to anybody, simply applied to one's own particular situation. Frequently, however, the practitioners of first-person moralities appear to have no such universal thoughts. Their first and last thought on an issue may be that this is how *we* do it. They simply do not care about the others. In like manner, I can claim that when some dirty work has to be done I very much want to keep *my* hands clean, but at the same I do not care whether other people dirty theirs. I may even be dependent upon them doing so. I would not care myself to work in the meat industry, but if I am a meat-eater, I have to be glad that somebody does.

Such thoughts may simply express a kind of squeamishness. But they may feel like matters of principle, and certainly they seem to many agents to define matters of principle. They may even be recognized as such, for instance by tribunals that release people from what would otherwise be a civic duty, if they can show that fulfilling it transgresses a principle that governs their lives. If a preference can be transmuted into a matter of principle, we expect people to respect it. More importantly, as we saw discussing contractarianism, it means we may be unwilling to drop it as we contemplate accommodations with other parties.

If we only ever think about what *we* are to do then we do not seek to place our particular practices within a wider understanding of duties applicable to all human beings. It is not only that *we* define ourselves as different from *them* by eating or dressing differently, but also by refusing to see our way as just one way amongst others, or as derivative from a universal frame of conduct that applies to them as well as to us. Quite apart from its lack of explanatory and justificatory backing, such moral complacency with our own position is not ethically all that admirable. The attitude is often one of simple superiority, or it may be simply one of not caring about the behaviour of those unfortunate enough not to be part of the favoured group. What this suggests is that a morality is only fundamentally first-person if it is more or less explicitly separatist in its intent. The thought is that *we* (or *I*) alone matter (my concern is to save my soul, and devil take the rest), and therefore we or I have no need to take *them* into account except perhaps as a potential nuisance. It is wrong to give an account of morality that ignores such thoughts, but it has to be recognized that they are dangerous and divisive. Of course, people are often egoistic and limited in their practical concerns, but the combination of limiting one's own concerns to the immediate circle, and then presenting the limitation as a matter of *principle*, and therefore requiring respect by those outside the circle, is difficult to admire.

We should notice that to retreat within a personal or community ethic in this sense is not to withdraw from attitudes such as encouragement or anger. Communities defined by their local prohibitions and practices are obviously primed to hostility against members who lapse. And even someone operating a solitary, first-person principle is primed towards anger with herself upon what she regards as falling short of her own standards: guilt or shame, for example. And they are typically disposed towards hostility to those who 'fail to respect' their principles.

Confining our concerns, then, issues in a certain kind of morality, but not one that is all that admirable, and certainly not one that is in any way compulsory. If this is all that relativism amounted to, it would be the recommendation of a particular ethic, but one which has only limited appeal.

But the second way in which relativism is expressed in practice is more familiar. It is in the plea for toleration towards those who do it differently. Such a plea is often well-placed. The astonishing moralistic imperialism of Western civilization, with its missionaries and magistrates and conviction of the superiority of its own ways, in confrontation with the peoples whose lands and lives it destroyed over the last five centuries, makes melancholy reading. For the relativist, the cure can usefully be thought of as involving three steps. First, before anything, you must understand the alien culture or form of life. Second, you must reflect whether it is not a proper, admirable, adaptation to whatever circumstances the people find themselves in. Third, says the first-order relativist, when you do this you will lose any inclination to colonial interference, and still less to outrage or indignation: you will replace such reactions by benign toleration. Live and let live: *tout comprendre, c'est tout pardonner*.

The first two stages are indeed required for any intelligent engagement with the lives of others. The problem is with the third step. For the obvious response is that although the third stage often follows on the first two, in good and sensitive people, there is no reason for it always to do so. It remains quite possible that one should understand an alien culture's attitudes and way of life, yet find oneself invoking moral indignation and outrage against them. This is typically so when, deep in a culture, lie norms that lead to the mistreatment of its own minorities, or its women, its children, its infirm, or its old people, or those of the wrong kind of birth or class. If a society institutionalizes practices that ruin the lives of many of its members, benign toleration seems simply blind. To understand such practices is not to forgive them, or to be happy coexisting with them, and still less to approve of them. Of course, the question of what to *do* is not then solved. I may regret ways of life that practise female circumcision, to take a nasty contemporary example, but I may not have any grasp of a practical way of doing much about it. And I may be vaguely aware that if it disappears certain kinds of ways of life, perhaps with other, admirable, features, will disappear with it. I must balance the disapproval against worry that the world may become a drabber and more uniform place, just as if I would welcome the destruction of some particularly unpleasant biological scourge, yet worry that the ecology will become impoverished if it goes.

The stance of increased toleration that may follow upon better understanding of a culture is sometimes used as a lever to unseat the moral relativist. The idea is that in one breath he is announcing that all values are relative to society; in another he is announcing, apparently as an 'absolute' value, that increasing understanding of societies should increase our toleration of their ways. The charge is that the relativist must shelter behind what has been called the 'Ishmael effect'. After the catastrophe at the end of *Moby Dick* the entire ship is destroyed, but, mysteriously, the narrator Ishmael escapes the wreck: 'I alone remain to tell the tale.' By analogy the relativist, on this view, inconsistently supposes that his moral opinions can escape the doom to which he consigns all others.

This is a venerable argument, and still popular.[2] But in the present application it is unconvincing. Consider the response to it given splendidly by William James, whose theory of truth was itself accused of asserting (absolutely) that all truth is relative to the person holding it:

---

[2] The argument goes back to the peritrope of Plato, *Theaetetus*, 171a. Hilary Putnam uses it in 'Why Reason can't be Naturalized', in his *Realism and Reason: Philosophical Papers*, vol. iii (Cambridge: Cambridge University Press, 1983), 237. Nagel mentions his discussion with approval, and gives his own rendering of it, in *The Last Word*, 15.

Can there be self-stultification in urging any account whatever of truth? 'Truth is what I feel like saying'— suppose that to be the definition. Well, I feel like saying that, and I want you to feel like saying it, and shall continue to say it until I get you to agree. Where is there any contradiction? Whatever truth may be said to be, that is the kind of truth which the saying can be held to carry.[3]

In the present application, the relativist asserts that we should fully tolerate some alien way of life. And he also holds that this is 'just us'—in other words, just us with our Western, Enlightenment, deep-rooted dislike of interference, for instance.

James's position may rightly make us nervous. There is something deeply wrong about the definition that truth is what I feel like saying. It makes it impossible to see our sayings as answering to the way things are, and therefore capable of success or failure. And without that much, the very notion of an assertion or a belief seems to vanish. But it is difficult to generalize this point to cover ethics. Nagel indeed protests that if the relativist makes James's move he 'does not call for a reply, since it is just a report of what the subjectivist finds it agreeable to say'. But this surely underestimates the position. The ethical relativist here has a distinct practical attitude, and one that might very well call for a reply. If we are bent on interfering with the alien way of life, and he is bent on our not doing so, we have practical, moral disagreement, and we need words to express it and words with which to try to resolve it.

The peritrope tries to catch the relativist out, by making him out to hold one claim, here a moral claim, 'absolutely'. But the canny relativist will not be caught in this trap: he will cheerfully apply his own conception of what a moral position is to his own moral position as well as those of others. The thinker who is impressed enough by cultural diversity to embrace toleration, while sometimes fatuous, is not thereby inconsistent, for she need not attribute to her attitude any further authority than she allows to attitudes in general. There is no kind of inconsistency in insisting on toleration of different ways of doing things, while at the same time recognizing that this insistence is 'just us'.

Nevertheless, the practical position remains insecure. Reticence at moralizing about the behaviour of other peoples is itself a moral position, and one that can coexist with admiration of their doings, or mere politeness, or blind and fatuous refusal to pay attention to them. And

---

[3] William James, 'What Pragmatism Means', in *Pragmatism* (New York: Longmans, 1908), 73 ff.

of course, there is a different kind of inconsistency in passionately advocating toleration, but doing so having climbed a way up the staircase of emotional ascent I identified in the first chapter. That is, it would be strange to campaign hard, but only against those who are intolerant, as if this were the worst thing people could be, and as if one's own campaign could somehow exempt itself, sheltering behind the Ishmael effect. It would be like beating children into eschewing violence, or murdering those who do not respect the sanctity of life. The attitude would be: 'Never be angry—and I shall be angry at you if you are.' We can easily recognize that there is something absurd about this combination. It could only begin to be defensible if, indeed, anger or indignation were dreadful states, but ones that only succumbed to doses of the same. One's own anger at the angry might then be defended as a necessary purgative.

Once more, it is not obvious that a practical or first-order relativist has to enter the trap. If she refuses to climb the staircase of emotional ascent, then she tolerates intolerance itself. Her practical life, however, is by then becoming fairly soggy. If nothing arouses her about other peoples' ways of behaving towards each other, she does not seem so much an advocate of a particular kind of morality, as something more like an ostrich, primarily concerned to notice and care about as little as possible.

The attitude of toleration is just that: an attitude. It is not all that admirable when the others do not deserve it, whether they belong to 'our group' or not. And this introduces one asymmetry with the relativist's favourite comparison, the rules of etiquette. These are indeed essentially *intra*-social. The convention that we do not burp appreciation of a meal coordinates our expectations of English or American eating habits, and it gives us no license to find ill-mannered other cultures who do it differently. But a moral claim can in principle regulate our attitude to outsiders who do not share it.

2. POSTMODERNIST RELATIVISM

Relativism as a first-order ethic has emerged as a general advocacy of toleration. But there is no reason to adopt this: it all depends on the case. Sometimes we admire the others, sometimes merely tolerate them, but sometimes it may be right to interfere. Still, the relativist says, it is important to remember that whatever we do it is just us, voicing our judgements, which therefore have no authority beyond that which we give them. This aspires to be a point *about* ethics, highlighting a lost authority. And it is supposed to have implications *within* ethics. How does that work?

The lost authority haunts us. This is why it can appear that in the rational mind any admission of relativism is a kind of surrender. It is an admission, one part of us thinks, that should itself paralyse judgement. And in practical discussion the spectre of relativism is frequently intended to unseat confidence. It is meant to deflate any claim to authority, and hence to moral commitment, including even a commitment to toleration. The relativist becomes someone who stands ready to disown his or her own convictions, and eventually, becomes unstable, incapable of conviction at all. This is the view we now turn to consider.

I shall illustrate what is involved in practical relativism by taking two examples of contemporary moral philosophizing: the views of Richard Rorty on the one hand, and those of Ronald Dworkin and Thomas Nagel on the other. Although apparently as divergent as can be, I shall suggest that they show a surprising tendency to coalesce, and that this should make us suspicious of many ways of drawing this debate.

Rorty is widely hailed as a 'brisk chronicler of our epistemological condition'.[4] And he is a clear example of someone who assents to a relativistic theory about ethics (and indeed, about other discourse as well), and who draws practical consequences from this theory about the nature of human thought, including moral thought. He is also a more than usually well-informed and articulate opponent of normal, or mainstream, or analytical philosophy. He thinks of the subject as embedded in a discourse that has had its day, an overarching 'Plato–Kant' tradition, within which its problems make sense, but outside which they make no sense. He wants us not to fight this tradition so much as to ignore it: to change the subject. Here Rorty and other postmodernists follow Thrasymachus in supposing that behind the façade of ethical discussion lie the realities of the will to power. Whatever moral and political thought feels like from the inside, it is ultimately the product of thinkers whose success is a matter of their power to impose vocabularies upon others. Rorty believes that philosophers no longer have that power, but the mantle has passed, happily, to literary theorists, psychoanalysts, and other commentators on the contemporary scene, and indeed it is such people who have proved his main constituency. His views therefore demand the gravest

---

[4] Stanley Fish, *Doing What Comes Naturally: Change, Rhetoric, and the Practice of Theory in Literary and Legal Studies* (Durham, N.C.: Duke University Press, 1989), 501–2.

attention from those of us who find them inadequate to life in its widest political and ethical dimensions, and inadequate especially as a guide to the proper direction of the humanities or social sciences.

Of course, Rorty is not a monster. He describes himself as a liberal, who thinks that 'cruelty is the worst thing we do'.[5] So far so good. But he is also an ironist: he takes his philosophical stance to make attractive, a figure who 'faces up to the contingency of his or her own most central beliefs and desires—someone sufficiently historicist and nominalist to have abandoned the idea that those central beliefs and desires refer back to something beyond the reach of time and chance'. This is the relativistic theme. Elsewhere the ironist is defined as fulfilling three conditions: (1) she has radical and continuing doubts about the final vocabulary she currently uses, because she has been impressed by other vocabularies, vocabularies taken as final by people or books she has encountered; (2) she realizes that argument phrased in her present vocabulary can neither underwrite nor dissolve these doubts; (3) in so far as she philosophizes about her situation, she does not think that her vocabulary is closer to reality than others, that it is in touch with a power not herself.[6] In short, the ironist is impressed by the thoughts that lead people to relativism. Ironists are therefore 'meta-stable': never quite able to take themselves seriously, because always aware that the terms in which they describe themselves are subject to change, always aware of the contingency and fragility of their final vocabularies and thus of themselves.

In the same sentence Rorty associates this tendency to instability with 'the realization that anything can be made to look good or bad by being redescribed'. We can usefully start by wondering what this might mean, and why people should be destabilized by thinking it. Trivially, people do redescribe events and they redescribe them in loaded ways: official dispatches and government reports like to redescribe the most awful atrocities as 'protecting legitimate interests', for example. An army may create a desert but it will call it peace. Someone might redescribe some awful event, such as the Holocaust, so that it looks good, by missing out all the detail, or just picking upon some incidental fact: 'The event that prompted the greatest diary of the Second World War', for instance. For his thought to be interesting, Rorty must have in mind more than this kind of casual, misleading, or vague description that merely serves to cover up all the important

---

[5] Richard Rorty, *Contingency, Irony and Solidarity* (Cambridge: Cambridge University Press, 1989), xv.
[6] Ibid. 73.

moral textures. Perhaps he is impressed by the thought that we may one day arrive at *better* descriptions of historical events than those we can manage at present. But it is one thing to wonder if we may one day find better words to describe some event or some aspect of life, but quite another to wonder whether those better words will involve a reversal of our valuations. I can easily imagine a better history of, say, the Holocaust than any written so far. But how can I imagine that a truer, fuller, and better description of it might represent it as anything other than abhorrent?

Perhaps Rorty means to emphasize '*looks* good', so his claim is only that there may be some audience and some description, such that a description of the Holocaust to that audience makes it look good to them. But who is this audience? Neo-Nazis, or sadistic fantasists of some equivalent stripe? Then we have to wonder why that has the significance he evidently attaches to it. Why should such a possibility make my own judgement of the Holocaust unstable? All it does is open up the melancholy possibility of people who don't understand the Holocaust in any way that exhibits its horrors, or who are inhuman enough to fail to respond to those horrors. But far from lightening the weight of my own commitment, the realization that there are such people, actual or possible, would better be seen as a reminder of the importance of keeping in good moral training, prepared and ready for my defence and my dissent whenever I am faced with them.

Suppose we do believe that there is a way of looking at practical life that is different from ours, root and branch. How are we to react to this discovery? As we have seen, at least as a matter of psychology, many civilized people find it very uncomfortable to recognize that a certain moral tone they have put on a situation is 'relative', in the sense that other ways of looking at the matter exist. But the right reaction is surely that these encounters are essentially opportunities for moral thought. Sometimes we can dismiss the rival attitudes as the unfortunate or even evil product of various defects. This is how we should react on learning that there is some audience that presents the Holocaust to itself in a way that makes it seem harmless or admirable. Sometimes, our old opinions may be destabilized, but only as they evolve into something else that commends itself more. We have learned something, and can incorporate the improvement. Sometimes, however, we may not know what to think, and we may withdraw from previous commitments into a kind of scepticism. In other words, a rival approach represents a challenge, and there will be different ways of meeting it. To anyone except the bigoted or prejudiced, it has to be met. But it is only sometimes that it causes instability in our views.

To agree with Rorty, we have to approve of a connection between the understanding of our commitments as in some important sense *ours*, and the playful and self-deprecating, ironical, standpoint that this is supposed to engender. Notice that this is itself a matter of taking one input, here an awareness of the origins of our commitments, to determine a definite output, namely the aesthetic and ironic response. Advocating this reaction is thus entering a moral claim. So should we agree with it as a general recipe? The ironic attitude can certainly be attractive: nobody ought to belittle the flexibility and humour that an appreciation of one's own peculiarities can engender. The Puritan, the Calvinist, the fanatic, is typically unselfconscious in the ways that the ironist is not. If Rorty sounds appealing at this point it is because such lack of self-awareness encourages various kinds of bigotry against which we want defences. But the defence we want is a *mean*. You do not want to be a prig or bigot, but neither do you want to be a weightless aesthete, to whom all real commitment is a subject of joke or parody. You need to be able to judge when the time for pastiche and irony is past, when the chips are down and people are counted and things need saying. You need to know when talk of 'other vocabularies' and different ways of looking at things is idle, and the moment for standing fast has arrived. Some judge it too quickly, and others too slowly, but it lies somewhere. Knowing where it lies may take the Aristotelian qualities of maturity and judgement: it is itself a piece of moral knowledge. Similarly, the judgement that the others, whose different opinions you hear, need to be taken seriously is a moral judgement. We may be destabilized when those other attitudes have their own credentials, being held by people who see situations clearly enough, and exhibit other undeniable virtues. But if they are not, then we may simply return from the encounter with our own commitments reaffirmed.

In his wonderful compendium of the reasons for doing nothing in university affairs, Francis Cornford lists 'This may block the way for far more sweeping reforms', along with 'The time is not yet ripe', as part of the self-serving rhetoric of conservatives.[7] But even Cornford did not add the blanket 'Someone may come along with a different way of looking at it'. The humour in Cornford arises because his academics were so clearly well-fed, well-contented men perfectly adapted to the social world they inhabited and perfectly supported by it. Nothing needed doing. Indeed, doing anything radical would be bad form, and sheltering behind the comfortable platitudes and doing

---

[7] Francis Cornford, *Microsmographica Academica* (Cambridge: Bowes & Bowes, 1908).

nothing shelves the problem. The aesthetic or ironic stance is the privilege of those for whom action is not a priority. The playful stance is appropriate to people for whom most of the decisions of life are play.

Rorty, and he is symptomatic of much postmodernism, frightens us into the aesthetic stance by a bogey. The bogey is one of 'truth' out there, God's truth, truth independent of vocabulary and the human perspective. We have to realize, he tells us, that truth, in so far as it means anything to us, is the same as comprehensible truth, and which truth is comprehensible depends in part on the make-up of the comprehender. Then we should remember the presence of historical and subjective conditions, the mutable and transient nature of vocabularies, and the endless revaluations and replacements brought about by processes of cultural and scientific change. The 'Plato–Kant' tradition is presented as a long search for a non-temporal, non-human anchorage—a contact-point between us and the Truth, a rational interpenetration, a mating of *nous* and *logos*—and it is the glory of the Nietzsche–Heidegger–Derrida revolt to have realized that this is an illusory ideal.

Now it is not at all clear what this bogey amounts to: what the mistake is that is shared so widely until Nietzsche, and is so clearly a mistake now. Relativism about truth in general faces the same choices that we have put in front of relativism about ethics. Certainly people 'look at things differently' in science as well as in practical living. But how can we conclude from this that no ways of looking at the world are better than any others? On the face of it, some ways of representing the world are distorted, inadequate, useless, and the products of ignorance, laziness, and superstition. The existence of these need not destabilize us. Nobody is sincerely inclined to retreat from the modern conception of the shape of the solar system by remembering that for centuries people thought about it differently. And the bare possibility of better ways of thinking about the world than any we happen to have here and now must only encourage us to build, carefully, on what we have got. It is just an armchair paradox that there is no such thing as progress in knowledge, in some areas, at some times.

There is also something perturbing about the picture supposed to replace a duly cautious belief in truth. For let us suppose that some philosophers, at some times, did indeed invest the word 'true' and its cognates with more weight than it will bear. Perhaps they gave it a mythical 'supersense' or invested it with properties that it does not have (perhaps they thought of truth as somehow luminous, or magnetic, for example, although I can think of no historical examples). Our problem is not then theirs, but is one of how much weight we can *our-selves* now invest in the notion of truth, once the contingencies of value and judgement have been put in front of us.

Let us then turn to a concrete example. In his essay on George Orwell's *1984*, Rorty recognizes that Orwell (and the hero, Winston) share a commitment to truth, and that one of the most frightening and dangerous things about the Party in the novel is its power to control beliefs. The Party has the nightmarish power to have people believe what it wants them to believe. (If the particular nightmare has faded now, let us substitute another. Consider the way in which the 'thera-peutical establishment' can manipulate what people believe them-selves to remember, for instance about childhood trauma or abuse.) Rorty recognizes that he must say something about why Winston's fear is so perfectly recognizable. For, if we have lost any sense of 'objective truth', as Rorty thinks we should, then all that is happening is that one kind of power—the Party—is filling a power vacuum left when it ousted other powers, such as the scientific academy. Why should we be so frightened of a change of government? Rorty is right to face the challenge. If he cannot understand the fear, and diagnoses it simply as expressing wrongly Platonized conception of ourselves and of truth, it is his own position, not the concerns of Orwell or Winston, that is revealed as inadequate. So what he offers as an inter-pretation of the fear is this: all that matters is that if you do believe something, you can say it without getting hurt. In other words, what matters is your ability to talk to other people about what seems to you to be true, not what is in fact true. It is the power of the Party to stop him from speaking his mind that emerges as Winston's fear.

But surely this is quite wrong. The nightmare is not one of being made to be quiet about one's beliefs, but that of having one's beliefs manipulated, and so formed in the wrong way. The Party is perfectly happy that if you believe something you can say it without getting hurt. It is happy about that because it has the technology to ensure that you only believe what it wants you to believe. It has no need to censor expressions of belief, just because it has the previous power to control the form belief will take. The nightmare is precisely that: your beliefs are not under control as they should be, but are instead under control of the political authorities. In response to this Rorty unveils his bogey—saying this implies collaborating with some Platonic, Kantian, myth about truth—but it is possible to demonstrate that he is wrong about that. The neatest demonstration comes from realizing that Orwell's nightmare, and Winston's commitment, are perfectly well statable by a minimalist or deflationist, without using *any* concept of truth at all.[8] Winston's commitment can usefully be presented in such a way as this:

> (i) He wants it to be the case that he believes p only if p.
> (ii) He wants to form beliefs only in areas in which, when he does believe p, then p.

These two desires can of course be combined with others. You may want to form beliefs about important matters rather than unimportant matters, or deep rather than superficial matters. But by themselves they capture the nature of Winston's nightmare. Winston is afraid that the Party can bring it about that he does believe that the government is wise, when the government is not wise, just as one might fear that the therapist can bring it about that you or others believe in certain events which did not occur. Winston will have such beliefs because the Party says so, not because investigations appropriate to determining whether the Party is wise have determined that it is.

Rather than worry about an inflated conception of truth, what we really need is to keep hold of the nature of *judgement*. Any proposition is given its sense by a set of rules or norms telling us what counts as proper evidence for it, and what are its implications. These norms also tell us that some situations yield better evidence than others. To know if there is a tomato in the cupboard, it is better to look than to toss a coin and guess. If I have the better evidence, I should not be destabilized by people who form their opinions on the worse. To conduct yourself so that you believe p only if p is to conform to such norms. The norms involved are the ones that bring about our understanding of what the proposition means. They are *enabling* norms, like the rules of chess. The rules of chess are what enables people to play the game; similarly, the rules surrounding a proposition are what enable people to think in terms of it. To depart from those norms, whether through self-deception, wishful thinking, political control, or anything else, is to begin to lose your right to be regarded as believing that p, and to depart enough is to forfeit your status as thinking about the topic at all. These norms are not 'social' or 'historical' 'conditionings' that a suitably light ironist or suitably acute social theorist can somehow fly away from. They are the structures that enable thought to take place.

We saw in Chapter 3 that the content of a statement exists only through its place in a norm-governed practice of application and withdrawal, determining proper evidence for it and proper inference from it. Participating in such a practice is not optional, if we would think

---

[8] Readers may wish to recollect the discussion of minimalism in Chapter 4.

and count as thinking at all. It is not play (and even those for whom all speech and all action has become play must play at accepting the norms). Winston's nightmare is that other things than the norms appropriate to propositions are forcing him to accept or reject them: the nightmare is one of being left no basis for trust in his judgement. It is the fear of being left unable to judge at all and so, in an entirely literal sense, the fear of losing his mind.

Rorty is a particularly acute example of the interaction between abstract metaphysics—the subject of the study, of dry academic forums—and practical politics. The detached, ironic, aesthetic posture is attractive, relaxing, essentially *civilized*. It is the state that the Greeks called *epoche*.[9] The Greeks (like Buddhists) thought that *epoche* leads to personal tranquillity. The highest form of living becomes merely spectating life, a kind of saintly fatalism, an indifference to the events around one. Such withdrawal is certainly pleasant enough in many circumstances. But it is itself an ethical and political action. Withdrawing from insisting upon an obligation, for instance, is equivalent to allowing an action or issuing a permission. It is not a purely private stance. It is a stance that can engage the attention of others, and inevitably it may prompt their hostility, and often needs defence. It is nice to think that your theory of truth supports it. But the position is only possible for those who can afford to think of their lives as play. It takes a certain amount of philosophical thought, of the kind Rorty believes himself to have floated above, to realize this.

The conclusion of this brush with postmodernism is, once more, that there is no way of escaping from ethics. But it also shows us that there is no reason to think we have to escape from it, if we would confront our situation clearly. Faced with different vocabularies and voices, we compare theirs with ours. If they seem to have got something right which we have not, we learn from them. If we have something right that they have not, we may be able to teach them. If their attitudes are foul and frightful, we may have to be at war with them.

3. RAMSEY'S LADDER

We saw Rorty attempting to support a practical attitude, that of the ironist, by means of reflection on truth and objectivity, or its absence. And we saw no reason to affirm the attitude, nor to take it to be sup-

---

[9] Julia Annas and Jonathan Barnes, *The Modes of Scepticism: Ancient Texts and Modern Interpretations* (Cambridge: Cambridge University Press, 1985).

ported by the views about description and language, or the 'situated' nature of human beings in a specific culture at a specific time.

So far as ethics goes, a similar case is made by Thomas Nagel and Ronald Dworkin, who also eschew the postmodernist ethical attitudes.[10] But what about the theory of ethics? At first sight, on any metatheoretical issue, they are as far from Rorty as can be, presenting themselves as Plato to Rorty's Protagoras. They announce themselves as cognitivists and realists, who celebrate truth, reason, and objectivity in ethics. These sound like just the 'Platonic–Kantian' terms with which to combat relativism. But the question will be what they come to in these writings. And when we see what they come to, it may be that the difference from the postmodernists begins to blur.

The reason for this is more obvious in the writings of Dworkin. Dworkin holds the view that all the relevant questions are internal, first-order, moral questions. The terms with which what seem to be metaethical positions are laid out are not fitted to sustain theory: we have to be metaethical minimalists. All the relativist can be intending is a moral claim (as in the first section of this chapter), and all that any opponent can do is meet that with moral claims and arguments of his own. What we do not have is a view *about* ethics. We only have views *within* ethics.

When presented as universal, applying to all claims in the vast world of the theory of ethics and practical reason, this is a rather peculiar position. It is one thing to say that Rorty, for example, improperly tries to support an ethical conclusion with a metaethical thought. It is a much stronger thing to say that there is no such thing as metaethical thought at all. When Hume, or Hare, or Gibbard, or I myself gives a story about our natures as beings who make decisions, who adopt attitudes, who have needs and desires and values, we are not on the face of it *moralizing*. We are doing the anatomy of philosophical psychology, and following Hume we distinguish the role of the anatomist from that of the painter. Is it credible that there is nothing to this distinction?[11]

We can approach this question by asking another. How does minimalism enable anyone to dub themselves a cognitivist, or a realist, or a defender of objectivity and an opponent of relativism? The answer is, by taking all the terms that might be used to frame metaethical debates onto Ramsey's ladder: the ladder we met in Chapter 3, taking us from 'p' to 'It is true that p' to 'It is really a fact . . . that it is true that p'. We saw that for the minimalist Ramsey's ladder is horizontal. From

---

[10] Dworkin, 'Objectivity and Truth: You'd Better Believe It'; Nagel, *The Last Word*.
[11] Hume, *Treatise*, III. iii. 7, p. 620.

its top there is no different philosophical view than from the bottom, and the view in each case is just, *p*. In other words, if it is minimalism that justifies the ascent, then the ascent gets nowhere that is inaccessible to anyone of decent first-order ethical views. To say that an ethical view is true is just to reaffirm it, and so it is if we add the weighty words 'really', 'true', 'fact', and so on. To say that it is objectively true is to affirm that its truth does not vary with what we happen to think about it, and once more this is an internal, first-order ethical position.[12]

Of course, these first-order ethical views might be shared by everyone, or by everyone decent, and that could in principle include the dreaded postmodernists. So there is suddenly less to Dworkin's stance than meets the eye. The rhetoric of 'realism' has stopped marking out a particular position, and retains only a talismanic quality: perhaps it is just, as James described the Absolute, the giver of moral holidays.[13] Dworkin called his main recent work on this area 'Objectivity and Truth: You'd Better Believe It'. But what is it that we are supposed to believe? The proposition that there is objective truth in ethics, once the minimalism is in place, can only serve as a summary for one of the lists we met in Chapter 3. It becomes a long disjunction of claims like 'Slavery is wrong: you'd better believe it, or slavery is permissible, you'd better believe it, or genocide is bad, you had better believe it, or genocide is good, you'd better believe it, or . . .'. The list would be given like other minimalist lists, in accordance with some principle for constructing possible objects of moral approbation or disapprobation. This is, of course, a list to which all can assent, since the 'you'd better believe it' element must be construed, in accordance with minimalism, simply as repetition or exhortation. Reverting to the older American tradition of a Longfellow or Whitman, Dworkin could equally have called his paper, 'Don't be worried!' or 'Affirm yourself!'

Yet Dworkin takes himself to be defending a 'face-value' view of ethics, a view held by ordinary unphilosophical folk who have not been tainted by postmodernism or expressivism. He thinks this face-value view is 'full-blooded' and 'shameless', a brave bulwark against the relativists.[14] But what can this mean? There is nothing full-blooded or shameless about saying, for example, that genocide is wrong, or

---

[12] Dworkin here makes the typical quasi-realist move, of insisting that claims about 'mind dependency' are read as first-order moral claims. Thus for me 'kicking friendly dogs would be wrong whatever we thought about it' enters an admirable moral claim rather than any kind of metaphysical or metaethical claim. See my *Essays in Quasi-Realism*, 4, and for the earliest discussion, 124–9.

[13] William James, 'What Pragmatism Means', in *Pragmatism*, 73 ff.

[14] Ibid. 127.

even repeating it, with the semantic terms of Ramsey's ladder added, since this just means banging a drum.

This suggests that Dworkin is only half aware that Ramsey's ladder is horizontal. At some level, he thinks the view from the top is different, superior, to the view from the bottom. Or perhaps he thinks that the view from the bottom, when all that is said is *p*, already includes philosophical theory, and especially a theory called realism, as part of its content. For when it suits, he interprets the face-value view as containing doctrines *about* morality. Thus he supposes that expressivists, who do have a view about morality, are held to require revision of what 'people' think.[15] But if the peoples' thoughts are entirely confined to the moral then there is absolutely nothing revisionary about expressivism. Expressivists aren't afraid of the list of disjunctions. Once the face-value views are interpreted as repetitions or emphatic ways of reaffirming moral convictions and the standards with which to hold them, no expressivist, from Hume onwards, has any reason to disagree with them. Nor do the folk, following their face-value ways, have the least reason to disagree with the expressivists.

We saw that for Ramsey and Wittgenstein minimalism about truth consorts with the most strict attention to the actual functions of judgement: the sifting of dispositions and stances and other propositional attitudes that underlie the 'language game' of practical reasoning. When this part is ignored minimalism offers no kind of view at all of the practice of judgement, and this is why any 'cognitivism' or 'realism' that supposes itself to be protecting actually marks no philosophical position. It amounts, at best to an ethical commitment: something like an injunction to get involved. A 'realist' of this stripe is simply someone who opposes the ironic attitudes of a Rorty, an unambitious piece of moral criticism that may, of course, be quite estimable in itself.

Nagel's discussion is avowedly influenced by Dworkin's and may seem similar in its upshot. But it is, in fact, not nearly so minimalist. This is partly because Nagel more explicitly holds a particular doctrine about the power of reason: he believes that there exist passions and desires that are 'themselves motivated and/or justified by reasons that do not depend on still more basic desires'.[16] He recognizes, in other words, that he is in opposition to Hume over the scope of reason and the nature of motivation. But the ground here is that we have already covered in the preceding two chapters. The question is whether there is scope for anything beyond a Hume-friendly conception of practical

[15] Ibid. 109. [16] Nagel, *The Last Word*, 102.

reasoning. Nagel believes that there is, but we have already discussed the mistaken picture of deliberation that motivates this opposition.

The other reason why Nagel is not a pure minimalist is more mysterious. He refers approvingly to a kind of Platonism he finds in Peirce, whereby we are sustained by an inward harmony between the way we think and the order of nature.[17] He takes seriously the quasi-religious hypothesis of some mysterious thing (not evolution, not anything visible to science) that is needed to explain the existence of minds in tune with the eternal verities of nature. This clashes badly with his stated sympathy for Dworkin's minimalism. For minimalism takes *everything*. We can happily climb the horizontal ladder from *p* as far as '*p* is in accord with the eternal and real normative order that governs the universe'. And there is doxastic minimalism as well, in which the topic is our own belief. Thus instead of 'we hold *p*' we might go in for locutions like 'in holding *p* our minds resonate in harmony with the eternal etc.' All this can mean is that we hold *p*. Yet Nagel seems to *intend* the reverse of minimalism. He intends Plato at full throttle. But making sense of that, and then believing it, seem high prices to pay for a defence of our right to go on deliberating as best we can.

4. RELATIVISM AND AUTHORITY

The relativist believes that arguing about ethical truth is like arguing about the true location of the rainbow. Or, it is like arguing about whether in an empty room a pot of flowers in front of a mirror appears in the mirror, a question which makes no sense except relativized to a point of view. And there are after all plenty of cases in which a set of sentiments with purely subjective origins can seem to the subject like the constraints of an independent authority. A lover feels that he or she must be with the beloved; a slave of fashion believes he or she must wear this year's colour or style. It feels not to be an expression of desire, but a necessity, even sometimes a burden, and certainly a condition of any possibility of happiness. To the subject, the idea that certain styles of dress are simply impossible can feel as certain, independent, and objective a constraint on choice as any ethical imperative. They can even be demanded of others, in the sense that those who choose such styles may condemn themselves socially as disastrously as those who behave badly (perhaps more so). But any picture

---

[17] Ibid. 129.

of human life will see the dictates of love or fashion as dependent entirely on subjective sentiments, without objective authority or validity.

For something to be fashionable it is necessary and sufficient that enough people (or people of some group with some status) give it their blessing. This tells us nothing about the process of reasoning these arbiters themselves go through in order to judge whether a thing is fashionable. But it is important to see that their thought-processes, if they can be so dignified, cannot themselves be exhaustively concerned with the question, 'Is this fashionable?' We can appreciate this by thinking of a parallel case. Suppose a thinker is very impressed by the extent to which scientific acceptance is determined by such things as social status or connections in the network of grant giving and prize awarding bodies. Suppose then they propose an overtly relativistic theory of truth:

> (*Relat*) X is true = X is what will prevail given the power struc-
> ture of the academy.

The interesting argument asks: what do you think happens in the deliberations of the academy? Any plausible answer has to admit that individuals advance statements against X or on behalf of X. That is, individuals advance statements that they take to be against or for the *truth* of X. So now we ask whether in doing this, can *they* be thinking of truth as it is represented in (*Relat*)? The answer has to be that they cannot. That must be the wrong place to turn. Suppose, for instance, the academy is wondering whether the Earth circles the Sun. They cannot at the same time be construed as wondering whether this is the opinion that will prevail, given the power structure of the academy. Members can certainly ponder that—as it were, making a book on their own voting—but it is a different thing altogether. Consider a piece of evidence that the Earth circles the Sun. This evidence is evidence that the opinion that it does so will prevail, only if it is evidence that the academy will take into account. But they cannot themselves stare at the issue of whether they *will* take it into account as determining whether they *should* take it into account. They have to deploy their independent standards of evidence in astronomy as they confront the last question, and it is what happens when they deploy those, that settles the first question. The point is that there has to be an *independent exercise* of adjudging evidence, apart from judging whether it is evidence that will be taken into account. This is a way of filling out the point just made, that the norms governing what counts as evidence in connection with a theoretical proposition determine the sense of the proposition. They are not avoidable, save at the cost of failing to think about the issue at all.

Note that this is not an argument that this independent exercise is well directed at the objective truth. It is only an argument that the academy must operate in terms that are *not* directed at the question of what they themselves will think. Otherwise they would face paralysis, in the same way that an electoral board would be paralysed if the *only* consideration each member cares about is whether a candidate is favoured by the others. If that is all, then none of them can cast a preference until they know what the preference of the others is. It is sometimes suggested that theatre critics are like this, none of them daring individually to make a judgement of a play until they know what the rest of the pack is going to say. It then takes a random event, a 'trembling hand', to set them off in one direction or another. Of course, if we are optimistic, as most people are in the case of science, we will suppose that the terms that break the implied log-jam are in fact adapted for the discovery of the truth.[18]

So even in the case of fashion, then, the arbiters of taste will not be exhaustively concerned with the question of whether something is or will be certified by the arbiters of taste. Instead, they select and compare and weigh features that in fact appeal to them.

The point strikes against relativism and subjectivism, at least in so far as it shows that ethical truth as it is conceived by us, as we debate, cannot be a truth about where we will end up or would end up after certain empirical procedures. Rather, as we insisted in Chapter 3, we conceive of it as truth about where we *ought* to end up, or would end up after *commendable* procedures, or where we would end up if we were *good*, just as in science we conceive of it as where we ought to end up, if we are to represent nature in the right way—which here means representing it to ourselves as it really is.

But a relativist will of course admit that participants will inevitably debate in terms of there being a truth at stake, rather than in terms of predicting where they themselves will end up agreeing. Still, as with

---

[18] I once attended a philosophy of science conference at which one of the participants, an adherent of a 'relativistic' philosophy of science of roughly the type indicated here, confronted the following paradox for his position. The physicist Michael Faraday has long been regarded as one of the great experimentalists. And the relativistic position implied that what he was concerned about, like everyone else, was such matters as power, prestige, and the likely acceptance of the academy. Yet, genius though he was, none of his instruments were apparently designed to locate or test for such things. They were instead designed to test for quite different things, such as electrostatic forces and electric potentials. The philosopher found this highly perplexing, and given his starting-point, maybe he was right to do so.

argument about the locus of the rainbow, or the flowers in the mirror, the subject may be an illusion. Perhaps there is really only the sway of power or politics; there is no genuine focus of debate. The image is one of participants in the grip of error, which the relativist or subjectivist has had the wit to see through. They are disputing about the real location of the rainbow. This is the 'error' theory of ethics associated with the philosopher John Mackie.[19] On this view, our first-order ethical practice is based on the presupposition that there are objective, independent, binding ethical facts, facts that exert pressure on all rational beings, whereas in truth there are no such facts. The view that there is an authoritative source for ethics is purely a fiction. It may be a useful fiction, but it is a mistake to take it for the truth.

How should the sentimentalist tradition respond? We can start by describing two near-misses. One is insufficient, and the other unnecessary. But by locating them we can see where the right answer lies. The first near-miss would take its stand on the actual convergence of attitude and sentiment among people 'in the long run'. The idea here is that, at least under some kinds of circumstances, the divergences of moral opinion we find would disappear. Peoples' emotional natures are sufficiently alike for them to acknowledge the same values, and the same rights and duties. Such diversity as we find is contextual, in which the same basic human nature works itself out in different environments:

The RHINE flows north, the RHONE south; yet both spring from the same mountain, and are also actuated, in their opposite directions, by the same principle of gravity. The different inclinations of the ground on which they run, cause all the difference of their courses.[20]

The second approach takes its stand on the *necessity* of this convergence. It is not that we just happen all to be alike, but that there is a necessity (of some kind) to converge on the truth. The formula offered by David Wiggins is that over a potentially disputed issue, one side can gain the high ground, justifiably talking of knowledge and truth, by showing that there is 'nothing else to think'.[21]

Actual convergence in opinion can well seem insufficient to allay

---

[19] J. L. Mackie, *Ethics: Inventing Right and Wrong* (Harmondsworth, Middx.: Penguin Books, 1977). Inventing is not quite the appropriate word, since we do not invent our attitudes and emotions. Only some parts of ethics concern the 'artificial' virtues, where an element of invention and convention comes into play.

[20] Hume, *Enquiry Concerning the Principles of Morals*, 'A Dialogue', 333.

[21] David Wiggins, 'Moral Cognitivism, Moral Relativism, and Motivating Beliefs', *Proceedings of the Aristotelian Society*, 91 (1990–1), 61–86. The formula is admired by Nagel, *The Last Word*, 69.

the problem of authority.[22] For we can think of ways in which people might actually converge on something pretty unpleasant. Across large tracts of human history, they may indeed have done so. Slavery, mistreatment of prisoners of war, mistreatment of women, of dissenters, and of strangers, have all flourished in many places and times, and indeed still do so. If the last word remains 'This is how we do it', it still falls short of funding the categorical claim to authority of ethics, even when 'we' as a matter of fact includes everybody, if, indeed, it ever does. Hence, Wiggins insists that 'There is nothing else to think' means more than 'There is nothing else for us to think'.[23]

What more? Wiggins is not entirely forthcoming. His favourite comparison is with '7 + 5 = 12'. Here indeed we may concede that there is nothing else to think in the strongest possible sense, because we have no conception of a genuine kind of mathematical thought that involves any different view (attempts have been made to sketch them, notably by Wittgenstein, but they quickly founder). Here we have that there is nothing else that it is *possible* to think. The enterprise of thinking any other way simply will not get off the ground. Of course, if this is true in ethics, then relativism does not get started. But it is not true: slave-owners and racists and misogynists and caste systems show all too plainly that there is something else to think.[24]

In explaining how his comparison works, Wiggins points us towards the kind of thing we might say, and eventually the kind of thing we would expect everyone to accept, if we are defending a fairly central moral certainty, for instance that slavery is unjust and intolerable. Here we work from within a moral scheme, reminding people of what they accept, and challenging the coherence or 'workability' of alternatives. I think this is exactly what needs to be done: it is, I think, a regulative principle of serious ethical thought that it contains the material for such exercises, and when dispute breaks out, they are compulsory. In Wiggins's terms, we are to follow a 'counsel of perseverance', step-by-step building up what we hope becomes an irresistible case.

But of course a relativist is apt to stay untroubled by this: she will insist that this is still just us, articulating our own attitudes as best we can. As with Dworkin's 'You'd better believe it', the words 'There is nothing else to think' simply becomes a badge of our own confidence,

---

[22] See also Crispin Wright, *Truth and Objectivity* (Cambridge, Mass.: Harvard University Press, 1992), ch. 3.   [23] 'Moral Cognitivism', 71.

[24] Cf. also Wittgenstein on ethics: 'There is no alternative does not mean what it does in logic', Rush Rhees, 'Wittgenstein's Lecture on Ethics: III', *Philosophical Review*, 74 (1965), 19.

or perhaps an injunction warning you not to think anything else on pain of my opposition. Such words, after all, are available in cases where relativism is more clearly attractive. The ardent slave of fashion supposes that there are *no two things to think* about the right height of skirt or the right material. She may well say that other lengths or materials are simply *impossible*.

Again, 'There is nothing else to think' may be heard in a way that carries insufficient weight for another reason. Consider again the use of 'thick' terms, which carry a certain evaluative weight, but are also tied quite closely to criteria of application that are relatively settled, at least in respect of being from a certain range of features. There may be nothing else to think than that Hengist is courageous, or that Horsa is chaste. This means that if we work in these terms at all, we will be bound to come to those judgements. Within communities that signal courage and chastity, this is how it is done. A dissident will need to work in other terms altogether, for he will not gain a hearing by denying that Hengist is courageous or Horsa chaste if they obviously are so. So there is only the one thing to think, provided, of course, that we think in these terms at all. But the problem lies with the proviso. In so far as the words in question signal a distinct evaluation of courage and chastity, there may well be something else to think, for it is perfectly possible to dislike and disapprove of Hengist's prowess in battle or Horsa's avoidance of erotic engagements. We can imagine a racist urging that there is nothing else to think than that so-and-so is a *****, but he is simply mistaken. The right thoughts are had by avoiding the terminology that insinuates attitudes possessed by a particular culture, and that therefore provide no defence against the charge of relativism.

So Wiggins needs to invest his formula with enough weight to disqualify the fashion editor or the racist from using it, but not so much as to identify it with what might be said about alternative arithmetics, for the comparison with arithmetic overshoots the mark. This is why relativism is a real issue in ethics, and only an unreal one in elementary arithmetic. In any interesting case, as Wiggins knows, historically there have been the other things which it has been possible to think.[25]

---

[25] In the particular case of the British abolition of slavery, Wiggins appeals to a class and period when there was general moral consensus, in order to suggest that there was nothing else to think. A wider trawl upsets this sunny picture, even amongst the English (or Scots): Wiggins may be fortunate enough not to have read, for instance, Carlyle's contribution to the question in *Fraser's Magazine*, December 1849, reprinted in *Critical and Miscellaneous Essays*, vol. iv (Boston, Mass.: Dama Estes & Company, 1869), although one could, I agree, pose a doubt about whether Carlyle was actually thinking. Other opponents of abolition clearly were, although doing so unpleasantly, of course.

It has been possible, for instance, to think that by failing to defend themselves in war people forfeit any right they may have had to decent treatment, or become appropriate objects of ownership by others. We can only hammer away at such a position by deploying our own values. 'Persevering' therefore is bound to mean working from within a particular set of values and concerns, and appealing to an audience to acknowledge them as theirs, and thence too to acknowledge their application to any disputed case. It is therefore quite unwarranted to think that optimism on the score of securing as wide a consensus as possible justifies us in supposing that there is nothing else that can be thought.

But this shows us the right way out, bypassing Hume's belief in actual convergence, without accepting the hyperbole of Wiggins's formula. For what the admirable policy of persevering requires is *not* strictly that there is nothing else which it is possible to think. The true formula does not settle for our actual shared commonalities of thought and feeling, but neither does it aspire to coerce any possible way of thought or feeling. Our actual practices of argument and persuasion require only the hope that there is nothing else for *decent* people to think. Certainly we are talking only of what *must* be thought ethically, but the necessity is itself *ethical*. The 'must' is the same as in: people must keep their promises. To try to show that something must be thought is no more, but no less, than to try to show that it is the right thing, or the best thing, to think. To do this we will be deploying values as we go. What we hope to show, as we persevere with analyses of social phenomena, deploying analogies, turning the values involved around in our minds, is that there is nothing else for good, decent people to think.

Faced with this, the relativist will, of course, suggest that we are using our left hand to give our right hand money. Certainly, she will say, you can work yourself into the frame of mind in which anybody dissenting reveals themselves as vicious or blind; you can link hands with the others in your community who feel the same way. But what you cannot do by such an exercise is to regain an authentic sense of the authority of your position. The sense of loss, when we found that we had to stand on our own feet, remains, or so says the relativist.

5. KNOWLEDGE, OBJECTIVITY, TRUTH

But should it really remain? We can put the point again in terms used by Thomas Nagel. For Nagel, it is a question of 'the last word'. The relativist thinks the last word in any discussion is 'that is just our opinion'. The relativist we are considering then derives a moral message from the fact that this is the last word. The absolutist or realist finds that shocking, and insists that the last word is something else: perhaps that our opinion conforms to the independent order of reason, for example.[26] But the right attitude may be neither: the right attitude, in my view, is that so far as this goes the last word is the first word. We stay with the original moral claim, and deliberate about it as best we can. In other words, the right course here is to rest on the horizontal position of Ramsey's ladder. Thus, consider an example:

(1) Slavery is a bad system.
(2) Our opinion is this: slavery is a bad system.
(3) Slavery is a bad system. That is just our opinion.
(4) Slavery is a bad system. That is an opinion reflecting an independent order of reason.

I introduce (2) simply to point out that in practice it is equivalent to (1): it does not function as a piece of psychological self-description, but as a way of giving the same verdict. Indeed in some situations a formula like it serves as the official way to deliver a verdict ('The opinion of this court is that . . .'). The relativist however goes on to intrude (3), and treats the introduction of the 'just' as a kind of qualification, or a step towards a qualification. It functions as a concessive move, one supposed to soften the conflict with people who deny (1). The realist or absolutist finds that shocking, and recoils to the philosophically charged (4). But (4) verges on the incoherent, for we have no conception of the nature of this independent order.

The right solution is not to oppose (3) with (4), but to neutralize it. Statement (3) reduces to (2), because there is nothing that the word 'just' can do. The word (like 'mere', as described in Chapter 4) insinuates a contrast: it is our opinion as opposed to something as good or better. But what as good or better is imagined? If the relativist is saying that it is just our opinion as opposed to a good or better opinion that approves of slavery, we are in moral dispute, certainly. But it is then up to him to locate this good or better opinion and defend it, and this we know he will be unable to do, for we are certain that slavery is a bad system. If he is saying it is just our opinion as opposed to e.g. the opinion of the gods, or an opinion with the quality gestured at in (4), then he is under a misapprehension about what opinion could ever be.

---

[26] Nagel, *The Last Word*, 129.

In other words, the relativist is sharing with the realist a mistaken vision of what powers might be conjured up by reflective thought. His problem was induced, as with nineteenth-century thinkers who felt morally lost when their religious faith vanished, purely by a mistaken vision of what things might be like. But the right response is not to share the vision and deny that it is mistaken, but to show that it never had any substance, and its loss is no loss at all. Statement (3) reduces to (2), which reduces to (1).

There is the platitude that different actual or possible sensibilities exist, and issue in different and sometimes conflicting attitudes. But relativism tries to go beyond the platitude and derive from it something significant for the concept of ethical truth. But what can it derive? It aims at something such as this: in some cases *it is equally true* that p and that not-p (one is true for us, and the other for them, for instance)? But if p is one of my commitments, I have no business allowing that it is true that not-p. Doing so induces incoherence in my set of attitudes. Of course, I can allow the solecism 'it is true for them that not-p' when this just means that they hold not-p, since that gets us nowhere beyond the platitude.

The idea I have been fighting is that I should not maintain the commitment to p, once I recognize the other sensibility. Why not? As I said above, it is only if the other sensibility commands some respect that my own commitment is even *prima facie* threatened, and then in balancing the respect, the threat, and the depth of my commitment I am back working from within my own framework of values, as of course I must do. There is no telling in advance whether it is the respect for the other sensibility, or the depth of my own commitment which is likely to lose in this process. The point is not that it is easy to know how to respond to a divergent sensibility. The point is that the response needs as full a range of imagination and thought as any other ethical matter. Because of this it is by no means given in advance that withdrawal, *epoche*, irony, or flabby aestheticism will win. On the contrary, given the real horror-show examples—the audience to whom the Holocaust seems fine—it is given in advance that they should *not* win. There is a time to tolerate and a time to fight. Such an audience simply serves to reinforce a proper sense of the gravity and indispensability of basic sympathies and concerns. Relativism and scepticism simply die away in the face of the obvious need to do this.

So can I talk of ethical knowledge? Across large tracts of human affairs, we know what to think. We can be fairly confident about the standards we use: to quote Hume for the last time, even a 'peevish delicacy' can never be carried so far as to make us deny the existence of every species of merit, and all distinction of manners and behaviour. Besides discretion, caution, enterprise, industry, assiduity, frugality, economy, good-sense, prudence, discernment; besides these endowments, I say, whose very names force an avowal of their merit, there are many others, to which the most determined scepticism cannot, for a moment, refuse the tribute of praise and approbation. Temperance, sobriety, patience, constancy, perseverance, forethought, considerateness, secrecy, order, insinuation, address, presence of mind, quickness of conception, facility of expression; these, and a thousand more of the same kind, no man will ever deny to be excellencies and perfections.[27]

Hume's list reflects a certain Scottish standpoint, but one sees what he is getting at. Perhaps I can contemplate as a bare possibility that some change should come along and 'improve' me into thinking that these are not after all standards for a good character. But I cannot really see how to take off the inverted commas, or in other words imagine how any such change would really be an improvement. The possibility remains idle, unreal. So I can quite properly claim to know that some things count as virtues and others do not. In other cases I may offer verdicts where I am not so sure. I may be in favour of a minimum wage. But I am uneasily aware that my understanding of economics is relatively poor, and that expert opinion differs. I know that there are processes that would almost certainly improve my grasp of the social consequences of a minimum wage. I predict they would reinforce my commitment to it. But I would not bet my shirt on that. So I think there is a real chance that improvement might undermine my verdict, and this means that due caution prohibits me from claiming knowledge. But in other cases I do have ethical knowledge: I know that happiness is better than pain, that promises deserve some respect, and so on for countless, fairly unambitious, pros and cons that make up my practical stance to the world.

What, then, of that other prized feature of good ethics, that it should be 'objective'? There are different ideals insinuated by the word. There is the degree of detachment to take up to issues, which may be too much or too little. It is difficult to know how much is right. Then there is the need to take up and respect the common point of view of Hume and Smith. There is objectivity in the sense of fairness and impartiality, the virtue above all of law courts and public administration. And of course, there is the objectivity mentioned above, of recognizing that it is not our own opinions that ground the rightness and wrongness of things. Cruelty is not bad because I think it is bad, but because it

---

[27] *Enquiry Concerning the Principles of Morals*, VI. 1, p. 242.

exhibits the intention to cause pain. Objectivity in all these senses is a moral virtue, and one to be striven for and respected.

Although this delivers a perfectly satisfactory answer to relativism, in many areas it can of course be strengthened with Hume's reminder of the basic building blocks of human living. While in the twentieth century we have all been impressed by the diversities of human nature and human culture, we should also remember the constancies that impressed earlier thinkers. We are social animals, with certain biological needs. We have to coordinate our efforts; we have to establish systems of property and promise-keeping and sometimes even government. We can then take comfort in reflecting that there are not so many admirable, coherent, mature, livable ethical systems on offer; indeed rather than being faced with a whole shopping basket of such things, our usual problem is to find as much as one that survives elementary critical reflection.

Relativism, then, can subside into the shadows. But perhaps we should not want it to disappear entirely. For it reminds us that there are choices to be made. It reminds us of the difficulty of even beginning to find One True System of Living, as many moral philosophers seem to try to do. It reminds us of the endless wrangles of moral theory, and the interminable casuistries it generates. So it may be appropriate to finish with a word about that.

First, let us return briefly to the dispute between universalists and particularists (Chapter 7). As I left it, the problem for particularists is to give an account of practical deliberation that makes it something other than the application of general principles to particular situations. The natural place to look would be to the 'valence' or direction of considerations. One might hold that it counts against an action that it is a lie, or for it that it causes pleasure, without committing oneself to the view that all lies are wrong, or all sources of pleasure good. It would be a matter of endorsing particular tendencies, without endorsing general principles.[28] In effect, we want our sensibilities to be reliable and projectible (pulling in the direction of general rules) but also sensitive and flexible (pulling in the direction of emphasis on particular contexts). Quasi-realism, I would urge, is well-placed to explain and to justify our tendency towards a mean here. We cannot think that each

---

[28] A more radical particularism, denying that there are even reliable tendencies of this kind, would be unable to make any sense of practical reasoning at all. If there was no pattern and no predicting which ways features would pull, from one occasion to another, deliberation would be an entirely arbitrary business. A view that seems to have this consequence is expressed in Jonathan Dancy, *Moral Reasons* (Oxford: Oxford University Press, 1993).

situation, in its full particularity, needs treating distinctly from each other situation, for then we have no ethic to communicate and to rely upon. And we do not want glacially abstract general principles, for then we miss the interesting textures of particular problems. Our sensibilities need to be firm, but flexible, for both these are virtues. As to whether all reflection and deliberation is a matter of bringing to bear universal or general principles, however complex, we may remain cautiously agnostic. Sometimes it surely is ('Don't commit adultery: full stop'). But sometimes the only evidence that universal principles are involved is that we are reasoning 'as if' we were bringing to bear some general principle. And then it may turn out that we are also reasoning as if we were bringing to bear any of a number of slightly different resembling principles. There are many ways of filling out the dots in a principle starting 'Never lie unless to someone who has no right to the truth, or if other obligations will not be met if you do . . . *and so on*', and it may simply be indeterminate which completed rule, if any, we are following. We may not have considered, and may not know what to think about, the remote possibilities that would distinguish them. If this is the position, practical deliberation is a matter of weighing tendencies and weights, rather than applying pre-existent principles.[29] This is not really 'particularism', but only a kind of indeterminacy. And we may be uneasy when we realize that we cannot formulate general principles. It may be that practical reasoning aspires to be universal, but goes on while falling short of it.

There is a tendency for moral philosophers to hope that truth in ethics is the inevitable upshot of coherence. I believe that coherence is important. A system of attitudes and beliefs is open to criticism if it shows any of a number of different kinds of incoherence. First, there is the coherence of possibility. If our beliefs are inconsistent, that is, if they cannot all be true together, then something is wrong. Similarly if our attitudes are inconsistent, in that what we recommend as policies or practices cannot all be implemented together then something is wrong. Second, there is the discipline of fairness. If our beliefs are somehow randomly held with different degrees of confidence, so that we are confident of some things and unconfident of others in apparently random patterns, then there is something wrong. We are not giving some beliefs a fair hearing. Similarly, if our attitudes show random attachments and rejections then we are not giving some of their objects a fair hearing. If we are fickle in what we recommend, either as a fit

---

[29] Cf. Wittgenstein, 'The expression "and so on" does not harbour a secret power by which the series is continued without being continued': *Philosophical Grammar*, 282.

object of belief or as a fit object of approval, we are likely to be a nuisance, to ourselves and others. Cleansing ourselves of such incoherences makes us better. As philosophers we are trained to isolate incoherent combinations of propositions and attitudes, and this is good. But it should not blind us to other virtues. As well as coherence, there are maturity, imagination, sympathy, and culture. An immature, unimaginative, unsympathetic, and uncultivated ethic might be quite coherent, in the way that the Decalogue is quite coherent. But the people who embody the attitudes it commends will not be particularly admirable.[30]

So what is the right method in ethics? How are we to be both flexible and firm, principled yet sensitive? Remember that for quasi-realism, an ethic is the propositional reflection of the dispositions and attitudes, policies and stances, of people. The virtues of a system of ethics are simply (and exactly) the virtues of the people who live it. But in that case there will be a limit to system, because sometimes single-mindedness is simplistic, and it is virtuous to be in two minds about things. Systematization should stop in theory just as it does in proper living. So what we need is not elaborate codifications and deductions. What we need to do is to make our responses mature, imaginative, cultured, sympathetic, and coherent, and we can accept what help we can from people who have thought more deeply about human life—people who have climbed further up the mountain. Persons on different mountains need not perturb us, except as it were politically, unless they can show that they are where we ought to be. But to show that they must do some ethics, and we in turn will be using our values as we respond to theirs. We stand on our own feet, and our feet are human feet. This is how it is, and how it must be.

---

[30] See especially Michael DePaul, *Balance and Refinement: Beyond Coherence Methods of Moral Inquiry* (New York: Routledge, 1993).

APPENDIX

Common Questions

In Spring 1997 I was invited by Russ Schafer-Landau to address his seminar at the University of Kansas. The students there had taken the trouble to prepare a careful list of questions about my position in ethics. I reproduce here their questions, and my answers, as a kind of template any reader might employ to see if they understand and agree with the position. I am grateful to Russ Schafer-Landau, and the students, for the stimulus. In fact, the first eighteen questions are from Kansas (sometimes very slightly reworded), the next two are other questions that I also face. The last is an objection quoted from a discussion of one of my papers by Colin McGinn.

Q. 1. For the quasi-realist, if there were no moral discourse, there would be no moral truths. How, then, can the quasi-realist claim that kicking friendly dogs would be wrong whatever anyone thought about it?

Ans. I distinguish. Certainly, if there were no moral discourse there would be nobody holding true moral sentences, and perhaps nobody with any moral commitments. But then that is true of discourse concerning anything. But even if there is no discourse, bad things could still be going on. If you describe for me a possible situation in which there is no moral discourse, but people are kicking friendly dogs, then that's a situation in which they are doing something wrong.

Q. 2. Your argument for mind-independence is based on what language users would say about the extensions of their own projections. At the meta-level, however, the projections are clearly mind-dependent. When philosophers ask whether moral truths are mind-dependent, the question appears to be asked at the meta-level. So, aren't the projectivist's moral truths mind-dependent after all?

Ans. The question *appears* to be asked at the meta-level, and perhaps is *intended* as a meta-level question. But there is no such meta-level question. According to me, 'moral truths are mind-dependent' can *only* summarize a list like 'If there were no people (or people with different attitudes) then X . . .', where the dots are filled in by some moral claim about X. One can then only assess things on this list by contemplating the nearest possible world in which there are no people or people with different attitudes but X occurs. And then one gives a moral verdict on that situation.

Sometimes the verdict may indeed change, because the present wrongness of a course of action *does* depend on the existence of other people and their attitudes. The clear examples are ones of etiquette and manners: it is only wrong to eat peas with a knife at an important dinner given in your honour because other people will take it as an implied insult. But there may also be subservient (bourgeois? religious?) moralities, in which either explicitly or implicitly people do think that it is the reaction of some person, or group, which literally makes things right or wrong, or good or bad. 'Voluntarism' is the idea that it is the will, either of the agent, or some other agent, that makes things right or wrong, in which case a world without that kind of willing is a world in which there are no obligations. I think that is morally repulsive: see the previous answer.

Q. 3. If it were possible to justify genuine realism on a 'slender' metaphysical basis, would you prefer such a theory? In other words, is the motivation for taking up projectivism and quasi-realism based on the belief that a naturalistic, realistic project is futile?

Ans. Partly. It is based firstly on the belief that my approach fits all the jigsaw pieces together in a natural and satisfying way. But I do also think that alternative approaches either violate some desideratum, or miss out some other pieces, or distort them to fit.

Q. 4. What do you take it that persons are disagreeing about when they disagree over moral judgements? If it is merely a matter of holding conflicting attitudes or dispositions, then what is problematic about their disagreement (i.e. what justifies whose judgement should prevail)?

Ans. They are disagreeing about what to allow or permit, or how to react, or what to do, or what to admire or condemn. There is nothing 'mere' about such disagreements. What justifies one position or another in such disputes are the concerns it meets, and how well it meets them. This can only be assessed from within a moral perspective, one acknowledging certain concerns, of course. If this sounds relativistic, read on.

Q. 5. Accord to the quasi-realist, what compels an agent to remain open-minded and actively disposed to re-evaluate her established attitudes? In other words, what motives does an individual have to be moral, and what motives to listen to other peoples' views and attitudes?

Ans. Nothing compels an agent to be virtuous in any respect, including these (the idea that something outside all our concerns and attitudes has a coercive force on them is the Kantian fantasy). But most people are concerned to do their bit, to care to some extent at least about others, and to pay attention to the views and attitudes of others. If we can hook onto these concerns, we can also argue that open-mindedness is a virtue. Taking up a common point of view, or respecting other voices in practical discourse, or trying to find collaborative solutions, are all Good Things.

Q. 6. What do you think of Allan Gibbard's suggestion that quasi-realism would more appropriately be named sophisticated realism?

Ans. I quite like it. But (as Gibbard would agree) it is the overall package that matters rather than the label. Once we find minimalists and quietists calling themselves realists, then my package deserves the label just as well as they do. But traditionally 'realism' referred to an ambition or aspiration—that of grounding ethics in a special kind of fact, or detecting a special source of authority for it—and although the aspiration may have been incoherent, as I suggest, it was still there. So if I co-opt the label, as some minimalists are happy to do, it risks being misleading, even if it is in fact appropriate.

Q. 7. You speak as though there is a best set of attitudes a person might have. Are there criteria for membership in the best set of attitudes and for improving one's set of attitudes, and if so, what are they exactly, apart from consistency?

Ans. The criteria are moral criteria, judged from within a moral perspective. That is, when I wonder how I might improve, I have to think about it deploying my current attitudes—there is no standing aside and apart from my present sensibility. But that does not mean that I have to deem myself perfect, or incapable of improvement. It just means that whatever flaws I suspect are judged as flaws in the light of other concerns (Neurath's boat). But I might certainly suspect flaws other than sheer inconsistency: immaturity, lack of imagination, bias, coarseness, and so on.

I am a little careful about saying that there is a 'best set of attitudes'. I think rather that improvement is a practical, real, goal, and thinking of improvement in terms of aiming at the best is natural enough. The 'best set of attitudes' becomes a *focus imaginarius* on which our efforts are targeted (rather like the way in which making larger samples of the frequency of heads, in order to make a robust judgement about whether a coin is biased, might be thought of as targeted on the *focus imaginarius* of the Limiting Frequency of heads in an infinite Long Run). What matters is the process, not the reality of its endpoint.

Q. 8. By what criterion would an agent, as seen by a quasi-realist, work to retain consistency in his/her attitudes and does this allow for a change in attitudes over time? Would the use of the Law of Non-Contradiction presuppose moral facts?

Ans. The criterion should be whether the set of attitudes can be jointly realized: whether, for instance, you find that you are both permitting and forbidding certain actions, or admiring the very same feature in some sayings that you denigrate in others. Using a form of words (indicatives, conjunctions, disjunctions, negations, conditionals) which allows application of the law of non-contradiction is an explicable strategy, and creates the appearance of what we call moral facts. It is this appearance that discomposes philosophers.

Change of mind is of course permissible, just as it is with straightforward beliefs, but unless the agent is to be a nuisance there has to be a speed-limit.

Q. 9. Quasi-realism seems to be a version of relativism. Is this so? If so, how can a moral theory have any force if it is relativistic?

Ans. No. Quasi-realism has us standing on our own feet. But it does not have us saying that everybody's feet are equally good. Your title to oppose other views is just the same as on any moral theory, except that others wrongly believe that they have added more. For example, Kantians wrongly believe they can support the authority of their position with the authority of pure reason.

Suppose I hold *p*. Relativism notices that other people hold a conflicting view, not-*p*. Then it tries to parlay 'they hold not-*p*' into 'not-*p* is true for them' into 'not-*p* is true (or as true as *p*)'. This last is then a moral claim, equivalent to 'not-*p*, or at any rate, not-*p* is no worse a view than *p*'. But the transition is illegitimate. Maybe the others hold not-*p* only because they are vicious, depraved, deprived, ignorant, misled, unimaginative, unsympathetic, cruel, and so on. Why should this put any pressure on me whatsoever to find these states admirable?

In a recent exchange, Judith Jarvis Thomson supposes that I think it possible that 'Smith has found out from within his moral framework that Bill acted wickedly and that Jones has found out from within his that Bill did not'.[1] And she rightly says that this would be intolerable, since 'find out' is factive: if you find out that *p*, I cannot find out that not-*p*. Fortunately I have not the least inclination to say that Smith can find out (moral) *p* and Jones find out that (moral) not-*p*. That would require that I myself assent both to *p* and to not-*p*, which I don't. If Smith and Jones are each saying that they have found out conflicting things, then at most I allow that one of them is right. I will say that Smith is right if I hold *p*, and Jones if I hold not-*p*. I shall hold that neither is right if, for instance, I think we should not talk in their terms at all.

Q. 10. You suggest that projectivists can avoid relativism by 'transcending the tree'. However, for moral projectors such open-mindedness may not be possible, if the nodes of the tree are based on deep cultural or religious differences. Is it only philosophers that need to reach the more absolute standpoint if relativism is to be avoided?

Ans. The tree structure referred to was a model of a journey towards an

[1] Judith Jarvis Thomson, 'Reply to Critics', *Philosophy and Phenomenological Research*, 58 (1998), 215–22.

improved perspective, solving some problem of how to react when faced with different opinions. Some people (those with deep 'cultural or religious' differences) may well react without reconsidering their own views. It may be part of a cultural and religious tradition that the right thing to do is to destroy people who don't share it, rather than to listen to them. Nothing can force such people to take a journey of self-examination. I would still say they would be better if they did, and in that sense they need to do so, and others need them to do so, if only to avoid conflict and war. But as the answer to the last question reminds us, sometimes the journey of self-examination simply reinforces our opposition to the others, and then it may become a case of conflict.

Q. 11. In the end, what trouble do you think your argument regarding supervenience makes for the moral realist? Has the realist a way out? What relation do you see between supervenience and causal explanation?

Ans. The argument proposed a challenge to the realist to describe how to account for supervenience. Since different positions call themselves realist, the argument makes more trouble for some than others. But I am encouraged that there is now a much more general awareness, amongst metaphysicians in many areas (especially the philosophy of mind) that supervenience is part of the problem, not part of the solution. That is, you could even be a Cartesian dualist and claim that the mental supervenes on the physical. But that would be by what Locke would have called God's good pleasure, or because of particular causal laws governing the actual world. In the case of ethics, supervenience seems to be built into the discourse—it is analytic—and I still see quasi-realism as the only genuine explanation of this. 'Minimalist' positions, for example, simply have to take it for granted, and this, to me, is letting the spade be turned far too soon.

I don't see any prospect of a causal explanation of this case of supervenience, both because it would not give us the analyticity, and because the idea that the moral stands in some (known?) *causal* relation to the natural is most unappealing.

Q. 12. If supervening properties do not do the explanatory work in the realm of ethics, then does this also hold for other realms? If so, how do you explain this, and if not, what is the difference?

Ans. This is quite tricky! Suppose we start with, for instance, biology and physics, and supposing that the former supervenes on the latter. I would nevertheless allow that biology is an autonomous explanatory science. Its patterns and classifications are biological (they can be 'variably realized' at the physical level). But it is perfectly proper to use them in explanations.

It is also proper, although often not very illuminating to say that things happened, e.g. because someone was a good man, or because a situation was unjust, or because someone did their duty. We all know what is suggested by this. But note that usually a better explanation would need to cite the specific ways in which he was a good man, or the situation unjust, or the duty performed.

For quasi-realism, the options are construing such explanations, or eliminating them. If I do not want to quarrel with them, I have to construe them. How? Well, there are only a certain number of things that count, for instance, as doing your duty, in a family context. So if I say that somebody did his duty, it is because I think that one of those actions was performed, and other actions that would have counted as dereliction of duty were not. In proffering the explanation, I do not *tell* you which action was done. But I express my view that some action was done, that I commend and am prepared to publicly salute as doing what you ought to do in a family context. And because of whatever action it was that was being done, some consequence followed. I use my *attitude*, rather than a higher-order property, to select the relevant class of actions (this can give rise to misunderstandings, because you may take me to regard one kind of action as dutiful, when I have a different one in mind).

I think there is a difference between this and the biology/physics case. In ethics we are invited to think of the underlying situation in virtue of which the father or soldier did his duty or whatever. In biology we are not: we may suppose there is a physical explanation, but we do not need to have any idea of what it is. Similarly, in physics citing a temperature rise may end the explanation of some event; there is no invitation to think in terms of the underlying micro-states (molecules gaining kinetic energy, for instance) that 'realize' the temperature rise. In ethics, by contrast, I think I am 'pointing towards' an underlying set-up in virtue of which a person counted as good, or a situation as unjust, although I remain silent about what the set-up is, relying on you to work it out.

Q. 13. Why not claim that supervenience is not important, and that what explains supervenience, morally speaking, is just that any property supervenes upon itself? If you claim that both the conceptual and referential content of (for example) 'is good' and 'creates happiness' are identical, then supervenience reduces to an uninteresting tautology.

Ans. This may indeed be the kind of thing that a certain kind of 'realist' (Cornell realism) might say, except that they would want to avoid an identity of 'conceptual' content. But then the idea that it is satisfactory comes from focusing exclusively on reference to properties. Generally speaking identity of properties does not explain the conceptual requirement that supervenience imposes in the case of ethics. For example, people say that the property of being water is identical with the property of being H_2O. But this does not make it a priori that being water supervenes on being H_2O, or indeed on any chemical composition (in one good sense, it doesn't supervene upon that, since you only get water from a certain chemistry at certain temperatures—otherwise you have ice or steam). It is the analyticity of the supervenience requirement, in ethics, that is the awkward problem for realism. Reference to properties does not explain it.

If the realist claims identity of conceptual content, between 'is good' and 'creates happiness' he escapes the problem, but the open question argument strikes. In a nutshell, evaluating things is different from describing them. One could describe something as creating happiness with a perfectly clinical detachment, or even with regret.

For an illustration of the importance of supervenience, think of particularist theories of ethics. In one version, these hold that moral truth only supervenes on an indefinitely extensible set of facts. For any finite specification of a situation could be filled out in further ways, reversing any moral verdict so far suggested. I am not sure how plausible this is, although I have heard it defended by Margaret Little. In any event, if it is true, anti-realism would surely be the only hope of explaining it (roughly, in terms of approving a policy of recognizing the defeasibility of verdicts). A realist would simply be left with a metaphysically bizarre and inexplicable structure. And, incidentally, one that would make it impossible to perceive or discern moral truth, unless we are credited with infinite powers of perception.

Q. 14. The quasi-realist takes moral talk to be truth-apt. By analogy would you say that the discourse of theology, astrology, and other pseudo-sciences is also truth-apt? If so, what is special or distinctive about the truth-aptitude of moral discourse? Can the quasi-realist consistently accept the truth-aptitude of moral languages, and reject the truth-aptitude of e.g. astrological talk?

Ans. I suppose sincere astrologers, if there are any, aspire to saying things about stars and their influence on us that are true. That is, they aspire to say or believe that being born under Saturn makes you melancholy, only if it is true that that being born under Saturn makes you melancholy, which means only if being born under Saturn makes you melancholy. That might, in principle, have been true. The problem with astrology is that together with other such remarks, it is false. The remark is truth-apt—it aspires to truth—but fails of it.

With ethics we similarly aspire to say or believe that teasing politicians is wrong only if it is true that teasing politicians is wrong, which means only if teasing politicians is wrong. But some such remarks are indeed true, if not this one. Kicking babies for fun is wrong.

Theology can be interpreted in different ways. In one way it is like astrology, and what is said is typically false. But interpreted in another, Wittgensteinian, way, it is more expressivist, and then the stances and pictures and attitudes it expresses need to be assessed in the light of others. Some (humility in the face of the universe, awe, wonder) may be good; others (spiritual pride, sectarianism, particular moral elements in particular religions) are horrible.

Q. 15. One of the charges against anti-realists is that they are unable to account for the common-sense notion that people may be mistaken in their moral views. How does the quasi-realist interpret this exactly?

Ans. Of course there is no problem thinking that other people may be mistaken, or indeed are mistaken. Anyone thinking that kicking babies for fun is OK is mistaken.

The problem comes with thinking of myself (or of us or our tradition) that I may be mistaken. How can I make sense of fears of my own fallibility? Well, there are a number of things I admire: for instance, information, sensitivity, maturity, imagination, coherence. I know that other people show defects in these respects, and that these defects lead to bad opinions. But can I exempt myself from the same possibility? Of course not (that would be unpardonably smug). So I can think that perhaps some of my opinions are due to defects of information, sensitivity, maturity, imagination, and coherence. If I really set out to investigate whether this is true, I stand on one part of the (Neurath) boat and inspect the other parts.

Q. 16. Rather than trying to accommodate truth-aptitude, why don't you argue that talking about morality in terms of truth and falsity is simply inappropriate? One might draw an analogy with aesthetics, or humour. And to many people it simply does not seem to make sense to talk in terms of TRUTH in these areas. Indeed, doing so would be sharing a realist muddle. Why not the same in ethics?

Ans. The question assumes that TRUTH is an identifiable 'robust' property, belonging for example to physical or scientific descriptions of the world, but not to others, even when those others are 'correct' in their own terms.

I am myself agnostic whether there is any way of defending this idea. If there is, then perhaps moral commitments would not be TRUE (just because this concept has been tailored for physics, or whatever). But there is an alternative: a more deflationary theory of truth. This simply acknowledges that in many areas we signal our own commitments, and our endorsements of those of others, using the word 'true'. The question then turns to the nature of the commitments we have, and the projectivist gives a story about that.

Some people think that if we go deflationary about truth the 'mere' syntactic form of moral (and comic and aesthetic) discourse justifies its truth-aptitude. I, on the other hand (together with Wittgenstein), think there is if there is something 'mere' about the syntactic form, then what becomes interesting is the variety of functional states that underlie this uniform clothing.

Q. 17. You allow talk of moral knowledge, but where there is knowledge, mustn't there also be truth?

Ans. Well, I allow talk of moral truth as well! I believe that the primary function of talking of 'knowledge' is to indicate that a judgement is beyond revision. That is, we rule out any chance that an improvement might occur, that would properly lead to revision of the judgement. Attempts to say just what counts as improvement and when revision is 'proper' lead to the post-Gettier salt mines in epistemology.

Applied to ethics, this means that I can deem us to know, for example, that kicking babies for fun is wrong, because I rule out the chance of any improvement reversing that view. I don't know whether a minimum wage is a good thing, although I am fairly sure that it is. But being modest about my economic education, I allow some chance that further knowledge of economics, which would be an improvement, might undermine my view.

Q. 18. Aren't you really trying to defend our right to talk 'as if' there were moral truths, although in your view *there aren't any really*?

Ans. No, no, no. I do not say that we can talk as if kicking dogs were wrong, when 'really' it isn't wrong. I say that it is wrong (so it is true that it is wrong, so it is really true that it is wrong, so this is an example of a moral truth, so there are moral truths).

This misinterpretation is curiously common. Anyone advancing it must believe themselves to have some more robust, metaphysically heavyweight conception of what it would be for there to be moral truths REALLY, and compared with this genuine article, I only have us talking *as if* there are moral truths REALLY. I deny that there is any such coherent conception.

Even if we sorted truth into TRUTH and truth (Q. 16) and decided that there was no moral TRUTH, this would only mean that you don't walk into rights and duties, or that they can't be cubic or solid or seen under a microscope.

Q. 19. Mustn't you depend upon a sharp fact/value distinction? And aren't there good grounds for scepticism about such a distinction?

Ans. No to both. I don't need the distinction between attitude and the rest on the one hand and representation on the other, to be sharper than it is. It might get drawn by a number of features, which do not always pull together, or give precise verdicts. As Wittgenstein said, when we talk of different functional states and different functions of parts of language, 'that is not to say that this contrast does not shade off in all directions. And that in turn is not to say that the contrast is not of the greatest importance.'[2]

I don't see any grounds for scepticism about the distinctions we do need. After all, we all think that evaluation is sufficiently distinct from describing for ethics to be a distinct subject! When people classify 'courageous' or 'treacherous' as thick, value-laden terms, they have something in mind that distinguishes them from 'cubic' or 'red'.

Q. 20. If all descriptions of human psychology, including descriptions of what people believe and desire, are implicitly normative, how can normativity be essentially a matter of attitude?

---

[2] Ludwig Wittgenstein, *Remarks on the Foundations of Mathematics* (Oxford: Blackwell, 1956), V. 6, p. 163.

Ans. All such descriptions are plausibly regarded as normative because they seem to imply views about what it 'makes sense' for a person to do, if they are in the states attributed to them. And affirming that something did or did not make sense is entering a normative judgement.

If we accept this line of reasoning, all I then add is that the verdict that a person's behaviour does or does not make sense itself expresses an attitude. And where is the harm in that? To give an example, suppose someone professes to have only one aim or goal, and to believe that some means is the only means to that end, and fails to take the means. I say his behaviour 'makes no sense', and part of what I convey is that I reject it, or am irritated by him, or find him alien or incredible (insincere). It's no good for anything; I cannot get on all fours with it.

Even here, I don't know whether it is useful to talk about defects of rationality. This agent somehow can't 'pull himself together' or get cracking, or perhaps he doesn't recognize other concerns that he in fact has and that prevent him from acting. Perhaps he is just depressed, and then it is his mood or emotional state that needs a kick-start, not his rationality.

Q. 21. Didn't Moore show us that morality 'stands above the flux of feelings and desires and tendencies to act, because you can ask of any of these whether it is morally good'? 'Goodness cannot be a mere projection from human sentiments because it is always possible to ask of a given sentiment whether it is a good sentiment to have. No matter whether everyone agrees on what they feel approval for, it never follows that what they approve is really good. Judgements of value are logically independent of the existence of patterns of desire. You cannot deduce an ought from an is—even at this late stage of the twentieth century.'[3]

Ans. You can certainly ask of any feeling or desire or tendency to act whether it is morally good. But this doesn't oppose 'morality' *en bloc*, to these other things, *en bloc* (you can ask of a perception whether it is an illusion, but you can't answer the question without relying on other perceptions). Just try answering the same question about an attitude without relying on other attitudes!

As for common agreement, of course it does not follow from it that what is approved of is really good. We are familiar with widespread flaws, the corruption of human nature, and may fear that we are subject to it (see also Q. 15).

And nobody is deducing an ought from an is. All that is claimed, and that is surely uncontroversial, is that we judge oughts because of something that is true: because of the shape of our prescriptions and attitudes and stances, because of our desires, and because of our emotional natures. I make no inference from the expressivism to any particular moral conclusion.

---

[3] Colin McGinn, 'Good Things', *London Review of Books*, 18, No. 17 (5 Sept. 1996), 23.

BIBLIOGRAPHY

ALLISON, HENRY. *Kant's Theory of Freedom*. Cambridge: Cambridge University Press, 1990.

ALTHAM, J. E. J. 'The Legacy of Emotivism', in McDonald and Wright, q.v.

ANNAS, JULIA, and BARNES, JONATHAN. *The Modes of Scepticism: Ancient Texts and Modern Interpretations*. Cambridge: Cambridge University Press, 1985.

AVINERI, SHLOMO, and DE-SHALIT, AVNEr, eds. *Contractarianism and Individualism*. Oxford: Oxford University Press, 1992.

BACON, FRANCIS. *The Advancement of Learning*, ed. G. W. Kitchin. London: J. M. Dent, 1973.

BAIER, ANNETTE. *Moral Prejudices*. Cambridge, Mass.: Harvard University Press, 1995.

BARON, MARCIA W. *Kantian Ethics Almost Without Apology*. Ithaca, N.Y.: Cornell University Press, 1995.

BENHABIB, SEYLA. *Situating the Self*. New York: Routledge, 1992.

—— and CORNELL, DRUCILLA, eds. *Feminism as Critique: On the Politics of Gender*. Minneapolis, Minn.: University of Minnesota Press, 1988.

BINMORE, KEN. *Game Theory and the Social Contract*, i. Cambridge, Mass.: MIT Press, 1994.

BLACKBURN, SIMON. 'Circles, Finks, Smells, and Biconditionals', in *Philosophical Perspectives*, 7: *Language and Logic* (1993), 259–79.

—— *Essays in Quasi-Realism*. New York: Oxford University Press, 1994.

—— 'Morality and Thick Concepts', *Proceedings of the Aristotelian Society*, supp. vol. 66 (1992), 285–99.

—— 'Practical Tortoise Raising', *Mind*, 104 (1995), 695–711.

—— 'Reply: Rule-Following and Moral Realism', in Holtzman and Leich, q.v., 163–87.

—— *Spreading the Word*. Oxford: Oxford University Press, 1984.

—— 'Trust, Cooperation and Human Psychology', in Levi and Braithwaite, q.v.

BOVENS, LUC. 'The Backward Induction Argument etc.', *Analysis*, 57 (1997), 179–86.

BRADLEY, F. H. *Ethical Studies*, 2nd edn. Oxford: Oxford University Press, 1927.

BRATMAN, MICHAEL. *Intention, Plans, and Practical Reason*. Cambridge, Mass.: Harvard University Press, 1987.

BRICKE, JOHN. *Mind and Morality*. Oxford: Oxford University Press, 1996.

BRIGHOUSE, M. H. 'Blackburn's Projectivism—An Objection', *Philosophical Studies*, 59 (1990), 225.

BROAD, C. D. *Broad's Critical Essays in Moral Philosophy*, ed. D. R. Cheney. London: George, Allen & Unwin, 1971.

BROOME, John. *Weighing Goods*. Oxford: Blackwell, 1991.

BUCHAN, JAMES. *Frozen Desire: An Inquiry into the Meaning of Money*. London: Picador, 1996.

BUTLER, JOSEPH. *Fifteen Sermons Preached at the Rolls Chapel*, ed. Revd. D. Matthews. London: Bell & Sons, 1953.

CARLYLE, THOMAS. *Critical and Miscellaneous Essays*, vol. iv. Boston, Mass.: Dama Estes & Co., 1869.

CARROLL, LEWIS. 'What the Tortoise Said to Achilles', *Mind*, 4 (1895), 278–80.

CAVELL, STANLEY. *Must we Mean what We Say?* New York: Charles Scribner's Sons, 1969.

CHILD, WILLIAM. *Causality, Interpretation, and the Mind*. Oxford: Oxford University Press, 1994.

COLLINGWOOD, R. *The Idea of History*. Oxford: Oxford University Press, 1946.

CORNFORD, FRANCIS. *Microsmographica Academica*. Cambridge: Bowes & Bowes, 1908.

DAMASIO, ANTONIO. *Descartes' Error*. New York: Putnam, 1994.

DANCY, JONATHAN. *Moral Reasons*. Oxford: Oxford University Press, 1993.

DARWALL, S., GIBBARD, A., and RAILTON, P., eds. *Moral Discourse and Practice*. New York: Oxford University Press, 1997.

DAVIDSON, DONALD. *Essays on Actions and Events*. Oxford: Oxford University Press, 1980.

DAVIES, NICK. *Dark Heart: The Shocking Truth about Hidden Britain*. London: Chatto & Windus, 1997.

DAWES, ROBYN M. *Rational Choice in an Uncertain World*. Orlando, Fla.: Harcourt, Brace, 1988.

DAWKINS, RICHARD. *The Selfish Gene*. Oxford: Oxford University Press, 1976; revised edn. 1989.

DENNETT, DAN. *The Intentional Stance*. Cambridge, Mass.: MIT Press, 1987.

DEPAUL, MICHAEL R. *Balance and Refinement: Beyond Coherence Methods of Moral Inquiry*. New York: Routledge, 1993.

DORIS, JOHN. *People Like Us: Personality and Moral Behavior*. Cambridge: Cambridge University Press, 1998.

DWORKIN, RONALD. 'Objectivity and Truth: You'd Better Believe It', *Philosophy and Public Affairs*, 25 (1996), 87–139.

EIBL-EIBESFELDT, IRENAUS. *Human Ethology*. New York: De Gruyter, 1989.

FERBER, MARIANNE, and NELSON, JULIE, eds. *Beyond Economic Man*. Chicago, Ill.: University of Chicago Press, 1992.

FISH, STANLEY. *Doing What Comes Naturally: Change, Rhetoric, and the Practice of Theory in Literary and Legal Studies*. Durham, N.C.: Duke University Press, 1989.

FRANK, ROBERT L. *Passions within Reason: The Strategic Role of Emotions*. New York: Norton, 1988.

FRANKFURT, HARRY. *The Importance of What we Care About*. Cambridge: Cambridge University Press, 1988.

GAUS, GERALD. *Value and Justification*. Cambridge: Cambridge University Press, 1990.

GAUTHIER, DAVID. *Morals by Agreement*. Oxford: Oxford University Press, 1986.

GHISELIN, M. T. *The Economy of Nature and the Evolution of Sex*. Berkeley, Calif.: University of California Press, 1974.

GIBBARD, ALLAN, 'A Natural Property Humanly Signified', forthcoming.

—— 'Morality and Thick Concepts', *Proceedings of the Aristotelian Society*, supp. vol. 66 (1992), 267–83.

—— *Wise Choices, Apt Feelings: A Theory of Normative Judgment*. Cambridge, Mass.: Harvard University Press, 1990.

GODFREY-SMITH, P. 'Signal, Decision, Action', *Journal of Philosophy*, 88 (1991), 709–22.

GOODIN, ROBERT E. *Motivating Political Morality*. Oxford: Blackwell, 1992.

—— *Utilitarianism as a Public Philosophy*. Cambridge: Cambridge University Press, 1995.

GORDON, ROBERT M. *The Structure of Emotions*. Cambridge: Cambridge University Press, 1987.

GRIFFITHS, PAUL E. *What Emotions Really Are*. Chicago, Ill.: University of Chicago Press, 1997.

HABERMAS, JÜRGEN. *The Theory of Communicative Action*, trans. Thomas McCarthy. Boston, Mass.: Beacon Press, 1987.

HALE, BOB. 'The Compleat Projectivist', *Philosophical Quarterly*, 36 (1986), 65–84.

HAMILTON, W. D. 'The Genetical Evolution of Social Behaviour', *Journal of Theoretical Biology*, 7 (1964), 1–52.

HAMPTON, JEAN. *Hobbes and the Social Contract Tradition*. Cambridge: Cambridge University Press, 1986.

HARDIN, RUSSELL. *Collective Action*. Baltimore, Md.: Johns Hopkins University Press, 1982.

HARE, R. M. *Moral Thinking: Its Levels, Method, and Point*. Oxford: Oxford University Press, 1981.

HARMAN, G., and THOMSON, J. J. *Moral Relativism and Moral Objectivity*. Oxford: Blackwell, 1996.

HARRÉ, ROM. *The Social Construction of the Emotions*. Oxford: Oxford University Press, 1986.

HEGEL, G. W. F. *Phenomenology of Spirit*, trans. A. V. Miller. Oxford: Oxford University Press, 1977.

HELD, VIRGINIA. *Feminist Morality*. Chicago, Ill.: University of Chicago Press, 1993.

HERMAN, BARBARA. *The Practice of Moral Judgment*. Cambridge, Mass.: Harvard University Press, 1993.

HOBBES, THOMAS. *Leviathan*, ed. John Gaskin. Oxford: Oxford University Press, 1996.

—— *The Citizen*, ed. B. Gert. New York: Doubleday, 1972.

—— *Human Nature*, ed. John Gaskin. Oxford: Oxford University Press, 1994.

HOLTON, RICHARD. 'Intentions, Response-Dependence and Immunity from Error', in Menzies, q.v.

HOLTZMAN, S., and LEICH, S., eds. *Wittgenstein: To Follow a Rule*. London: Routledge, 1981.

HORWICH, PAUL. *Truth*. Oxford: Blackwell, 1990.

HUME, DAVID. *Enquiries Concerning Human Understanding and Concerning the Principles of Morals*, ed. L. A. Selby-Bigge. 3rd edn. revised by P. H. Nidditch. Oxford: Oxford University Press, 1975.

—— *Essays Moral, Political, and Literary*, ed. T. H. Green and T. H. Grose. London: Longmans, Green, 1875.

—— *Letters*, ed. J. Y. T. Greig. Oxford: Oxford University Press, 1932.

—— *Treatise of Human Nature*, ed. L. A. Selby Bigge. Oxford: Oxford University Press, 1888.

HUTCHESON, FRANCES. *An Inquiry into the Original of our Ideas of Beauty and Virtue*, 4th edn. (1725). London: reprinted by Gregg International, 1969.

JACKSON, FRANK, and PETTIT, PHILIP. 'Moral Functionalism and Moral Motivation', *Philosophical Quarterly*, 45 (1995), 20–40.

JAMES, WILLIAM. *Pragmatism*. New York: Longmans, 1908.

JOHNSTON, MARK. 'Dispositional Theories of Value', *Proceedings of the Aristotelian Society*, supp. vol. 63 (1989), 139–74.

JONES, KAREN. 'Trust as an Affective Attitude', *Ethics*, 107 (1996), 4–25.

KANT, IMMANUEL. *Critique of Judgement*, trans. James Meredith. Oxford: Oxford University Press, 1952.

—— *Critique of Practical Reason*, trans. Lewis White Beck. New York: Macmillan, 1959.

—— *Critique of Pure Reason*, trans. Norman Kemp Smith. London: Macmillan, 1963.

—— *Groundwork of the Metaphysics of Morals*, trans. H. J. Paton. Harper Torchbooks, 1964.

—— *The Metaphysics of Morals*, trans. Mary Gregor. Cambridge: Cambridge University Press, 1996.

KAVKA, GREGORY. *Hobbesian Moral and Political Theory*. Princeton, N.J.: Princeton University Press, 1986.

KORSGAARD, CHRISTINE. *The Sources of Normativity*. Cambridge: Cambridge University Press, 1996.

KRAUS, JODY. *The Limits of Hobbesian Contractarianism*. Cambridge: Cambridge University Press, 1993.

KREPS, DAVID M. *Game Theory and Economic Modelling*. Oxford: Oxford University Press, 1990.

LATANÉ, BIBB, and DARLEY, J. M. *The Unresponsive Bystander: Why Doesn't He Help?* New York: Appleton-Crofts, 1970.

LEVI, MARGARET, and BRAITHWAITE, VALERIE, eds. *Trust and Governance*. New York: Russell Sage Foundation, 1998.

LEWIS, DAVID. *The Plurality of Worlds*. Oxford: Blackwell, 1986.

LOCKE, JOHN. *Essay Concerning Human Understanding*, ed. P. H. Nidditch. Oxford: Oxford University Press, 1975.

LOVEJOY, A. O. *Reflections on Human Nature*. Baltimore, Md.: Johns Hopkins University Press, 1961.

LUKER, KRISTIN. *Taking Chances: Abortion and the Decision not to Contracept*. Berkeley, Calif.: University of California Press, 1975.

McDONALD, GRAHAM, and WRIGHT, CRISPIN, eds. *Fact, Science and Morality: Essays on A. J. Ayer's Language, Truth and Logic*. Oxford: Blackwell, 1986.

McDOWELL, JOHN. 'Are Moral Requirements Hypothetical Imperatives?' *Proceedings of the Aristotelian Society*, supp. vol. 52 (1978), 13–29.

—— 'Non-Cognitivism and Rule-Following', in Holtzman and Leich, q.v., 141–62.

—— 'Projection and Truth in Ethics', in Darwall, Gibbard, and Railton, q.v., 215–25.

McGINN, COLIN. 'Good Things', *London Review of Books*, 18, no. 17 (1996), 22–3.

MACINTOSH, DUNCAN. 'Preference's Progress: Rational Self-Alteration and the Rationality of Morality', *Dialogue*, 30 (1991), 3–32.

MACINTYRE, ALASDAIR. *After Virtue*. London: Duckworth, 1981.

MACKIE, J. L. *Ethics: Inventing Right and Wrong*. Harmondsworth, Middx.: Penguin Books, 1977.

McLENNEN, EDWARD. *Rationality and Dynamic Choice*. New York: Cambridge University Press, 1990.

MANDEVILLE, BERNARD. *The Fable of the Bees*, ed. F. B. Kaye. Oxford: Oxford University Press, 1924.

MARX, KARL, and ENGELS, FRIEDRICH. *The German Ideology*, in *The Marx–Engels Reader*, ed. Robert C. Tucker. 2nd edn. New York: Norton, 1978.

MENZIES, PETER, ed. *Response-Dependent Concepts*. Canberra: Philosophy Program, Research School of Social Sciences, 1993.

MEYERS, DIANA. *Subjection and Subjectivity*. New York: Routledge, 1994

MILL, JOHN STUART. *Utilitarianism*, ed. John Gray. Oxford: Oxford University Press, 1991.

MILLER, WILLIAM IAN. *The Anatomy of Disgust.*. Cambridge, Mass.: Harvard University Press, 1997.

MONROE, KRISTEN RENWICK, and MAHER, KRISTEN HILL. 'Psychology and Rational Actor Theory', *Political Psychology*, 16 (1995), 1–21.

MOORE, G. E. *Principia Ethica*. Cambridge: Cambridge University Press, 1903.

NAGEL, THOMAS. *The Last Word*. New York: Oxford University Press, 1997.

NODDINGS, NEL. *Caring: A Feminine Approach to Ethics and Moral Education*. Berkeley, Calif.: University of California Press, 1984.

PARFIT, DEREK. *Reasons and Persons*. Oxford: Oxford University Press, 1984.

PETTIT, PHILIP, and SMITH, MICHAEL. 'Backgrounding Desire', *Philosophical Review*, 99 (1990), 569–92.

—— and SUGDEN, ROBERT. 'The Backward Induction Paradox', *Journal of Philosophy*, 86 (1989), 169–82.

PRICE, HUW. 'Truth and the Nature of Assertion', *Mind*, 96 (1987), 202–20.

PRIEST, GRAHAM. *Beyond the Limits of Thought*. Cambridge: Cambridge University Press, 1995.

PUTNAM, HILARY. *Philosophical Papers*, vol. 3: *Realism and Reason*. Cambridge: Cambridge University Press, 1983.

QUINE, W. V. *Philosophy of Logic*. Englewood Cliffs, N.J.: Prentice-Hall, 1970.

RAHE, PAUL. 'Antiquity Surpassed: The Repudiation of Classical Republicanism', in Wooton, q.v.

RAMSEY, F. P. *Foundations: Essays in Philosophy, Logic, Mathematics and Economics*, ed. D. H. Mellor. Atlantic Highlands, N.J.: Humanities Press, 1978.

RAWLS, JOHN. *A Theory of Justice*. Cambridge, Mass.: Harvard University Press, 1972.

—— 'Justice as Fairness: Political not Metaphysical', in Avineri and de-Shalit, q.v., 186–204.

—— 'Kantian Constructivism in Moral Theory', in Darwall, Gibbard, and Railton, q.v., 247–66.

—— *Political Liberalism*. New York: Columbia University Press, 1993.

RAYNOR, DAVID. 'Hume's Abstract of Adam Smith's *Theory of Moral Sentiments*', *Journal of the History of Philosophy*, 22 (1984), 51–79.

RHEES, RUSH. 'Wittgenstein's Lecture on Ethics', *Philosophical Review*, 74 (1965), 3–26.

RORTY, RICHARD. *Contingency, Irony and Solidarity*. Cambridge: Cambridge University Press, 1989.

ROSE, STEVEN, KAMIN, LEON J., and LEWONTIN, R. C. *Not in Our Genes*. Harmondsworth, Middx.: Penguin Books, 1984.

ROSENBAUM, S. P., ed. *English Literature and British Philosophy*. Chicago, Ill.: University of Chicago Press, 1971.

ROSS, IAN SIMPSON. *The Life of Adam Smith*. Oxford: Oxford University Press, 1995.

ROSS, LEE, and NESBITT, RICHARD. *The Person and the Situation*. Philadelphia, Pa.: Temple University Press, 1991.

ROUSSEAU, JEAN-JACQUES. *Émile: or, On Education*, trans. Allan Bloom. New York: Basic Books, 1979.

—— *Discourse on Political Economy and The Social Contract*, trans. Christopher Betts. Oxford: Oxford University Press, 1994.

RUSHDIE, SALMAN. *The Satanic Verses*. Dover: The Consortium, 1992.

RYLE, GILBERT. 'Jane Austen and the Moralists', *Oxford Review* (1966), repr. in Rosenbaum, q.v.

SAHLINS, MARSHALL. *The Use and Abuse of Biology*. Ann Arbor, Mich.: University of Michigan Press, 1976.

SAMUELSON, P. A. *Foundations of Economic Analysis*. Cambridge, Mass.: Harvard University Press, 1947.

SANDEL, MICHAEL. *Liberalism and the Limits of Justice*. Cambridge: Cambridge University Press, 1982.

SAYRE-MCCORD, GEOFF. 'Why the Common Point of View Isn't Ideal—And Shouldn't Be', *Social Philosophy and Policy*, 9 (1994), 202–28.

SCANLON, THOMAS. 'Levels of Moral Thinking', in Seanor and Fotion, q.v.

Scarry, Elaine. *The Body in Pain*. New York: Oxford University Press, 1985.

Schmidt, Alfred. *The Concept of Nature in Marx*. London: NLB, 1971.

Schopenhauer, Arthur. *On the Freedom of the Will*, trans. Konstantin Kolenda. Oxford: Blackwell, 1985.

Schueler, G. F. 'Modus Ponens and Moral Realism', *Ethics*, 98 (1988), 492–500.

Seanor, Douglas, and Fotion, N., eds. *Hare and Critics*. Oxford: Oxford University Press, 1988.

Sellars, W. F. *Science, Perception and Reality*. London: Routledge & Kegan Paul, 1963.

Sen, Armartya. *Choice, Welfare and Measurement*. Cambridge, Mass.: MIT Press, 1982.

Sidgwick, Henry. *The Methods of Ethics*. London: Macmillan, 1874.

Singer, Peter. *How are We to Live?* Cambridge: Cambridge University Press, 1993.

Skyrms, Brian. *Evolution of the Social Contract*. Cambridge: Cambridge University Press, 1996.

Smith, Adam. *The Theory of Moral Sentiments*, ed. D. D. Raphael and A. L. Macfie. Oxford: Oxford University Press, 1976.

Smith, Michael. *The Moral Problem*. Oxford: Blackwell, 1994.

—— 'Response Dependence without Reduction', *European Review of Philosophy* (1997).

Sobel, J. 'Backward Induction Arguments: A Paradox Regained', *Philosophy of Science*, 60 (1993), 114–33.

Spinoza, Baruch. *Ethics*, trans. Andrew Boyle. London: J. M. Dent, 1959.

Tarski, Alfred. *Logic, Semantics, Metamathematics*. Oxford: Oxford University Press, 1956.

Taylor, Charles. 'Atomism', in Avineri and de-Shalit, q.v.

Thomson, Judith Jarvis. 'Reply to Critics', *Philosophy and Phenomenological Research*, 58 (1998), 215–22.

Trivers, Robert. 'The Evolution of Reciprocal Altruism', *Quarterly Review of Biology*, 46 (1971), 35–57.

—— *Social Evolution*. Menlo Park, Calif.: Benjamin/Cummings, 1985.

Tronto, Joan. *Moral Boundaries*. New York: Routledge, 1993.

Ullmann-Margalit, Edna. *The Emergence of Norms*. Oxford: Oxford University Press, 1977.

Unger, Peter. *Living High and Letting Die*. New York: Oxford University Press, 1996.

Van Roojen, Mark. 'Expressivism and Irrationality', *Philosophical Review*, 105 (1996), 311–35.

Von Neumann, J., and Morgenstern, O. *The Theory of Games and Economic Behaviour*. Princeton, N.J.: Princeton University Press, 1944.

Walker, Margaret Urban. 'Feminism, Ethics, and the Question of Theory', *Hypatia*, 7 (1992), 23–38.

—— *Moral Understandings: A Feminist Study in Ethics*. New York: Routledge, 1998.

WALZER, MICHAEL. *Spheres of Justice*. New York: Basic Books, 1983.

WEBER, MAX. *The Protestant Ethic and the Spirit of Capitalism*, trans. Talcott Parsons. London: Allen & Unwin, 1930.

WIGGINS, DAVID. 'Moral Cognitivism, Moral Relativism, and Motivating Beliefs', *Proceedings of the Aristotelian Society*, 91 (1990–1), 61–86.

——'Towards a Sensible Subjectivism', in Darwall, Gibbard, and Railton, q.v., 227–44.

WILLIAMS, BERNARD. *Ethics and the Limits of Philosophy*. London: Fontana, 1985.

—— *Making Sense of Humanity*. Cambridge: Cambridge University Press, 1995.

—— *Moral Luck*. Cambridge: Cambridge University Press, 1981.

—— *Problems of the Self*. Cambridge: Cambridge University Press, 1973.

—— *Shame and Necessity*. Berkeley, Calif.: University of California Press, 1993.

WILSON, JAMES Q. *The Moral Sense*. Montreal: The Free Press, 1993.

WILSON, KEITH, ed. *Decisions for War 1914*. New York: St Martin's Press, 1995.

WITTGENSTEIN, LUDWIG. *Philosophical Grammar*, ed. Rush Rhees, trans. Anthony Kenny. Berkeley, Calif.: University of California Press, 1974.

—— *Philosophical Investigations*, trans. G. E. M. Anscombe. Oxford: Blackwell, 1953.

—— *Remarks on the Foundations of Mathematics*, trans. G. E. M. Anscombe. Oxford: Blackwell, 1956.

WOOTON, DAVID, ed. *Republicanism, Liberty, and Commercial Society, 1649–1776*. Stanford, Calif.: Stanford University Press, 1994.

WRIGHT, CRISPIN, *Truth and Objectivity*. Cambridge, Mass.: Harvard University Press, 1992.

YOUNG, IRIS MARION. 'Impartiality and the Civic Public', in Benhabib and Cornell, q.v.

ZANGWILL, NICK. 'Moral Modus Ponens', *Ratio*, 5 (1992), 177–93.

INDEX

MO TU WED THURS FRI

| NT | (PR) | NT | (PR) | NT |

p–r (DIY) r   t   ed

r — 1
t — 2.5 ⇒ (1.5)
g — 1
p-r — 0.5

t

music — 1
art — 1 → ¼
Kant — ¼
Humstt — ¼